Apache Server Administrator's Handbook

Apache Server Administrator's Handbook

Mohammed J. Kabir

IDG Books Worldwide, Inc.
An International Data Group Company
Foster City, CA ■ Chicago, IL ■ Indianapolis, IN ■ New York, NY

Apache Server Administrator's Handbook

Published by
IDG Books Worldwide, Inc.
An International Data Group Company
919 E. Hillsdale Blvd., Suite 400
Foster City, CA 94404
`www.idgbooks.com` (IDG Books Worldwide Web site)

Library of Congress Catalog Card Number: 99-13763

ISBN: 0-7645-3306-1

Printed in the United States of America

10 9 8 7 6 5 4 3 2 1

1P/TR/QT/ZZ/FC

Distributed in the United States by IDG Books Worldwide, Inc.

Distributed by CDG Books Canada Inc. for Canada; by Transworld Publishers Limited in the United Kingdom; by IDG Norge Books for Norway; by IDG Sweden Books for Sweden; by Woodslane Pty. Ltd. for Australia; by Woodslane (NZ) Ltd. for New Zealand; by TransQuest Publishers Pte Ltd. for Singapore, Malaysia, Thailand, Indonesia, and Hong Kong; by ICG Muse, Inc. for Japan; by Norma Comunicaciones S.A. for Colombia; by Intersoft for South Africa; by Le Monde en Tique for France; by international Thomson Publishing for Germany, Austria and Switzerland; by Distribuidora Cuspide for Argentina; by Livraria Cultura for Brazil; by Ediciones ZETA S.C.R. Ltda. for Peru; by WS Computer Publishing Corporation, Inc., for the Philippines; by Contemporanea de Ediciones for Venezuela; by Express Computer Distributors for the Caribbean and West Indies; by Micronesia Media Distributor, Inc. for Micronesia; by Grupo Editorial Norma S.A. for Guatemala; byChips Computadoras S.A. de C.V. for Mexico; by Editorial Norma de Panama S.A. for Panama; by American Bookshops for Finland. Authorized Sales Agent: Anthony Rudkin Associates for the Middle East and North Africa.

For general information on IDG Books Worldwide's books in the U.S., please call our Consumer Customer Service department at 800-762-2974. For reseller information, including discounts and premium sales, please call our Reseller Customer Service department at 800-434-3422.

For information on where to purchase IDG Books Worldwide's books outside the U.S., please contact our International Sales department at 317-596-5530 or fax 317-596-5692.

For consumer information on foreign language translations, please contact our Customer Service department at 800-434-3422, fax 317-596-5692, or e-mail rights@idgbooks.com.

For information on licensing foreign or domestic rights, please phone +1-650-655-3109.

For sales inquiries and special prices for bulk quantities, please contact our Sales department at 650-655-3200 or write to the address above.

For information on using IDG Books Worldwide's books in the classroom or for ordering examination copies, please contact our Educational Sales department at 800-434-2086 or fax 317-596-5499.

For press review copies, author interviews, or other publicity information, please contact our Public Relations department at 650-655-3000 or fax 650-655-3299.

For authorization to photocopy items for corporate, personal, or educational use, please contact Copyright Clearance Center, 222 Rosewood Drive, Danvers, MA 01923, or fax 978-750-4470.

Library of Congress Cataloging-in-Publication Data
Kabir, Mohammed J., 1971-
Apache Servier adminstrator's handbook / Mohammed J. Kabir
p. cm.
ISBN 0-7645-3306-1 (alk. paper)
1. Apache (Computer file : Apache Group)
2. Web servers--Computer programs.
I. Title.
TK5105.8885.A63K32 1999
005.7'13769--dc21 99-13763
CIP

ABOUT IDG BOOKS WORLDWIDE

Welcome to the world of IDG Books Worldwide.

IDG Books Worldwide, Inc., is a subsidiary of International Data Group, the world's largest publisher of computer-related information and the leading global provider of information services on information technology. IDG was founded more than 30 years ago by Patrick J. McGovern and now employs more than 9,000 people worldwide. IDG publishes more than 290 computer publications in over 75 countries. More than 90 million people read one or more IDG publications each month.

Launched in 1990, IDG Books Worldwide is today the #1 publisher of best-selling computer books in the United States. We are proud to have received eight awards from the Computer Press Association in recognition of editorial excellence and three from Computer Currents' First Annual Readers' Choice Awards. Our best-selling *...For Dummies®* series has more than 50 million copies in print with translations in 31 languages. IDG Books Worldwide, through a joint venture with IDG's Hi-Tech Beijing, became the first U.S. publisher to publish a computer book in the People's Republic of China. In record time, IDG Books Worldwide has become the first choice for millions of readers around the world who want to learn how to better manage their businesses.

Our mission is simple: Every one of our books is designed to bring extra value and skill-building instructions to the reader. Our books are written by experts who understand and care about our readers. The knowledge base of our editorial staff comes from years of experience in publishing, education, and journalism — experience we use to produce books to carry us into the new millennium. In short, we care about books, so we attract the best people. We devote special attention to details such as audience, interior design, use of icons, and illustrations. And because we use an efficient process of authoring, editing, and desktop publishing our books electronically, we can spend more time ensuring superior content and less time on the technicalities of making books.

You can count on our commitment to deliver high-quality books at competitive prices on topics you want to read about. At IDG Books Worldwide, we continue in the IDG tradition of delivering quality for more than 30 years. You'll find no better book on a subject than one from IDG Books Worldwide.

John Kilcullen
Chairman and CEO
IDG Books Worldwide, Inc.

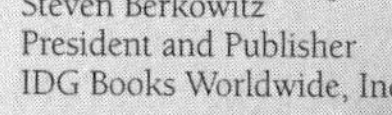

Steven Berkowitz
President and Publisher
IDG Books Worldwide, Inc.

Eighth Annual Computer Press Awards 1992

Ninth Annual Computer Press Awards 1993

Tenth Annual Computer Press Awards 1994

Eleventh Annual Computer Press Awards 1995

IDG is the world's leading IT media, research and exposition company. Founded in 1964, IDG had 1997 revenues of $2.05 billion and has more than 9,000 employees worldwide. IDG offers the widest range of media options that reach IT buyers in 75 countries representing 95% of worldwide IT spending. IDG's diverse product and services portfolio spans six key areas including print publishing, online publishing, expositions and conferences, market research, education and training, and global marketing services. More than 90 million people read one or more of IDG's 290 magazines and newspapers, including IDG's leading global brands — Computerworld, PC World, Network World, Macworld and the Channel World family of publications. IDG Books Worldwide is one of the fastest-growing computer book publishers in the world, with more than 700 titles in 36 languages. The "...For Dummies®" series alone has more than 50 million copies in print. IDG offers online users the largest network of technology-specific Web sites around the world through IDG.net (http://www.idg.net), which comprises more than 225 targeted Web sites in 55 countries worldwide. International Data Corporation (IDC) is the world's largest provider of information technology data, analysis and consulting, with research centers in over 41 countries and more than 400 research analysts worldwide. IDG World Expo is a leading producer of more than 168 globally branded conferences and expositions in 35 countries including E3 (Electronic Entertainment Expo), Macworld Expo, ComNet, Windows World Expo, ICE (Internet Commerce Expo), Agenda, DEMO, and Spotlight. IDG's training subsidiary, ExecuTrain, is the world's largest computer training company, with more than 230 locations worldwide and 785 training courses. IDG Marketing Services helps industry-leading IT companies build international brand recognition by developing global integrated marketing programs via IDG's print, online and exposition products worldwide. Further information about the company can be found at www.idg.com. 1/24/99

Credits

Acquisitions Editor
Jim Sumser

Development Editors
Norma Emory
Jennifer Rowe

Technical Editor
John Dupuy

Copy Editors
Anne Friedman
Adam Newton
Julie M. Smith

Project Coordinator
Susan Parini

Book Designer
Kurt Krames

Cover Design
Peter Kowaleszyn

Cover Image
Cyndra Robbins

Graphics and Production Specialists
James Kussow
Jude Levinson

Quality Control Specialists
Mick Arellano
Mark Schumann

Proofreader
York Production Services

Indexer
York Production Services

About the Author

Mohammed J. Kabir is the Chief Technology Officer and a cofounder of Integration Logic, Inc. His company specializes in Web-based software development and provides various custom software solutions to companies all around the globe. When he is not busy managing software projects or writing books, he enjoys riding mountain bikes and watching sci-fi movies. Kabir studied computer engineering at California State University, Sacramento, and is also the author of *Apache Server Bible* and *CGI Primer Plus for Windows*. You can contact Kabir at `kabir@integrationlogic.com`.

To the memory of my mother, Nazma Bathen

Preface

Welcome to *Apache Server Administrator's Handbook*. This handbook is one of the first of its kind on the market. Its sole purpose is to be the only source of information for people who are responsible for administering Apache Web servers. There is no introductory information (which is often meant for beginners), no cross-references, no screenshots, and no sidebars in this book. Everything you need to know about a topic is located in a single chapter. This means that information may be repeated, as necessary, to save you the trouble of flipping back to find information that's already been presented. All chapters are designed to be to-the-point, self-contained, and free from extraneous information.

Unlike many other Web server books, you will not find any chapters on how to create pretty HTML pages or write CGI scripts. What you will find is pure and solid information on how to configure and use the Apache Web server. This book will help you take advantage of all the powerful features that make Apache the best Web server in the world. You also will find a complete alphabetical reference for both core directives and the standard modules (see Chapters 3 and 4).

If you are looking for an indispensable Apache book that you will use on a daily basis . . . well, you've found it!

Is This Book for You?

This book is for people who do not need to read a lot of introductory information before getting started. It's a single, yet complete source of how-to and reference information that empowers an administrator on a day-to-day basis. It is meant for the professional administrators and others who work under deadlines and do not have the time or need for handholding every single step of the way. The reader is expected to know the basics of the Web but does not necessarily need to be a C programmer or a computer scientist to understand any of the topics discussed in this book.

How This Book Is Organized

I organized this book into three parts, as follows:

Part I: Installation and Configuration

The first part of the book deals with new server installation, server configuration files, core directives, the standard modules, and the virtual Web services. I primarily discuss the new APACI-based installation and upgrade technique that make it very easy to handle server customization tasks. The complete alphabetical reference for both core directives and the standard modules will prove to be really handy for serious Apache administrators. The virtual Web services chapter is a must read for almost everyone.

Part II: Server Side Commands and Scripts

In this part of the book, you learn about Server Side Includes (mod_include), CGI configuration (mod_cgi), FastCGI (mod_fastcgi), and how to embed a Perl interpreter in Apache using mod_perl. All the chapters are focused on covering the configuration issues related to these topics. Do not expect to learn CGI/FastCGI/Perl programming in these chapters. Covering the programming aspects of these topics is beyond the scope of this book. Hence, I refrained from providing mediocre coverage of script development in various languages and instead focused solely on how you can create an ideal execution environment for the previously mentioned technologies.

Part III: Common Administration Tasks

This part of the book deals with various administrative tasks involving authentication schemes, server monitoring, logging, security, Secured Socket Layer (SSL), URL rewriting, and proxy service. You will learn how to configure Apache to provide multiple types of authenticated access to restricted areas, how to monitor the server, how to customize logging, how to enhance server security, how to use SSL, how to use mod_rewrite to provide URL rewriting services, and how to create both forward and reverse proxy services using Apache.

Conventions Used in This Book

Here are a couple of icons that you should know about before reading this book:

Tip

The Tip icon is used to tell you something that is likely to save you time and effort.

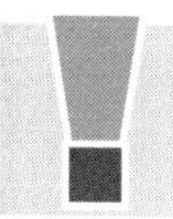

Caution

The Caution icon is used to make sure you are aware of a potential danger.

Tell Us What You Think

Both IDG Books Worldwide and I would like to know what you think of this book. Please register this book online at the IDG Books Worldwide Web site (`http://www.idgbooks.com`) and give us your feedback. If you are interested in communicating with me directly, send e-mail to `kabir@integrationlogic.com`. I will try my best to respond promptly.

Acknowledgments

First, I'd like to thank Jim Sumser for entrusting me with the task of writing the very first Administrator's Handbook for IDG Books Worldwide. This book would not exist if he hadn't come up with the handbook series idea.

Overwhelming thanks to Norma Emory who has been very kind from the beginning. I don't know how I could have done this book without her patience, hard work, and insight.

John Dupuy has been helping me with technical details for a while now. His friendly advice and suggestions have been incorporated all over the book. Thanks, John.

Jennifer Rowe is very good at taking the pressure out of writing for IDG Books. She has been kind and friendly to me since my first project with the publisher. It is a pleasure to work with her. Thanks Jennifer.

I owe much to Julie Smith who worked very hard in the final development phase of the manuscript. Her quick response and feedback ensured a timely delivery of the book.

I would also like to thank the rest of the IDG Books Worldwide team that made this book a reality. They are the people who turned a few files into a beautiful and polished book.

Finally, I would like to thank my wife, Sheila Kabir, for everything.

IDG Books Worldwide would like to give special thanks to Lisa Spencer, who realized the need for this kind of book and came up with the concept.

Contents at a Glance

Contents

Part I

Installation and Configuration

Chapter

Chapter 1

New Server Installation

Apache for UNIX

You can configure Apache manually or you can use the Autoconf-style interface called APACI. I prefer the APACI method since it is the new and quick way of configuring Apache, as well as the recommended method. I assume that you have already downloaded the source distribution from the Apache Web site or from one of its mirror sites. I also assume that you have extracted the source distribution into a directory.

Configuring Apache Using APACI

In the top-level directory of the source distribution, you will find a script called `configure`, which is what you need for configuring Apache using APACI. You can run this script as follows:

```
./configure --help
```

This enables you to see all the available options.

The first step in configuring Apache is to determine where you want to install it. For example, to install Apache in a directory called /usr/local/apache, you can run the configuration script as follows:

```
./configure --prefix=/usr/local/apache
```

This will install all Apache files under the specified directory. However, if for some reason you need to install certain files outside the directory, you can use the `--prefix` options:

- exec-prefix=DIR — Installs architecture-dependent files in DIR
- bindir=DIR — Installs executables in DIR
- sbindir=DIR — Installs sysadmin executables in DIR
- libexecdir=DIR — Installs program executables in DIR
- mandir=DIR — Installs manual (man) pages in DIR
- sysconfdir=DIR — Installs configuration files in DIR
- datadir=DIR — Installs read-only data files in DIR
- includedir=DIR — Installs includes files in DIR
- localstatedir=DIR — Installs modifiable data files in DIR
- runtimedir=DIR — Installs runtime data in DIR
- logfiledir=DIR — Installs logfile data in DIR
- proxycachedir=DIR — Installs proxy cache data in DIR
- compat — Installs according to the the Apache 1.2 installation paths

For example, if you keep your logs in a separate partition called /logs and you want Apache to write logs there, you can run the `configure` script as follows:

```
./configure --prefix=/usr/local/apache --logfiledir=/logs
```

If you want to be 100 percent sure about which file is going to be installed in what directory, use the `--layout` option. For example:

```
./configure --prefix=/usr/local/apache --layout
```

This will show the following output:

```
Configuring for Apache, Version 1.3.3
Installation paths:
prefix: /usr/local/apache
```

```
exec_prefix: /usr/local/apache
bindir: /usr/local/apache/bin
sbindir: /usr/local/apache/sbin
libexecdir: /usr/local/apache/libexec
mandir: /usr/local/apache/man
sysconfdir: /usr/local/apache/etc
datadir: /usr/local/apache/share
includedir: /usr/local/apache/include
localstatedir: /usr/local/apache/var
runtimedir: /usr/local/apache/var/run
logfiledir: /usr/local/apache/var/log
proxycachedir: /usr/local/apache/var/proxy

Compilation paths:
HTTPD_ROOT: /usr/local/apache
SUEXEC_BIN: /usr/local/apache/sbin/suexec
SHARED_CORE_DIR: /usr/local/apache/libexec
DEFAULT_PIDLOG: var/run/httpd.pid
DEFAULT_SCOREBOARD: var/run/httpd.scoreboard
DEFAULT_LOCKFILE: var/run/httpd.lock
DEFAULT_XFERLOG: var/log/access_log
DEFAULT_ERRORLOG: var/log/error_log
TYPES_CONFIG_FILE: etc/mime.types
SERVER_CONFIG_FILE: etc/httpd.conf
ACCESS_CONFIG_FILE: etc/access.conf
RESOURCE_CONFIG_FILE: etc/srm.conf
```

The `--layout` option allows you to verify the directory structure before it is actually used. If you are upgrading Apache from 1.2 and you want to keep the old directory structure, you can use `compat`, which uses the old-style directory structure.

The next step in configuring Apache is to decide if you want to use the standard module configuration provided by the developers of Apache. If this is your first time compiling Apache, you might stick to the standard configuration just to get used to the entire process.

The standard or default configuration file for APACI-based configuration is stored in the SRC subdirectory. It is called Configuration.apaci and is shown in Listing 2-1.

Listing 1-1 *The default configuration file without the comments and blank lines.*

```
EXTRA_CFLAGS= '$(SRCDIR)/apaci'
EXTRA_LDFLAGS=
EXTRA_LIBS=
EXTRA_INCLUDES=
EXTRA_DEPS=

Rule SHARED_CORE=default
Rule SHARED_CHAIN=default
Rule SOCKS4=no
Rule SOCKS5=no
Rule IRIXNIS=no
Rule IRIXN32=yes
Rule PARANOID=no
Rule WANTHSREGEX=default

AddModule modules/standard/mod_env.o
AddModule modules/standard/mod_log_config.o
AddModule modules/standard/mod_mime.o
AddModule modules/standard/mod_negotiation.o
AddModule modules/standard/mod_status.o
AddModule modules/standard/mod_include.o
AddModule modules/standard/mod_autoindex.o
AddModule modules/standard/mod_dir.o
AddModule modules/standard/mod_cgi.o
AddModule modules/standard/mod_asis.o
AddModule modules/standard/mod_imap.o
AddModule modules/standard/mod_actions.o
```

```
AddModule modules/standard/mod_userdir.o
AddModule modules/standard/mod_alias.o
AddModule modules/standard/mod_access.o
AddModule modules/standard/mod_auth.o
AddModule modules/standard/mod_setenvif.o
```

There are three types of information in this file. The `EXTRA_*` lines are used by the `--configure` script to add extra flags in the Makefile which, in turn, is needed to compile Apache. The `Rule` lines are used by the script to turn on/off certain functions. And the `AddModule` lines enable Apache modules that should be part of your Apache executable.

Makefile Configuration Options

For most systems, you do not need to modify any of these extra flags. Also note that the `configure` script will try to figure out which C compiler you use on your system. In case you think it might fail to find your compiler for some reason, you can uncomment the `#CC=` line and send it to your compiler: For example: CC = gcc

In such a case, you also might have to supply extra compiler flags in the following lines:

```
EXTRA_CFLAGS=
EXTRA_LDFLAGS=
```

If your system requires special libraries or include files, you can specify them using the following lines:

```
EXTRA_LIBS=
EXTRA_INCLUDES=
```

Note that the `configure` script automatically sets code optimization to –O2. If you want a different setting, first, uncomment the following line:

```
#OPTIM=-O2
```

Then, change the value to whatever you desire, as long as your C compiler supports it. For most installations, the default settings work just fine, just as they did for me on a RedHat 5.1 Linux system.

Rules Configuration Options

Like the Makefile flags, you should not need to modify the `Rules` lines. However, if you must modify these rules, you can use the `configure` script. To enable a rule use the `--enable-rule=NAME` option, where NAME is the name of the rule. For example:

```
./configure --prefix=/usr/local/apache --enable-rule=SOCKS4
```

Similarly, you can disable a rule using the `disable-rule` option.

The first two `Rule` lines (SHARED_CORE, SHARED_CHAIN) relate to Dynamic Shared Object (DSO) support and should be left as is.

The SOCKS4 functionality is turned off by default. SOCKS is a middleware in which all TCP/IP network application data flows through the SOCKS daemon. This enables SOCKS to collect, audit, screen, filter, and control the network data. Most people use it as a software-based firewall. If you want to make Apache SOCKS4-compliant, you need to turn this feature on by setting it to Yes using the `--enable-rule=SOCKS4` option in the command line of the `configure` script. Also, make sure you modify the `EXTRA_LIBS` setting in the Makefile configuration area to point to your SOCKS4 library file. Similarly, if you want SOCKS5 support, turn it on by setting it to Yes using the `--enable-rule=SOCKS5` option in the command-line of the `configure` script.

The IRIXNIS rule is for people who want to use Apache on a Silicon Graphics system running IRIX and NIS. The IRIXN32 option is also meaningful for systems running IRIX operating system. It tells Apache to use n32 libraries instead of o32 libraries.

The PARANOID rule allows you to see if any Apache module is executing any shell scripts during configuration. Apache 1.3 allows modules to execute custom shell scripts when the `configure` script is run. This rule is turned off by default. If you want to enable it, set this to Yes using the --enable-rule=PARANOID option in the command-line of the configure script.

The WANTHSREGEX option is automatically set to default. This specifies that you want to use the regular expression package included with Apache. If you'd rather use your own system's regular expression package, however, you can set this option to No using the --disable-rule=WANTHSREGEX option in the command-line of the configure script.

Modules Configuration Options

The default set of modules is added to the standard Apache using the AddModule lines. The modules are listed in reverse priority order. If you plan to add other modules, do not manually modify this file. I recommend using the configure script to add, remove, enable, or disable modules.

To enable a module that is not already enabled by default, you can use the --enable-module=NAME option. To disable a module, use the --disable-module=NAME option. For example, to disable CGI module you can use:

```
./configure --prefix=/usr/local/apache
--disable-module=cgi
```

Or, to enable the user-tracking module, you can run configure as follows:

```
./configure --prefix=/usr/local/apache
--enable-module=usertrack
```

Once you have run the configure script successfully using one or more of the options discussed above, you are ready to compile and install Apache.

Compiling and Installing Apache

Compiling and installing Apache is very simple after you have already run the configure script. Just run the make command from the top-level directory of your Apache source distribution. If everything goes well, you will not see any error messages. In such a case, you can install Apache by running the `make install` command. If you get error(s) when running `make`, note the error message(s) and go through the configuration steps again.

Once you have compiled and installed Apache, you can run `make clean` to remove all the object files that get created during compilation.

Compiling and Installing Support Tools

When you configure Apache using the `configure` (or `config.status`) script, it automatically installs a set of support tools. So, you do not need to do anything extra to install any of the support tools. The only exception is the `logresolve.pl` script. You will need to install this Perl script manually. Also, if you do not want to install any of the support tools, you can supply the `–without-support` option when running the `configure` (or `config.status`) script. I highly recommend leaving the default alone since the support tools are very helpful in administering various aspects of Apache. In the following section, you will learn more about these support tools.

apachectl

Using this script you can now control Apache. To learn about the command-line options it accepts, just run it without any command-line options or use the `help` option as follows:

```
/path/to/apache/sbin/apachectl help
```

To start the server, just run the script as follows:

```
/path/to/apache/sbin/apachectl start
```

To stop the server, just run the script as follows:

```
/path/to/apache/sbin/apachectl stop
```

To restart the server, just run the script as follows:

```
/path/to/apache/sbin/apachectl restart
```

To perform a graceful restart, run the script as follows:

```
/path/to/apache/sbin/apachectl graceful
```

For the curious, the restart command sends a SIGHUP signal, and the graceful command sends a SIGUSR1 signal to Apache. Because the latter is user defined (that is, defined by the Apache developers), it is much more agreeable to the running server.

To get the full status of the running server, run the script as follows:

```
/path/to/sbin/dir/apachectl fullstatus
```

You get a page full of information showing various server status data. It is probably a good idea to redirect the status information in a file, because it is most likely to be more than a screenfull. Here is how you can redirect the data to a file called /tmp/status:

```
/path/to/apache/sbin/dir/apachectl fullstatus >\
/tmp/status
```

To test the server configuration files for syntax errors, you can run the `apachectl` script as follows:

```
/path/to/apache/sbin/dir/apachectl configtest
```

ab

This utility allows you to run benchmarks on your Web server. Just run the program without any options to find out about the command-line options it takes.

apxs

This utility helps in compiling modules for dynamic loading. It is not useful unless you have Dynamic Module Support (DSO) enabled on your Apache server, and your operating system supports DSO.

logresolve.pl

This Perl script does not get installed automatically, but you can manually copy it in an appropriate place from the src/support directory of your Apache source distribution. This script resolves IP addresses found in an Apache log file to their hostnames. This script spawns child processes and uses the parent process to provide caching support to speed up DNS lookups, which are often very slow.

logresolve

This utility works practically the same way as the `logresolve.pl` script. However, this executable program gets installed by default. To learn about the command-line syntax, just run it with `h` option.

htpasswd

This utility allows you to create username/password pairs for per-directory authentication schemes. To see the usage syntax, run the program without any arguments. Unlike the previously mentioned support tools, this utility gets installed in the bin directory of your Apache server installation directory.

dbmmanage

This utility allows you to manage DBM-based username/password pairs for DBM-based authentication schemes. To see the usage syntax, run the program without any arguments. Unlike the previously mentioned support tools, this utility gets installed in the bin directory of your Apache server installation directory.

htdigest

This utility allows you to create username/password pairs for MD5 digest-based authentication schemes. To see the usage syntax, run the program without any arguments. Unlike the previously mentioned support tools, this utility gets installed in the bin directory of your Apache server installation directory.

Apache for Windows

Apache for Windows is still considered beta grade software. I do not recommend using the Windows version of Apache for production purposes yet. Unlike most UNIX systems, Windows systems do not come with free C compilers, so it is not practical for most people to compile Windows version of Apache. You will need Microsoft Visual C++ 5.0 or above to compile Apache under Windows. Also, the Apache group is targeting Windows NT as the viable Apache platform, so other Windows platforms such as Windows 95, Windows 98, or Windows NT 3.5x are not likely to be widely tested. In any event, the best deal for now is to download the precompiled binary distribution and install it. You can download the self-extracting Windows version of Apache binaries from the Apache Web site and run it. The self-extract version of the distribution includes an installation program that will install Apache on your system.

The installation process is quite simple. After you run the self-extracting executable file by clicking it, the installer will launch automatically.

The installer program will give you the option to change the default directory location where Apache will be installed. The default location is C:\PROGRAM FILES\APACHE GROUP\APACHE, where C: is your hard drive. You can change the default directory by clicking the Browse button and selecting another existing directory. However, if you want to install it in a new directory, just type the path in the dialog window that pops up after you click on the Browse button. The installer is smart enough to create the new directory for you.

After you have selected the destination directory, you will be asked to select installation types. Currently, there are three types available: Typical, Compact, or Custom. I choose Custom so that I can see what is getting installed, and I recommend that you do the same. The custom option will show you that the installer is going to install the Application Files, Source Code, Apache Manual, Additional Modules, Icons, and Required Directories. If you are not planning on compiling Apache using a C compiler, you might want to deselect the Source Code component from being installed. This will save you 3MB of disk space.

Next, you will have to select the program folder where the installer should put the Apache program icons. The default is a new folder called APACHE WEB SERVER, which should be fine for most installation.

The installer will now install all the necessary files. Once installation is complete, you will be asked to view the README file. You should take a look at this file because it contains valuable information for the Windows version of Apache. This information includes the list of known problems so that you don't spend hours and hours trying to solve a problem when it is already known to have no fix available yet.

If you are using Apache on a Windows NT platform, you have the choice to install Apache as a service. This allows you to run the Apache server automatically when you boot or reboot your NT workstation or server. In order to run Apache as service, select the Install Apache as service (NT only) option from the newly installed Program Folder for Apache (default is APACHE WEB SERVER) This will install Apache as a service. Now if you want the Apache server to run at boot or reboot automatically, do the following:

1. Click the Services icon inside the Control Panel to bring up the service control panel options.
2. Select the Apache service from the listed services and click the Startup button.
3. Select the Startup Type to be automatic by clicking the appropriate radio button; then click the OK button and close the services option dialog box by clicking the Close button.

The service option is not available for Windows 95/98 systems.

Chapter 2

Getting Apache Up and Running

Customizing the Default Configuration Files

Every Apache source distribution comes with the following set of default configuration files:

- access.conf
- httpd.conf
- srm.conf
- magic
- mime.types

The last two files, magic and mime.types, should be left as is in most cases. The magic file is used for a special module called `mod_mime_magic`, and the mime.types file controls what MIME types are sent to the client for a given file extension. If for some reason you need to create additional MIME types for your server, I recommend you use AddType directive instead of modifying this file.

The httpd.conf, access.conf, and the srm.conf are the files that you have to customize. Although there are three files, they all share the same structure. In fact, you can put all the directives in the httpd.conf and keep the other two files empty. In a future version,

Apache Group is likely to drop the requirements of configuration files to just one. However, since traditionally there have been three files, I will assume that you will go with the tradition as well. These text files have two types of information: optional comments and server directives. Lines that contain a # symbol as the first character are comments; these comments have no purpose for the server software, instead they serve as a form of documentation for the server administrator. You can add as many comment lines as you want; the server simply ignores all comments when it parses these files.

Except for the comments and blank lines, the server treats all other lines as either complete or part of directives. While editing these files, you need to make certain decisions regarding how you want the server to behave. In the following sections, you learn what these directives mean and how you use them to customize your server.

httpd.conf

httpd.conf is the primary configuration file. It is used to tell the server how it is to run. Listing 4-1 shows the default httpd.conf file. I removed the comments because it is easier to understand the configuration when you can see it in one piece.

Listing 2-1 *Default httpd.conf without comments*

```
ServerType standalone
Port 80
User nobody
Group nobody
```

ServerName: `wormhole.nitec.com`
ServerAdmin: `kabir@wormhole.nitec.com`
ServerRoot: `/usr/local/apache`

```
ErrorLog /usr/local/apache/var/log/error_log\
LogLevel warn
```

```
LogFormat "%h %l %u %t \"%r\" %>s %b \"%{Referer}i\"\
\"%{User-Agent}i\"" combined
LogFormat "%h %l %u %t \"%r\" %>s %b" common
LogFormat "%{Referer}i -> %U" referer
LogFormat "%{User-agent}i" agent
CustomLog /usr/local/apache/var/log/access_log common
PidFile /usr/local/apache/var/run/httpd.pid
ScoreBoardFile /usr/local/apache/var/run/httpd.scoreboard

HostnameLookups off
UseCanonicalName on

Timeout 300
KeepAlive On
MaxKeepAliveRequests 100
KeepAliveTimeout 15
MinSpareServers 5
MaxSpareServers 10
StartServers 5
MaxClients 150
MaxRequestsPerChild 30
```

Now let's take a close look at each of these directives.

Running Apache as a Standalone or inetd Server

The first directive in the default httpd.conf configuration file is ServerType. This directive specifies how the Web server is run. The server can be run using one of two methods: standalone or inetd. It may appear that the standalone and the inetd methods are virtually identical in their functionality, but there's a big difference. The difference lies in the performance of the server. An inetd-run server process exits as soon as it finishes servicing a request. In the standalone mode, the child Web server processes hang out for a certain amount of time before they cease to exist. This gives them a chance to be reused by future requests. Because the overhead of launching a new process per request is absent in the standalone mode, this mode is more efficient. So the default value (standalone) should work for most sites. If you have decided to stick with this default value, you can skip the rest of this section. However, if you prefer to run Apache as an inetd server, then set this directive to inetd value.

Then you need to edit your /etc/inetd.conf file to add a new record for Apache. This text file has a specific record format, which you should be able to determine by looking at the existing entries in the file. Unless you have an unusual UNIX system, however, you will probably have an inetd.conf file that uses the following record definition:

```
<service_name> <sock_type> <proto> <flags> <user>
<server_path> <args>
```

As you can see in the preceding line, the service is run as a particular user so you need to decide which user you want to run with the Apache server. The simplest method is either to use the *nobody* user or to create a special user named *httpd* to run the server process. If you use the nobody user for other services, then don't use it again for Apache. Reusing nobody for Web service might affect what is accessible to the Web server when you modify a directory/file setting for the other service using the nobody account. I recommend creating a special httpd account and using it as follows:

```
httpd stream tcp nowait httpd /path/to/httpd -f\
/path/to/httpd.conf
```

Once you have modified the inetd.conf file, you need to modify the /etc/services file, which has a record structure as follows:

```
<service name>       <port number>/<protocol name>
<service entry in inetd.conf>
```

So, the line to add in the /etc/services is:

```
httpd 80/tcp httpd
```

The preceding entry describes the httpd service available and used by the inetd server. It specifies that the HTTP service is available on port 80. If you want to use a different port for your Web (HTTP) service, replace 80 with a port number that is not already being used by another service. Since all port numbers below 1024 are reserved for standard services, you want to use a port address higher than 1024 (for example, 8080) and lower than 65535.

Now you need to restart your inetd process. First, you need its process ID (PID), which you can obtain using the following commands:

```
ps auxw | grep inetd
```

Depending on your UNIX system, you may have to use different arguments for the ps utility (see the main pages for ps, if necessary). Piping the output of ps to the grep utility enables grep to search the lines for any line that matches the word inetd, and print out the line on the screen (standard output). Although ps output format varies on different systems, usually the first numeric column in the output is the process ID for the process on that line. Now, use the kill utility as follows:

```
kill -HUP <PID of inetd>
```

Don't forget to replace the <PID of inetd> part with the actual process ID. The kill utility sends a SIGHUP (HUP is the shortened name) signal to the named PID. This restarts your inetd server and enables it to re-read the configuration files you modified. Now your inetd configuration is complete.

Once you assign the Apache directive ServerType to inetd and configure the /etc/inetd.conf and the /etc/services files, the User and Group directives in the httpd.conf file have no effect. However, make sure the user name you used in the /etc/inetd.conf file has access privileges both to your Web directories and where you store the log files for the server.

I recommend that you run Apache as an inetd server only if your system has very little RAM to spare, or if you do not expect to have a high-traffic Web site.

Port for the Standalone Server. The Port directive has no effect if you choose to run your Apache server as an inetd process. On the other hand, if you kept the default ServerType setting (standalone), you can use this directive to tell Apache which port address to listen to.

The default HTTP port is 80, and this should be used in typical Web sites. If you are not the root user of the system, however, and you want to run the Web server, you need to use a port number greater than 1023 and lower than 65535. All ports below 1024 are considered standard reserved ports and require inetd-level (root-level) access to start a service on these ports. If you are just experimenting with Web servers on a non-root account on a system, you can use a port higher than the mentioned range, as long as it has not already been taken. If you try to use a port address that is already in use by another server, you will get an error message when you try to start the server. Also, note that if you use any port other than the standard HTTP port 80, you will have to supply a port number along with all URL requests to the server. For example, if you set this directive as `Port 8080`, you need to request resources (such as a page called `mypage.html`) on this server as follows:

```
http://www.domain.tld:8080/mypage.html
```

User and Group for the Standalone Server. Like the Port directive, the User and the Group directives in the httpd.conf file are meaningful only for a standalone server. The syntax for these directives is as follows:

```
User  [username    |   #UID]
Group [group name  |   #GID]
```

These two directives are very important for security reasons. When the primary Web server process launches a child server process to fulfill a request, it changes the child's UID and GID according to the values set for these directives.

If the child processes are run as root user processes, this may create a security hole vulnerable to hackers. Allowing the capability to interact with a root user process would maximize a potential breach of security in the system; hence, I do not recommend that you use this username. Rather, I highly recommend that you choose to run the child server processes as a very low-privileged user belonging to a very low-privileged group. In most UNIX systems, the user named nobody (usually UID = -1) and the group named nogroup (usually GID = -1) are low-privileged. You should consult your /etc/group and /etc/passwd files to determine these settings.

If you plan to run the primary Web server as a non-root (regular) user, it will not be able to change the UID and GID of child processes, because only root user processes can change the UID or GID of other processes. Therefore, if you run your primary server as the user named foobar, then all child processes will have the same privileges of foobar. Similarly, whatever GID you have also will be the GID for the child processes.

Note that if you plan to use the numeric format for user and/or group ID, you need to insert a # symbol before the numeric value, which can be found in /etc/passwd and in /etc/group files.

Common Directives for Both inetd and Standalone Servers

The standalone and inetd-based servers share the common directives discussed below.

CustomLog. This directive sets the log file path for storing logs for successful access requests. It also sets the log format that needs to be used in logging the access requests. For example, the default setting uses the common log format specified using the LogFormat directive earlier. If you choose to use a different log format such as combined, then make sure you change the default value from common to combined.

ErrorLog. This directive specifies the log file used for logging error messages. If you set this directive to a relative path (that is, a path that does not start with a slash character), then the path is assumed to be relative to the ServerRoot directory. For example, if your ServerRoot directory is set as serverroot/usr/local/apache and ErrorLog is set to var/logs/error_log, then it is the equivalent of the following:

```
ErrorLog /usr/local/apache/var/log/error_log
```

Whatever directory you keep the logs in, make sure that only the primary server process has write access in that directory. This is a major security issue; allowing other users or processes to write to the log directory can potentially mean someone unauthorized could be able to take over your primary Web server process UID, which is normally the root account.

HostnameLookups. When this directive is set to off it tells Apache not to do DNS lookups to determine host names of requesting clients. Since DNS lookups are time consuming, the default value off is a very good idea. Turning this on may cause clients to time out if their ISP has not properly set up the client's reverse-DNS settings.

LogFormat. The LogFormat specifies the format for server log files and also assigns a nickname to that format. The default httpd.conf contains multiple LogFormat directives but uses only one with the CustomLog directive. For example:

```
LogFormat "%h %l %u %t \"%r\" %>s %b \"%{Referer}i\"\
\"%{User-Agent}i\"" combined
```

This log format nicknamed *combined* specifies all the Common Log Format (CLF) fields and adds the referrer and the user-agent fields. The next format in the default configuration is as follows:

```
LogFormat "%h %l %u %t \"%r\" %>s %b" common
```

This format is simply the Common Log Format , and hence it is nicknamed common. The last two LogFormat directives in the default httpd.conf file are:

```
LogFormat "%{Referer}i -> %U" referer
LogFormat "%{User-agent}i" agent
```

These two create nicknames for log formats that only store the referrer and user-agent information. By default, the 'common' format is used with the CustomLog directive. However, since most log analysis programs accept the combined format, you may want to set that as the default. After all, more log information is always better for determining who is accessing your site and how.

LogLevel. This directive specifies the level of logging for the ErrorLog directive. The default value warn is normally sufficient. It will tell Apache to log all emergency (emerg) error conditions, alert (alert) conditions, critical (crit) errors, and all the warnings (warn). If you are planning on doing a great deal of debugging, you might want to set this to debug, which will catch just about all types of errors, warnings, and informative messages from the server. Also remember that the more disk I/O that you have the server perform, the slower it gets. So keeping the LogLevel at debug is not ideal for production servers.

ServerAdmin. This directive sets the email address of the server admin. The email address is displayed when the server generates an error message page. Typically it is set as follows:

```
ServerAdmin webmaster@domain.tld
```

ServerName. This directive sets the server's Internet host name. Normally, you want to enter a host name such as `www.yourcompany.com`. Be sure, however, that the host name you enter here has proper DNS records that point it to your server machine.

ServerRoot. This directive specifies the top-level directory where the server's configuration, error, and log files are kept. This is the parent directory for all server-related files. If you compiled and installed Apache using APACI interface, the default ServerRoot is set to the value of the `prefix` value you supplied as the parameter to the configure script. For example, if you run the `configure` script from your Apache distribution directory as follows, then ServerRoot will be set to /usr/local/apache by default:

```
./configure --prefix=/usr/local/apache
```

However, if you compiled Apache manually, you might have to change the default value to point to an appropriate directory.

Timeout. This directive is set to the number of seconds that the server will wait for the client. The default value should be just fine.

UseCanonicalName. When set to On, this directive tells Apache to use ServerName and Port directive specified values when creating self-referencing URLs. On the other hand, when it is set to Off, the server will construct self-referencing URLs using the server name and port information the client supplied. If the client does not supply any such information, the server then uses ServerName and Port specified values. Most sites do not use self-referencing URL addresses, so this is not going to be an important directive for most of us.

Directives for a Standalone Server

The following directives in the default httpd.conf file are meaningful only for Apache running in the standalone mode.

KeepAlive. This directive enables or disables the KeepAlive feature built into Apache. Simply speaking, KeepAlive is a feature that allows persistent connection between the server and the client. Having a persistent connection helps speed up the delivery of the content, because no time is lost in establishing new connections for each request. Keep the default as is because it is a part of the HTTP 1.1 specification.

KeepAliveTimeout. This directive specifies the maximum time (in seconds) the server will wait for a subsequent connection before it disconnects from the client. Keep the default as is.

MaxClients. This directive sets the limit on the number of simultaneous requests that can be supported. The maximum possible value is 256. If you feel that you need to handle more than 256 simultaneous connections, you will have to edit the src/include/httpd.h header file and set the `HARD_SERVER_LIMIT` constant to the desired limit. Once you compile the new server, you will be able to set this directive to the desired limit.

MaxKeepAliveRequests. This directive specifies the maximum number of requests to be serviced per KeepAlive connection. You should keep the default as is. Note that setting the value to zero will disable the KeepAlive feature.

MaxRequestsPerChild. This directive sets the limit on the number of requests a child server process will service before it dies. If you set the value to zero, the child server processes will never die. Keep the default as is.

MaxSpareServers. This directive specifies the maximum number of spare (idle) servers that Apache will run. You should experiment with this directive only if you are running Apache to host very busy Web sites.

This directive is useless with the Windows version of Apache.

MinSpareServers. This directive sets the minimum number of spare (idle) servers that the primary server will keep around. You should experiment with this directive only if you are running Apache to host very busy Web sites. Apache can automatically adjust to load, so I recommend that you do not use a large number here.

This directive is useless with the Windows version of Apache because it does not use a pool of servers to service requests.

PidFile. This directive is used to specify a filename for storing the primary server's process ID information. This file can be used by scripts to easily determine what the process ID of the primary server is. For example, if the PidFile is set as follows:

```
PidFile /usr/local/apache/var/run/httpd.pid
```

I can restart the Apache server using the UNIX kill command as follows:

```
kill -HUP `cat /usr/local/apache/var/run/httpd.pid`
```

Whatever directory you keep this file in, make sure that only the primary server process has write access in that directory. This is a major security issue; allowing other users or processes to write to this directory can potentially mean someone unauthorized could be able to take over your primary Web server process UID, which is normally the root account.

ScoreBoardFile. This directive is set to a file name which the primary server uses to communicate with its child server processes. This is needed for only a few OS platforms. If you have to use a ScoreBoardFile, then you may see improved speed by placing it on a RAM disk. Consult your OS manuals.

StartServers. This directive sets the initial number of child server processes that Apache will launch at startup. Apache can automatically adjust to load, so there is no real need to change the default.

This directive is useless with the Windows version of Apache.

srm.conf

srm.conf is the resource configuration file, which is used to tell the server what resources you want to offer from your Web site, and where and how to offer them. Listing 2-2 shows the default srm.conf file without comments.

Listing 2-2 *Default srm.conf without comments.*

```
DocumentRoot /usr/local/apache/share/htdocs
UserDir public_html

DirectoryIndex index.html
FancyIndexing on
AddIconByEncoding (CMP,/icons/compressed.gif) x-compress
x-gzip
AddIconByType (TXT,/icons/text.gif) text/*
AddIconByType (IMG,/icons/image2.gif) image/*
AddIconByType (SND,/icons/sound2.gif) audio/*
AddIconByType (VID,/icons/movie.gif) video/*
AddIcon /icons/binary.gif .bin .exe
AddIcon /icons/binhex.gif .hqx
AddIcon /icons/tar.gif .tar
AddIcon /icons/world2.gif .wrl .wrl.gz .vrml .vrm .iv
AddIcon /icons/compressed.gif .Z .z .tgz .gz .zip
AddIcon /icons/a.gif .ps .ai .eps
AddIcon /icons/layout.gif .html .shtml .htm .pdf
AddIcon /icons/text.gif .txt
AddIcon /icons/c.gif .c
AddIcon /icons/p.gif .pl .py
AddIcon /icons/f.gif .for
AddIcon /icons/dvi.gif .dvi
AddIcon /icons/uuencoded.gif .uu
AddIcon /icons/script.gif .conf .sh .shar .csh .ksh .tcl
AddIcon /icons/tex.gif .tex
AddIcon /icons/bomb.gif core
```

```
AddIcon /icons/back.gif ..
AddIcon /icons/hand.right.gif README
AddIcon /icons/folder.gif ^^DIRECTORY^^
AddIcon /icons/blank.gif ^^BLANKICON^^

DefaultIcon /icons/unknown.gif
ReadmeName README
HeaderName HEADER
IndexIgnore .??* *~ *# HEADER* README* RCS
AccessFileName .htaccess
TypesConfig /usr/local/apache/etc/mime.types

DefaultType text/plain

AddEncoding x-compress Z
AddEncoding x-gzip gz

AddLanguage en .en
AddLanguage fr .fr
AddLanguage de .de
AddLanguage da .da
AddLanguage el .el
AddLanguage it .it

LanguagePriority en fr de
Alias /icons/ /usr/local/apache/share/icons/

BrowserMatch "Mozilla/2" nokeepalive
BrowserMatch "MSIE 4\.0b2;" nokeepalive downgrade-1.0
force-response-1.0
BrowserMatch "RealPlayer 4\.0" force-response-1.0
BrowserMatch "Java/1\.0" force-response-1.0
BrowserMatch "JDK/1\.0" force-response-1.0
```

The directives in srm.conf are discussed in the following sections. There are several directory configuration directives that need to be configured in srm.conf. These directives are needed to tell the server where to find Web pages and scripts.

AccessFileName

This directive sets the directory access control file name. Some Web administrators change the default (.htaccess) to enhance security, because the .htaccess name is widely known. If you are planning on changing the name, make sure you choose a name that starts with a period so that it will not show up in directory listings. Also note that the default access.conf file prohibits Apache from looking into any directory level access control file. If you plan to use such access control files, make sure you modify the access.conf file accordingly. For example, the default access.conf file has the following configuration segment:

```
<Directory />
Options FollowSymLinks
AllowOverride None
</Directory>
```

This configuration uses the AllowOverride directive to prohibit Apache from looking into AccessFileName specified File. If you are interested in allowing Apache to look for an access control file in a certain subsection of your site, use the following configuration:

```
<Directory /path/to/your/dir>
Options FollowSymLinks
AllowOverride All
</Directory>
```

This configuration allows you to have an access control file such as .htaccess in the /path/to/your/dir directory or any of the subdirectories below it. It also allows you to override all the allowed directives. If you are interested in a more restricted setting, you may set AllowOverride to:

- **AuthConfig**. Allows the authorization directives, such as AuthDBMGroupFile, AuthDBMUserFile, AuthGroupFile, AuthName, AuthType, AuthUserFile, require, and so on.
- **FileInfo**. Allows the document types directives, such as AddEncoding, AddLanguage, AddType, DefaultType, ErrorDocument, LanguagePriority, and so on.
- **Indexes**. Allows the directory indexing directives, such as AddDescription, AddIcon, AddIconByEncoding, AddIconBy Type, DefaultIcon, DirectoryIndex, FancyIndexing, Header Name, IndexIgnore, IndexOptions, ReadmeName, and so on.
- **Limit**. Allows the host access directives, such as allow, deny, and order.
- **Options**. Allows the directory options directives, such as Options and XbitHack.

AddEncoding

This directive assigns MIME encoding information with filename extensions. Keep the defaults as they are.

AddIcon

This directive sets the icon filename for a specific file extension. When FancyIndexing is turned on, Apache will display this icon next to each file matching the extension specified in this directive. Keep the default as is.

AddIconByEncoding

This directive sets the icon to display next to files with mime-encoding for FancyIndexing. Keep the default as is.

AddIconByType

This directive also sets the icon to display next to files with mime-encoding for FancyIndexing. Keep the default as is.

AddLanguage

This directive assigns language specific MIME encoding information with filename extensions. Keep the defaults as they are.

Alias

This directive allows you to create an alias for a physical directory. The default alias /icons/ points to the directory where the server's icon images are stored. If the path is incorrect, modify it as appropriate. The icon images are used to create fancy directory listings.

BrowserMatch

This directive defines environment variables based on the User-Agent HTTP request header field. Keep the defaults as they are.

DefaultIcon

This directive sets the icon to display for files when no specific icon is known. Keep the default as is.

DefaultType

This directive sets the default content type. When the server cannot determine a document's MIME type using the mapping information stored in mime.types or other means (such as AddType directives), it uses the value set by this directive. Keep the default as is.

DirectoryIndex

This directive specifies which file the Apache server should consider as the index for the directory being requested. For example, when a URL such as `http://www.yourcompany.com/` is requested, the Apache server determines that this is a request to access the /

(document root) directory of the Web site. If the DocumentRoot directive is set as follows:

```
DocumentRoot /www/www.yourcompany.com/public/htdocs
```

then the Apache server looks for a file named `/www/www.yourcompany.com/public/htdocs/index.html`; if the server finds the file, Apache services the request by returning the content of the file to the requesting Web browser. If the DirectoryIndex is assigned welcome.html instead of the default index.html, however, the Web server will look for `/www/www.yourcompany.com/public/htdocs/welcome.html` instead. If the file is absent, Apache returns the directory listing by creating a dynamic HTML page. You also can specify multiple index filenames in the DirectoryIndex directive.

```
DirectoryIndex index.html index.htm welcome.htm
```

The example above tells the Web server that it should check for the existence of any of the three files, and if any one is found, it should be returned to the requesting Web client.

Listing many files as the index may create two problems. First, the server will now have to check for the existence of many files per directory request; this could potentially make it a bit slower than usual. Second, having multiple files as indexes could make your site a bit difficult to manage from the organizational point of view. If your Web site content developers use various systems to create files, however, it may be a practical solution to keep both index.html and index.htm as index files. For example, a Windows 3.*x* machine is unable to create filenames with extensions longer than three characters, so a user working on such a machine may need to manually update all of his or her index.htm files on the Web server. Using the recommended index filenames eliminates this hassle.

DocumentRoot

This directive tells the server to treat the supplied directory name as the root directory for all documents. The default is typically set to

Apache's own htdocs directory where server documentation is kept. Most likely you will have to change the default to make your Web site more than yet another "It Works!" site. This is a very important decision for you to make. For example, if the directive is set as follows then every file on the system becomes accessible by the Web server.:

```
DocumentRoot /
```

Of course, you can protect files by providing proper file permission settings, but setting the document root to the physical root directory of your system is definitely a major security risk. Instead, you want to point the DocumentRoot to a specific subdirectory of your file system. A potentially better option, however, would be to create a Web directory structure for your organization. For example, if you are planning to host more than one Web site (such as virtual hosts) using your Apache server, you may want to create a partition specific for Web documents and scripts. I typically use a separate disk partition such as /www to store all the Web sites I manage. I keep each site as a subdirectory of /www directory. However, it is often good to go one step further. For example:

- Directory structure for www.nitec.com on port 80

/www/www.nitec.com/public	
/www/www.nitec.com/public/htdocs	Document Root Dir
/www/www.nitec.com/public/cgi-bin	CGI Script Dir

- Directory structure for www.nitec.com on port 8080

/www/www.nitec.com/staging	
/www/www.nitec.com/staging/htdocs	Document Root Dir
/www/www.nitec.com/staging/cgi-bin	CGI Script Dir

- Directory structure for www.nitec.com on port 9000

  /www/www.nitec.com/dev

/www/www.nitec.com/dev/htdocs	Document Root Dir
/www/www.nitec.com/dev/cgi-bin	CGI Script Dir

This is the directory structure I use for the entire production of my company Web site (`www.nitec.com`.) Having such a directory structure allows me to develop, stage, and produce the Web site in a systematic fashion. For example, when some new development work is done for the site, it is accessible from the `www.nitec.com:9000` site. Then, once it is approved, the newly developed content moves to `www.nitec.com:8080`. Finally, the content moves to the public site.

Just because your document root points to a particular directory does not mean the Web server cannot access directories outside your document tree. You can easily enable it to do so using symbolic links (with proper file permission) or aliases. From an organizational and security perspective, I don't recommend using a lot of symbolic links or aliases to access files and directories outside your document tree. Nonetheless, it is sometimes necessary to keep a certain type of information outside the document tree, even if you need to keep the contents of such a directory accessible to the server on a regular basis.

If you have to add symbolic links to other directory locations outside the document tree, make sure that when you backup your files, your backup program is instructed to backup symbolic links properly.

FancyIndexing

This directive sets the FancyIndexing option for a directory. When a request for a directory is made and none of the files in the directory matches any name specified in the DirectoryIndex directive, the server generates a dynamic directory listing. This feature is turned on/off by this directive. Also, note that FancyIndexing and IndexOptions directives will override each other. Instead of using the FancyIndexing directive, you can use IndexOptions directive as follows:

```
IndexOptions FancyIndexing
```

This directive also turns on fancy indexing for server-generated directory listings.

HeaderName

This directive sets the filename that will be embedded in the directory listings created by the server. This file is inserted before the actual listing, thus creating the effect of a header.

IndexIgnore

This directive sets the filenames that will be ignored by the server when creating a dynamic directory listing. The filenames can be simple regular expressions separated by space characters. Keep the default.

LanguagePriority

This directive sets the precedence of languages in order of decreasing preference. Keep the default as is if English (en) is your preferred language.

ReadmeName

This directive sets the filename that will be appended at the end of a directory listing created by the server. This file is inserted after the actual listing, thus creating the effect of a footer. This file must be in the same directory.

TypesConfig

This directive sets the location of the mime types configuration file. Keep the default unless you move the mime.types file.

UserDir

This directive is used to tell Apache which directory to consider as the DocumentRoot for users on your system. This applies only if you have multiple users on the system and want to allow each one to have his or her very own Web directory. The default value is public_html which means that if you set up your Web server's name to be www.yourcompany.com, and you have two users (Joe and Jenny), their personal Web site URLs and Web directories would be as follows:

```
~joe/public_html
~jenny/public_html
```

On UNIX systems, the tilde (~) character extends to a user's home directory. The directory specified by the UserDir directive resides in each user's home directory, and Apache must have read and execute permissions to read files and directories within the public_html directory. This can be accomplished using the following commands on a UNIX system:

```
chown -R <user>.<Apache server's group name> \
  ~<user>/<directory assigned in UserDir>
chmod -R 770 ~<user>/<directory assigned in UserDir>
```

For example, if the username is joe and Apache's group is called httpd, and public_html is assigned in the UserDir directive, the preceding commands will look like this:

```
chown -R joe.httpd  ~joe/public_html
chmod -R 2770 ~joe/public_html
```

The first command, chown, changes ownership of the ~joe/public_html directory (as well as all files and subdirectories within it) to joe.httpd. In other words, it gives the user joe and the group httpd full ownership of all the files and directories in the public_html directory. The next command, chmod, sets the access rights to 2770—in other words, only the user (joe) and the group (httpd) have full read, write, and execute privileges in public_html and all files and subdirectories under it. It also ensures that when a new file or subdirectory is created in the public_html directory, the newly created file has the group ID set. This enables the Web server to access the new file without the user's intervention.

If you create user accounts on your system using a script (such as /usr/sbin/useradd script on Linux systems), you may want to incorporate the Web site creation process in this script. Just add an mkdir command to create a default public_html directory (if that's what you assign to the UserDir directive) to create the Web directory. Add the chmod and chown commands to give the Web server user permission to read and execute files and directories under this public directory.

access.conf

The final configuration file you need to modify is the access.conf file. The access.conf file is used to set access permissions for items such as files, directories, and scripts on your Web site. Listing 2-3 shows the default access.conf file without comments.

Listing 2-3 *Default access.conf*

```
<Directory />
Options FollowSymLinks
AllowOverride None
</Directory>

<Directory /usr/local/apache/share/htdocs>
Options Indexes FollowSymLinks
AllowOverride None
order allow,deny
allow from all
</Directory>

<Directory /usr/local/apache/share/cgi-bin>
AllowOverride None
Options None
</Directory>
```

This is the only configuration file in which you need to modify directives that span multiple lines. The first directive you need to modify has the following syntax:

```
<Directory path> ... </Directory>
```

`<Directory>` and `</Directory>` are used to enclose a group of directives. The scope of the enclosed directive is limited to the named directory path (with subdirectories.); however, you may use only directives that are allowed in a directory context. The named directory is either the full path to a directory or a wild-card string.

The first `<Directory /> . . . </Directory>` container configuration segment is very restrictive; it enables the server to follow only symbolic links and disables per-directory based access control files (.htaccess) for all directories starting with the root directory of the system. You should keep this configuration segment as is. The idea here is to open things that need to be opened and to lock up everything else. For example, the next `<Directory /usr/local/etc/httpd/htdocs> . . . </Directory>` configuration segment allows directory indexing and the FollowSymLinks feature for the DocumentRoot directory.

You may need to change the directory `/usr/local/etc/httpd/htdocs` to whatever you set earlier as the argument for the DocumentRoot directive in the httpd.conf file. The default setting, which includes multiple directives such as Options and AllowOverride, tells the server the following:

- The named directory and all subdirectories under it can be indexed. In other words, if there is an index file, it will be displayed; in the absence of an index file, the server will create a dynamic index for the directory. The Options directive specifies this.
- The named directory and all subdirectories under it can have symbolic links that the server can follow (that is, use as a path) to access information. The Options directive also specifies this.

- No options specified in the Directory directive can be overridden by a local access control file (specified by the AccessFileName directive in srm.conf; the default is `.htaccess`). This is specified using the AllowOverride directive.
- Access is permitted for all.

The default setting should be sufficient at this early stage. If your server is going to be on the Internet, however, you may want to remove the FollowSymLinks option from the Options directive line. Leaving this option creates a potential security risk. For example, if a directory in your Web site does not have an index page, the server displays an automated index that shows any symbolic links you may have in that directory. This could cause sensitive information to be displayed or may even allow anyone to run an executable that resides in a carelessly linked directory.

The final configuration segment in Listing 2-3 disables all options and per-directory (.htaccess) overrides for a special directory called `/usr/local/apache/share/cgi-bin`. This is the directory where the distributed CGI scripts are kept. Since the content of the CGI scripts is not to be browsed or made available via directory indexing, there is no need to allow any per-directory control on that directory; hence, the default is to remove all options. However, one thing the default configuration does not enable is the CGI script directory.

If you plan on running CGI scripts, you'll want to store these scripts in a directory other than the one pointed to by DocumentRoot (or one of its subdirectories). You need to do this for security reasons. Keeping scripts in the publicly accessible document tree might enable someone to take a look at your scripts and find vulnerabilities in them. So, keep the CGI script directory outside your DocumentRoot directory. As you might have guessed already, you will need an alias to point to that directory, because technically the server cannot access a directory outside the document tree. You will be right in guessing so. However, since you are keeping CGI scripts in this directory, you will need more than an

Alias directive for making that alias. You need a ScriptAlias directive, which not only aliases a directory but also tells the server to treat it as a script directory. In other words, a request that falls in a ScriptAlias directory is not serviced by sending out the content of the requested file. Instead, the requested file is executed as a script and the output of the script is returned to the client.

You can use the ScriptAlias directive in either of the three configuration files to create an alias for the directory as follows:

```
ScriptAlias [/alias/] [fully qualified path for script
directory]
```

The alias is just a name that you arbitrarily assign to the physical directory that stores the scripts, applets, and so on. The standard alias for the CGI script directory is cgi-bin; however, you are free to call it anything you like. For example:

```
ScriptAlias /cgi-bin/ /www/www.nitec.com/public/cgi-bin/
```

Here the `/www/www.nitec.com/public/cgi-bin/` directory has been aliased as /cgi-bin/.

When referring to a script in a URL or an HTML link in your document tree, you should use the alias instead of the physical file location. For example:

```
http://www.nitec.com/cgi-bin/finger.cgi
```

requests the finger.cgi script in the `/www/www.nitec.com/public/cgi-bin/` directory. Another way to look at this directive would be:

```
ScriptAlias fakename realname
```

Controlling the Apache Server

Apache 1.3.*x* comes with a nifty shell script called `apachectl`, which can be used to control the server in many ways. In this section, I will discuss this script in detail. However, before you can control Apache, you must become the super user on your system, unless you have configured Apache to run on a port above 1023.

Note that if you properly set up the inetd configuration for httpd, you don't need to do anything to start or stop the Apache server, because inetd runs it when it receives a request for access on the HTTP port.

Starting the Server

To start the server, just run the apachectl script as follows:

```
/path/to/your/apache/sbin/dir/apachectl start
```

If you want your server to start up automatically after a system reboot, you should add the above line to your /etc/rc.local or a similar file in your rc.d directory. On a RedHat Linux system, I use the script shown in Listing 2-4 for automatic Apache startup and shutdown at boot and reboot respectively.

Listing 2-4 *The httpd.sh script*

```
#!/bin/sh
#
# httpd   This shell script starts and stops the Apache
# server
# It takes an argument 'start' or 'stop' to receptively
# start and stop the server process.
#
# Notes: You might have to change the path information
# used in the script to reflect your system's
# configuration.
#
[ -f /usr/local/apache/sbin/apachectl ] || exit 0

# See how the script was called.
case "$1" in
  start)
        # Start daemons.
        echo -n "Starting httpd:"
        /usr/local/apache/sbin/apachectl start
        touch /var/lock/subsys/httpd
```

```
        echo
        ;;
  stop)
        # Stop daemons.
        echo -n "Shutting down httpd:"
        /usr/local/apache/sbin/apachectl stop

        echo "done"
        rm -f /var/lock/subsys/httpd
        ;;
  *)
        echo "Usage: httpd {start|stop}"
        exit 1
esac
exit 0
```

I put this script in the /etc/rc.d/init.d/ directory and made the following symbolic links:

```
/etc/rc.d/rc3.d/S80httpd -> /etc/rc.d/init.d/httpd.sh
/etc/rc.d/rc3.d/K80httpd -> /etc/rc.d/init.d/httpd.sh
```

When the system starts up, it loads the Apache server automatically. The script also stops the Apache server at system shutdown or reboot.

Stopping the Server

To stop the server, just run the apachectl script as follows:

```
/path/to/your/apache/sbin/dir/apachectl stop
```

Restarting the Server

To restart the server, just run the apachectl script as follows:

```
/path/to/your/apache/sbin/dir/apachectl restart
```

To perform a graceful restart, run the apachectl script as follows:

```
/path/to/your/apache/sbin/dir/apachectl graceful
```

For the curious, the restart command sends a SIGHUP signal and the graceful command sends a SIGUSR1 signal to Apache. Because the latter is user defined (that is, defined by the Apache developers), it is much more agreeable to the running server.

Getting Full Status of the Server

Before you can get the full status of the server, you will need to make sure you have the Lynx text-based Web browser installed on your system. You can get this nifty Web browser from the following URL:

```
http://lynx.browser.org/
```

Once you have Lynx installed, you can get the full status of the running server when you run the `apachectl` script as follows:

```
/path/to/your/apache/sbin/dir/apachectl fullstatus
```

You will get a page full of information showing various server status data. It is probably a good idea to redirect the status information in a file because it is most likely to be more than a full screen. Here is how you can redirect the data to a file called /tmp/status:

```
/path/to/your/apache/sbin/dir/apachectl fullstatus >\
/tmp/ status
```

Checking Server Configuration Files

To test the server configuration files for syntax errors, you can run the `apachectl` script as follows:

```
/path/to/your/apache/sbin/dir/apachectl configtest
```

Testing the Apache Server

Run your favorite Web browser and point it to the Web site running your newly configured Apache server. If you are running the Web browser on the same system running Apache, you can use the following URL:

```
http://localhost/
```

In all other cases, however, you need to specify the exact host name (such as `www.yourcompany.com`). If you have not made any changes to the default htdocs directory, you will see a page that tells you "It Works!" This page is shipped with the Apache distribution and needs to be changed with your own content.

Finally, you want to make sure the log files are updated properly. To check your log files, enter the log directory and run the following UNIX command:

```
tail -f  [/path/to/access_log]
```

The `tail` part of the command is a UNIX utility that enables viewing of a growing file (when the -f option is specified). Now, use a Web browser to access the site, or if you are already there, simply reload the page you currently have on the browser. You should see an entry added to the listing on the screen. Press the reload button a few more times to ensure the access file is updated accordingly. If you see the updated records, your access log file is working. Press Ctrl+C to exit the `tail` command session. If you do not see any new records in the file, you should check the permission settings for the log files and the directory in which they are kept.

Another log to check is the error log file. Use the example below to view the error log entries as they come in:

```
tail -f  [/path/to/error_log]
```

Simply request nonexistent resources (such as a file you don't have) on your Web browser, and you will see entries being added. If you observe this, the error log file is properly configured.

If all of these tests were successful, then you have successfully configured your Apache server. Congratulations!

Chapter 3

The Core Directives

Apache Directive Contexts

Before you decide to use any of the core directives, it is important that you understand in which context a directive is usable; in other words, you need to know the scope of a directive and understand the terminology needed to discuss the core directives.

There are three major contexts for using a directive. A directive can appear anywhere in the primary server configuration files (server config context) outside any containers (which look very much like HTML tags), between containers (container context), or in per-directory configuration files (per-directory context).

Server Config Context

Directives may appear anywhere in the primary server configurations files outside any containers. You can think of this context as the global context or scope. Directives that apply in this context affect all other contexts by default. A rule of thumb is to treat a directive that is not enclosed in a container as a global directive. These directives may be used anywhere in the server configuration files (such as httpd.conf, srm.conf, and access.conf), but not within any containers or a per-directory configuration file (.htaccess).

Container Context

To limit the scope of a directive, you can use containers. A container tag pair encloses a set of directives and thus restricts the scope of the directives within itself. Apache offers the following standard containers:

- `<VirtualHost …> . . . </VirtualHost>` is used to apply one or more directives to the virtual host specified in the opening tag of the container.
- `<Directory …> . . . </Directory>` is used to apply one or more directives to a certain directory. If you specify one or more directives for a directory using this container tag, the directives automatically apply to all the subdirectories as well. If this is not a desirable side effect, however, you can create a separate directory container for each subdirectory and control the server's behavior differently in each sublevel of the directory.
- `<DirectoryMatch regex> . . . </DirectoryMatch>` is the same as the `<Directory>` container, however, it takes a regular expression (regex) as an argument instead of a regular directory name.

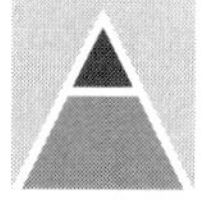

TIP

A regular expression is typically composed of both normal and special characters to create a pattern. This pattern is used to match one or more substrings or an entire string. To learn more about regular expressions, see Appendix B.

- `<Files …> . . .</Files>` is used to apply one or more directives to a certain file or group of files.
- `<FilesMatch regex. . .</FilesMatch regex>` is the same as the `<Files>` container, however, it takes a regular expression (regex) as an argument instead of one or more filenames.
- `<Location …>. . .</Location>` is used to apply one or more directives to a certain URI.

- URI (Uniform Resource Identifier) is the generic term for the family of Uniform Resource Identifiers, of which URL is but one member. The others are Uniform Resource Names (URN), Uniform Resource Characteristics (URC), and Location Independent File Names (LIFN). Only URL is widely used, however.
- `<LocationMatch regex>. . .</LocationMatch regex >` is the same as the `<Location>` container, however, it takes a regular expression (regex) as an argument instead of a URI.
- `<Limit ...>. . .</Limit>` is used to apply one or more directives to control access to certain areas of a Web site or a particular HTTP request method. This container has the narrowest scope of all containers.

Let's look at an example of container scope. The following shows a segment of an httpd.conf file:

```
<VirtualHost 206.171.50.50>

ServerName www.nitec.com
DocumentRoot /www/nitec/public/htdocs
DirectoryIndex welcome.html

<Location /secured/>
              DirectoryIndex login.html
</Location>

</VirtualHost>
```

In this example, a virtual host called `www.nitec.com` is defined using the `<VirtualHost>` container. The three directives, ServerName, DocumentRoot, and DirectoryIndex, are in the virtual host context and therefore apply to the entire virtual host. The DirectoryIndex directive specifies that if a request is made to access a directory in this virtual server, a file named welcome.html should be returned if available. However, the Location container specifies that a different file, login.html, be returned when someone tries to access the `www.nitec.com/secured/` URL. The directives in a narrower scoped container always override the directives in a higher scoped container.

Keep a few rules in mind when using any of the containers to define a behavior for a section of your Web space:

- A `<VirtualHost>` container cannot be nested within another container of any kind.
- There can be no container within the narrowest context container `<Limit>`.
- A `<Files>` container can have only the narrowest container `<Limit>` within itself.
- The `<Location>` and the `<Directory>` containers do not mix, so do not use one inside another.

Per-Directory Context

You also can include directives in per-directory configuration files. A per-directory configuration file (the default filename is .htaccess) is a text file containing one or more directives that apply only to the current directory. These directives can also be enclosed in containers such as `<Files . . .>` or `<Limit . . .>`. Using this file, you can control how Apache behaves when a request is made for a file in a directory. If a directive is valid in this context, it means that it appears inside per-directory access configuration files.

It is possible to disable all or part of what can be overridden in a per-directory configuration file in the server config or virtual host context. Therefore, all directives in this context may not be processed, depending on the overrides currently active.

General Configuration Directives

These directives are fundamental in nature and generally apply to both the primary server (server config context) and the virtual servers (virtual host context).

AccessConfig

Syntax: `AccessConfig filename`

Default: `AccessConfig conf/access.conf`

Context: `server config, virtual host`

Apache server reads a set of configuration files during startup. One of these files is the global access configuration file called access.conf. This file is located by default in the conf directory under the server's root directory, which is specified by the ServerRoot directive.

Using the AccessConfig directive, you can instruct Apache to read a different file than the default conf/access.conf file. For example, if you want to load global access information from a file called conf/globalaccess.conf, you need to use the following directive in the httpd.conf file:

```
AccessConf conf/globalaccess.conf
```

The filename has to be relative to the ServerRoot path name.

If you like to have a single configuration file for each Apache server you run, you can disable the loading of conf/access.conf file by setting AccessConfig as follows:

```
AccessConfig /dev/null
```

You also need to disable the loading of the conf/srm.conf file by using the ResourceConfig directive in a similar fashion. See the ResourceConfig directive for details.

Until recently, the access.conf file contained only `<Directory>` sections; now, it can contain any server directive allowed in the server config context. It is also valid in virtual host contexts, so you can use it to load a configuration file from within the `<VirtualHost>` directive. However, only one instance of AccessConfig is permitted in a `<VirtualHost>` section. This can come in handy if you have many virtual hosts to support. Use this directive to load a separate virtual host configuration file and thus increase the readability of your primary server configuration file.

The file specified by the AccessConfig directive is read after the file specified by the ResourceConfig directive is read.

AccessFileName

Syntax: `AccessFileName filename filename ...`

Default: `AccessFileName .htaccess`

Context: `server config, virtual host`

Compatibility: `more than one filename option is available in Apache 1.3 and later.`

This directive specifies the name of the per-directory access control file. The default setting (.htaccess) makes Apache look for the .htaccess file each time an access request is made by a client system. For example, let's say the DocumentRoot directive of an Apache-powered Web site called `www.mycompany.com` is set as follows:

```
DocumentRoot /www/mycompany/public/htdocs
```

And then a Web browser requests the following URL:

```
http://www.mycompany.com/feedback.html
```

This causes Apache to search for the following access control files:

- /.htaccess
- /www/.htaccess
- /www/mycompany/.htaccess
- /www/mycompany/public/.htaccess
- /www/mycompany/public/htdocs/.htaccess

After Apache has checked for all these files, it looks for the feedback.html file. If this seems like a lot of disk I/O, it is! If you do not make use of the per-directory access control file and would like Apache to stop checking for it, simply use the `<Directory>` directive to disable privileges to override options as follows:

```
<Directory />
AllowOverride None
</Directory>
```

BindAddress

Syntax: `BindAddress IP address`
Default: `BindAddress *`
Context: `server config`

Apache running on a UNIX system can listen for connections on one or more IP addresses. This directive enables you to specify an IP address, which Apache will service. The default value of this directive is `*` (wildcard), which means that Apache listens on all IP addresses attached to a server machine. Look at the following code:

```
BindAddress 206.171.50.50
```

This will make Apache listen to only the given IP address. Only one BindAddress directive can be used. For more control over which addresses and ports Apache listens to, use the Listen directive instead of BindAddress. BindAddress can be used as an alternative method for supporting virtual hosts using multiple independent servers, instead of using `<VirtualHost>` sections. This is done by putting a unique BindAddress into different httpd.conf files and launching the different servers with the command-line parameters pointing to them.

CoreDumpDirectory

Syntax: `CoreDumpDirectory directory`

Default: `the same location as ServerRoot`

Context: `server config`

If you are capable of exploring a core dump file and want Apache to dump core in a certain file in case of a crash, set this directive to the location where you want the core dump file to reside. The default is in the ServerRoot directory, however, since your ServerRoot should not be writable by the user that the server runs as, core dumps won't get written there. Therefore, the default value is likely to be wrong.

DefaultType

Syntax: `DefaultType mime-type`

Default: `DefaultType text/html`

Context: `server config, virtual host, directory, .htaccess`

Override: `FileInfo`

This directive is used to establish a default content type, so when Apache receives a request for a document whose file type is unknown (in other words, it cannot be determined from the MIME type map available to the server), it uses the predetermined default type.

For example, if you have a directory in which you keep a lot of text files with no extensions, you can use the DefaultType directive inside a `<Directory>` container that points to this directory. In this case, setting the DefaultType to text/plain would enable the server to tell the other side (the Web browser) that these are plain text files. Here's an example:

```
<Directory /www/mycompany/public/htdocs/plaindata>
DefaultType plain/text
```

</Directory>

Here, all the files in the /www/mycompany/public/htdocs/plaindata/ directory are treated as plain text files unless the files have a matching mime type.

DocumentRoot

Syntax: DocumentRoot directory

Default: DocumentRoot /usr/local/apache/htdocs

Context: server config, virtual host

The directory specified by this directive becomes the top-level directory for all the documents serviced by Apache. For example, if

```
DocumentRoot /www/mycompany/public/htdocs
```

is set for the server www.mycompany.com, then an access request for http://www.mycompany.com/corporate.html makes the server look for the following file:

```
/www/mycompany/public/htdocs/corporate.html
```

If the file is found, it is returned to the client (that is, the Web browser). Similarly, an access request for http://www.mycompany.com/info/corporate.html makes the server look for

```
/www/mycompany/public/htdocs/info/corporate.html
```

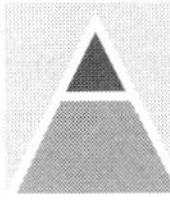

TIP

A bug in one of the core modules (mod_dir) causes a problem when the DocumentRoot has a trailing slash (for example, documentroot /usr/web/), so you should avoid entering a slash (/) character at the end of any path for any directive.

It is possible to have the server look for files in a directory outside the documentroot directory. In other words, if you want to access some files outside the documentroot tree, you can use the Alias directive to create a virtual directory name that can point to a physical directory anywhere in your server's file system. For example:

```
Alias   /foobar/     /some/dir/
```

Here, the /foobar/ alias is mapped to a physical path called /some/dir/ so whenever a request contains the alias /foobar/, Apache will internally map the request to /some/dir/ path. For example, a request for /foobar/index.html page will really map to /some/dir/index.html page. The ScriptAlias directive also can point to a directory outside the documentroot-specified directory.

ErrorDocument

Syntax: `ErrorDocument error-code filename | error message | URL`

Context: `server config, virtual host, directory, per-directory`

Override: `FileInfo`

Compatibility: `the directory and per-directory (.htaccess) contexts are available in Apache 1.1 and later.`

When the server encounters a problem, it generates a standard error message with the error code in it. This is not very user-friendly for most people, however, so a more customized version of the error message or possibly a recovery measure is more desirable. If you nccd such customization, use the ErrorDocument directive to override standard error messages.

The directive requires two arguments. The first one is the standard HTTP error code, which you can find in Appendix A, and the second one is the action item for the error. Depending on your needs, you can define what action you want the server to take for a particular error condition.

For example, if you want to provide a custom message for all requests that result in a standard "file not found" message, all you have to do is find the server status code for that error condition and use the ErrorDocument directive. Since the server status code for missing files is 404, the following directive setting enables Apache to display a custom message:

```
ErrorDocument 404 "Sorry, this is an invalid request
since %s "
```

Notice that the entire message is quoted, and the server replaces %s with whatever information is available regarding the error. If you find this a bit limiting, however, you can use a file as your error message response. For example:

```
ErrorDocument 404 /errors/404.html
```

Whenever the missing file error occurs, the 404.HTML file found in the errors directory under the documentroot directory is returned to the client (the Web browser). If you want to do more than just return a static page, you can use a CGI script to perform some specific action. In such a case, you replace the filename with a call to your CGI script:

```
ErrorDocument 404 /cgi-bin/missingurl.cgi
```

This calls a CGI script called missingurl.cgi every time a 404 error occurs. You can also redirect the client to another site using a URL instead of a filename:

```
ErrorDocument 404 http://www.newsite.com/we.moved.html
```

This can be used when a page or an entire site has moved to another location.

You cannot point the client to a remote server if an error 401 (unauthorized) occurs. The value of this directive must be a local file or a message.

Group

Syntax: `Group Unix-group`
Default: `Group #-1`
Context: `server config, virtual host`

The Group directive should be used in conjunction with the User directive. Group determines the group under which the standalone server answers requests. In order to use this directive, the standalone server must be run initially as root. The group directive can be assigned a group number as well. Look up group names and their corresponding numeric values in your /etc/group file.

All the warnings and recommendations I provide for the User directive apply to this directive as well. Make sure you read the User directive details.

<IfDefine>

Syntax: `<IfDefine [!]parameter-list> ... </IfModule>`

Default: `None`

Context: `all`

Compatibility: `only available in 1.3.1 and later.`

This directive is useful if you want to activate one or more directives when you supply a specific parameter at server startup. For example:

```
<IfDefine cgi>

ScriptAlias /cgi-bin/     /www/nitec/public/cgi-bin/

</IfDefine>
```

Here, the ScriptAlias directive will be activated if the server is started as follows:

```
/path/to/apache/sbin/httpd -Dcgi
```

The -D option defines a name that Apache uses to match a corresponding <IfDefine> container. When -d<name> is supplied in the command-line at server startup, the matching <IfDefine name> container is activated. In other words, the directives within the matching <IfDefine> are loaded as part of the current configuration. On the other hand, if you wanted to load a certain set of directives only when a name is not supplied in the command line, you can use the ! operator. For example:

```
<IfDefine !nocgi>

ScriptAlias /cgi-bin/     /www/nitec/public/cgi-bin/

</IfDefine>
```

When the server is started without a -Dnocgi option, the server will load the ScriptAlias.

<IfModule>

Syntax: `<IfModule [!]module-name> ... </IfModule>`
Default: `None`
Context: `all`
Compatibility: `only available in 1.2 and later.`

Use this directive if you have directives that are available from a custom module that may not always be present in your Apache installation. For example, if you want to use certain directives only if a module is available, then you can use the following conditional construct:

```
<IfModule module-name>
# assign the following directives their respective value
# your directives goes here
</IfModule>
```

On the other hand, if you need a conditional statement that is the reverse of the preceding one, all you need to do is insert a ! (bang or exclamation symbol) before the module name. The module name argument is the filename of the module at the time it was compiled (for example, mod_rewrite.c). <IfModule> sections are nestable; this is a method that can be used to implement simple multiple-module condition tests.

Include

Syntax: `Include filename`

Context: `server config`

Compatibility: `available in Apache 1.3 and later.`

If you want to include other configuration files from within the server configuration files, use this directive.

Listen

Syntax: `Listen [IP address:] port number`

Context: `server config`

By default, Apache responds to requests on all the IP addresses attached to the server machine, but only to the port address specified by the Port directive. The Listen directive can be used to make this situation more configurable. You can use the Listen directive to tell Apache to respond to a certain IP address, an IP address and port combination, or just a port by itself.

Although Listen can be used instead of BindAddress and Port, you may have to use the Port directive if your Apache server generates URLs that point to the server itself.

Multiple Listen directives may be used to specify a number of addresses and ports to listen to. The server will respond to requests from any of the listed addresses and ports. For example, to make the server accept connections on both port 80 and port 8080, use:

```
Listen 80
Listen 8080
```

The following example makes Apache accept connections on two IP addresses and port numbers:

```
Listen 11.22.33.1:80
Listen 11.22.33.2:8080
```

Options

Syntax: `Options [+|-]option [+|-]option ...`

Context: `server config, virtual host, directory, .htaccess`

Override: `Options`

The Options directive controls which server features are available in a particular directory. When this directive is set to None, none of the extra features are enabled for the context in which the directive is used. All the possible settings for this directive are:

- **None**. No options are enabled.
- **All**. All options, except for MultiViews, are enabled.
- **ExecCGI**. Execution of CGI scripts is permitted.
- **FollowSymLinks**. The server follows symbolic links in the directory.
- **Includes**. Server Side Include (SSI) commands are permitted.
- **IncludesNOEXEC**. A restricted set of Server Side Include (SSI) commands can be embedded in the SSI pages. The SSI commands that are not allowed are #exec and #include.
- **Indexes**. If a URL that maps to a directory is requested, and there is no DirectoryIndex (for example, index.html) in that directory, then the server returns a formatted listing of the directory.
- **SymLinksIfOwnerMatch**. The server follows only symbolic links for which the target file or directory is owned by the same user as the link.
- **MultiViews**. Content negotiated based on a document's language.

Use the + and – signs to enable or disable an option in the Options directive. Let's look at an example to make this a bit clearer. The following configuration segment shows two directory containers in a single configuration file such as access.conf:

```
<Directory /www/myclient/public/htdocs >
```

```
Options Indexes MultiViews
</Directory>

<Directory /www/myclient/public/htdocs>
Options Includes
</Directory>
```

The /www/myclient/public/htdocs will only have the Includes option set. However, if the second <Directory> section uses the + and – signs as follows, then the options MultiViews and Includes are set for the specified directory:

```
<Directory /www/myclient/public/htdocs>
Options +Includes -Indexes
</Directory>
```

When you apply multiple Options, be aware that the narrowest context always takes precedence over the broader ones. For example:

```
ServerName
Options ExecCGI Includes
<VirtualHost 11.22.33.1>
ServerName www.myclient.com
Options -ExecCGI -Includes
<Directory /www/myclient/public/htdocs/ssi >
       Options Includes
</Directory>
</VirtualHost>
```

In this example, the main server enables both CGI execution and Server Side Includes by setting the Options directive to ExecCGI and Includes. The virtual host `www.myclient.com` disables both of these options, however, using the -ExecCGI and -Includes settings in its own Options directive. Finally, the virtual host has another Options directive for the /www/myclient/public/htdocs/ssi directory that enables the Server Side Include execution. Includes is the only option that is set for the /www/myclient/public/htdocs/ssi directory.

As you can see, if the Options directive uses the + or – signs, then the values are added or subtracted from the current Options list. On the other hand, if the Options directive does not use the relative + or – signs, then the values for that container will completely override any previous Options directives.

Port

Syntax: `Port number`

Default: `Port 80`

Context: `server config`

This directive assigns a port number in the range of 0 to 65535 to a host. In the absence of any Listen or BindAddress directives specifying a port number, the Port directive sets the network port on which the server listens. If any Listen or BindAddress directives specify a port number, then the Port directive has no effect on which address the server listens at. The Port directive sets the SERVER_PORT environment variable (for CGI and SSI) and is used when the server must generate a URL that refers to itself.

Although you can specify a port number between 0 and 65535, there is one restriction you should keep in mind. All the port numbers below 1024 are reserved for standard services such as TELNET, SMTP, POP3, HTTP, and FTP. You can locate all the port number assignments to standard services in your /etc/services file. Or, if you want to be safe, use any port number other than 80 for your Apache server (use a high address such as 8000, for example).

If you are a non-root user and want to run Apache for experimentation or some other noble cause, you need to use ports higher than 1024, because only root users can run services such as Apache on these restricted ports.

The <VirtualHost> container can also be used to set up which port is used for a virtual host.

ResourceConfig

Syntax: `ResourceConfig filename`

Default: `ResourceConfig conf/srm.conf`

Context: `server config, virtual host`

This directive is the same as the AccessConfig directive. If you want to disable loading of the default conf/srm.conf file, just set it as follows in your httpd.conf file:

```
ResourceConfig /dev/null
```

ServerAdmin

Syntax: `ServerAdmin email-address`

Context: `server config, virtual host`

This directive assigns an email address that appears in conjunction with many error messages issued by the server. If you host a large number of virtual Web sites, you may want to use a different email address for each virtual host so you can immediately figure out which server a problem reporter is talking about.

Tip

In order to give your virtual sites the professional look and feel they deserve, do not use an email address that does not include the virtual site as the host part of the address. For example, if your company is an Internet Service Provider (ISP) named `mycompany.net`, and you have a client site called `www.myclient.com`, then set the `www.myclient.com` site's ServerAdmin to a `user@myclient.com` address such as `webmaster@myclient.com`, instead of `webmaster@mycompany.net`. This way, when the server displays an error message to someone visiting `www.myclient.com`, the visitor will see an email address that belongs to `myclient.com`. This would be considered a bit more professional. Of course, if the client Web site is not administered by the client, you can forward `webmaster@myclient.com` to your tech-support address.

ServerName

Syntax: `ServerName fully qualified domain name`

Context: `server config, virtual host`

The ServerName directive sets the host name of the server. When this directive is not used, Apache tries to determine the host name by doing a DNS request at startup. Depending on your DNS setup, however, this may not be desirable, because the lookup done by Apache may choose an undesirable name for your server if you have canonical name records for your server. Therefore, it is best to just set this to whatever host name you prefer.

Make sure you enter a fully qualified domain name instead of just a shortcut. For example, if you have a host called `wormhole.mycompany.com`, you should not set the ServerName to `wormhole`. The valid choice is:

```
ServerName wormhole.mycompany.com
```

ServerRoot

Syntax: `ServerRoot directory-filename`

Default: `ServerRoot /usr/local/apache`

Context: `server config`

The ServerRoot directive sets the directory in which the server files reside. Do not confuse this with DocumentRoot directive, which is used for pointing the server to your Web contents. The ServerRoot directory is used for locating all the server configuration files and log files. The standard distributions include conf, src, and logs directories under the ServerRoot directory. If you do not specify the ServerRoot directive, however, you can use the -d option to tell Apache what your ServerRoot directory is.

The AccessConfig and ResourceConfig directives use the ServerRoot directory to locate configuration files. For example, if you have the directives set as follows:

```
ServerRoot /usr/local/httpd
```

```
AccessConfig conf/access.conf
ResourceConfig conf/srm.conf
```

then AccessConfig and ResourceConfig will tell Apache to load the /usr/local/httpd/conf/access.conf and /usr/local/httpd/conf/srm.conf files, respectively.

ServerSignature

Syntax: `ServerSignature on | off | EMail`

Default: `ServerSignature off`

Context: `server config, virtual host, per-directory configuration`

This directive lets the server insert a footer in server-generated pages. When this directive is set to On, the server will simply insert a line with the server version number and ServerName in the server generated page such as an error message or dynamically generated directory listing pages. The EMail option additionally creates a `mailto:` link to the ServerAdmin of the requested ServerName.

ServerTokens

Syntax: `ServerTokenson Min | OS | Full`

Default: `ServerTokens Full`

Context: `server config`

This directive allows Apache to send information about the server in the server response header. When set to Min, only Apache version information is sent in the header. When set to OS, the response header contains the generic name for the underlying operating system. If this directive is not specified or is set to Full, Apache sends its version information, OS type, and any additional compiled-in module information available. If you have a strict security need, set this directive to Min.

UseCanonicalName

Syntax: `UseCanonicalName on | off`

Default: `UseCanonicalName off`

Context: `server config, virtual hosts, per-directory configuration`

This directive is useful when dealing with self-referencing URLs. If your server can be accessed via different ServerNames, use the default value. When this directive is set to Off, Apache uses server name and port information supplied by the client. On the other hand, when this directive is set to On, Apache will use the server name set by the ServerName directive and the port address set by the Port directive.

User

Syntax: `User unix-userid`

Default: `User #-1`

Context: `server config, virtual host`

This directive sets the user ID that is used by the child Apache server processes that respond to requests. In order to use this directive, Apache must be configured to run as a standalone server (see the ServerType directive), and the standalone server must be run initially by the root. Once the Apache server is started, it launches child processes to respond to requests. However, these child processes are not run as a root. The parent Apache process (often called the daemon) changes the child process user ID to whatever is set in the User directive, as long as it is a valid user ID.

If you start the server as a non-root user, it fails to change to the user ID specified by the User directive, and instead continues to run as the original user. If you do start the server as a root, then it is normal for the parent Apache process to remain running as a root; however, it runs the child processes as the user specified by the User directive.

You can also employ user ID numbers, which you can usually find in your /etc/passwd file. If you plan on using a numeric value instead of the actual user name, the number should be preceded by a # sign.

Many Apache administrators use the default *nobody* user for their sites. This user is not available on all UNIX systems, and is not always desirable. I highly recommend that you employ a unique user and group ID (see the Group directive) for your Apache server. Doing so will give you better control of what the server can or cannot access. The user ID you decide to use for Apache child processes should have very few access privileges. It should not be able to access files that are not intended to be visible to the outside world, and similarly, the user should not be able to execute applications that are not meant for HTTP requests.

Use of this directive in the <VirtualHost> container requires a properly configured suEXEC wrapper. When the wrapper is used inside a <VirtualHost> container in this manner, only the user that CGIs are run as is affected. Non-CGI requests are still processed with the user specified in the main User directive. So, the primary User directive is not completely overridable.

Finally, never set the User (or Group) directive to root unless you know exactly what you are doing and what the dangers are.

Performance and Resource Configuration Directives

These directives enable you to fine-tune Apache for higher performance and better control. You can fine-tune the Apache processes in many ways. Almost all of these directives require a clear understanding of how your system works in terms of the operating system, hardware, and so on. Therefore, it would be helpful to browse your operating system manuals and/or man pages to learn how your system limits system resources to processes, how it controls TCP/IP connectivity, and so on.

The directives in this section are further divided into sub-functions.

Controlling Apache Processes

The following directives are used to control how Apache executes in your system. Using these directives also enables you to control how Apache uses resources on your system. For example, you can decide how many child server processes to run on your system, or how many threads you should allow Apache to use on a Windows platform.

A few things to remember when configuring these directives:

- The more processes you run, the more load your CPU(s) experiences.
- The more processes you run, the more RAM you need.
- The more processes you run, the more operating system resources (such as file descriptors, shared buffers) are used.

Of course, more processes also could mean more requests serviced and thus more hits for your site. So, setting these directives should be based on a combination of experimentation, requirements, and available resources.

ListenBacklog

Syntax: `ListenBacklog backlog`

Default: `ListenBacklog 511`

Context: `server config`

Compatibility: `only available in Apache versions after 1.2.0.`

This directive enables you to take defensive action against a known security attack called Denial of Service (DOS) by enabling you to set the maximum length of the queue of pending connections. Increase this if you detect that you are under a TCP SYN flood attack, which is a type of DOS attack; otherwise, you can leave it alone.

MaxClients

Syntax: `MaxClients number`

Default: `MaxClients 256`

Context: `server config`

This directive limits the number of simultaneous requests that Apache can service. Because Apache uses one child server for each request, this is also the effective limit for the number of child servers that can exist at the same time. The default limit is really the hard limit set in the httpd.h file in the Apache source distribution. This setting should be fine for most typical to moderate load sites. The Apache programmers put the hard limit there for two reasons: they do not want the server to crash the system by filling out some kernel table, and, this maximum limit keeps the scoreboard file small enough to be easily readable.

If you have a high-performance server system and have the necessary bandwidth, you can recompile the server with a higher hard limit by modifying the httpd.h file. Look for the following conditional define statements and change the number 256 to a higher number.

```
#ifndef HARD_SERVER_LIMIT
#define HARD_SERVER_LIMIT 256
#endif
```

So, what happens when the server reaches the maximum request count? Well, it puts the incoming requests in a wait state until it is free to service them.

MaxRequestsPerChild

Syntax: `MaxRequestsPerChild number`

Default: `MaxRequestsPerChild 0`

Context: `server config`

Apache launches a child server process to service a request, however, a child server can process multiple requests. The number of requests a child server can process is limited by the MaxRequestsPerChild directive. After servicing the maximum number of requests, the child process terminates.

If the MaxRequestsPerChild is 0 (zero), then the process will never expire. If you suspect there are libraries on your operating system (for example, Solaris) that have memory-leaking code, you may want to set this directive to a non-zero value. This enables you to define a life cycle for a child process, and therefore reduces the chances of a process consuming leaked memory and slowly eating up all available memory. It also provides you with a small load average number for your system, since the Apache-related load is reduced as your Web server becomes less busy.

MaxSpareServers

Syntax: `MaxSpareServers number`

Default: `MaxSpareServers 10`

Context: `server config`

This directive lets you set the number of idle Apache child processes you want on your server. If the number of idle Apache child processes exceeds the maximum number specified by the MaxSpareServers directive, then the parent process kills off the excess processes. Turning off this parameter should only be necessary for very busy sites. Unless you know what you are doing, do not change the default.

MinSpareServers

Syntax: `MinSpareServers number`

Default: `MinSpareServers 5`

Context: `server config`

The MinSpareServers directive sets the desired minimum number of idle child server processes. An idle process is one that is not handling a request. If there are fewer idle Apache processes than the number specified by the MinSpareServers directive, then the parent process creates new children at a maximum rate of one per second. Turning of this parameter should be necessary only on very busy sites. Unless you know what you are doing, do not change the default.

SendBufferSize

Syntax: `SendBufferSize bytes`

Context: `server config`

This directive sets the TCP send buffer size to the number of bytes specified. On a high-performance network, setting the directive to a higher value than the operating system defaults may increase server performance.

ServerType

Syntax: `ServerType inetd | standalone`

Default: `ServerType standalone`

Context: `server config`

The ServerType directive tells Apache how it should be run by a UNIX system. There are two values for this directive: inetd and standalone.

Use the inetd value to run your server by the system process called -inetd. In this system, for each HTTP connection received, a new copy of the Apache server is started; after the connection is serviced by the Apache server, it exits. This increases the amount of work the system must do to service a request and therefore is not efficient performance-wise. However, inetd has been around for a long time, and various security options (such as TCP wrappers) are available for it. Many Internet server administrators prefer running services this way. For low-traffic sites, the difference in performance may not be noticeable.

Running Apache as an inetd-run server does not automatically make it more secure than running it in standalone mode. Since inetd has been around for a long time, many veteran administrators consider it less prone to attack.

Use the standalone value to run your system in standalone mode, in which Apache runs as a daemon process. In other words, a primary Apache server listens for a connection request to the specified ports, and as new connection requests come, it launches child Apache processes to service the requests; it never services any HTTP request by itself. The child processes are run with the user ID and the group ID specified in the User and Group directives. You should consult these directives to learn more about their settings. I recommend this option for busy, high-traffic sites.

StartServers

Syntax: `StartServers number`

Default: `StartServers 5`

Context: `server config`

The StartServers directive is useful only when the Apache server is running as a standalone server. In other words, you need to have ServerType set to standalone for this directive to be effective.

This directive sets the number of child Apache server processes that are created on startup. The number of Apache child processes needed for a certain time period is dynamically controlled. The primary Apache server (the daemon process) launches new child processes as it encounters a higher load of requests. The actual number of child processes is controlled by the MinSpareServers, MaxSpareServers, and MaxClients directives. Therefore, you have little to gain by adjusting this parameter.

When running with Microsoft Windows, this directive sets the total number of child processes running. Because the Windows version of Apache is multithreaded, one process handles all the requests. The rest of the processes are held in reserve until the primary process dies.

ThreadsPerChild

Syntax: `ThreadsPerChild number`

Default: `ThreadsPerChild 50`

Context: `server config (Windows)`

Compatibility: `only with Apache 1.3 and later with Windows`

The Windows version of Apache is a multithreaded server. The ThreadsPerChild directive tells the server how many threads it should use. It also decides the maximum number of connections the server can handle at any given time. Therefore, this value should be set reasonably high to allow the maximum number of possible hits.

TimeOut

Syntax: `TimeOut number`

Default: `TimeOut 300`

Context: `server config`

As you may already know, the Web is really a client/server system where the Apache server responds to requests. The requests and responses are transmitted via packets of data and Apache must know how long to wait for a certain packet. This directive enables you to configure the time in seconds. The time you specify here is the maximum time Apache will wait before it breaks a connection; the default setting allows Apache to wait for 300 seconds before it disconnects itself from the client. If you are on a slow network, however, you may want to increase the time out value to decrease the number of disconnects.

Currently, this time out setting applies to:

- The total amount of time it takes to receive a GET request.
- The amount of time between receipt of TCP packets on a POST or PUT request.
- The amount of time between ACKs on transmissions of TCP packets in responses.

Making Persistent Connections

Using the KeepAlive directives discussed in this section, you can instruct Apache to use persistent connections so that a single TCP connection can be used for multiple transactions. Normally, every HTTP request and response uses a separate connection. This means that every time the server gets a request, it opens a connection to retrieve the request and then closes it. Once the server has received the request, it opens another TCP connection to respond, and finally closes the connection after completing the service. This method increases the toll on high performance. Reuse of a single connection for multiple transactions reduces the overhead needed for setting up and closing a TCP connection repeatedly, and thereby increases performance.

To establish a persistent connection, however, both the server and the client need to have the persistent connection facility. Most popular browsers, such as Netscape Navigator and Microsoft Internet Explorer, have KeepAlive features built in.

Not all transactions can take advantage of the persistent connections. One of the requirements for a persistent connection is that the resources being transmitted must have a known size. Because many CGI scripts, SSI commands, and other dynamically generated contents do not have a known length before transmission, they are unable to take advantage of this feature.

KeepAlive

Syntax: `(Apache 1.2) KeepAlive On | Off`

Default: `(Apache 1.2) KeepAlive On`

Context: `server config`

Compatibility: `only available in Apache 1.1 and later`

This directive enables you to activate/deactivate persistent use of TCP connections in Apache.

Older Apache servers (prior to version 1.2) may require a numeric value instead of On/Off. This value corresponds to the maximum number of requests you want Apache to entertain per request. A limit is imposed to prevent a client from taking over all your server resources. To disable KeepAlive in the older Apache versions, use 0 (zero) as the value.

KeepAliveTimeout

Syntax: `KeepAliveTimeout seconds`

Default: `KeepAliveTimeout 15`

Context: `server config`

If you have the KeepAlive directive set to On, you can use this directive to limit the number of seconds Apache will wait for a subsequent request before closing a connection. Once a request has been received, the timeout value specified by the Timeout directive applies.

MaxKeepAliveRequests

Syntax: `MaxKeepAliveRequests number`

Default: `MaxKeepAliveRequests 100`

Context: `server config`

Compatibility: `only available in Apache 1.2 and later.`

The MaxKeepAliveRequests directive limits the number of requests allowed per connection when KeepAlive is set to On. If it is set to 0 (zero), unlimited requests will be allowed. I recommend that this setting be kept to a high value for maximum server performance.

Controlling System Resources

Apache is quite flexible in allowing you to control the amount of system resources (such as CPU time and memory) it consumes. These control features come in handy for making your Web server system more reliable and responsive. Many typical hacking attempts try to make a Web server consume all system resources like a hog and thus try to make the system non-responsive and virtually halted. Apache provides a set of directives to combat such a situation. These directives are discussed in this section.

LimitRequestBody

Syntax: `LimitRequestBody number`

Default: `LimitRequestBody 0`

Context: `all`

Compatibility: `only available in Apache 1.3.2 and later`

This directive sets a limit on the allowed size of an HTTP request message body. The default value is 0 (zero), which means that the size of the message body is unlimited. The allowed range is 0 to 2147483647. You should change this directive only if you notice abnormal client requests in log files. Such requests might be made by hackers trying to exploit the server's request handling buffers.

A client that sends a request message that exceeds the message body size limit specified in this directive will see an error message and the request will not be serviced. This protects the server from a form of denial of service attack.

LimitRequestFields

Syntax: `LimitRequestFields number`

Default: `LimitRequestFields 100`

Context: `server config`

Compatibility: `only available in Apache 1.3.2 and later`

This directive sets a limit on the number of fields in an HTTP request header. The default value of 100 should be more then enough as a typical request header includes only approximately 20 fields or so. You can use a number between 0 (zero—meaning unlimited) to 32767. You should not have to change the default. If you do want to change the maximum value of the limit, you will have to modify the DEFAULT_LIMIT_REQUEST_FIELDS constant in the src/include/httpd.h include file. Client request headers that contain more than the specified fields will generate an error message and the request will not be serviced to protect the server from a denial of service attack.

LimitRequestFieldsize

Syntax: `LimitRequestFieldsize number`

Default: `LimitRequestFieldsize 8190`

Context: `server config`

Compatibility: `only available in Apache 1.3.2 and later`

This directive sets a limit on the number of fields in an HTTP request header. The default value of 8190 should be more then enough for typical request headers. You should not have to change the default. However, if you want to change this, you will have to change the DEFAULT_LIMIT_REQUEST_FIELDSIZE constant in the src/include/httpd.h include file. Client request headers that contain more then the specified fields will generate an error message and the request will not be serviced to protect the server from a denial of service attack.

LimitRequestLine

Syntax: `LimitRequestLine number`

Default: `LimitRequestLine 8190`

Context: `server config`

Compatibility: `only available in Apache 1.3.2 and later`

This directive sets a limit on the number of lines in an HTTP request header. The default value of 100 should be more then enough for typical request headers. You should not have to change the default. However, if you want to change this you will have to change the DEFAULT_LIMIT_REQUEST_LINE constant in the src/include/httpd.h include file. Client request headers that contain more then the specified fields will generate an error message and the request will not be serviced to protect the server from a denial of service attack.

RLimitCPU

Syntax: `RLimitCPU n | 'max' [ n | 'max']`
Default: `Unset; uses operating system defaults`
Context: `server config, virtual host`
Compatibility: `only available in Apache 1.2 and later`

This directive enables you to control Apache's CPU usage. The directive takes two parameters. The first parameter sets a soft resource limit for all processes, and the second parameter sets the maximum resource limit. Raising the maximum resource limit requires that the server be running as a root or in the initial startup phase. The second parameter is optional.

For each of these parameters, there are two possible values:

- n is the number of seconds per process
- max is the maximum resource limit allowed by the operating system

RLimitMEM

Syntax: `RLimitMEM n | 'max' [ n | 'max']`
Default: `Unset; uses operating system defaults`
Context: `server config, virtual host`
Compatibility: `only available in Apache 1.2 and later`

This directive limits the memory (RAM) usage of Apache processes. The directive takes two parameters. The first parameter sets a soft resource limit for all processes, and the second parameter sets the maximum resource limit. Raising the maximum resource limit requires that the server be started by the root user. The second parameter is optional.

For each of these parameters, there are two possible values:

- n is the number of bytes per process
- max is the maximum resource limit allowed by the operating system

RLimitNPROC

Syntax: `RLimitNPROC n | 'max' [ n | 'max']`

Default: `Unset; uses operating system defaults`

Context: `server config, virtual host`

Compatibility: `only available in Apache 1.2 and later`

This directive sets the maximum number of simultaneous processes per user. It takes one or two parameters. The first parameter sets the soft resource limit for all processes, and the second parameter sets the maximum resource limit. Each parameter can be either of the following:

- n is the number of bytes per process
- max is the maximum resource limit allowed by the operating system

Raising the maximum resource limit requires that the server be running as a root or in the initial startup phase.

If your CGI processes are run under the same user ID as the server process, use of this directive limits the number of processes the server can launch (or "fork"). If the limit is too low, you will see a message similar to the following in your server error log file:

```
"Can not fork process"
```

In such a case, you should increase the limit or just leave it as the default. I highly recommend that you leave this limit as the default.

Using Dynamic Modules

Apache loads all the precompiled modules when it starts up; however, it also provides a dynamic module loading and unloading feature that may be useful on certain occasions. When you use the following dynamic module directives, you can change the list of active modules without recompiling the server.

AddModule

Syntax: `AddModule module module ...`

Context: `server config`

Compatibility: `only available in Apache 1.2 and later`

This directive can be used to enable a precompiled module that is currently not active. The server can have modules compiled that are not actively in use. This directive can be used to enable these modules. The server comes with a preloaded list of active modules; this list can be cleared with the ClearModuleList directive. Then, new modules can be added using the AddModule directive.

ClearModuleList

Syntax: `ClearModuleList`

Context: `server config`

Compatibility: `only available in Apache 1.2 and later`

You can use this directive to clear the list of active modules and enable the dynamic module-loading feature. Then, use the AddModule directive to add modules that you want to activate.

Standard Container Directives

In this section, I discuss the standard containers that are part of the base Apache server. These containers are widely used to apply a group of other directives to a certain directory, file, or location.

The <VirtualHost> container is discussed later in this chapter.

You cannot randomly mix and match the containers. The general guidelines are:

- Use the <Directory> or <Files> containers to specify directives for file system objects such as files and directories. You cannot use <Directory> inside an .htaccess file, because an .htaccess file applies only to the directory where it is found.

- Use the <Location> container for matching URL objects. You cannot use this directive inside an .htaccess file.
- When using the regular expression version of a directive (for example, <DirectoryMatch>), follow the same guidelines as for the regular version. Use the regular expression version of the containers only if you are confident that your regular expressions are tightly expressed.
- Due to a mistake in the early stage of Apache, the proxy control is still done with the <Directory> container, whereas the <Location> container is more appropriate for it. This may be corrected in a future version. However, this really doesn't cause any harm, other than making things a bit more difficult to conceptualize.

<Directory>

Syntax: `<Directory directory> ... </Directory>`
Context: `server config, virtual host`

<Directory> and </Directory> are used to enclose a group of directives that apply only to the named directory and its subdirectories.

Any directive that is allowed in a directory context may be used. The argument can be a fully qualified path name. For example:

```
<Directory /www/mycompany/public/htdocs/download>
Options +Indexes
</Directory>
```

Here, the directory /www/mycompany/public/htdocs/download is used as a fully qualified path name. This example enables directory indexing in this directory. You also can use wildcard characters such as `*` and `?` in specifying the path. For example:

```
<Directory /www/mycompany/public/htdocs/downloa?>
Options +Indexes
</Directory>
```

Here, the ? will match any single character; therefore, directories such as /www/mycompany/public/htdocs/download and /www/mycompany/public/htdocs/downloaD will be matched. You can use * (asterisk) to match any sequence of characters other than the / (forward slash) character. Extended regular expressions can also be used, with the addition of the ~ (tilde) character. For example, the following would match any subdirectory under /www/:

```
<Directory ~ "^/www/.*/">
```

Regular expression-based <Directory> containers may not be applied until all normal (that is, without regular expression) <Directory> containers and .htaccess files have been applied. Then, all the regular expressions are tested in the order in which they appeared in the configuration file.

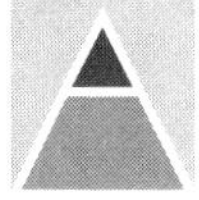

TIP

For a detailed explanation of the regular expressions, see Appendix B.

If you specify more than one <Directory> container for the same directory space, the <Directory> container with the narrowest scope is applied first. For example:

```
<Directory /www>
AllowOverride None
</Directory>

<Directory ~ "/www/mycompany/public/htdocs/*">
AllowOverride FileInfo
</Directory>
```

According to this, when a request for /www/mycompany/public/htdocs/somefile.cvs arrives, Apache disables the per-directory access control file (.htaccess) for /www and then enables it for /www/mycompany/public/htdocs. It also accepts any FileInfo directive such as DefaultType from within the /www/mycompany/public/htdocs/.htaccess file.

Also, <Directory> containers defined in a virtual host configuration override corresponding <Directory> containers in the main server.

<DirectoryMatch>

Syntax: `<DirectoryMatch regex> ... </DirectoryMatch>`
Context: `server config, virtual host`
Compatibility: `only in Apache 1.3 and later`

This is exactly the same as the <Directory> container, except that it takes a regular expression as the argument and does not require the ~ (tilde) character. <DirectoryMatch> and </DirectoryMatch> are used to enclose a group of directives that apply only to the named directory and its subdirectories. For example, the following would match all subdirectories of /www/mycompany/public/htdocs that have exactly eight uppercase letters as a name:

```
<DirectoryMatch "^/www/mycompany/pubic/htdocs/[A-
Z]{8}/*">
```

Therefore, `/www/mycompany/public/htdocs/AAAABBBB/` would match the preceding regular expression. For more details on regular expressions, see Appendix B.

Also, <DirectoryMatch> containers are taken into considerations after all <Directory> containers have been applied. In other words, this type of container gets lower priority over <Directory> containers.

<Files>

Syntax: `<Files filename> ... </Files>`
Context: `server config, virtual host, .htaccess`
Compatibility: `only available in Apache 1.2 and above.`

To control access by filename, you need to use this directive. <Files> sections are processed in the order in which they appear in the configuration file, after the <Directory> sections and .htaccess files are read, but before the <Location> sections are read. The filename argument should include a filename, or a wildcard string, where ? matches any single character, and * matches any sequence of characters except the / character. Using the ~ (tilde) character, you can enable extended regular expression checking on the argument. As an example, the following would match any file with the .zip, .tar, .tgz, .arj, and .zoo extensions:

```
<Files ~ "\.(zip|tar|tgz|arj|zoo)$">
```

Unlike <Directory> and <Location> sections, <Files> sections can be used inside .htaccess files. When using these from within an .htaccess file, you don't need to append the path name, because an .htaccess file applies only to the directory where it is found.

<FilesMatch>

Syntax: `<FilesMatch regex> ... </Files>`
Context: `server config, virtual host, .htaccess`
Compatibility: `only available in Apache 1.3 and above.`

This is the same as the <Files> directive, except that it takes a regular expression as its argument. For example, the following would match any file with the .zip, .tar, .tgz, .arj, and .zoo extensions:

```
<FilesMatch "\.( zip|tar|tgz|arj|zoo)$">
```

Notice that you do not need the ~ (tilde) character in this directive to use a regular expression.

<Location>

Syntax: `<Location URL> ... </Location>`
Context: `server config, virtual host`

This directive provides access control by URL. <Location> containers are processed in the order in which they appear in the configuration file, after the <Directory> containers and .htaccess files are read.

The URL argument cannot have the http://servername prefix. You can use wildcard characters such as ? (matches any single character) or * (matches any sequence of characters except for the / character). You also can use an extended regular expression using the ~ character before the expression. For example, the following would match URLs such as /my/file or your/file:

```
<Location ~ "/(my|your)/file">
```

<Location> containers defined in a virtual host configuration override corresponding < Location > containers in the main server.

<LocationMatch>

Syntax: `<LocationMatch regex> ... </LocationMatch>`
Context: `server config, virtual host`
Compatibility: `only available in Apache 1.3 and later`

This directive is identical to the <Location> directive except that its argument (URL) is a regular expression, and it does not require a ~ (tilde) before the expression. For example, the following would match URLs such as /my/file or your/file:

```
<LocationMatch "/(my|your)/file">
```

Virtual Host Specific Directives

These directives are used for creating virtual hosts. By default, Apache services only the Web site host specified by the ServerName directive. It is possible, however, to make Apache serve other Web sites using a virtual host container directive. Many directives I discussed in the General Configuration Directives section are also applicable to virtual hosts.

NameVirtualHost

Syntax: `NameVirtualHost addr[:port]`

Context: `server config`

Compatibility: `only available in Apache 1.3 and later`

If you plan on using name-based virtual hosts, you need to use this directive. Although addr can be the host name, I recommend that you always use an IP address.

For example, for a virtual host named `www.mycompany.com` that uses the IP address 11.22.33.44, the directive and virtual host definition will be:

```
NameVirtualHost 11.22.33.44
<VirtualHost 11.22.33.44>
ServerName www.mycompany.com
</VirtualHost>
```

If you have multiple name-based hosts on multiple addresses, repeat the directive for each address. For example:

```
NameVirtualHost 11.22.33.44

# First virtual host that corresponds to the preceding
# NameVirtualHost directive
<VirtualHost 11.22.33.44>
ServerName www.mycompany.com
</VirtualHost>

# Second virtual host that corresponds to the preceding
# NameVirtualHost directive
<VirtualHost 11.22.33.44>
ServerName www.friendscompany.com
</VirtualHost>

#  Another NameVirtualHost directive for
#  a new set of name-based virtual hosts that
```

```
#  use a different IP.
NameVirtualHost 11.22.33.55

<VirtualHost 11.22.33.55>
ServerName www.myclient.com
</VirtualHost>
<VirtualHost 11.22.33.55>
ServerName www.herclient.com
</VirtualHost>
```

Here, the first NameVirtualHost directive is used for the `www.mycompany.com` and `www.friendscompany.com` virtual hosts. The second one is used for the `www.myclient.com` and `the www.herclient.com` virtual hosts. Optionally, you can specify a port number on which the name-based virtual hosts should be used. For example:

```
NameVirtualHost 11.22.33.44:8080
```

ServerAlias

Syntax: `ServerAlias host1 host2 ...`
Context: `virtual host`
Compatibility: `only available in Apache 1.1 and later.`

When you have a name-based virtual host with multiple IP names (CNAME records in the DNS database), you can use a single virtual host definition to service all of them. For example:

```
NameVirtualHost 11.22.33.55

<VirtualHost 11.22.33.55>
ServerName www.myclient.com
ServerAlias www.sac-state.edu  www.csu.sacramento.edu
</VirtualHost>
```

Here, `www.sac-state.edu` and `www.csu.sacramento.edu` are aliases for the `www.csus.edu` virtual host. You also can use wildcard characters such as `*` in defining aliases.

ServerPath

Syntax: `ServerPath pathname`
Context: `virtual host`
Compatibility: `only available in Apache 1.1 and later.`

This directive sets the legacy URL (in other words, the URL used when browsers do not indicate the domain name with their requests) path name for a host, for use with name-based virtual hosts. Typically, this is used to support browsers that are not HTTP/1.1-compliant.

<VirtualHost>

Syntax: `<VirtualHost addr[:port] ...> ... </VirtualHost>`
Context: `server config`
Compatibility: `multiple address support only available in Apache 1.2 and later.`

This container directive specifies a virtual host configuration. All the enclosed directives found within the <VirtualHost> and the closing </VirtualHost> apply only to the named virtual host. Any directive that is allowed in a virtual host context may be used. When the server receives a request for a document on a particular virtual host, it uses the configuration directives enclosed in the <VirtualHost>.

To specify which IP address or IP name is to be used for a particular virtual host, you can use any of the following:

- An IP address. Example: <VirtualHost 11.22.33.44> ... </VirtualHost>.

- An IP address with a port number. Example: <VirtualHost 11.22.33.44:8080> … </VirtualHost>.
- Multiple IP addresses. Example: <VirtualHost 11.22.33.1 11.22.33.2> … </VirtualHost>.
- Multiple IP addresses with port numbers. Example: <VirtualHost 11.22.33.1:8000 11.22.33.2:10000> … </VirtualHost>.

You can replace IP addresses with IP names, but this is not recommended; if the DNS lookup necessary to determine the address fails for some reason, the server may get confused and not service the virtual site at all.

The special name _default_ can be specified, in which case this virtual host will match any IP address that is not explicitly listed in another virtual host. In the absence of any _default_ virtual host, the primary server config, which consists of all the definitions outside any VirtualHost section, is used when no match occurs.

If a port is unspecified, then it defaults to the same port as the most recent Port directive of the primary server. You also may specify :* to match all ports on that address.

Logging Directives

Logging server transactions is a must for any system running Apache. Server logs provide you with valuable information, such as who accesses your Web site(s), which pages are accessed, and which errors the server generates.

LogLevel

Syntax: `LogLevel level`

Default: `LogLevel error`

Context: `server config, virtual host`

This directive specifies the level of logging for the ErrorLog directive. The available log levels are as follows:

- **emerg**. Log only when Apache is unstable.
- **alert**. Log all of the above and incidents that require immediate attention.
- **crit**. Log all of the above and critical errors.
- **Error**. Log all of the above and regular error messages.
- **warn**. Log all of the above and warnings as well.
- **notice**. Log all of the above and server notices as well.
- **info**. Log all of the above and informative messages.
- **debug**. Log everything.

When debugging a problem with your Apache server, you may want to set the log level to debug. However, making server log do more would take away server performance as more disk I/O is needed to write more data.

ErrorLog

Syntax: `ErrorLog filename`

Default: `ErrorLog logs/error_log`

Context: `server config, virtual host`

This directive specifies the log filename used to log error messages that the server produces. If the filename does not begin with a slash (/), then it is assumed to be relative to the ServerRoot.

If you need to disable error logging, you can use the following:

```
ErrorLog /dev/null
```

It is very important that the permission settings for your server log directory indicate that only the Apache user (specified by the User directive) is allowed read/write access. Allowing anyone else to write in this directory could potentially create security holes.

ScoreBoardFile

Syntax: `ScoreBoardFile filename`

Default: `ScoreBoardFile logs/apache_status`

Context: `server config`

This directive sets the path to the file used for storing internal process data. If the filename does not begin with a slash (/), then it is assumed to be relative to the ServerRoot.

This file is used by the primary server process to communicate with the child processes. If you want to find out if your system requires this file, just run the Apache server and see if a file gets created in the specified location. If your system architecture requires the file, then you must ensure that this file is not used at the same time by more than one invocation of Apache. Also, make sure that no other user has read or write access to this file, or even to the directory in which it is kept.

Because the processes have to perform disk I/O to communicate, this could potentially cause a performance bottleneck; therefore, you should create a RAM disk for this file, if possible. Consult your operating system manuals for details.

PidFile

Syntax: `PidFile filename`

Default: `PidFile logs/httpd.pid`

Context: `server config`

Using this directive, you can tell Apache to write the primary server (that is, the daemon process) process ID (PID) in a file. If the filename does not begin with a slash (/), then it is assumed to be relative to the ServerRoot. The PidFile is used only in standalone mode.

Its primary use is to make it convenient for the Apache administrator to find the primary Apache PID, which is needed to send signals to the server. For example, if the PID file is kept in the /usr/local/httpd/logs directory, and its name is httpd.pid, an administrator can force Apache server to reread its configuration by sending a SIGHUP signal from the shell prompt (as root) as follows:

```
kill -HUP `cat /usr/local/httpd/logs/httpd.pid`
```

The same command makes Apache reopen the ErrorLog and TransferLog.

As with any other log files, make sure the PID file is not writeable or even readable by anyone other than the server process. For better security, you should make the log directory read/write-able only by the Apache server user.

LockFile

Syntax: `LockFile filename`

Default: `LockFile logs/accept.lock`

Context: `server config`

If Apache is compiled with the USE_FCNTL_SERIALIZED_ACCEPT or USE_FLOCK_SERIALIZED_ACCEPT options, a lock file is used to cordinate which Apache process should take the next incoming request. You can use this directive to set the path to the filename of the lock file. Make sure that only the Apache server has read and write access to the file.

Storing the lock file on a Network File System (NFS) mounted partition is not a good idea because NFS is known to be problematic when it comes to file locking and security. If you are using a server firm where NFS mounted file systems are in use, make sure the lock file is kept in each server machine's hard disk.

Authentication and Security Directives

The authentication and security directives discussed in this section enable you to define access policies for your server.

AllowOverride

Syntax: `AllowOverride override override ...`

Default: `AllowOverride All`

Context: `directory`

This directive tells the server which directives declared in an .htaccess file (as specified by AccessFileName) can override earlier directives found in configuration files.

When Override is set to NONE, the server does not read the file specified by AccessFileName (default .htaccess). This could speed up the response time of the server, because the server does not have to look for an AccessFileName specified file for each request (see the AccessFileName section for details).

If you do want to allow AccessFileName-based control, however, you can specify one or more of the options. The override options are:

- **AuthConfig**. Allows use of the authorization directives (such as AuthDBMGroupFile, AuthDBMUserFile, AuthGroupFile, AuthName, AuthType, AuthUserFile, and require).
- **FileInfo**. Allows use of the directives controlling document types (such as AddEncoding, AddLanguage, AddType, DefaultType, ErrorDocument, and LanguagePriority).
- **Indexes**. Allows use of the directives controlling directory indexing (such as AddDescription, AddIcon, AddIconByEncoding, AddIconByType, DefaultIcon, DirectoryIndex, FancyIndexing, HeaderName, IndexIgnore, IndexOptions, and ReadmeName).
- **Limit**. Allows use of the directives controlling host access (allow, deny, and order).

- **Options**. Allows use of the directives controlling specific directory features (Options and XBitHack).

AuthName

Syntax: `AuthName label`

Context: `directory, .htaccess`

Override: `AuthConfig`

This directive sets a label for a resource (such as a directory) that requires authentication. The label is usually displayed by a Web browser in a popup dialog window when prompting for a username and password to access the requested (controlled) resource. There is no default label. The primary purpose of this label is to inform users on the client side about what resource they are trying to access. For example, the following informs users that they are requesting to enter the "Secured Game Zone" area of a site:

```
AuthName "Secured Game Zone"
```

The double-quotes are necessary only if the label contains whitespace characters as shown in this example.

In order for this directive to work, it must be accompanied by AuthType, require directives, and directives such as AuthUserFile, and AuthGroupFile.

AuthType

Syntax: `AuthType type`

Context: `directory, .htaccess`

Override: `AuthConfig`

This directive selects the user authentication type for a directory. Currently, only basic HTTP authentication type is implemented in Apache. This type of authentication should not be used for serious needs; the password and username are transmitted in clear (plain) text. The password and username are retransmitted for each subsequent request that maps in the same restricted directory or its subdirectories.

This directive must be accompanied by AuthName and requires other directives such as AuthUserFile and AuthGroupFile to work.

HostNameLookups

Syntax: `HostNameLookups on | off | double`

Default: `HostNameLookups off`

Context: `server config, virtual host, directory, .htaccess`

Compatibility: `double available only in Apache 1.3 and above.`

This directive instructs Apache to enable or disable a DNS lookup for each request. When enabled, Apache stores the host name of the client in the REMOTE_HOST environment variable of each CGI and SSI process it runs.

The on and off values should be obvious. The double value refers to doing a double-reverse DNS lookup—that is, after a reverse lookup is performed, a forward lookup is then performed on that result. At least one of the IP addresses in the forward lookup must match the original address. However, the CGI and SSI processes do not get the results from the double DNS lookups.

No matter what you set this directive to, when mod_access is used for controlling access by host name, a double reverse lookup is performed.

I recommend that you keep the default setting for this directive. This will rid the Internet of a lot of unnecessary DNS traffic. If you want to turn it on just so your log files contain IP names instead of IP addresses, you may want to consider another option, such as running the logresolve utility to resolve IP addresses to IP names.

IdentityCheck

Syntax: `IdentityCheck boolean`

Default: `IdentityCheck off`

Context: `server config, virtual host, directory, .htaccess`

This directive tells Apache to log remote usernames by interacting with the remote user's identd (identification daemon) process, or something similar and RFC1413-compliant. This is rarely a useful directive because it will not work for all systems. Most systems do not run identd processes to provide user identifications to remote servers.

If you decide to use this directive in your configuration, be aware that the information you log is not to be trusted in any way except for usage tracking. This directive can also cause major performance problems because the server has to perform checking for each request. Also, when a remote user is either not providing an identd service or is behind a firewall or proxy, the checking process has to time out.

<Limit>

Syntax: `<Limit method method ... > ... </Limit>`

Context: `any`

This container is used to enclose a group of access control directives, which will then apply only to the specified HTTP methods. The method names listed can be one or more of the following: GET, POST, PUT, DELETE, CONNECT, and OPTIONS. If GET is used, it will also restrict HEAD requests. If you wish to limit all methods, do not include any method in the <Limit> directive at all.

This container cannot be nested, and a <Directory> container cannot appear within it either. Also, the method names are matched in a case-insensitive manner.

require

Syntax: `require entity-name entity entity...`

Context: `directory, .htaccess`

Override: `AuthConfig`

Using this directive, Apache determines which users or group can access a restricted directory. There are three types of entity-names available:

- user
- group
- valid-user

For example, this line tells Apache to allow only joe or jenny to enter the area after successful authentication:

```
require user joe jenny
```

Only the named users can access the directory. An example of a group-based access requirement would be as follows:

```
require group my-group your-group his-group her-group
```

Only users in the named groups can access the directory.

```
require valid-user
```

With the preceding line, all valid users can access the directory.

If the require directive appears in a <Limit> section, then it restricts access to the named methods; otherwise it restricts access for all methods. For example:

```
AuthType Basic
AuthName "Game Zone Drop Box"
AuthUserFile /www/netgames/users
AuthGroupFile /web/ntgames/groups
<Limit GET>
require group coders
</Limit>
```

If the preceding configuration is found in an .htaccess file in a directory, only a group called coders is allowed access to the directory to retrieve files via the HTTP GET method. In order to work correctly, the require directive must be accompanied by AuthName and AuthType directives, and directives such as AuthUserFile and AuthGroupFile.

Satisfy

Syntax: `Satisfy 'any' | 'all'`

Default: `Satisfy all`

Context: `directory, .htaccess`

Compatibility: `only available in Apache 1.2 and later`

If you have created a basic HTTP authentication configuration in which both allow and require directives are used, you can use this directive to tell Apache what will Satisfy the authentication requirements. The value of the Satisfy directive can be either all or any. If the value is all, then the authentication succeeds only if both allow and require succeed. If the value is any, then the authentication succeeds if either allow or require succeeds.

This directive is useful only if access to a particular area is being restricted by both the username/password and the client host address. In this case, the default behavior (all) requires that the client pass the address access restriction and enter a valid username and password. With the any option, the client is granted access if he or she either passes the host restriction or enters a valid username and password. This directive can be used to restrict an area using passwords, and at the same time, all clients from a particular IP address pool (that is, a set of IP addresses) are let in without being required to enter passwords.

Chapter 4

Apache Modules

This chapter covers the Apache modules.

mod_access

This module is built into the default for Apache. It enables access control based on the Internet hostname of a Web client. The hostname can be either a fully qualified domain name (FQDN), such as `blackhole.nitec.com`, or an IP address, such as 206.171.50.50. The module provides this access control support using the following Apache directives.

allow

Syntax: `allow from host1 host2 host3`
Context: `directory, location, per-directory access control file`
Override: `Limit`

This directive enables you to define a list of hosts (containing one or more hosts or IP addresses) that are allowed access to a certain directory. When more than one host or IP address is specified, they should be separated with space characters. Table 4-1 shows the possible values for the directive.

Table 4-1 *Possible Values for the allow Directive*

Value	Example	Description
All	allow from all	This reserved word allows access for all hosts. The example shows how to use this option.
A fully qualified domain name (FQDN) of a host	allow from `wormhole.nitec.com`	Only the host that has the specified FQDN is allowed access. The allow directive in the example allows access only to `wormhole.nitec.com`. Note that this compares whole components; `toys.com` would not match `etoys.com`.
A partial domain name of a host	allow from `.mainoffice .nitec.com`	Only the hosts that match the partial host name are allowed access. The example permits all the hosts in the `.mainoffice.nitec.com` network to access the site. For example, `developer1.mainoffice.nitec.com` and `developer2.mainoffice.nitec.com` have access to the site. However, `developer3.baoffice.nitec.com` is not allowed access.
A full IP address of a host	allow from 206.171.50.50	Only the specified IP address is allowed access. The example shows a full IP address (all four octets of IP are present), 206.171.50.50, that is allowed access.
A partial IP address	Example 1: allow from 206.171.50 Example 2: allow from 130.86	When not all four octets of an IP address are present in the allow directive, the partial IP address is matched from left to right, and hosts that have the matching IP address pattern (that is, it is part of the same subnet) are allowed access. In the first example, all hosts with IP addresses in the range of 206.171.50.1 to 206.171.50.255 have access. In the second example, all hosts from the 130.86 network are allowed access.

Value	Example	Description
A network/netmask pair	allow from 206.171.50.0/255.255.255.0	This enables you to specify a range of IP addresses using the network and the netmask address. The example allows only the hosts with IP addresses in the range of 206.171.50.1 to 206.171.50.255 to have access. This feature is available in Apache 1.3 or above.
A network/nnn CIDR specification	allow 206.171.50.0/19	Similar to the previous entry, except the netmask consists of nnn high-order 1 bits. The example is equivalent to allow from 206.171.50.0/255.255.224.0. This feature is available in Apache 1.3 or above.

deny

Syntax: `deny from host1 host2 host3`

Context: `directory, location, per-directory access control file`

Override: `Limit`

This directive is the exact opposite of the allow directive. It enables you to define a list of hosts that are denied access to a specified directory. Like the allow directive, it can accept all the values shown in Table 4-1.

order

Syntax: `order deny, allow | allow, deny | mutual-failure`

Default: `order deny, allow`

Context: `directory, location, per-directory access control file`

Override: `Limit`

This directive controls how Apache evaluates both allow and deny directives. For example:

```
<Directory /mysite/myboss/rants>
order deny, allow
deny from myboss.mycompany.com
allow from all
</Directory>
```

This example denies the host `myboss.mycompany.com` access and allows all other hosts to access the directory. The value for the order directive is a comma-separated list, which indicates which directive takes precedence. Typically, the one that affects all hosts is given lowest priority. In the preceding example, because the allow directive affects all hosts, it is given the lower priority.

Although allow, deny and deny, allow are the most widely used values for the order directive, you can use another value, mutual-failure. This indicates that only those hosts appearing on the allow list and not on the deny list are granted access.

In all cases, every allow and deny directive is evaluated.

allow from env=variable

Syntax: `allow from env=variable`
Context: `directory, location, per-directory access control file`
Override: `Limit`

This directive, a variation of the allow directive, allows access when the named environment variable is set. This is useful only if you are using other directives such as BrowserMatch to set an environment variable. For example, say you want to allow Microsoft Internet Explorer 4.01, the latest version of Internet Explorer, to access a directory where you stored some HTML files with embedded VBScript. Because the other leading Web browser, Netscape

Navigator, does not support VBScript directly, you'd rather not have Navigator users go into the directory. In such a case, you can use the BrowserMatch directive to set an environment variable when Internet Explorer 4.01 is detected. The directive would be as follows:

```
BrowserMatch "MSIE 4.01" ms_browser
```

Now you can use a <Directory> container to specify the allow directive, as follows:

```
<Directory /path/to/Vbscript_directory >
order deny,allow
deny from all
allow from env=ms_browser
</Directory>
```

Here the Apache server will set the ms_browser environment variable for all browsers that provide the "MSIE 4.01" string as part of the user-agent identifier. The allow directive will allow only browsers for which the is set.

deny from env=variable

Syntax: `deny from env=variable`
Context: `directory, location, per-directory access control file`
Override: `Limit`

This directive, a variation of the deny directive, denies access capability for all hosts for which the specified environment is set. For example, if you want to deny all hosts using Microsoft Internet Explorer access, you can use the BrowserMatch directive to set a variable called ms_browser whenever a browser identifies itself to the server with the string "MSIE".

```
BrowserMatch "MSIE" ms_browser
```

Now you can use a <Directory> container to specify the deny directive, as follows:

```
<Directory /path/to/Vbscript_directory >
order allow,deny
allow from all
deny from env=ms_browser
</Directory>
```

If you are interested in blocking access to a specific HTTP request method, such as GET, POST, and PUT, you can use the <Limit> container to do so. For example:

```
<Location /cgi-bin>
<Limit POST>
order deny,allow
deny from all
allow from yourdomain.com
</Location>
```

This example allows POST requests to the cgi-bin directory only if they are made by hosts in the `yourdomain.com` domain. In other words, if this site has some HTML forms that send user input data via the HTTP POST method, only the users in `yourdomain.com` will be able to use these forms effectively. Typically, CGI applications are stored in the cgi-bin directory, and many sites feature HTML forms that use the POST method to dump data to CGI applications. Using the preceding host-based access control configuration, a site can allow anyone to run a CGI script but only allow a certain site (in this case, `yourdomain.com`) to actually post data to one or more CGI scripts. This gives the CGI access in such a site a bit of read-only character. Everyone can run applications that generate output without taking any user input, but only users of a certain domain can provide input.

mod_actions

This module is compiled by default. It enables you to run a CGI script based on MIME-type or the HTTP request method and offers the following directives.

Action

Syntax: `Action MIME-type cgi-script`

Context: `server config, virtual host, directory, per-directory configuration (.htaccess)`

Override: `FileInfo`

Status: `Base`

This directive enables you to associate an action for a specific MIME-type. The action is usually a CGI script that processes the file being requested. For example:

```
Action text/html/cgi-bin/somescript.pl
```

This makes Apache run the specified script whenever an HTML file is requested. The script receives the URL and file path of the requested document via the standard CGI PATH_INFO and PATH_TRANSLATED environment variables. This can be useful in developing filter scripts. This section discusses one such filter script.

When a text file (.txt) is requested via the Web, it appears on the Web browser in a less-than-desirable format, because the line breaks are not translated by Web browsers in any manner. Usually, most text files appear as a large paragraph. Using the Action directive, you can develop a better solution. To make this example a bit more interesting, let's also say that you want to develop a solution that not only displays the text files better on the Web browser but also inserts a copyright message at the end of each text file.

To accomplish this, you need to do two things. First, add the following directive in an Apache configuration file (such as srm.conf.):

```
Action plain/text /cgi-bin/textfilter.pl
```

Then, develop the Perl script, textfilter, that will display the text file the way you wish. Listing 4-1 shows one such script.

Listing 4-1 *textfilter.pl*

```
#!/usr/local/bin/perl
#
# Script: textfilter.pl
#
# Purpose: this filter script converts plain text files
# into an HTML document but keeps the text layout
# as is.
#
# $Author$
# $Revision$
# $Id$
# $Status
#

# The copyright message file will be always stored on
# the server's document root
# directory and is called copyright.html.
#
my $copyright_file = $ENV{DOCUMENT_ROOT} .
"/copyright.html";

# Get the requested document's path.
my $path_translated = $ENV{PATH_TRANSLATED};

# Other variables needed for storing data:
my $line;
my @text;
```

```
my @html;

# Store the path info and the file name of
# requested doc in an array.
@filename = split(/\//,$path_translated);

# Since HTML tags will be used to display the text file,
# let's print the text/html content header.
print "Content-type: text/html\n\n";

# Read the document requested and store the data
# in @text array variable.
@text = &readFile($path_translated);

# Now print the following HTML document tags.
# These tags will be sent before the actual
# document content.
#
print <<HEAD;
<HTML>
<HEAD>
<TITLE>$filename[-1] </TITLE>
</HEAD>
<BODY BGCOLOR="white">

<BLOCKQUOTE>

<PRE>

<FONT FACE="Arial">

HEAD

# Now print each line stored in the @text array
```

Continued

Listing 4-1 *Continued*

```
# (i.e., the content of the document requested).
#
foreach $line (@text){ print $line; }

# Now read the copyright file and store the content
# in the @html array variable.
#
@html = &readFile($copyright_file);

# Print each line stored in the @html array (i.e.,
# the content of the copyright message file).
#
foreach $line (@html){ print $line; }

# Exit the filter.
exit 0;

sub readFile{
#
# Subroutine: readFile.
# Purpose: reads a file if it exists or else prints
# an error messages and exits script.
#

# Get the name of the passed file name and store
# it in variable $file.
 my $file = shift;

# Local buffer variable.
 my @buffer;

# If the file exists, then open it and read all the
# lines into the @buffer array variable.
 if(-e $file){
```

```
    open(FP,$file) || die "Can not open $file.";

    while(<FP>){
      push(@buffer,$_);
      }

    close(FP);
    }

  else{
      push(@buffer,"$file is missing.");
      }

# Return the content of the buffer.
 return (@buffer);
 }
```

This script reads the requested text file and prints out the content inside a few HTML tags that enable the content to be displayed as is. This trick is done using the HTML tag <PRE>. After the content is printed, a copyright message file content is inserted at the end of the output. This enables a copyright message to be printed with each requested text file. The document is block quoted, and a custom copyright message is printed. The copyright message file is stored in the document root directory. The one used in this example is:

```
<BLOCKQUOTE>
<CENTER>
<HR>
Copyright © 1998 Mohammed J. Kabir () ({Hyperlink
Mail to:kabir@nitec.com})
</CENTER>
</BODY>
</HTML>
```

Script

Syntax: `Script method cgi-script`

Context: `server config, virtual host, directory`

This directive is like the Action directive, but instead of associating an action with a MIME-type, it associates the action with an HTTP request such as GET, POST, PUT, or DELETE. The CGI script receives the URL and file path of the requested document using the standard CGI PATH_INFO and PATH_TRANSLATED environment variables. This directive defines default action. In other words, if you have defined the following in an Apache configuration file (such as srm.conf):

```
Script POST /cgi-bin/deafult_post.pl
```

Then, whenever a request is made via the HTTP POST method, it will be processed as usual unless the default action specified by the directive needs to be used. For example, the following HTML form does not specify a CGI script as its action:

```
<FORM METHOD="POST">
Enter Name: <INPUT TYPE=TEXT NAME="name" SIZE=25>
<INPUT TYPE=SUBMIT VALUE="Click Here">
</FORM>
```

If a name is submitted by a user via this form, there is no specified CGI script to process the information, in which case the default POST action /cgi-bin/default_post.pl script is run. However, if the <FORM ...> tag is changed to:

```
<FORM ACTION="/cgi-bin/form_processor.pl" METHOD="POST">
```

Then whenever the form is submitted, the /cgi-bin/form_processor.pl script will be called as usual. What you do in the default action script is up to you. In an Internet service provider setup, I recommend making the default script print out meaningful messages, so the HTML form developer user can get a clue about what he or she is not doing right.

In case of the GET request, the default action is used only if the request accompanies query data. For example, `www.yoursite.com/somefile.html` will be processed as usual, but if a request such as `www.yoursite.com/somefile.html?some=data` is received, then the default action for GET will be run.

mod_alias

This module is compiled into the default for Apache. It provides the following directives that can be used to map one part of the server's file system to another or even perform URL redirection services.

Alias

Syntax: `Alias URL-path path`
Context: `server config, virtual host`

This directive enables you to map a path to anywhere in your system's file system. For example:

```
Alias /data  /web/data
```

This maps /data to /web/data; therefore, when a request such as `www.yoursite.com/data/datafile.cvs` is received, the file called /web/data/datafile.cvs is returned. The aliased path does not have to reside inside your document root tree, so be careful when you create aliases — you might accidentally reveal some part of your file system to the entire world.

If you use a trailing / (slash) in defining an alias, the requests that are able to access the aliased directory also need to contain a trailing /. For example:

```
Alias /data/  /web/data
```

This is used only to service `www.yoursite.com/data/` and not `www.yoursite.com/data`. In the latter case, Apache looks for a data directory under the document tree and not the /web/data directory.

AliasMatch

Syntax: `AliasMatch regex path`

Context: `server config, virtual host`

This is similar to the Alias directive, except it can make use of regular expressions. For example:

```
AliasMatch ^/data(.*)  /web/data$1
```

This matches `www.yoursite.com/data/index.html` to the /web/data/index.html file.

Redirect

Syntax: `Redirect [status] old-URL new-URL`

Context: `server config, virtual host, directory, per-directory configuration (.htaccess)`

This directive redirects a URL request to another URL. For example:

```
Redirect /data      www.your-new-site.com/data
```

This redirects all URL requests containing the /data path to the new URL. Therefore, requests for `www.yoursite.com/data/somefile.txt` are redirected to `www.your-new-site.com/data/somefile.txt` instead. The redirect directive generates an HTTP redirect header, which the client must use to find the requested resource.

The Redirect directive takes precedence over the Alias and ScriptAlias directives. By default, the status code sent to the client is Temp (HTTP status code 302). If you want to specify a different status code, use the following:

- Permanent. Tells the client that the redirect is permanent. The HTTP status code 301 is returned.

- Temp. Returns a temporary redirect status (302). This is the default.
- See other. Returns a See Other status (303), indicating that the resource has been replaced.
- Gone. Returns a Gone status (410) indicating that the resource has been permanently removed. When this status is used, the URL argument should be omitted.

You can provide valid HTTP status codes in numeric format as well. If the status you provide is between 300 and 399, the new-URL must be present; otherwise, it must be omitted. You may wonder about the use of different status codes. In the future, clients may be smart enough to recognize the status codes in a more meaningful manner. For example, if a proxy server receives a permanent redirect status code, it can store this information in a cache so it can directly access the new resource in a later request.

RedirectMatch

Syntax: `RedirectMatch [status] regex URL`
Context: `server config, virtual host`

This directive is similar to the Redirect directive, but it accepts regular expressions instead of the simple old-URL. For example:

```
RedirectMatch (.*)\.htm$ http://www.yourserver.com$1.html
```

This redirects all requests that end with .htm to an .html version of the same request. For example, the following request:

```
http://www.yoursite.com/some/old/dos/files/index.htm
```

is redirected to:

```
http://www.yoursite.com/some/old/dos/files/index.html
```

RedirectTemp

Syntax: `RedirectTemp old-URL new-URL`

Context: `server config, virtual host, directory, per-directory configuration (.htaccess)`

This is similar to the Redirect directive. It lets the client know that the redirect is only temporary. The Redirect directive also produces a temporary status by default.

RedirectPermanent

Syntax: `RedirectPermanent old-URL new-URL`

Context: `server config, virtual host, directory, per-directory configuration (.htaccess)`

This is similar to the Redirect directive. It lets the client know that the redirect is permanent. Note that the Redirect directive produces a temporary status by default, but you can use the status code 301 or the keyword permanent, as the status does the same as this directive.

ScriptAlias

Syntax: `ScriptAlias URL-path  path`

Context: `server config, virtual host`

This directive creates an alias (URL-path) for path. Additionally, any filename supplied in the request is treated as a CGI script, and the server attempts to run the script. For example:

```
ScriptAlias /cgi-bin/  /www/nitec/public/cgi-bin/
```

This can be used to process a request such as `www.nitec.com/cgi-bin/somescript.pl`. The server tries to run somescript.pl if proper permission is verified. Note that the scriptAlias directory is not browsable.

ScriptAliasMatch

Syntax: `ScriptAliasMatch regex directory-filename`

Context: `server config, virtual host`

Status: `Base`

This directive is equivalent to the ScriptAlias directive except it uses regular expression. For example:

```
ScriptAliasMatch ^/cgi-bin(.*)\
/www/nitec/public/cgi-bin$1
```

will do exactly the same as:

```
ScriptAliasMatch  /cgi-bin/ /www/nitec/public/cgi-bin/
```

mod_asis

This module is compiled into the default for Apache. It enables you to send a document as is — in other words, the document is sent to the client without HTTP headers. This can be useful in redirecting clients without the help of any scripting. To send a file as is, you need to make sure that one of your Apache configuration files (for example, srm.conf) contains an entry such as:

```
AddType httpd/send-as-is asis
```

This assigns the MIME-type httpd/send-as-is to file extension .ASIS. If you create a file called foobar.asis and a client requests it, the file will be sent to the client without any HTTP header. It will be your job to include appropriate headers in the file. For example, if you want to provide a redirect mechanism via the .ASIS files, you can create files with headers such as:

Status: `301 Text Message`

Location: `new-URL`

Content-type: `text/html`

For example, Listing 4-2 shows a file called redirect.asis, which redirects the clients to a new location.

Listing 4-2 *redirect.asis*

```
Status: 301 We have moved.
Location: http://www.our-new-site/
Content-type: text/html

<H1>Notice to Visitors</H1>
Please update your bookmark to point to <A HREF="www.our-
new-site/"> www.our-new-site/ </A><BR>
<BR>

Thanks.
```

When a client requests this file, the 301 status message tells the client to use the location information to redirect the request. You do not have to add the Date: and Server: headers, because the server automatically adds them. However, the server does not provide a Last-Modified header.

mod_auth

This module is compiled by default in the standard distribution. Standard mod_auth-based basic HTTP authentication uses usernames, groups, and passwords stored in text files to confirm authentication. This works well when dealing with a small number of users. However, if you have a lot of users (thousands or more), use of mod_auth might have a performance penalty. In such a case, you can use something more advanced, such as DBM files, Berkeley DB files, or even a SQL database.

This module offers the following directives.

AuthUserFile

Syntax: `AuthUserFile filename`

Context: `directory, per-directory access control file`

Override: `AuthConfig`

This directive sets the name of the text file that contains the usernames and passwords used in the basic HTTP authentication. You must provide a fully qualified path to the file to be used. For example:

```
AuthUserFile /www/nitec/secrets/.htpasswd
```

This file is usually created using a utility called htpasswd, which is available as a support program in the standard Apache distribution. The format of this file is very simple. Each line contains a single username and an encrypted password. The password is encrypted using the standard crypt() function.

It is important that the AuthUserFile-specified file resides outside the document tree of the Web site. Putting it inside a Web-accessible directory might enable someone to download it.

AuthGroupFile

Syntax: `AuthGroupFile filename`

Context: `directory, per-directory access control file`

Override: `AuthConfig`

This directive specifies a text file to be used as the list of user groups for basic HTTP authentication. The file name is the absolute path to the group file.

You can create this file using any text editor. The format of this file is as follows:

```
groupname: username username username
```

For example:

```
startrek: kirk spock picard data
```

This creates a group called startrek, which has four users: kirk, spock, picard, and data.

It is important that the AuthGroupFile-specified file resides outside the document tree of the Web site. Putting it inside a Web-accessible directory might enable someone to download it.

AuthAuthoritative

Syntax: `AuthAuthoritative on | off`

Default: `on`

Context: `directory, per-directory access control file`

Override: `AuthConfig`

If you are using more than one authentication scheme for the same directory, you can set this directive to On so that when a username/password pair fails with the first scheme, it is passed on to the next (lower) level.

For example, if you are using mod_auth_db (discussed in a later section) and the standard mod_auth module to provide authentication services, and a username/password pair fails for one of them, the next module is used to authenticate the user, if possible. Which module is considered as a lower- or higher-level authentication module is determined by its appearance in the Configuration file. Say the Configuration file looks like this:

```
AddModule modules/standard/mod_auth.o
AddModule modules/standard/mod_auth_db.o
```

The mod_auth_db will have higher priority because the modules in the Configuration file are listed in reverse priority order.

In any case, when a username/password pair fails all modules, the server reissues a 401 status header and sends the WWW-Authenticate response header for reauthentication. However, if a username/password pair is successfully authenticated by a particular module, the lower-level modules never receive the username/password pair.

mod_auth_anon

This module allows anonymous access to authenticated areas. If you are familiar with anonymous FTP servers, this is very similar to such a setup. All users can use a user ID called "anonymous" and their e-mail addresses as the password to get access. The e-mail address entered is stored in log files and can be used to perform user tracking or even creation of a mailing list of prospective clients.

Anonymous

Syntax: `Anonymous user user ...`
Context: `directory, per-directory access control file (.htaccess)`
Override: `AuthConfig`

Using this directive, you can specify one or more usernames that can be used to access the restricted area. It is a good idea to keep the username "anonymous" in your chosen list because it is widely associated with anonymous access. If the username you choose has a space character in it, make sure the username is surrounded by quote marks. For example:

```
Anonymous "Unregistered User" anonymous
```

Or

```
Anonymous 'Unregistered User' anonymous
```

The strings are not case sensitive.

Anonymous_Authoritative

Syntax: `Anonymous_Authoritative on | off`
Default: `Anonymous_Authoritative off`
Context: `directory, per-directory access control file (.htaccess)`
Override: `AuthConfig`

When set to on, the anonymous authentication becomes the authoritative authentication scheme for a directory. In other words, there will be no fall-through to other authentication methods.

Anonymous_LogEmail

Syntax: `Anonymous_LogEmail on | off`

Default: `Anonymous_LogEmail on`

Context: `directory, per-directory access control file (.htaccess)`

Override: `AuthConfig`

When this directive is set to on, whatever is entered in the password field of the browser's popup authentication window will be logged in the Apache access log file.

Anonymous_MustGiveEmail

Syntax: `Anonymous_MustGiveEmail on | off`

Default: `Anonymous_MustGiveEmail on`

Context: `directory, per-directory access control file (.htaccess)`

Override: `AuthConfig`

When set to on, this directive enables the module to reject access requests that do not provide passwords in the form of e-mail addresses. However, you should not trust the e-mail addresses that people will enter when this directive is set to on, as there is no way of checking who entered whose e-mail address.

Anonymous_NoUserID

Syntax: `Anonymous_NoUserID on | off`

Default: `Anonymous_NoUserID off`

Context: `directory, per-directory access control file (.htaccess)`

Override: `AuthConfig`

If you want the users to leave the username field of the pop-up window empty, set this directive to on; otherwise, a username that matches the values provided in the Anonymous directive is required.

Anonymous_VerifyEmail

Syntax: `Anonymous_VerifyEmail on | off`

Default: `Anonymous_VerifyEmail off`

Context: `directory, per-directory access control file (.htaccess)`

Override: `AuthConfig`

When this directive is set to on, it requires that the password be a valid e-mail address. However, the validity check is limited. The module checks for only an @ symbol and a period (.) in the password field. If the entered password has either of these symbols in it, it is accepted.

mod_auth_db

If your system is not capable of using DBM, but Berkeley DB file support is available, you can use mod_auth_db to use DB files instead. Like the mod_auth_dbm module, this module is not compiled in the standard Apache distribution.

AuthDBUserFile

Syntax: `AuthDBUserFile filename`

Context: `directory, per-directory access control file (.htaccess)`

Override: `AuthConfig`

This directive sets the fully qualified pathname of the user DB file that contains the list of users and encrypted passwords.

The DB user file is also keyed using the username and the value is the crypt()-encrypted password.

Always make sure your user files are kept outside the Web document tree and are readable only by Apache. No one but the owner should have write access to these files.

AuthDBGroupFile

Syntax: `AuthDBGroupFile filename`

Context: `directory, per-directory access control file (.htaccess)`

Override: `AuthConfig`

This directive sets the fully qualified pathname of the group DB file, which contains the list of user groups for user authentication. Like the DBM counterpart, the group file uses the username as the key and the comma-separated group list is treated as the value. There must be no white space within the value, and it must never contain any colons.

If you prefer not to use a separate group file, you can use a single DB file to provide both password and group information. The format of the file would be as follows:

```
username: encrypted password: comma-separated group list
```

Here username is the key, and the password and group lists are two fields of the value. Other data may be left in the DB file after another colon; it is ignored by the authentication module. If you use a single DB to provide both group and password information, you will have to point both AuthDBGroup and AuthDBUserFile directives to the same file.

AuthDBAuthoritative

Syntax: `AuthDBAuthoritative on | off`

Default: `on`

Context: `directory, per-directory access control file (.htaccess)`

Override: `AuthConfig`

When using multiple authentication schemes such as mod_db, mod_dbm, and standard mod_auth in the same directory, you can use this directive to define whether mod_auth_db is the authoritative authentication scheme. The default value of the directive allows mod_auth_db to become the authoritative authentication for the directory. This means that if the DB-based authentication fails for a particular user, the user's credentials will not be passed on to a lower-level authentication scheme. When set to the off value, the credentials of a failed authentication will be passed on to the next authentication level.

Although using DBM or DB files makes it easier to administer a large user base, they often are not suitable for organizations that have the user information already stored in a relational SQL database. A SQL database provides a great deal of functionality that is not available to either DBM or DB files. Apache also provides support for a popular SQL database called mSQL.

mod_auth_dbm

The .htpasswd and .htgroup file-based authentication scheme is inefficient for high-speed processing and could negatively affect a Web server's performance when thousands of users (or more) need authenticated access to restricted areas. The mod_auth_dbm module is a better choice in such a case. This module uses DBM files instead of text files to store data.

Once you have recompiled Apache with DBM support, you can use the module mod_auth_dbm to provide DBM-based basic HTTP authentication. For Berkeley DB you will have to use mod_auth_db instead of mod_auth_dbm. The following directives are provided by this module.

AuthDBMUserFile

Syntax: `AuthDBMUserFile filename`

Context: `directory, per-directory access control file (.htaccess)`

Override: `AuthConfig`

This directive sets the fully qualified pathname of a DBM file to be used as the user file for DBM authentication. The file contains a key=value pair per record, where the username is the key and the crypt()-encrypted password is the value. Note that each field in the record is separated by a colon, and arbitrary data can be appended after the initial username and password fields.

Tip

Never store user database files inside your Web document tree.

AuthDBMGroupFile

Syntax: `AuthDBMGroupFile filename`

Context: `directory, per-directory access control file (.htaccess)`

Override: `AuthConfig`

This directive sets the fully qualified pathname of the group file that contains the list of user groups. Each record in the file is a key=value pair, where the key is the username and the value is a comma-separated list of group names to which the user belongs.

If you prefer not to use a separate group file, you can use a single DBM file to provide both password and group information. The format of the file is as follows:

```
username: encrypted password: comma-separated group list
```

Here, username is the key, and the password and group lists are two fields of the value. Other data may be left in the DBM file after another colon, if desired; it is ignored by the authentication module. If you use a single DBM to provide both group and password information, you will have to point both AuthDBMGroup and AuthDBMUserFile directives to the same file.

AuthDBMAuthoritative

Syntax: `AuthDBMAuthoritative on | off`

Default: `on`

Context: `directory, .per-directory access control file (.htaccess)`

Override: `AuthConfig`

When using multiple authentication schemes such as mod_dbm and standard mod_auth in the same directory, you can use this directive to define whether mod_auth_dbm is the authoritative authentication schema.

The default value of the directive enables mod_auth_dbm to become the authoritative authentication for the directory. What this means is if the DBM-based authentication fails for a particular user, the user's credentials will not be passed on to a lower-level authentication scheme. When set to the off value, the credentials of a failed authentication will be passed on to the next authentication level.

A common use for this is in conjunction with one of the basic authentication modules, such as mod_auth.c. Whereas this DBM module supplies the bulk of the user credential checking, a few (administrator) related accesses fall through to a lower level with a well-protected .htpasswd file.

mod_auth_external

Apache can use external authentication programs if the mod_auth_external module is compiled into the server executable. This module is bundled in a compressed tar file containing all the contributed modules found at the following URL:

```
http://www.apache.org/dist/contrib/modules/1.3/
```

You will need to install this module as you install any other third-party module. Let's look at the directives that this module provides.

AddExternalAuth

Syntax (system call and pipe version): `AddExternalAuth keyword path/to/authenticator`
Syntax (function version): `AddExternalAuth keyword type: path/to/configuration`
Context: `server config`

This directive associates the keyword with the specified user authenticator. For example:

```
AddExternalAuth archive_auth /usr/local/bin/authcheck
```

This associates archive_auth with an external authentication program called /usr/local/bin/authcheck. An example of the directive for a hard-coded function would look like:

```
AddExternalAuth archive_auth RADIUS:
```

where RADIUS is the name of the hard-coded function. If the function requires a configuration file, the file can be passed to it as follows:

```
AddExternalAuth archive_auth RADIUS:/usr/local/raddb
```

External user authentication programs are passed the client-entered username, the password, and, optionally, a configuration filename (only for hard-coded function-based authentication). By default the external authentication program receives the username and password as USER and PASS environment variables, respectively. If pipe mode is specified in the SetExternalAuthMethod directive, the username and password are passed as key=value pairs in the form of USER=username and PASS=password. For the hard-coded function version, the data is passed as C function parameters.

If the external user authentication program exits with an exit code of 0, authentication is assumed to be successful. A nonzero value indicates either a failure to authenticate or a failure to execute the authenticator.

Note that you can use multiple types of authentication in one server by providing multiple directives in the srm.conf file. Just make sure each group has a different keyword.

AddExternalGroupAuth

Syntax (system call and pipe version): `AddExternalGroupAuth keyword path/to/authenticator`

Syntax (function version): `AddExternalGroupAuth keyword type: path/to/configuration`

Context: `server config`

This directive associates the keyword with the specified group authenticator. For example, the following associates archive_auth with an external authentication program called /usr/local/bin/groupcheck:

```
AddExternalGroupAuth archive_auth \
/usr/local/bin/groupcheck
```

External group authentication programs are passed the username, the group, and, optionally, a configuration filename (only for hard-coded function-based authentication). By default, the external authentication program receives the username and group as USER and GROUP environment variables, respectively. If pipe mode is specified in the SetExternalGroupMethod directive, the username and password are passed as key=value pairs in the form of USER=username and GROUP=group. For the hard-coded function version, the data is passed as C function parameters.

If the external group authentication program exits with an exit code of 0, authentication is assumed to be successful. A nonzero value indicates either a failure to authenticate or a failure to execute the authenticator.

SetExternalAuthMethod

Syntax: `SetExternalAuthMethod keyword method`

Context: `server config`

This directive sets the method for passing data to the external user authentication program. Currently there are three methods available:

- **The environment method**. In this method, the username and password are passed via the method environment. The USER variable contains the username, and the PASS variable contains the password. This is the default method.

  Consider the following example:

  ```
  AddExternalAuth archive_auth \
  /usr/local/bin/authcheck
  SetExternalAuthMethod archive_auth environment
  ```

  Here, the /usr/local/bin/authcheck program will receive the client-entered username and password via environment variables USER and PASS.

- **The function method**. This method is used when a hard-coded function is defined to handle the authentication.

  Take a look at the following:

  ```
  AddExternalAuth archive_auth RADIUS:
  SetExternalAuthMethod archive_auth function
  ```

  Here, the hard-coded function RADIUS is used, and the function receives the data as function parameters.

- **The pipe method**. This method sends the data via a pipe to the external authenticator's standard input device (STDIN). The data is passed as key=value pairs, where USER=username and PASS=password.

  Look at the following example:

  ```
  AddExternalAuth archive_auth /
  /usr/local/bin/authcheck
  SetExternalAuthMethod archive_auth pipe
  ```

  Here, the /usr/local/bin/authcheck program will receive the client-entered username and password via a pipe to its standard input device (STDIN), where USER=username and PASS=password.

SetExternalGroupMethod

Syntax: `SetExternalGroupMethod keyword method`

Context: `server config`

This directive sets the method, which is to be used for passing data to the external group authentication program. Currently three methods are available: environment, function, and pipe. See the preceding section, "SetExternalAuthMethod," for examples and more details.

AuthExternal

Syntax (system call and pipe version): `AddExternalAuth keyword`

Syntax (function version): `AddExternalAuth function name: path/to/configuration file`

Context: `directory, per-directory access control file (.htaccess)`

This directive is used in the directory context or per-directory access control file (.htaccess) to tell Apache which external user authenticator program to use for authentication. The server matches the keyword or the function name (in the case of hard-coded function) to determine what to do. For example:

```
AuthExternal archive_auth
```

If this line is found in a .htaccess file, Apache will run the user authenticator associated with that keyword.

GroupExternal

Syntax (system call and pipe version): `GroupExternal keyword`
Syntax (function version): `GroupExternal function name: path/to/configuration file`
Context: `directory, per-directory access control file (.htaccess)`

This directive is used in the directory context or per-directory access control file (.htaccess) to tell Apache which external group authenticator program to use for group authentication. The server matches the keyword or the function name (in the case of hard-coded function) to determine what to do.

For example, if the following line is found in an .htaccess file, Apache will run the group authenticator associated with that keyword. For example:

```
GroupExternal archive_auth
```

mod_autoindex

This module is compiled into the default for Apache. When a request for a directory is received by Apache, it looks for one or more directory index files specified by the DirectoryIndex directive. Typically, this file is index.html or index.htm. In the absence of such an index file, however, Apache can generate a dynamic directory listing. This module enables you to control how Apache creates the dynamic directory listing.

Apache generates two types of dynamic directory indices—simple and fancy. Fancy indexing is available through either the FancyIndexing or IndexOptions directives found in this module.

This fancy index and many other indexing options are available from this module. The directives for mod_autoindex follow:

AddAlt

Syntax: `AddAlt "text" file file...`

Context: `server config, virtual host, directory, per-directory configuration (.htaccess)`

Override: `Indexes`

When FancyIndexing is on, this directive sets the specified text as an alternative to the icon that is displayed for one or more files or file extensions specified as arguments. This is done for nongraphical browsers such as Lynx. For example:

```
AddAlt "Pictures" gif jpeg jpg bmp
```

This enables Apache to display the alternative text "Pictures" in place of the icon for each type of graphics file specified here. For graphical browsers such as Netscape Navigator or Internet Explorer, the alternative text is displayed as help text under popular Windows platforms. In such systems, users can get a tip or help about the file when they move their mouse cursor on top of the icon representing one of the file types.

AddAltByEncoding

Syntax: `AddAltByEncoding "text" MIME-encoding MIME-encoding`

Context: `server config, virtual host, directory, per-directory configuration (.htaccess)`

Override: `Indexes`

If you do not like to assign alternative text to filenames or file extensions via the AddAlt directive, you can use this directive to assign such text for one or more MIME-encodings. Like AddAlt, this directive is also usable only when FancyIndexing is turned on. For example:

```
AddAltByEncoding "Compressed File" x-compress
```

AddAltByType

Syntax: `AddAltByType "text" MIME-type MIME-type...`
Context: `server config, virtual host, directory, per-directory configuration (.htaccess)`
Override: `Indexes`

Like the AddAltByEncoding directive, this directive sets alternative text for a file, instead of an icon for FancyIndexing. However, it uses MIME-type instead of MIME-encoding. For example:

```
AddAltByType "HTML FILE" text/html
```

This shows the "HTML FILE" text in place of the icon for non-graphical browsers. In the case of graphical browsers, this text may appear as a tip or help.

AddDescription

Syntax: `AddDescription "text" file file...`
Context: `server config, virtual host, directory, per-directory configuration (.htaccess)`
Override: Indexes

This directive sets the description text for a file, partial, or wildcard filename when FancyIndexing is turned on. For example:

```
AddDescription "Graphics File" *.gif *.jpeg *.jpg *.bmp
```

This displays the description for all GIF, JPEG, JPG, and BMP files.

AddIcon

Syntax: `AddIcon icon name name ...`
Context: `server config, virtual host, directory, per-directory configuration (.htaccess)`
Override: `Indexes`

This directive enables you to assign icons to files and directory names that are displayed for FancyIndexing. For example:

```
AddIcon /icons/picture.gif .gif .jpg .bmp
```

This tells Apache to show /icons/picture.gif next to files that have extensions such as .gif, .jpg, and .bmp. If you also want to provide alternative text for the file extension listed, you can use a format such as:

```
AddIcon (IMG, /icons/picture.gif) .gif .jpg .bmp
```

Here, IMG is the alternative text displayed for nongraphical browsers. If you want to display an icon for a directory, you can use the directive as follows:

```
AddIcon /path/to/your/directory/icon   ^^DIRECTORY^^
```

Similarly, if you want to display an icon for each blank line displayed by the fancy indexing scheme, you can use:

```
AddIcon /path/to/your/blank/line/icon   ^^BLANKICON^^
```

AddIconByEncoding

Syntax: `AddIconByEncoding icon mime-encoding mime-encoding ...`
Context: `server config, virtual host, directory, per-directory configuration (.htaccess)`
Override: `Indexes`

This directive lets you assign icons to MIME-encodings. For example:

```
AddIconByEncoding  /icons/zip.gif   x-gzip
```

AddIconByType

Syntax: `AddIconByType icon MIME-type MIME-type ...`
Context: `server config, virtual host, directory, per-directory configuration (.htaccess)`
Override: `Indexes`

This directive also enables you to assign icons to MIME-types. For example:

```
AddIconByType (HTML,/icons/html.gif) text/html
```

DefaultIcon

Syntax: `DefaultIcon url`
Context: `server config, virtual host, directory, per-directory configuration (.htaccess)`
Override: `Indexes`

When no AddIcon, AddIconByEncoding, or AddIconByType is matched for a file, a default icon can be displayed. This directive enables you to set that icon. For example:

```
DefaultIcon/icon/idontknow.gif
```

This shows idontknow.gif whenever a file's icon association is unknown.

FancyIndexing

Syntax: `FancyIndexing on | off`
Context: `server config, virtual host, directory, per-directory configuration (.htaccess)`
Override: `Indexes`

This directive lets you enable and disable fancy indexing of directories. You can achieve the same with the IndexOptions directive.

HeaderName

Syntax: `HeaderName filename`

Context: `server config, virtual host, directory, per-directory configuration (.htaccess)`

Override: `Indexes`

If you use FancyIndexing, you can insert a file's content at the top of the index listing. This directive lets you specify the name of the file for such an insertion. For example:

```
HeaderName welcome
```

This makes Apache look for a file called welcome or welcome.html in the directory of the listing. If such a file is found, the content is inserted before the actual listing.

IndexIgnore

Syntax: `IndexIgnore file file ...`

Context: `server config, virtual host, directory, per-directory configuration (.htaccess)`

Override: `Indexes`

If you need some files or file extensions to be invisible in the directory listing, you can use this directive to accomplish this. For example:

```
IndexIgnore welcome welcome.html per-directory
configuration (.htaccess)
```

This ensures that Apache does not list welcome, welcome.html, or per-directory configuration (.htaccess) files in directory listings. The dot (.) character is automatically in the IndexIgnore list; thus, files that start with this character are not listed. However, I still prefer to add per-directory configuration (.htaccess) in the list just to feel safer.

IndexOptions

Syntax: `IndexOptions option option ...`

Context: `server config, virtual host, directory, per-directory configuration (.htaccess)`

Override: `Indexes`

The IndexOptions directive specifies the behavior of the directory indexing. Options are:

- **FancyIndexing.** This turns on fancy indexing of directories. The FancyIndexing and IndexOptions directives will override each other.
- **IconHeight[=pixels].** This option enables Apache to include the HEIGHT=pixels attribute in the IMG tag of the icon, which makes the loading of the icon faster on most browsers. If you do not specify a pixel count, a default value of 22 is used.
- **IconsAreLinks.** This makes the icons part of the anchor for the filename, for fancy indexing.
- **IconWidth[=pixels].** This enables Apache to include the WIDTH=pixels attribute in the IMG tag of the icon, which makes the loading of the icon faster on most browsers. If you do not specify a pixel count, a default value of 20 is used.
- **ScanHTMLTitles.** If you want Apache to read the title (denoted by the <TITLE> and </TITLE> tag pair) of an HTML document for fancy indexing, use this option. If you have already specified a description using the AddDescription directive, however, this option is not used. Note that reading each file's content and searching for title information is a time-consuming task that may slow down the delivery of directory listings. I do not recommend this option.
- **SuppressColumnSorting.** By default, Apache makes clickable column headings for a fancy directory index, which enables users to sort information in that column. This option disables that feature.

- **SuppressDescription.** If you do not want to display file descriptions in the fancy directory listing, use this option.
- **SuppressHTMLPreamble.** If the directory actually contains a file specified by the HeaderName directive, the module usually includes the contents of the file after a standard HTML preamble (<HTML>, <HEAD>, and so on). The SuppressHTMLPreamble option disables this behavior.
- **SuppressLastModified.** This suppresses the display of the last modification date in fancy indexing listings.
- **SuppressSize.** This suppresses the file size in fancy indexing listings.

ReadmeName

Syntax: `ReadmeName filename`

Context: `server config, virtual host, directory, per-directory configuration (.htaccess)`

Override: `Indexes`

If you want to insert a file at the end of the fancy directory listing, use this directive. For example:

```
ReadmeName readme
```

Apache looks for a file called readme.html or readme to insert at the end of the listing.

mod_cern_meta

This module is not compiled by default. It provides support for metainformation. This information can either be additional HTTP headers such as:

```
Expires: Saturday, 3-Oct-98 12:00:00 GMT
```

or it can be any other information such as:

```
Foo=Bar
```

The meta information is stored in a file and appears along with the HTTP response header.

MetaFiles

Syntax: `MetaFiles on/off`

Default: `MetaFiles off`

Context: `per-directory config (.htaccess)`

This directive enables or disables metaheader file processing.

MetaDir

Syntax: `MetaDir directory name`

Default: `MetaDir .web`

Context: `per-directory config (.htaccess)`

This directive specifies the name of the directory that is used to store metaheader files. For example, if you have a directory called /www/mycompany/public/htdocs and you want to store metainformation files for that directory, you need to create a subdirectory called .web if you use the default value for the MetaDir directive. The .web directory is used to store metaheader files.

MetaSuffix

Syntax: `MetaSuffix .suffix`

Default: `MetaSuffix .meta`

Context: `per-directory config (.htaccess)`

This directive specifies the filename extension for metainformation files. For example, if you have an HTML file called mypage.html, you need to create mypage.html.meta (using the default value of this directive) to store your metaheaders. The mypage.html.metafile must reside in the directory specified by the MetaDir directive.

To enable Apache to send out metainformation for a directory called /www/mycompany/public/htdocs, you need to do the following:

1. Set the MetaFiles directive to on in the per-directory configuration file (.htaccess) for /www/mycompany/public/htdocs. You also can set the MetaDir and MetaSuffix directive in this file.
2. Create a subdirectory called .web (assuming you are using the default for the MetaDir directive).
3. Create a text file with extension .meta (assuming you are using the default value for MetaSuffix directive).
4. Put all the HTTP headers that you want to supply in this file.

For example, to provide metaheaders for a file named /www/mycompany/public/htdocs/mypage.html, you need to create a file called /www/mycompany/public/htdocs/.web/mypage.html.meta.

This file could include lines such as:

```
Expires: Saturday, 3-Oct-98 12:00:00 GMT
Anything=Whatever
```

mod_cgi

Apache's CGI support comes from the mod_cgi.c module. This module is compiled into Apache by default. In the following sections, I discuss the environment variables that are available from the standard CGI module compiled into Apache.

Using Server-specific Environment Variables

These variables are set by Apache to inform the CGI program about itself. Using server variables, a CGI program can determine various server-specific information, such as a version of the Apache software, administrator's e-mail address, and so on.

SERVER_SOFTWARE

The value of this variable is usually the name and version number of the server software running the CGI program.

GATEWAY_INTERFACE

This variable tells the CGI program what version of CGI specification the server currently supports.

SERVER_ADMIN

If you use the ServerAdmin directive in the httpd.conf file to set the e-mail address of the site administrator, this variable will be set up to reflect that.

DOCUMENT_ROOT

This variable is set to the value of the DocumentRoot directive of the Web site being accessed.

Using Client-request-specific Environment Variables

Apache creates a set of environment variables from the HTTP request header it receives from a client requesting a CGI program. It provides this information to the CGI program by creating the following set of environment variables:

AUTH_TYPE

If the CGI program is stored in a section of the Web site where authentication is required to gain access, this variable is set to specify the authentication method used.

CONTENT_LENGTH

When the HTTP POST request method is used, Apache stores input data (attached to the request) in the stdin of the CGI program.

CONTENT_TYPE

This variable specifies the MIME type of any data attached to the request header.

HTTP_ACCEPT

This variable is set to the list of MIME types that the client is capable of accepting.

HTTP_ACCEPT_CHARSET

This variable specifies which character set is acceptable to the client.

HTTP_ACCEPT_LANGUAGE

This variable specifies which language is acceptable to the client.

HTTP_CONNECTION

This variable is set to the type of connection being used by the client and the server.

HTTP_HOST

This variable also tells a CGI program which server host is being accessed.

HTTP_REFERER

This variable is set to the URI that forwarded the request to the CGI program being called. Using this variable, you can tell if a request is coming from a link on one of your Web pages or a remote URI.

HTTP_USER_AGENT

This variable specifies what client software the requesting system is running and what operating system it is running on.

PATH_INFO

If input data for a CGI program is part of the URI, the extra path (which is really some data for the program being called) is stored as the value of the variable.

PATH_TRANSLATED

This is the absolute path of the requested file.

REMOTE_ADDR

This is the IP address of the client system.

REMOTE_HOST

This variable tells a CGI program about the IP address or IP name of the client.

REMOTE_IDENT

This will be set only if the IdentityCheck directive is set. This variable stores the user identification information returned by the remote identd (identification daemon).

REMOTE_PORT

This port number was used by the client to originate the connection to request the CGI program.

REMOTE_USER

This will be set only when access to the CGI program requires HTTP basic authentication. The username used in the basic authentication is stored in this variable for the CGI program.

REQUEST_METHOD

This variable is set to the HTTP request method used by the client to request the CGI program.

REQUEST_URI

This variable is set to the URI of the request.

SCRIPT_FILENAME

This is the physical, fully qualified pathname of the requested CGI program.

SCRIPT_NAME

This is the URI of the requested CGI program.

SERVER_NAME

This variable tells a CGI program which server host is being accessed.

SERVER_PORT

The value of this variable tells a CGI program which server port is currently being used to access the program.

SERVER_PROTOCOL

This is the protocol and version number the client used to send the request for the CGI program.

```
SERVER_PROTOCOL = HTTP/1.1
```

Configuring Apache for CGI

Configure Apache to process CGI requests includes telling Apache where you store your CGI programs, setting up CGI handlers for specific file extensions, and indicating which file extensions should be considered CGI programs. It is a good idea to keep your CGI programs in one central directory. This permits better control of them. Scattering CGI programs all over the Web space may make the site unmanageable; it also could create security holes that would be hard to track.

Making a central CGI program directory is just the beginning to setting up a secured CGI environment. It is best to keep this central CGI program directory outside of your DOCUMENTROOT directory so CGI programs cannot be accessed directly. Why? Well, when it comes to CGI programs, you want to provide as little information as possible to the outside world. This will ensure better security for your site(s). The less someone knows about where your CGI programs are physically located, the less harm that person can do.

The first step is to create a directory outside of your documentroot directory. For example, if /www/mycompany/public/htdocs is the documentroot directory of a Web site, then /www/mycompany/public/cgi-bin is a good candidate for the CGI program directory. To create the alias for your CGI program directory, you can use the ScriptAlias directive.

If you are setting up CGI support for the primary Web server, edit the httpd.conf file and insert a ScriptAlias line with the following syntax:

```
ScriptAlias  /alias/ /path/ \
/to/the/CGI/program/directory/ending/with/
```

For example:

```
ScriptAlias /cgi-bin/    /www/mycompany/public/cgi-bin/
```

If you are setting up CGI support for a virtual site, add a ScriptAlias line in the <VirtualHost . . . > container that defines the virtual host. For example:

```
NameVirtualHost 206.171.50.60
<VirtualHost 206.171.50.60>
ServerName blackhole.nitec.com
ScriptAlias /apps/   /www/nitec/blackhole/public/cgi-bin/
</VirtualHost>
```

Here the /apps/ alias is used to create a CGI program directory alias. If there is a CGI program called feedback.cgi in the

/www/nitec/blackhole/public/cgi-bin directory, it can ONLY be accessed via the following:

```
http://blackhole.nitec.com/apps/feedback.cgi
```

After you set up the ScriptAlias directive, make sure that the directory permission permits Apache to read and execute files found in the directory.

The directory pointed to by ScriptAlias should have very strict permission settings. No one but the CGI program developer or the server administrator should have full (read, write, and execute) permission for the directory. Note that you can define multiple CGI program directory aliases, and the ScriptAlias specified directory is not browseable (by default) for security reasons.

When requested, Apache will attempt to run any executable (file permission-wise) file found in the ScriptAliased directory. For example:

```
http://blackhole.nitec.com/apps/foo.cgi
http://blackhole.nitec.com/apps/foo.pl
http://blackhole.nitec.com/apps/foo.bak
http://blackhole.nitec.com/apps/foo.dat
```

All of the preceding URL requests will prompt Apache to attempt running the various foo files.

Debugging CGI Programs

To log CGI output in Apache, use the following directives, which are found in the mod_cgi module.

ScriptLog

Syntax: `ScriptLog filename`
Context: `resource config`

This directive sets the log filename for CGI program errors. If the log file name is relative (that is, it does not start with a leading /), it is taken to be relative to the server root directory set by the ServerRoot directive.

When you use this directive, make sure that the log directory is writeable by the user specified by the UserDir directive. Using this directive on a daily basis might not be a good idea as far as efficiency or performance goes. I recommend using it when needed and turning it off when the debugging is completed.

ScriptLogLength

Syntax: `ScriptLogLength size`

Default: `10385760`

Context: `resource config`

This directive limits the size of the log file specified by the ScriptLog directive. The script log file can log a lot of information per CGI error and, therefore, can grow rapidly. Using this directive, you can limit the log so that once the file is at the maximum length, no more information will be logged.

ScriptLogBuffer

Syntax: `ScriptLogBuffer size`

Default: `1024`

Context: `resource config`

This directive limits the size of POST or PUT data that is logged. Using these directives, you can set up the logging of CGI programs that you are developing or attempting to install on your system.

mod_digest

This provides user authentication using the MD5 digest authentication scheme. It is not compiled by default. It offers the following directive.

AuthDigestFile

Syntax: `AuthDigestFile filename`

Override: `AuthConfig`

Context: `directory, per-directory configuration (.htaccess)`

This directive sets the fully qualified filename that contains the list of users and passwords for MD5-based authentication.This file can be created by the htdigest utility supplied as a support utility with the Apache distribution. Unfortunately, the majority of Web browsers still do not support digest authentication; hence, this module is not practical just yet.

mod_dir

This module is compiled in the default for Apache. Using this module, Apache can redirect any request for a directive that does not include a trailing slash character. For example, this module can redirect `www.yoursite.com/somedirectory` to `www.yoursite.com/somedirectory/`. It also provides a directive called DirectoryIndex to help with indexing a directory's content.

DirectoryIndex

Syntax: `DirectoryIndex local-URL local-URL...`

Default: `DirectoryIndex index.html`

Context: `server config, virtual host, directory, per-directory configuration (.htaccess)`

Override: `Indexes`

This directive specifies the name(s) of files that Apache should look for before creating a dynamic directory index. The files can be anything from an HTML file to a CGI script. The default setting enables Apache to look for the index.html file for any request that ends with a directory name. For example, `http://www.yoursite.com/some/directory/` causes Apache to look for a file called /some/directory/index.html. If the file exists, its content is delivered to the client. In the absence of this file, Apache creates a dynamic directory listing.

You can specify one or more files as the default directory index files. For example:

```
DirectoryIndex index.html index.htm welcome.html\
welcome.htm
```

This tells Apache to look for all the named files for each directory request. Apache will look for files in the same order (from left to right) as they appear in the preceding configuration. In other words, if Apache finds index.html, it will no longer look for index.htm, welcome.html, or welcome.htm. You can specify a CGI script name as the default index, as well. For example:

```
DirectoryIndex/cgi-bin/show_index.cgi
```

This makes Apache run the /cgi-bin/show_index.cgi script every time Apache gets a directory request.

mod_env

This module is not compiled by default. It enables you to pass environment variables to CGI or SSI scripts. It has the following directives.

PassEnv

Syntax: `PassEnv variable variable ...`
Context: `server config, virtual host`

This directive tells the module to pass one or more environment variables from the server's own environment to the CGI and SSI scripts. For example:

```
PassEnv HOSTTYPE PATH
```

SetEnv

Syntax: `SetEnv variable value`

Context: `server config, virtual host`

This directive sets an environment variable, which is then passed on to CGI/SSI scripts. For example:

```
SetEnv CAPITAL_CITY   SACRAMENTO
```

UnsetEnv

Syntax: `UnsetEnv variable variable ...`

Context: `server config, virtual host`

This directive removes one environment variable or more from those that are passed to CGI/SSI scripts. For example:

```
UnsetEnv PATH
```

mod_expires

This module is not compiled in Apache by default. It lets you determine how Apache deals with Expires HTTP headers in the server's response to requests. Expires HTTP headers provide you with means for telling the client about the time when the requested resource becomes invalid. This is useful when documents are cached by the client and need to be requested again. Most smart clients will determine the validity of a rerequested document by investigating the cached document's expiration time provided by the Expires HTTP headers. This module enables you to control the setting of the Expires HTTP headers.

ExpiresActive

Syntax: `ExpiresActive on | off`

Context: `server config, virtual host, directory, per-directory configuration (.htaccess)`

Override: `Indexes`

This directive enables or disables the generation of the Expires header. It does not guarantee that an Expires header will be generated. If the criteria are not met, no header is sent.

ExpiresByType

Syntax 1: `ExpiresByType MIME-type M<seconds> | A<seconds>`
Syntax 2: `ExpiresByType MIME-type "<base time> [plus] <num> <years|months|weeks|days|hours|minutes|seconds>"`
Context: `server config, virtual host, directory, per-directory configuration (.htaccess)`
Override: `Indexes`

This directive specifies the value of the Expires HTTP header for documents of a specified MIME-type. The expiration time is specified in seconds. You can define the time in two ways. If you choose to use the M<seconds> format to specify expiration time, then the file's last modification time is used as the base time. In other words, M3600 means that you want the file to expire one hour after it was last modified. On the other hand, if you use the A<seconds> format, then the client's access time is used as the base time. Following are some examples:

The following expires all plain text files after an hour in the client's cache:

```
ExpiresByType text/plain A3600
```

This expires all GIF files after a week from the last modified time:

```
ExpiresByType image/gif M604800
```

If you want to use the second syntax for specifying expiration times, you need to determine the appropriate value of <base time> using the following options:

- **Access.** Time when client accessed the file.
- **Now.** Current time. This is the same as the access time.
- **Modification.** Time when the file was last changed.

For example:

```
ExpiresByType text/html "access plus 7 days"
ExpiresByType image/gif "modification plus 3 hours 10
minutes"
```

ExpiresDefault

Syntax 1: `ExpiresDefault M<seconds> | A<seconds>`
Syntax 2: `ExpiresDefault "<base time> [plus] <num> <years|months|weeks|days|hours|minutes|seconds>"`
Context: `server config, virtual host, directory, per-directory configuration (.htaccess)`
Override: `Indexes`

This directive sets the default expiration time for all documents in the context in which it is specified. For example, if this directive is specified in the virtual host context, it will only apply to the documents accessible via the virtual host. Similarly, you can specify this directive in a per-directory context, which allows all documents in that directory to expire at a specified interval. See ExpiresByType for details on the syntax. Here are some examples:

- ExpiresDefault M3600
- ExpiresDefault "access plus 2 days"

The first example sets the expiration time to one hour after the last modification time of the documents. The second one sets the expiration time to two days after access by the client.

mod_headers

This module is not compiled by default. It enables you to manipulate HTTP response headers, and it offers a single directive called Header.

Header

Syntax: `Header <action> <header> <value>`
Context: `server config, virtual host, directory, per-directory configuration (.htaccess)`
Override: `FileInfo`

This directive enables you to manipulate the HTTP response header. The allowed actions are:

- **Set.** Sets a header. If an old header with the same name existed, its value is changed to the new value.
- **Add.** Adds a header. This can cause multiple headers with the same name when one or more headers with the same name exist.
- **Append.** Appends the value to an existing header value.
- **Unset.** Removes a header.

For example:

```
Header add Author "Mohammed J. Kabir"
```

This adds the Author header with the value "Mohammed J. Kabir". The following line removes this header:

```
Header unset Author
```

mod_imap

This module is compiled in Apache by default. It provides imagemap support, which used to be provided by the CGI program called imagemap. You can use the AddHandler directive to specify the imap-file handler (built into this module) for any file extension. For example:

```
AddHandler imap-file map
```

This makes Apache treat all files with the .map extension as image maps, and Apache processes the file using this module. The older format, as shown below, is still supported by this module; however, it is not recommended:

```
AddType application/x-httpd-imap map
```

The lines in an imagemap file can have any of the following formats:

```
directive value [x,y ...]
directive value "Menu text" [x,y ...]
directive value x,y ... "Menu text"
```

The allowed image-map directives are:

- **base.** Relative URLs used in map files are considered relative to the value of this directive. The Imapbase directive setting is overridden by this directive when found in a map file. It defaults to http://server_name/. base_uri is synonymous with base.
- **default.** Specifies the action to take when the coordinates do not fit into any poly, circle, or rect, and no point directives are given. The default value for this directive is nocontent, which tells the client to keep the same page displayed.
- **poly.** Defines a polygon using at least three points to a maximum of one hundred points. If user-supplied coordinates fall within the polygon, this directive is activated.
- **circle.** Defines a circle using the center coordinates and a point on the circle. If user-supplied coordinates fall within the circle, this directive is activated.
- **rect.** Defines a rectangle using two opposing corner coordinates. If user-supplied coordinates fall within the rectangle, this directive is activated.
- **point.** Defines a single point coordinate. The point directive closest to the user-supplied coordinate is used when no other directives are satisfied.

The value is an absolute or relative URL, or one of the special values in the following list. The coordinates (x, y) are separated by white space characters. The double-quoted text is used as the text of the link if an imagemap menu is generated. Any line with a leading # character is considered a comment and is ignored.

The special imagemap file directive values are:

- **A URL.** A relative or absolute URL. Relative URLs resolve relative to the base.
- **Map.** Same as the URL of the imagemap file itself. Unless ImapMenu is set to none, a menu will be created.
- **Menu.** Same as Map.
- **Referer.** Same as the URL of the referring document. Defaults to http://servername/ if no Referer: header is present.
- **Nocontent.** A status code of 204 is sent to tell the client to keep the same page displayed. This is not valid for base.
- **Error.** A status code of 500 is sent to inform the client about a server error.

The coordinates are written in *x,y* format, where each coordinate is separated by a white space character. The quoted text string is used as the link when a menu is generated. In the absence of such a string, the URL will be the link shown in the following imagemap file example:

```
# Comments go here
#  Version 1.0.0

base http://www.yoursite.com/some/dir
rect thisfile.html "Customer info" 0,0 100,200
circle http://download.yoursite.com/index.html 295,0
100,22
```

If this imagemap file is called imagemap.map, it can be referenced as follows from another HTML file, such as:

```
<A HREF="/path/to/imagemap.map"><IMG ISMAP
SRC="/path/to/imagemap.gif"></A>
```

ImapMenu

Syntax: `ImapMenu {none, formatted, semiformatted, unformatted}`
Context: `server config, virtual host, directory, .htaccess`
Override: `Indexes`

This directive determines the action for a request for an imagemap file without any valid coordinates. It allows the following actions:

- **None.** No menu is generated, and the default action is performed.
- **Formatted.** The simplest menu is generated. Comments are ignored. A level one header is printed, then an hrule, then the links — each on a separate line.
- **Semiformatted.** In the semiformatted menu, comments are printed. Blank lines are converted into HTML breaks. No header or hrule is printed.
- **Unformatted.** In the unformatted menu, comments are printed. Blank lines are ignored.

ImapDefault

Syntax: `ImapDefault {error, nocontent, map, referer, URL}`
Context: `server config, virtual host, directory, .htaccess`
Override: `Indexes`

This defines the default action for imagemaps. This default setting can be overridden in the imagemap file using the default directive.

ImapBase

Syntax: `ImapBase {map, referer, URL}`
Context: `server config, virtual host, directory, .htaccess`
Override: `Indexes`

This directive sets the default base used in the imagemap files. This base setting can be overridden by using the base directive within the imagemap file. If this directive is not present, the base defaults to `http://servername/`.

mod_include

This module is compiled by default in the standard Apache distribution. However, to enable SSI support for Apache you need to perform the following steps:

1. Add a new handler for SSI pages.
2. Add a new file extension for SSI pages.
3. Enable SSI parsing for a directory.

By default, Apache does not parse HTML files when requested. If it did, the HTML pages that do not have SSI commands in them would still need to be parsed, and the unnecessary parsing would make the delivery of these pages slower. The solution to this problem is to identify pages that have SSI commands with a different file extension than the typical HTML file extensions (.html or .htm). Let's say you want to use .shtml as the SSI file extension for all HTML pages that will contain one or more SSI commands. You need to tell Apache that the file extension .shtml should be treated as an SSI-enabled page. You can do that using the AddHandler directive as follows:

```
AddHandler server-parsed .shtml
```

The AddHandler directive tells Apache that an .shtml file needs to be handled by the server-parsed handler, which is found in the mod_include module.

If, for some reason, you have to use .html and .htm extension as the SSI extension, do not use:

```
AddHandler server-parsed .html
AddType text/html .html

AddHandler server-parsed .htm
AddType text/html .htm
```

This would degrade your server performance. Apache would process all the .html and .htm files, which would mean that files without any SSI commands would be parsed, therefore increasing the delay in file delivery. You should try hard to avoid using the .html or .htm extensions for SSI; if you must use them, however, then use the XbitHack directive found in the mod_include module.

XBitHack

Syntax: `XBitHack on | off | full`
Default: `XBitHack off`
Context: `server config, virtual host, directory, .per-directory access control file (.htaccess)`
Override: `Options`

Typically, only .html and .htm files are associated with text/html. The default value Off tells the server not to parse these files. When this is set to On, any HTML file that has execute permission for the file owner is considered an SSI file and is parsed. When the directive is set to FULL, it makes the server check the owner and the group executable bits of the file permission settings. If the group executable bit is set, then Apache sets the last-modified date of the returned file to be the last modified time of the file. If it is not set, then no last-modified date is sent. Setting this bit enables clients and proxies to cache the result of the request. Use of the value FULL is not advisable for SSI pages that produce a different output when parsed and processed.

Although Apache now knows how to handle the .shtml file, it needs to be told what to tell the Web browser about this file. Web servers send header information for each request to tell the Web browser what type of content is being sent as the response. Therefore, you need to tell Apache that when responding to an .shtml file request, it should tell the browser, by setting the content type, that the information being sent is still an HTML document. This way, the Web browser will render the content onscreen as usual. The MIME type for HTML content is text/html. The following line shows how Apache can be told to generate a text/html content type header when transmitting the output of an .shtml page:

```
AddType text/html  .shtml
```

Both Apache and Web browsers know how to handle the new .shtml files; however, Apache is still not ready to parse the .shtml pages.

Using the Options directive, you need to tell Apache that you want to enable Includes support. First, however, you need to determine where to put this Options directive.

If you want to enable SSI support in the entire (primary) Web site, add the following directive in one of the global configuration files (such as access.conf):

```
Options +Includes
```

If you want to enable SSI support for a virtual Web site, you need to put the preceding directive inside the appropriate <VirtualHost ...> container. Or if you want to be able to control this option from directory to directory, you can put this directive inside a <Directory ...> container or in the per-directory access control file (.htaccess).

If you use the per-directory access control file (.htaccess) to enable SSI support, make sure the AllowOverride directive for the site owning that directory allows such an operation. The AllowOverride directive for such a site must allow the Includes option to be overridden. For example, if the AllowOverride is set to None for a site, no SSI parsing will occur.

mod_info

This module provides a comprehensive overview of the server configuration, including all installed modules and directives in the configuration files. It is not compiled into the server by default. It provides the AddModuleInfo directive:

Syntax: `AddModuleInfo module-name descriptive text`
Context: `server config, virtual host`

This directive enables you to add descriptive text in the module listing provided by the mod_info module. The descriptive text could be anything including HTML text. For example:

```
AddModuleInfo mod_auth.c 'See <A
HREF="http://www.apache.org/docs/mod/mod_auth.html">http:
//www.apache.org/docs/mod/mod_auth.html</A>'
```

This will show an HTML link next to the listing of mod_auth.c. This link provides a quick way to get more information on the module from the Apache Web site. To view server configuration information via the Web, add the following to your access.conf file:

```
<Location /server-info>
SetHandler server-info
</Location>
```

You may wish to add a <Limit> clause inside the location directive to limit access to your server configuration information. Once configured, the server information is obtained by accessing:

```
http://your.host.dom/server-info
```

This returns a full configuration page for the server and all modules.

To return server configuration only, use:

```
http://your.host.dom/server-info?server
```

To return configuration for a single module, use:

```
http://your.host.dom/server-info?module_name
```

To return a quick list of included modules, use:

```
http://your.host.dom/server-info?list
```

mod_log_agent

This module enables you to store user agent (Web browsers, robots) information in a separate log file. It is not compiled into the standard Apache distribution. It provides a single directive:

AgentLog

Syntax: `AgentLog filename | "| /path/to/external/program"`
Default: `AgentLog logs/agent_log`
Context: `server config, virtual host`

This directive tells Apache the file or program name to be used to send the UserAgent header for incoming requests. As with the TransferLog directive, you can provide either a log filename or a fully qualified pathname to a program.

Note that when using the LogFormat and CustomLog directives, you can add the percent{User-agent}i format specifier to log the UserAgent header without the use of this module. For example:

```
LogFormat "%h %l %u %t   \"%r\"  %>s  %b \
         \"%{Referer}i\"  \"%{User-agent}i\"" combined

CustomLog log/access.log combined
```

This example, the access.log file will have both user-agent and referrer information. In other words, this module does not provide any functionality that is not present in the standard mod_log_config module. If this module had a way of ignoring local accesses made by you and people on your network, then the data would be more interesting.

mod_log_config

By default, the standard Apache distribution includes this module, which is responsible for the basic logging; it writes CLF log files by default. You can alter this behavior using the LogFormat directive. However, CLF covers logging requirements in most environments.

The CLF file contains a separate line for each request. A line is composed of several tokens separated by spaces:

```
host ident authuser date request status bytes
```

If a token does not have a value, then it is represented by a hyphen (-). Tokens have the following meanings:

- **Host.** The fully qualified domain name of the client, or its IP address
- **Ident.** The identity information reported by the client, if the IdentityCheck directive is enabled and the client machine runs identd
- **Authuser.** The username, if the requested URL required a successful Basic HTTP authentication
- **Date.** The date and time of the request
- **Request.** The request line from the client, enclosed in double quotes (“)
- **Status.** The three-digit HTTP status code returned to the client.
- **Bytes.** The number of bytes in the object returned to the client, excluding all HTTP headers

See Appendix A for a list of all HTTP/1.1 status codes.

The date field can have the following format:

```
date = [day/month/year:hour:minute:second zone]
```

For example:

```
[02/Jan/1998:00:22:01 -0800]
```

The date field sizes are:

Day	2 digits	
Month	3 letters	
Year	4 digits	
Hour	2 digits	
Minute	2 digits	
Second	2 digits	
Zone	(`+' | `-')	4 digits

The four directives available in mod_log_config are discussed in the following sections.

TransferLog

Syntax: `TransferLog filename | "| /path/to/external/program"`

Context: `server config, virtual host`

This directive sets the name of the log file or program where the log information is to be sent. By default, the log information is in the Common Log File (CLF) format. This format can be customized using the LogFormat directive (discussed in the next section). When the TransferLog directive is found within a virtual host container, the log information is formatted using the LogFormat directive found within the context. If a LogFormat directive is not found in the same context, however, the server's log format is used.

The TransferLog directive takes either a log file path or a pipe to an external program as the argument. The log filename is assumed to be relative to the ServerRoot setting if no leading / character is found. For example, if the ServerRoot is set to /etc/httpd, then the following tells Apache to send log information to the /etc/httpd/logs/access.log file:

```
TransferLog logs/access.log
```

When the argument is a pipe to an external program, the log information is sent to the external program's standard input (stdin).

A new program is not started for a VirtualHost if it inherits the TransferLog from the main server. If a program is used, then it is run under the user who started httpd. This will be the root if the server was started by the root. Be sure that the program is secure.

LogFormat

Syntax: `LogFormat format [nickname]`

Default: `LogFormat "%h %l %u %t \"%r\" %s %b"`

Context: `server config, virtual host`

This directive sets the format of the default log file named by the TransferLog directive. If you include a nickname for the format on the directive line, you can use it in other LogFormat and CustomLog directives rather than repeating the entire format string. A LogFormat directive that defines a nickname does nothing else—that is, it only defines the nickname, it doesn't actually apply the format.

CustomLog

Syntax: `CustomLog file-pipe format-or-nickname`

Context: `server config, virtual host`

Like the TransferLog directive, this directive enables you to send logging information to a log file or an external program. Unlike the TransferLog directive, however, it enables you to use a custom log format that can be specified as an argument.

The argument format specifies a format for each line of the log file. The options available for the format are exactly the same as for the argument of the LogFormat directive. If the format includes any spaces (which it will do in almost all cases), it should be enclosed in double quotes.

Instead of an actual format string, you can use a format nickname defined with the LogFormat directive.

CookieLog

Syntax: `CookieLog filename`

Context: `server config, virtual host`

The CookieLog directive sets the filename for the logging of cookies. The filename is relative to the ServerRoot. This directive is included only for compatibility with mod_cookies and is deprecated — therefore, I do not recommend that you use this directive. Use the user-tracking module's directive instead. The user-tracking module mod_usertrack is discussed later in this chapter.

mod_log_referer

The mod_log_referer provides you with the facility to log the incoming Referer headers from requests. Of course, the standard mod_log_config with the CustomLog directive enables you to do the same using the percent{Referer}I format specifier. So, what's the advantage of using this module? Well, this module, unlike mod_log_config, enables you to ignore certain hosts. This way, you can log only your real users and not references from your own host(s).

You need to compile this module into your Apache executable by yourself. It provides the directives discussed in the following sections.

RefererLog

Syntax: `RefererLog filename | "| /path/to/external/program"`
Default: `RefererLog logs/referer_log`
Context: `server config, virtual host`

This directive sets the name of the log file or program that receives the Referer headers of incoming requests.

RefererIgnore

Syntax: RefererIgnore string string ...
Context: server config, virtual host

The RefererIgnore directive adds to the list of strings to be ignored in Referer headers. If any of the strings in the list are contained in the Referer header, then no referrer information will be logged for the request. For example:

```
RefererIgnore yourcompany.com
```

This avoids logging references from `yourcompany.com`. If `yourcompany.com` is the domain name for your internal network, you will be able to ignore all references that have been generated from within your network.

The log file format is quite simple. It contains a separate line for each referral. Each line has the following format:

```
uri -> document
```

where uri is the (percent-escaped) URI for the document that references the one requested by the client, and document is the (percent-decoded) local URL to the document being referred to.

mod_mime

This module is compiled in Apache by default. It is used to provide clients with metainformation about documents. It also enables you to define a handler for a document to determine how the document is processed by Apache.

AddEncoding

Syntax: `AddEncoding MIME-encoding file-extension file-extension...`
Context: `server config, virtual host, directory, per-directory configuration (.htaccess)`
Override: `FileInfo`

This directive maps one or more file extensions to a MIME-encoding scheme. For example:

```
AddEncoding x-gzip gz
AddEncoding x-tar tar
```

This causes a file called backup.gz to be mapped as an x-gzip-encoded file, and a file called tarball.tar to be mapped as an x-tar-encoded file.

AddHandler

Syntax: `AddHandler handler-name file-extension file-extension...`
Context: `server config, virtual host, directory, per-directory configuration (.htaccess)`

This directive is used to define a handler for one or more file extensions. For example:

```
AddHandler server-parsed  .shtml
```

This specifies that all .shtml files be processed by a handler called server-parsed, which is found in mod_include.

AddLanguage

Syntax: `AddLanguage MIME-language file-extension file-extension...`
Context: `server config, virtual host, directory, per-directory configuration (.htaccess)`
Override: `FileInfo`

This directive maps a list of file extensions to a MIME-language. For example:

```
AddLanguage en .en .english
```

This maps all files with extensions .en or .english to be mapped as English language files. This becomes useful in content negotiation, where the server can return a document based on the client's language preference. For example:

```
AddLanguage en .en
AddLanguage fr .fr
```

If the client prefers an English document, and both document.fr.html and document.en.html are available, the server should return document.en.html.

AddType

Syntax: `AddType MIME-type file-extension file-extension...`
Context: `server config, virtual host, directory, per-directory configuration (.htaccess)`
Override: `FileInfo`

This directive maps a list of file extensions to a MIME-type. For example:

```
AddType text/html htm html. HTM HTML
```

ForceType

Syntax: `ForceType MIME-type`

Context: `directory, per-directory configuration (.htaccess)`

This directive is used to force a certain MIME-type for all files in a directory. The directory can be specified by a <Directory> or <Location> container. For example:

```
<Directory
/www/nitec/public/htdocs/files/with/no/extensions>
ForceType text/html
</Directory>
```

This forces the text/html MIME-type for all files in the specified directory, regardless of their extensions.

SetHandler

Syntax: `SetHandler handler-name`

Context: `directory, per-directory configuration (.htaccess)`

This directive is used to define a handler for a directory or a URL location. For example:

```
<Location /ssi>
SetHandler server-parsed
</Location>
```

This forces all files in the /ssi location to be treated as Server Side Includes, which are handled by the server-parsed handler.

TypesConfig

Syntax: `TypesConfig filename`

Default: `TypesConfig conf/mime.types`

Context: `server config`

This directive specifies the default MIME configuration file. The default value should be fine for most Apache installations. If you want to add your own MIME-types, use the AddType directive instead of modifying this file.

TIP

If you need additional support for handling MIME-types, you may want to look at the mod_mime_magic module.

mod_mime_magic

This module can be used to determine the MIME type of a file by looking up a few bytes from within the file. This module is not compiled by default and offers the following directive.

MimeMagicFile

Syntax: `MimeMagicFile filename`

Context: `server config, virtual host`

This directive enables the module and also specifies the magic file that is needed to determine MIME types for files. The standard Apache distribution comes with a magic file called MAGIC, which is installed in the conf directory when you install Apache using APACI.

Using this module could affect your server performance heavily and is not recommended for sites that expect heavy traffic.

mod_negotiation

This module is compiled by default. It provides support for content negotiations. In a typical content negotiation scenario, the client provides information about what type of content it can handle, and the server attempts to provide the most appropriate content. The server performs this with the help of type maps and the MultiViews search.

A type map provides a description of documents. Each document description contains one or more headers. It also can contain comment lines that start with a # character. Document descriptions are separated by blank lines. The document description headers are:

- **Content-Encoding.** The encoding type of the file. Only x-compress and x-gzip encoding are allowed at present.
- **Content-Language.** The language of the document.
- **Content-Length.** The length of the file, in bytes.
- **Content-Type.** The MIME type of the document. Optional key=value parameters are allowed. The allowed parameters are level and qs. The first one provides the version number (as an integer) of the MIME type, and the second one is used to indicate the quality (as a floating point number) of the document.
- **URI.** The path to the document relative to the map file.

A MultiViews search tries to determine the closest match for the missing document using the information it knows from the client and returns the match if possible. When you enable the MultiViews option in the Options directive, the server is able to perform the MultiViews search when a requested document is not found.

Mod_negotiation provides the directives discussed in the next two sections.

CacheNegotiatedDocs

Syntax: `CacheNegotiatedDocs`

Context: `server config`

This directive allows content-negotiated documents to be cached by proxy servers. The new HTTP/1.1 specification provides much better control for caching negotiated documents, and CacheNegotiatedDocs has no effect in response to HTTP/1.1 requests. This directive is likely to disappear after HTTP/1.1 is widely used. Use of CacheNegotiatedDocs is not recommended.

LanguagePriority

Syntax: `LanguagePriority MIME-language MIME-language...`
Context: `server config, virtual host, directory, per-directory configuration (.htaccess)`
Override: `FileInfo`

This directive specifies what language preference the server should use in a MultiViews search scenario, when the client does not provide language preference information. For example:

```
LanguagePriority en fr de
```

If the MultiViews option is turned on and the client does not provide language preference information for a file that is missing, the server first tries to serve the English version of the closest match, and then the French version, and so on. Like the CacheNegotiatedDocs directive, this directive is not effective in the HTTP/1.1 environment.

mod_proxy

The proxy support in Apache comes from the mod_proxy module. This module is not compiled by default. It offers the following set of directives.

ProxyRequests

Syntax: `ProxyRequests on/off`
Default: `ProxyRequests off`
Context: `server config, virtual host`

This directive allows you to enable or disable the caching proxy service. However, it does not affect the functionality of the ProxyPass directive.

ProxyRemote

Syntax: `ProxyRemote <match> <remote-proxy-server-URL>`

Context: `server config, virtual host`

This directive enables you to interface your proxy server with another proxy server. The value of match can be one of the following:

- The name of an URL scheme that the remote server supports
- A partial URL for which the remote server should be used
- To indicate the server should be contacted for all requests

The <remove-proxy-server-URL> can be `http://remove-proxy-hostname:port`. Currently, only the HTTP protocol is supported. In other words, you can only specify a proxy server that deals with the HTTP protocol; however, you can forward FTP requests from your proxy server to one that supports both HTTP and FTP protocols as follows:

```
ProxyRemote ftp http://ftp.proxy.nitec.com:8000
```

This will send all FTP requests that come to the local proxy server to `ftp://ftp.proxy.nitec.com`. The requests will be sent via HTTP, so the actual FTP transaction will occur at the remote proxy server.

If you just want to forward all proxy requests for a certain Web site to its proxy server directly, you can do that with this directive. For example:

```
ProxyRemote http://www.bigisp.com/ \
http://web-proxy.bigisp.com:8000
```

This will send all requests that match `www.bigisp.com` to `web-proxy.bigisp.com`. If you want to forward all of your proxy requests to another proxy, however, you can use the asterisk as the match phrase, for example:

```
ProxyRemote * http://proxy.domain.com
```

This will send all local proxy requests to the proxy server at proxy.domain.com.

ProxyPass

Syntax: ProxyPass <relative-URL> <destination-URL>
Context: server config, virtual host

This directive enables you to map a Web server's document tree onto your proxy server's document space. For example:

```
ProxyPass /internet/microsoft       www.microsoft.com/
```

This directive found in the httpd.conf file of a proxy server called proxy.nitec.com will permit users of the proxy server to access the Microsoft Web site using the URL:

```
http://proxy.nitec.com/internet/microsoft
```

This acts like a mirror of the remote Web site. Any request that uses the <relative-URL> will be converted internally into a proxy request for the <destination-URL>.

ProxyPassReverse

Syntax: ProxyPassReverse <relative-URL> <destination-URL>
Context: server config, virtual host

This directive is useful when you want to create a reverse proxy server using Apache. In such a reverse proxy setup, this directive fixes the Location headers that might be returned by the actual Web server. For example:

```
<Virtualhost 206.171.50.50>
ServerName www.nitec.com
ProxyRequests  on
ProxyPass / realserver.nitec.com/
ProxyPassReverse / realserver.nitec.com/
</VirtualHost>
```

Here, the `www.nitec.com` is the proxy server that gets all the pages from another server called `realserver.nitec.com`. The ProxyPass directive enables this feature. However, if a page on the `realserver.nitec.com` sends a Location header in response, the ProxyPassReverse directive fixes it so that the proxy server `www.nitec.com` is not bypassed by the client.

ProxyBlock

Syntax: `ProxyBlock <partial or full host name> . . .`
Context: `server config, virtual host`

This directive enables you block access to a named host or domain, for example:

```
ProxyBlock gates
```

This will block access to any host that has the word gates in its name. This way, access to `http://gates.ms.com` or `http://gates.friendsofbill.com` will be blocked. You also can specify multiple hosts as follows:

```
ProxyBlock apple orange.com banana.com
```

This blocks all access to any host that matches any of the preceding words or domain names. The mod_proxy module attempts to determine the IP addresses for these hosts during server start-up, and caches them for matching later.

To block access to all hosts, use:

```
ProxyBlock *
```

This effectively disables your proxy server.

NoProxy

Syntax: `NoProxy <Domain name| Subnet | IP Address | Hostname>`
Context: `server config, virtual host`

This directive gives you some control over the ProxyRemote directive in an intranet environment. You can specify a domain name, a subnet, an IP address, or a hostname not to be served by the proxy server specified in the ProxyRemote directive. For example:

```
ProxyRemote  *  http://firewall.yourcompany.com:8080
NoProxy         .yourcompany.com
```

Here all requests for <anything>`.yourcompany.com` (such as `www.yourcompany.com`) will be served by the local proxy server and everything else will go to the `firewall.yourcompany.com` proxy server.

ProxyDomain

Syntax: `ProxyDomain <Domain>`

Context: `server config, virtual host`

This directive specifies the default domain name for the proxy server. When this directive is set to the local domain name on an intranet, any request that does not include a domain name will get this domain name appended in the request, for example:

```
ProxyDomain  .nitec.com
```

When a user of `nitec.com` domain sends a request for a URL such as `http://marketing/us.html`, the request will be regenerated as the following URL:

```
http://marketing.nitec.com/us.html
```

The domain name you specify must have a leading period.

ProxyReceiveBufferSize

Syntax: `ProxyReceiveBufferSize <bytes>`

Context: `server config, virtual host`

This directive sets the network buffer size for all outgoing requests from the proxy server. The buffer size has to be greater than

512. However, you can set this to zero (0) to use the default buffer size of your system.

CacheRoot

Syntax: `CacheRoot <directory>`

Context: `server config, virtual host`

This directive allows you to enable disk caching. You can specify a directory name where the proxy server can write cached files. The Apache server running the proxy module must have write permission for the directory, for example:

```
CacheRoot /www/proxy/cache
```

This will tell Apache to write proxy cache data to the /www/proxy/cache directory. You will need to specify the size of the cache using the cachesize directory before the proxy server can start using this directory for caching. You also may need to use other cache directives shown later to create a useable disk-caching proxy solution.

CacheSize

Syntax: `CacheSize  <n kilobytes>`

Default: `CacheSize 5`

Context: `server config, virtual host`

This directive specifies the amount of disk space (in K) that should be used for disk caching. The cached files are written in the directory specified by the CacheRoot directive. Note that it is possible for the proxy server to write more data than the specified limit, but the proxy server's garbage collection scheme will delete files until the usage is at or below this setting. The default setting (5K) is unrealistic; I recommend anywhere from 10MB to 1GB, depending on your user load.

CacheGcInterval

Syntax: `CacheGcInterval <n hour>`

Context: `server config, virtual host`

This directive specifies the time (in hours) when Apache should check the cache directories for deleting expired files. This is also when Apache will enforce the disk space usage limit specified by the CacheSize directive.

CacheMaxExpire

Syntax: `CacheMaxExpire <n hour>`

Default: `CacheMaxExpire 24`

Context: `server config, virtual host`

This directive specifies the time (in hours) when all cached documents expire. In other words, if you specify this directive as written below, then all the cached documents will expire in 48 hours or two days.

```
CacheMaxExpire 48
```

This directive overrides any expiration date specified in the document itself; so, if a document has a expiration date later then the maximum specified by this directive, the document is still removed.

CacheLastModifiedFactor

Syntax: `CacheLastModifiedFactor <floating point number>`

Default: `CacheLastModifiedFactor 0.1`

Context: `server config, virtual host`

This directive specifies a factor used to calculate expiration time when the original Web server does not supply an expiration date for a document. The calculation is done using the following formula:

```
expiry-period =  (last modification time for the document
) *  (floating point number)
```

So, if a document was last modified 24 hours ago, then the default factor of 0.1 will make Apache calculate the expiration time for this document to be 2.4 hours. If the calculated expiration-period is longer than that set by CacheMaxExpire, then the latter takes precedence.

CacheDirLength

Syntax: `CacheDirLength <length>`

Default: `CacheDirLength 1`

Context: `server config, virtual host`

When disk caching is on, Apache creates subdirectories in the directory specified by the CacheRoot directive. This directive specifies the number of characters used in creating the subdirectory names. You really do not need to change the default for this directive. For curious users who want to know how or why these subdirectories are created, a simplified answer follows.

Apache uses a hashing scheme when creating the path and file name for a URL's data to be cached. For example, when you have caching turned on and access a URL (such as `www.microsoft.com`) via your proxy Apache server, the server hashes this URL so it can retrieve the data quickly later on. This hash could look like `1YSRxSmB20Q_HkqkTuXeqvw`. If the defaults are used for both the CacheDirLength and CacheDirLevels directives, Apache will store the data found on `www.microsoft.com` in a file called:

```
%CacheRoot%/1/Y/S/RRxSmB20Q_HkqkTuXeqvw
```

Here percentCacheRootpercent is the directory specified by the CacheRoot directive. The 1/Y/S directories get created because of the default value of the CacheDirLevels directive. When this document is requested again using the same URL, Apache need only recalculate the hash and retrieve the page from the specified path.

CacheDirLevels

Syntax: `CacheDirLevels <levels>`

Default: `CacheDirLevels 3`

Context: `server config, virtual host`

This specifies the number of subdirectories that Apache will create to store cache data files. See CacheDirLength above for related information.

CacheDefaultExpire

Syntax: `CacheDefaultExpire <n hour>`

Default: `CacheDefaultExpire 1`

Context: `server config, virtual host`

This directive provides a default time (in hours) that is used to expire a cached file when the last modification time of the file is unknown. CacheMaxExpire does not override this setting.

CacheForceCompletion

Syntax: `CacheForceCompletion <percentage>`

Default: `CacheForceCompletion 90`

Context: `server config, virtual host`

This directive tells the proxy server to continue transferring a document from the remote HTTP/FTP server even if the request is cancelled. The percentage specified in the directive makes the proxy server determine if it should continue or not with the transfer. The default value is 90 percent which tells the proxy server to continue transferring when 90 percent of the document is already cached. You can change the value from 1 to 100.

NoCache

Syntax: `NoCache <Domain name|  Subnet | IP Address | Hostname> . . .`

Context: `server config, virtual host`

The NoCache directive specifies a list of hosts, domain names, and IP addresses, separated by spaces, for which no caching is performed. This directive should be used to disable caching of local Web servers on an intranet. The proxy server also matches partial names of a host. If you want to disable caching altogether, use the following:

```
NoCache *
```

mod_rewrite

By default, the mod_rewrite module is compiled into the standard Apache distribution. You will have to enable it and recompile and reinstall Apache to make use of it. To use the module properly, you will need to know about the following variables:

API_VERSION	Version of API used
AUTH_TYPE	Type of authentication used
DOCUMENT_ROOT	Top-level document directory of the Web site
HTTP_ACCEPT	MIME types that are acceptable by the Web client
HTTP_COOKIE	Cookie received from the Web client
HTTP_FORWARDED	Forwarding URL
HTTP_HOST	Web server's host name
HTTP_PROXY_ CONNECTION	The HTTP proxy connection information
HTTP_REFERER	The URL that referred to the current URL

HTTP_USER_AGENT	Information about the Web client
IS_SUBREQ	Set if request is a subrequest
PATH_INFO	Path of the requested URL
QUERY_STRING	Query data sent along with the requested URL
REMOTE_ADDR	IP address of the Web client
REMOTE_HOST	Host name of the Web client
REMOTE_USER	Username of the authenticated user
REMOTE_IDENT	Information about the remote user's identification
REQUEST_METHOD	HTTP request method used to request the current URL
REQUEST_URI	Requested URI
REQUEST_FILENAME	Same as SCRIPT_FILENAME
SCRIPT_FILENAME	Physical path of the requested script file
SERVER_ADMIN	Web server administrator's e-mail address
SERVER_NAME	Host name of the Web server
SERVER_PORT	Port address of the Web server
SERVER_PROTOCOL	Version of HTTP protocol being used by the Web server
SERVER_SOFTWARE	Name of the Web server vendor
SERVER_VERSION	Version of the Web server software
THE_REQUEST	Requested URL
TIME	Current time
TIME_YEAR	Current year
TIME_MON	Current month
TIME_DAY	Current day
TIME_HOUR	Current hour

TIME_MIN	Current minute
TIME_SEC	Current second
TIME_WDAY	Current weekday

The directives available from mod_rewrite module are discussed in the following sections.

RewriteEngine

Syntax: `RewriteEngine on | off`

Default: `RewriteEngine off`

Context: `server config, virtual host, per-directory config (.htaccess)`

This directive provides you with the ON/OFF switch for the URL rewrite engine in the mod_rewrite module. By default, all rewriting is turned off. To use the rewrite engine, you must turn the engine on by setting this directive to on.

When enabling URL rewriting per-directory configuration (.htaccess) files, you must enable (set to ON) this directive inside the per-directory configuration file and make sure that you have enabled the following directive in the appropriate context for the directory:

```
Options FollowSymLinks
```

In other words, if the directory belongs to a virtual host site, make sure this option is enabled inside the appropriate virtual host container. Similarly, if the directory in question is part of the main server's Web document space, make sure this option is enabled in the main server configuration.

Note that enabling rewrite rules in per-directory configurations could degrade the performance of your Apache server. This is because mod_rewrite employs a trick to support per-directory rewrite rules, and this trick involves increasing the server's processing load. Therefore, you should avoid using rewrite rules in per-directory configuration files whenever possible.

RewriteOptions

Syntax: `RewriteOptions option1 option2 ...`
Context: `server config, virtual host, per-directory config (.htaccess)`

This directive enables you to specify options to change the rewrite engine's behavior. Currently, the only available option is inherit. By setting this directive to the inherit option, you can force a higher-level configuration to be inherited by a lower-level one. For example, if you set this directive in your main server configuration area, a virtual host defined in the configuration file will inherit all the rewrite configurations, such as the rewrite rules, conditions, maps, and so on.

Similarly, when this directive is set as mentioned in a per-directory configuration file (.htaccess), it will inherit the parent directory's rewrite rules, conditions, and maps. By default, the rewrite engine does not permit inheritance of rewrite configuration, but this directive permits you to alter the default.

RewriteRule

Syntax: `RewriteRule search-pattern substitution-string [flag list]`
Context: `server config, virtual host, per-directory config (.htaccess)`

This directive enables you to define a rewrite rule. The rule must have two arguments. The first argument is the search pattern that must be met to apply the substitution string. The search pattern is written using regular expression (see Appendix B for basics of regular expression). The substitution string can be constructed with plain text, back-references to substrings in the search pattern, values from server variables, or even map functions. The flag list can contain one or more flag strings, separated by commas, to inform the rewrite engine about what to do next with the substitution. Let's take a look back at the previous example:

```
RewriteRule /~([^/]+)/?(.*)  /users/$1/$2 [R]
```

Here, the search pattern is `/~([^/]+)/?(.*)`, and the substitution string is `/users/$1/$2`. Notice the use of back-references in the substitution string. The first back-reference string `$1` corresponds to the string found in the first set of parentheses (from the left). So `$1` is set to whatever is matched in `([^/]+)`, and `$2` is set to the next string found in `(.*)`. When a URL request is as follows:

```
http://blackhole.nitec.com/~kabir/welcome.html
```

The value of `$1` is `kabir`, and `$2` is welcome.html; so the substitution string looks like:

```
/users/kabir/welcome.html
```

When you have more than one RewriteRule specified, the first RewriteRule operates on the original URL and if a match occurs, the second rule will no longer operate on the original URL. Instead, it gets the URL substituted by first rule as the URL on which to apply rules. In a scenario where a match occurs at every step, a set of three rewrite rules will function as follows:

```
RewriteRule  search-pattern-for-original-URL\
substitution-string-1  [flags]
RewriteRule  search-pattern-for-substitution-string-1\
substitution-string-2  [flags]
RewriteRule  search-pattern-for-substitution-string-2\
substitution-string-3  [flags]
```

Is it possible to apply more than one rule to the original URL? Yes, you can use the C flag to instruct the rewrite engine to chain multiple rules. In such a case, you may not want to substitute until all rules are matched so you can use a special substitution string to disable a substitution in a rule.

The details of the possible flags are as follows:

C | chain. This flag specifies that the current rule be chained with the next rule. When chained by a C flag, a rule is looked at if and only if the previous rule in the chain results in a match. Each rule in the chain must contain the flag, and if the first rule does not match, the entire chain of rules is ignored.

E=var:value | . You can set an environment variable using this directive. The environment variables you set using this directive are accessible from rewrite conditions, Server Side Includes and CGI scripts.

F | forbidden. When a rule using this flag is matched, an HTTP response header called FORBIDDEN (status code 403) is sent back to the browser. This effectively disallows the requested URL.

G | gone. When a rule using this flag is matched, an HTTP response header called GONE (status code 410) is sent back to the browser. This informs the browser that the requested URL is no longer available on this server.

L | last. This tells the rewrite engine to end rule processing immediately so that no other rules are applied to the last substituted URL.

N | next. This tells the rewrite engine to restart from the first rule. However, the first rule no longer tries to match the original URL, because it now operates on the last substituted URL. This effectively creates a loop. You must have terminating conditions in the loop to avoid an infinite loop.

NS | nosubreq. Use this flag to avoid applying a rule on an internally generated URL request.

P | proxy. Using this flag will convert a URL request to a proxy request internally. This will work only if you have compiled Apache with the mod_proxy module and configured it to use the proxy module.

PT | passthrough. This is a hack and likely to disappear in a later version of Apache. This flag forces the rewrite engine to modify the internal request record structure such that the URL member variable of the structure is set to the value of the filename member variable. Use this directive only when you are using directives from mod_rewrite with other modules that contain URL-to-filename translators. An example of such module is the mod_alias module.

QSA | qsappend. This flag allows you to append data (such as key=value pairs) to the query string part of the substituted URL.

S=n | skip=n. Skips n rules.

T=mime-type |. Forces the specified MIME-type to be the MIME-type of type=mime-type — the target file of the request.

You can add conditions to your rules by preceding them with one or more RewriteCond directives, which are discussed in the following section.

RewriteCond

Syntax: `RewriteCond test-string condition-pattern [flag list]`

Context: `server config, virtual host, perl-directory config (.htaccess)`

This directive is useful when you want to add an extra condition for a rewrite rule specified by the RewriteRule directive. You can have several RewriteCond directives per RewriteRule. All rewrite conditions must be defined before the rule itself.

The test string may be constructed with plain text, server variables, or back-references from both the current rewrite rule and the last rewrite condition. To access the first back-reference from the current RewriteRule directive, use `$1`; to access the first back-reference from the last RewriteCond directive, use percent1.

To access a server variable, use the percent{variable name} format. For example, to access the REMOTE_USER variable, specify percent{REMOTE_USER} in the test string.

There are a few special data access formats:

%{ENV:variable}. Use this to access any environment variable that is available to the Apache process.

%{HTTP:header}. Use this to access the HTTP header used in the request.

%{LA-U:variable}. Use this to access the value of a variable that is not available in the current stage of processing. For example, if you need to make use of the REMOTE_USER server variable in a rewrite condition stored in the server's configuration file (httpd.conf), you cannot use %{REMOTE_USER}, because this variable is only defined after the server has performed the authentication phase, which comes after mod_rewrite's URL processing phase. To look ahead at what the username of the successfully authenticated user is, you can use %{LA-U:REMOTE_USER} instead. However, if you are accessing the REMOTE_USER data from a RewriteCond in a per-directory configuration file, you can use %{REMOTE_USER} because the authorization phase has already finished and the server variable has become available as usual. The lookup is performed by generating a URL-based internal subrequest.

%{LA-F:variable}. Same as the %{LA-U:variable}in most cases, but lookup is performed using a filename-based internal subrequest.

The condition pattern also can use some special notations in addition to being a regular expression. For example, you can perform lexical comparisons between the test string and the condition pattern by prefixing the condition pattern with a <, >, or = character. In such a case, the condition pattern is compared with the test string as plain text string.

Also note that there may be times when you want to check if the test-string is a file, directory, or symbolic link. In such a case, you can replace the condition pattern with the following special strings:

-d. Tests whether the test-string specified directory exists.

-f. Tests whether the test-string specified file exists.

-s. Tests whether the test-string specified nonzero size file exists.

-l. Tests whether the test-string specified symbolic link exists.

-F. Tests the existence and accessibility of the test-string-specified file.

-U. Tests the validity and accessibility of the test-string-specified URL.

The optional flag list can consist of one or more comma-separated strings as follows:

NC | nocase. Performs a case-insensitive condition test.

OR | ornext. Normally, when you have more than one RewriteCond for a RewriteRule directive, these conditions are ANDed together for the final substitution to occur. However, if you need to create an OR relationship between two conditions, use this flag.

RewriteMap

Syntax: `RewriteMap name-of-map type-of-map:source-of-map`
Context: `server config, virtual host`

This directive facilitates a key-to-value lookup through the use of a map. Think of a map as a table of data in which each row has a key and a value. Typically, a map will be stored in a file. However, the map can be either a text file, a DBM file, internal Apache functions, or an external program. The type of the map corresponds to the source of the map. The applicable types are:

txt. Plain text file that has key value lines such that each key and value pair are on a single line and are separated by at least one white space character. The file can contain comment lines starting with #

characters or can have blank lines. Both comments and blank lines are ignored. For example:

```
Key1    value1
Key2    value2
```

defines two key value pairs. Text file-based maps are read during Apache startup and reread only if the file has been updated after the server is already up and running. The files are also reread during server restarts.

rnd. A special plain text file which has all the restrictions of txt type but allows a flexibility in defining the value. The value for each key can be defined as a set of ORed values using the | (vertical bar) character. For example:

```
Key1    first_value_for_key1 | second_value_for_key1
Key2    first_value_for_key2 | second_value_for_key2
```

defines two key value pairs where each key has multiple values. The value selected is decided randomly.

Int. The internal Apache functions toupper(key) or tolower(key) can be used as a map source. The first function converts the key into all uppercase characters and the second one converts the key to lowercase characters.

dbm. A DBM file can be used as a map source. This can be very useful and fast (compared to text files) when you have a large number of key value pairs. Note that DBM-file-based maps are read during Apache startup and reread only if the file has been updated after the server is already up and running. The files also are reread during server restarts.

Prg. An external program can generate the value. When a program is used, it is started at the Apache startup, and data (key, value) is transferred between Apache and the program via standard input (stdin) and standard output (stdout). Make sure you use the RewriteLock directive to define a lock file when using an external program. When constructing such a program, make sure you read the input from the stdin and write it on stdout in a nonbuffered I/O mode.

RewriteBase

Syntax: `RewriteBase <base URL>`

Default: `current directory path of per-directory config (.htaccess)`

Context: `per-directory config (.htaccess)`

This directive is useful only if you are using rewrite rules in per-directory configuration files. It is also required only for URL paths that do not map to the physical directory of the target file. Set this directive to whatever alias you used for the directory. This will ensure that mod_rewrite will use the alias instead of the physical path in the final (substituted) URL. For example, when an alias is set as follows:

```
Alias /icons/  /www/nitec/htdocs/icons/
```

and rewrite rules are enabled in the /www/nitec/htdocs/icons/.htaccess file, the RewriteBase directive should be set as follows:

```
RewriteBase /icons/
```

RewriteLog

Syntax: `RewriteLog path/to/logfile`

Context: `server config, virtual host`

If you want to log the applications of your rewrite rules, use this directive to set a log filename. Like all other log directives, it assumes that a path without a leading slash (/) means that you want to write the log file in the server's root directory, for example:

```
RewriteLog logs/rewrite.log
```

This will write a log file in the logs subdirectory under your server's root directory. As mentioned before, a log written by the server should be writeable only by the server user.

RewriteLogLevel

Syntax: `RewriteLogLevel level`

Default: `RewriteLogLevel 0`

Context: `server config, virtual host`

This directive allows you to specify what gets logged in the log file. A default value of zero (0) means that nothing will be logged. In fact, a log level of zero (0) means no log-related processing is done inside the module. Therefore, if you wanted to disable logging, keep it set to zero (0).

If you set the RewriteLog directive to /dev/null and the RewriteLogLevel to a nonzero value, the internal log-related processing will still be done, but no log will be produced. This is a waste of your system's computing resources, so if you don't want logging, keep this directive set to its default value. You have a choice between zero (0) and nine (9) for log levels. The higher the level, the more logging data is written.

RewriteLock

Syntax: `RewriteLock filename`

Context: `server config, virtual host`

If you use an external mapping program for creating rewrite maps, you will need to specify a filename with this directive. This file is used as a lock file for synchronizing communication with external mapping programs.

mod_setenvif

This module is compiled in Apache by default. It enables you to create custom environment variables that can later be used to make decisions.

BrowserMatch

Syntax: `BrowserMatch regex variable[=value] [...]`
Context: `server config`

This directive is used to set and remove custom environment variables when a pattern is matched by the regular expression. For example:

```
BrowserMatch ^Mozilla vbscript=no javascript
```

This sets a variable called vbscript to the value no if the User-Agent HTTP request header field contains the word Mozilla, and an environment variable called javascript is set to one (1) because no value was specified for this variable. Let's take a look at another example:

```
BrowserMatch IE vbscript !javascript
```

Here, the variable javascript is removed and the vbscript is set to one (1) if the word IE is found in the User-Agent HTTP request header.

The regular expression matches are case-sensitive.

BrowserMatchNoCase

Syntax: `BrowserMatchNoCase regex variable[=value] [...]`
Context: `server config`

This directive is the same as the BrowserMatch directive, except that it provides case-insensitive matching for regular expressions. For example:

```
BrowserMatchNoCase ^MSIE vbscript=yes
```

This matches MSIE, msie, Msie, and so on.

SetEnvIf

Syntax: `SetEnvIf attribute regex envar[=value] [...]`
Context: `server config`

Like the BrowserMatch and BrowserMatchNoCase directives, this directive enables you to set and unset custom environment variables. Actually, BrowserMatch and BrowserMatchNoCase are two special versions of SetEnvIf. These two directives can perform the regular expression only on the User-Agent HTTP request header field, whereas SetEnvIf can be used for all request header fields. For example:

```
SetEnvIf Remove_Host "yourdomain\.com" local_user=true
```

Some of the other variables you can use are: Remote_Addr, Remote_User, Request_Method, Request_URI, and Referer, if they are available.

SetEnvIfNoCase

Syntax: `SetEnvIfNoCase attribute regex variable[=value] [...]`
Context: `server config`

This is the same as SetEnvIf, but it offers case-insensitive regular expression matches.

mod_speling

This module is not compiled in Apache by default. It enables you to handle misspelled or miscapitalized URL requests. It compares the requested (misspelled or miscapitalized) document name with all the document names in the requested directory for one or more close matches.

In the case of a misspelled document request, the module allows a single spelling error, such as an extra character insertion, a character omission, or a transposition. In the case of a miscapitalized document request, it performs a case-insensitive filename comparison. Either way, if the module locates a single document that closely resembles the request, it sends a redirect request to the client. If there's more than one match, it sends the list to the client for selection.

The single directive offered by this module is called CheckSpelling.

CheckSpelling

Syntax: `CheckSpelling on | off`

Default: `CheckSpelling off`

Context: `server config, virtual host`

This directive enables or disables the module. Note that when the spelling correction is on, the server may experience performance loss due to extra searches that are needed for serving a misspelled document request. You also should be aware that the module works only with file and directory names.

mod_status

This enables Apache administrators to monitor the server via the Web. An HTML page is created with server statistics. It also produces another page that is machine-readable. The information displayed on both pages includes:

- Server version and compilation date/time stamp
- Current time on the server system
- Time when the server was last restarted
- Server uptime
- Total number of accesses served so far
- Total bytes transferred so far
- The number of idle servers and their status

- Averages giving the number of requests per second, the number of bytes served per second, and the average number of bytes per request
- CPU usage by each child server and total load placed on the server by Apache processes
- The list of virtual hosts and requests currently being processed

This module is not compiled by default in the standard Apache distribution, so you will need to compile it into your Apache executable (httpd) yourself. It provides the following directive.

ExtendedStatus

```
Syntax: ExtendedStatus on|off
Default: ExtendedStatus off
Context: server config
```

This directive turns on or off whether the server keeps track of extended status information for each request.

Once you have the mod_status module compiled and built into your Apache server, you need to define a URL location, which Apache should use to display the information. In other words, you need to tell Apache which URL will bring up the server statistics on your Web browser.

Let's say that your domain name is `yourdomain.com`, and you want to use the following URL:

```
www.mydomain.com/apache-status
```

Using the <Location ...> container, you can tell the server that you want it to handle this URL using the server-status handler found in the mod_status module. The following will do the job:

```
<Location /apache-status>
SetHandler server-status
</Location>
```

Here, the SetHandler directive sets the handler (server-status) for the previously mentioned URL. This configuration segment should typically go in the access.conf file, but it really can go inside any of the three configuration files. Once you have added the configuration in one of the three files, you can restart the server and access the preceding URL from a browser. The <Location ...> container in this example enables anyone to see the server status using this URL; this may not be a good thing as far as security is concerned. To make sure that only machines on your domain can access the status page, you can replace the preceding configuration with the following:

```
<Location /apache-status>
SetHandler server-status
order deny, allow
deny from all
allow from .yourdomain.com
</Location>
```

where `yourdomain.com` should be replaced with your own domain name. If you want only one or more selected hosts to have access to this page, you can simply list the hostnames in the allow directive line.

TIP

You can have the status page update itself automatically if you have a browser that supports the refresh command. Access the page http://www.yourdomain.com/server-status?refresh=N to refresh the page every N seconds.

mod_unique_id

This module provides a magic token for each request that is guaranteed to be unique across "all" requests under very specific conditions. The unique identifier is unique even across multiple machines in a properly configured cluster of machines. The environment variable UNIQUE_ID is set to the identifier for each request. This module currently is not available for the Windows version of Apache.

mod_userdir

This module allows you to specify the user directory which is to be used as a document root directory when a request contains a ~username. This module is compiled by default and offers the following directive.

UserDir

Syntax: `UserDir directory`

Default: `UserDir public_html`

Context: `server config, virtual host1`

This directive sets the directory name which will be used as a user's document root directory. The default setting will translate `http://www.nitec.com/~kabir` to /home/dir/of/kabir/public_html.

You can use "*" as a wildcard as well. For example:

```
UserDir/public/*/www
```

This setting will translate a request such as `http://www.nitec.com/~kabir/publications.html` to /public/kabir/www/publications.html. I like this example since it allows me to keep the publicly readable Web files outside a user's home directory in a /public partition.

Also, you can enable/disable users who can have Web sites or not using UserDir. For example:

```
UserDir disabled root
```

This disables the root user's UserDir-specified directory to be accessible via the Web. In other words, if you had the following UserDir settings:

```
UserDir  public_html
UserDir disabled root
```

the http://domain.tld/~root will not translate as usual. It is highly recommended (for security reasons) that you disable the root user's Web directory as shown in the preceding code. You also can enable user directories using the enabled keyword. For example:

```
UserDir public_html
UserDir disabled root kabir
UserDir enabled sheila
```

Here, only the user Sheila has her Web directory enabled.

mod_usertrack

The mod_usertrack module is not compiled into the standard distribution version of Apache, so you need to compile it before you can use it. The module provides the following directives.

CookieExpires

Syntax: `CookieExpires expiry-period`
Context: `server config, virtual host`

This directive is used to set the expiration period of the cookies that are generated by the module. The expiration period can be defined in terms of number of seconds or in a format such as "1 month 2 days 3 hours." For example:

```
CookieExpires 3600
CookieExpires "2 days 3 hours"
```

Here, the first directive defines the expiration period in seconds, and the second one defines the expiration period using the special format. When the expiration period is not defined in a numeric form, the special form is assumed. However, the special format requires that you put double quotes around the format string. If this directive is not used, cookies last only for the current browser session.

CookieTracking

Syntax: `CookieTracking on | off`

Context: `server config, virtual host, directory, per-directory configuration file ( .htaccess)`

Override: `FileInfo`

This directive enables or disables the generation of automatic cookies. When it is set to on, Apache starts sending a user-tracking cookie for all new requests.

The CookieTracking directive can be used to turn this behavior on or off on a per-server or per-directory basis. By default, compiling mod_usertrack does not activate cookies. If you plan to use this directive, you might want to consider enabling it only in the directories in which you have HTML documents. Enabling it for the entire Web site will generate tracking cookies for everything including the images you embed in your HTML documents.

Chapter 5

Hosting Virtual Sites

Apache supports two types of virtual hosts — IP-based virtual hosts and name-based virtual hosts. IP-based virtual hosts will work with all old and new browsers, but name-based virtual hosts might not work, because they rely on the latest HTTP/1.1 protocol. However, HTTP/1.1 is becoming widely supported by major browser vendors, so this particular difference will soon become a non-issue. I recommend using a name-based virtual host, because it allows you to create virtually unlimited numbers of hosts. On the other hand, the total number of IP-based virtual hosts is limited by the IP class of your network. For example, if you have a class C IP network, you have a total of 256 IP addresses, and not all of them can be used for virtual hosting.

No matter what type of virtual host you choose to implement, proper Domain Name Service (DNS) configuration is a prerequisite. All the DNS examples in this chapter use syntax for the most commonly used Berkley Name Daemon. This name server is the default for many operating systems such as Linux, FreeBSD, and so on. If your name server is not named compatible, make sure you use appropraite syntax. There are two ways you can configure your DNS server to support virtual hosts.

DNS Configuration for IP-Based Virtual Hosts

IP-based virtual host configuration requires unique IP addresses for each virtual host. Therefore the first step in creating an IP-based virtual host is to add an Address record in your forward DNS server configuration file. For example, to create a virtual host called `vhost1.domain.com`, you need to add the following A (address) record:

```
vhost1.domain.com.        IN    A     x.y.z.n.
```

Or, if you prefer to use the shortened version, you can add:

```
vhost1                    IN    A     x.y.z.n.
```

where `x.y.z.n` is the IP address you would like to assign `vhost1.domain.com`. Next, you will need to create a PTR (pointer) record in the reverse DNS configuration file. This record for the previous example would be as follows:

```
n.z.y.x.in-addr.arpa.     IN    PTR   vhost1.domain.com.
```

Again, the shortened version is as follows:

```
n                         IN    PTR   vhost1.domain.com.
```

For example, if I wanted to create three IP-based virtual hosts such as www.classifiedworks.com, `www1.classifiedworks.com`, and `www2.classfiedworks.com` for a domain called `classified-works.com`, I would add the following lines in the forward DNS configuration file:

```
; A Records (shortened version)
www                       IN    A     192.168.0.50
www1                      IN    A     192.168.0.51
www2                      IN    A     192.168.0.52
```

Then, I would add the following PTR records in the reverse DNS configuration file for the preceding domain:

```
; PTR Records (shortened version)
50     IN     PTR    www.classifiedworks.com.
51     IN     PTR    www1.classifiedworks.com.
52     IN     PTR    www2.classifiedworks.com.
```

Once you have created the necessary A and PTR records in your DNS configuration files, you should restart your DNS server and test the new configuration. Using the widely available (both on UNIX and NT systems) nslookup utility program, you can test the new DNS configuration quite easily. For example, to test the DNS configuration for the `www.classifiedworks.com`, I needed to run two instances of nslookup command as follows:

```
nslookup –query=a www.classifiedworks.com
nslookup –query=ptr www.classifiedworks.com
```

The first nslookup command is told to find an A record for `www.classifiedworks.com`; the second one is told to look for a PTR record for the same host. If nslookup fails to find the appropriate information, revisit your DNS configuration and check for mistakes or typos.

DNS Configuration for Name-Based Virtual Hosts

Name-based virtual hosts do not require unique IP addresses. All you need to do is to create a CNAME (canonical name) record for each virtual host. In other words, you just need to create an alias for an existing host. Let's say that you have an existing host called `www.domain.com` with appropriate DNS configuration. Now, if you wanted to create a virtual host called `vhost1.domain.com` that uses the same Apache server as the `www.domain.com`, all you need to do is create the following alias in the forward DNS configuration file for `domain.com`:

```
vhost1.domain.com.  IN    CNAME    www.domain.com.
```

The shortened version is as follows:

```
vhost1    IN      CNAME     www
```

For example, if I wanted to create two name-based virtual hosts, such as www1.classifiedworks.com and www2.classifiedworks.com, for a domain called classifiedworks.com with an existing host called www.classifiedworks.com, I would add the following lines in the forward DNS configuration file:

```
; CNAME Records (shortened version)
www1      IN      CNAME     www
www2      IN      CNAME     www
```

Here www.classifiedworks.com already has the following A and PTR records in forward and reverse DNS configuration files, respectively:

```
; A Records (shortened version) in forward DNS file

www       IN      A         192.168.0.50

; PTR Records (shortened version) in reverse DNS file

50        IN      PTR       www.classifiedworks.com.
```

To test your CNAME record addition(s), use nslookup utility. For example, to test the DNS configuration for the www1.classifiedworks.com and www2.classifiedworks.com, I needed to run two instances of the nslookup command as follows:

```
nslookup —query=cname www1.classifiedworks.com
nslookup —query=cname www2.classifiedworks.com
```

The nslookup commands are told to find a CNAME (canonical name) record for www1.classifiedworks.com and www2.classifiedworks.com. If nslookup does not show the appropriate canonical name for the host specified in the command line, there must be a mistake or typo in the configuration.

Apache Configuration for Virtual Hosts

You can configure Apache in two ways to enable it to support multiple hosts (the main server and the virtual servers). You can either run multiple daemons, so that each host has a separate httpd daemon, or you can run a single daemon, which supports all the virtual hosts and the primary server host.

For typical needs, you would want to run a single primary Apache daemon. If sharing httpd configurations between virtual hosts is not acceptable, however, because of differences in ServerType, user, group, TypesConfig, ServerRoot, and so on, then you need to run multiple main Apache processes. These separate primary httpd processes would require separate configuration files.

Let's take a look at how to configure each of your options: setting up multiple daemons and setting up a single daemon.

Setting Up Multiple Apache Daemons

To set up multiple Apache daemons, you first need to create a separate httpd installation for each virtual host. Basically, you have to create a separate set of Apache configuration files for each daemon process. For each installation, use the Listen directive in the configuration file to select which IP address (or virtual host) the daemon services.

There are two ways to tell Apache which addresses and ports to listen to: You can either use the BindAddress directive to specify a single address or port or use the Listen directive to specify any number of specific addresses or ports. For example, if you run your primary server on IP address 192.168.0.50 port 80 and a virtual host on IP 192.168.0.54 port 8080, you would use:

```
Listen 192.168.0.50:80
Listen 192.168.0.54:8080
```

TIP

It is better to use IP addresses instead of hostnames in Listen directives, because it reduces the domain name lookup needed to resolve the hostname to the IP address at server startup.

Assuming that you have multiple IP addresses bound to the network interface of the server, you can use the Listen directives (as shown earlier) to have Apache listen to different IP addresses. For example, to create two virtual hosts called `www.nitec.com` and `www.ad-engine.com`, you would have to do the following:

1. Make two copies of your Apache ServerRoot directory. For example, if you installed Apache in /usr/local/apache, you need to make two more copies of the entire /usr/local/apache directory structure. For this example, I will assume that these two copies are /usr/local/apache-nitec and /usr/local/apache-ad-engine.
2. Edit the httpd.conf files in /usr/local/apache-nitec/etc/ and /usr/local/apache-ad-ngine/etc, and insert appropriate Listen directives as shown earlier.
3. Now, modify the httpd.conf file for each virtual host per your liking. For example, you will have to change the ServerName, DocumentRoot, ScriptAlias, ErrorLog, and TransferLog directives to point to different locations.
4. Run both Apache daemons using the -d command line option, which requires that you specify the fully qualified path name of the server root directory. Run two Apache daemons as follows:

```
/usr/local/apache-nitec/sbin/httpd -d \
/usr/local/apache-nitec

/usr/local/apache-ad-engine/sbin/httpd -d \
/usr/local/apache-ad-engine
```

You also can run your main Apache daemon as usual. It is possible to just make multiple copies of the configuration files in the main server's ETC directory and run the virtual server daemons using the -f option, which requires that you specify the full path of the httpd.conf file. However, if you are going to use multiple Apache daemons for virtual hosts, you are better off copying the entire server root directory structure as shown in the previous example. This way, you can have three different Apache executables. This allows you to customize (by compiling with different options) each executable to be different if needed.

Using multiple main servers for virtual Web sites puts a heavy load on the system and is not recommended for sites that are likely to experience high traffic.

Setting Up a Single Apache Daemon

This is the default configuration for Apache. A single httpd daemon launches child processes to service requests for the primary Web site and all the virtual sites. By default, Apache listens to port 80 on all IP addresses of the local machine, and this is often sufficient. If you have a more complex requirement, such as listening on various port numbers or listening only to specific IP addresses, you can use the BindAddress or Listen directives.

Apache uses the special container <VirtualHost> in the httpd.conf file to handle all the virtual host-specific configurations. An example of a minimal virtual host configuration might look like this:

```
<VirtualHost 192.168.0.50>
DocumentRoot /www/apachehandbook/public/htdocs
ServerName  www.apachehandbook.com
</VirtualHost>
```

In the code above, the first line marks the start of a virtual host (`www.apachehandbook.com`) configuration. The enclosed IP address needs to be a valid IP for `www.apachehandbook.com`. If a nonstandard (that is, not 80) port address needs to be used, it can be supplied as follows:

```
<VirtualHost IP-address:port>
```

For example:

```
<VirtualHost 192.168.0.50:8080>
```

WARNING

You may be wondering if you can use hostnames instead of IP addresses inside the <VirtualHost> container. Yes, you can; but please don't, unless the developers of Apache tell you it's OK to do so. If you use a hostname instead of an IP address, Apache must do a DNS lookup to determine the IP address of that host. If, for some reason, the DNS lookup fails, the virtual host is likely to be unavailable until you restart Apache. Like many people, I personally do not like to keep hard-coded IP addresses in configuration files, but until Apache developers come up with a better way of handling this situation, hard-coded IP addresses should be used.

Any directive inside a <VirtualHost> container applies only to that virtual host. Any directive that has been used outside the <VirtualHost> directives constitutes the primary server's configuration. Each virtual host inherits the primary server's configuration unless there is a conflict. In a case in which the same directive is used both in the main server configuration and in a virtual host configuration (that is, inside a <VirtualHost> container), the directive inside the virtual host configuration overrides the primary server's setting for only that particular virtual host. For example, if you have ServerName set to `www.yourcompany.com` in your primary server configuration (that is, outside any <VirtualHost> container), and you have a ServerName directive in a <VirtualHost> container set to `www.yourclient.com`, then obviously you want the virtual host to respond to `www.yourclient.com`, right? That's exactly what happens; the directive within the virtual host section overrides the main server's corresponding directive. It may be easier to think of the main server configuration as the global default configuration for all virtual hosts that you create using the <VirtualHost>. So, when configuring virtual hosts, you need to decide what changes need to be made in each of the virtual host configurations.

The directives either override the configuration given in the primary server or supplement it, depending on the directive. For example, the DocumentRoot directive in a <VirtualHost> section overrides the primary server's DocumentRoot, whereas AddType supplements the main server's MIME types.

Now, when a request arrives, Apache uses the IP address and port on which it arrived to find a matching virtual host configuration. If no virtual host matches the address and port, it is handled by the primary server configuration. If it does match a virtual host address, Apache uses the configuration of that virtual server to handle the request.

In the previous example, the virtual host configuration used is the same as the primary server, except that the DocumentRoot is set to /www/apachehandbook/public/htdocs, and the ServerName is set to `www.apachehandbook.com`. Directives commonly set in <VirtualHost> containers are: DocumentRoot, ServerName, ErrorLog, and TransferLog.

You can put almost any configuration directive in the VirtualHost directive, with the exception of ServerType, StartServers, MaxSpareServers, MinSpareServers, MaxRequestsPerChild, BindAddress, Listen, PidFile, TypesConfig, ServerRoot, and NameVirtualHost. User and Group may be used inside VirtualHost containers if the suEXEC wrapper is used.

You can have as many <VirtualHost> containers as you want. You can choose to have one or more of your virtual hosts handled by the primary server, or have a <VirtualHost> for every available address and port and leave the primary server with no requests to handle.

Apache Configuration for IP-Based Virtual Hosts

Setting up IP-based virtual hosts in a single primary Apache server configuration is very simple. All you need to do is create a <VirtualHost> container per virtual IP-address. For example, to create a virtual host called `vhost1.domain.com` (192.168.0.50) with /www/vhost1/ as the DocumentRoot directory, you need to add the following lines in the httpd.conf file.

```
<VirtualHost 192.168.0.50>
DocumentRoot /www/vhost1
ServerName vhost1.domain.com
</VirtualHost>
```

Here are some practical examples of IP-based virtual host configurations.

IP-Based Virtual Hosting on a Server with Multiple IP Addresses

In this example, you want to configure an IP-based virtual host, `www.myclient.com`, on a host called `webserver.mycompany.com`. This host also needs to run a main server called `www.mycompany.com`. Also, assume that the Web server machine has two IP addresses that have the following DNS records:

```
www.webserver.mycompanycom.  IN A      192.168.0.1
www.myclient.com.            IN A      192.168.0.2
www.mycompany.com.           IN CNAME  webserver.
                                       mycompany.com.
```

The simplified httpd.conf configuration file looks like this:

```
...
Port 80
DocumentRoot /www/mycompany
ServerName www.mycompany.com

<VirtualHost 192.168.0.2>
DocumentRoot /www/myclient
ServerName www.myclient.com
...
</VirtualHost>
```

The host www.myclient.com can be reached only through the address 192.168.0.2, while the server www.mycompany.com can be reached only through the 192.168.0.1 address.

IP-Based Virtual Hosting without a Main Server

This example is similar to the previous one; the difference is that only the local users (that is, users who are running their Web browsers on the webserver.mycompany.com machine) can see the main server pages. In other words, there will be no dedicated main server.

The simplified httpd.conf configuration file looks like this:

```
...
Port 80
ServerName webserver.mycompany.com
DocumentRoot /www/localinfo

<VirtualHost 192.168.0.1>
DocumentRoot /www/mycompany
ServerName www.mycompany.com
...
</VirtualHost>
<VirtualHost 192.168.0.2>
DocumentRoot /www/myclient
ServerName www.myclient.com
...
</VirtualHost>
```

In such a setup, the main server can only service the requests of local users who are running their Web browsers on this machine. So, when a local user enters http://localhost/, he or she will be able to access the main server pages stored in /www/localinfo. Calls such as http://www.mycompany.com/ and http://www.myclient.com/, however, are serviced by their respective virtual servers.

IP-Based Virtual Hosts on Different Ports

This example uses the same hosts as in the previous two examples, but this time I want to show how you can configure Apache to have one virtual host listening to one port and another to a different port.

The simplified httpd.conf configuration file looks like this:

```
...
Listen 192.168.0.1:80
Listen 192.168.0.2:10000
ServerName webserver.mycompany.com
DocumentRoot /www/localinfo

<VirtualHost 192.168.0.1>
DocumentRoot /www/mycompany
ServerName www.mycompany.com
...
</VirtualHost>
<VirtualHost 192.168.0.2>
DocumentRoot /www/myclient
ServerName www.myclient.com
...
</VirtualHost>
```

As in the previous example, the main server can catch requests only from the local users. The `www.mycompany.com` server can be reached via the standard port (valid URLs are `www.mycompany.com/` and `www.mycompany.com:80/`). The `www.myclient.com` site, however, can be reached only through the port 10000. Therefore, to access this site, the following URL needs to be used:

```
http://www.mycompany.com:10000/
```

Apache Configuration for Name-Based Virtual Hosts

Setting up name-based virtual hosts is also very easy. The very first step is to set the NameVirtualHost directive to the IP address of the name-based virtual hosts. This directive specifies an IP address that should be used as a target for name-based virtual hosts. For example, say that you want to set up two virtual hosts, `www.client1.com` and `www.client2.com`, on an Apache server that listens to IP address 192.168.0.50. Here is an example configuration for such a setup:

```
NameVirtualHost 192.168.0.50

<VirtualHost 192.168.0.50>
ServerName www.client1.com
DocumentRoot /www/client1
</VirtualHost>

<VirtualHost 192.168.0.50>
ServerName www.client2.com
DocumentRoot /www/client2
</VirtualHost>
```

You only need a single NameVirtualHost directive per IP address for all the name-based virtual hosts using that IP address. When a request comes for one of these virtual hosts from an HTTP/1.1-compliant browser, Apache matches the ServerName with the hostname provided in the Host header of the request. Thus, Apache is able to determine which virtual host was requested.

Once you have created the virtual host configuration for Apache, you can start (or restart) the Apache server for the configuration to take effect. Also, don't forget to create any directories that you might be using in a virtual host configuration before restarting your Apache server.

This example shows you how to configure a single-IP-based host, `webserver.mycompany.com`, to host two name-based virtual Web sites: `www.mycompany.com` and `www.myclient.com`. The Web server machine has a single IP address with the following DNS records:

```
www.webserver.mycompany.com.  IN A      192.168.0.1
www.mycompany.com. IN CNAME   webserver.mycompany.com.
www.myclient.com. IN CNAME    webserver.mycompany.com.
```

Two aliases (CNAME records) for `webserver.mycompany.com` are `www.mycompany.com` and `www.myclient.com`.

The simplified httpd.conf configuration file looks like this:

```
...
Port 80
ServerName webserver.mycompany.com

NameVirtualHost 192.168.0.1

#
# primary virtual server
#
<VirtualHost 192.168.0.1>
DocumentRoot /www/mycompany
ServerName www.mycompany.com
...
</VirtualHost>

<VirtualHost 192.168.0.1>
DocumentRoot /www/myclient
ServerName www.myclient.com
...
</VirtualHost>
```

The main server services only the local users on the system. The first virtual host is what users with non-HTTP/1.1-compliant browsers see. Other than that, all HTTP/1.1-compliant browsers can request the proper virtual host, and the server services them according to the virtual host settings found in the configuration file.

Compatibility with Pre-HTTP/1.1 Browsers

Prior to HTTP/1.1, there was no way for a Web server to know which hostname the browser user entered to request service. The new HTTP/1.1 specification adds a facility in which the browser must tell the server the hostname it is using, on the Host: header. Of course, if someone is using a browser that is not HTTP/1.1-compliant, it will not send the necessary Host: header information, and the server will fail to find the appropriate site. There is a workaround that involves using the ServerPath directive in the first virtual host configuration. Here is an example configuration:

```
NameVirtualHost 192.168.0.44

#
# primary virtual host
#
<VirtualHost 192.168.0.44>
DocumentRoot /www/subdomain
...
</VirtualHost>

<VirtualHost 192.168.0.44>
DocumentRoot /www/subdomain/client1
ServerName www.client1.com
ServerPath /client1/
...
</VirtualHost>
```

```
<VirtualHost 192.168.0.44>
DocumentRoot /www/subdomain/client2
ServerName www.client2.com
ServerPath /client2/
...
</VirtualHost>
```

In the first virtual host's index page (`/www/subdomain/index.html`), you would need to establish links with a URL prefix to the name-based virtual hosts. You also need to locate all name-based virtual hosts under the first virtual host's document root directory, each in its own subdirectory. In the preceding example, the first virtual host's document root directory is /www/subdomain/. The document roots for `www.client1.com` and `www.client2.com` are located in the /www/subdomain/client1 directory and the /www/subdomain/client2 directory, respectively. The final piece of discipline you need to add in this virtual Web site is that all links should be relative links (for example, file.html or ../icons/image.gif) or links containing the prefacing /domain/ (for example, `www.domain.tld/domain/misc/file.html` or /domain/misc/file.html).

The ServerPath directive causes a request to the URL `www.client1.com/client1/` to always be served from the client1 virtual host. A request to the URL `www.client1.com/` is served from the client1 virtual host only if the client sent a correct Host: header using HTTP/1.1. If no Host: header is sent, the client receives the information page from the first virtual host.

This solution may appear cumbersome and difficult to manage, but adherence to these guidelines will, for the most part, ensure that your pages work with all browsers, new and old.

Mixing IP-Based and Name-Based Virtual Hosts

Now let's take a look at an example in which both IP-based and name-based virtual hosts are configured. In this example, I use the following DNS records:

```
; A Records
www.webserver.mycompany.com.  IN A   192.168.0.1
www.myclient.com.             IN A   192.168.0.2

; CNAME Records
www.mycompany.com.     IN CNAME  webserver.mycompany.com.
```

The simplified httpd.conf configuration file looks like this:

```
...
Port 80
ServerName webserver.mycompany.com

NameVirtualHost 192.168.0.1

<VirtualHost 192.168.0.1>
DocumentRoot /www/client1
ServerName www.client1.com
...
</VirtualHost>

<VirtualHost 192.168.0.1>
DocumentRoot /www/client2
ServerName www.client2.com
...
</VirtualHost>

<VirtualHost 192.168.0.2>
DocumentRoot /www/mycompany
ServerName www.mycompany.com
...
</VirtualHost>
```

When you are combining both IP-based and name-based virtual hosts, remember to use the NameVirtualHost directive before all the name-based virtual hosts with the same IP. If you want to keep your configuration files readable, simply enter the NameVirtualHost once per IP and list all the name-based virtual hosts using that IP afterward, as I did in the preceding example.

Using Default Virtual Hosts

This example shows how to catch every request to any unspecified IP address and port, that is, an address/port combination that is not used for any other virtual host.

The simplified httpd.conf configuration file looks like this:

```
...

<VirtualHost default:*>
DocumentRoot /www/default
...
</VirtualHost>
```

Using such a default virtual host with a wildcard port effectively prevents any request from going to the primary server. A default virtual host never serves a request that was sent to an address/port that is used for name-based Virtual Hosts. If the request contains an unknown or no Host: header, it is always served from the primary name-based virtual host (with the virtual host for that address/port appearing first in the configuration file).

If you want to provide a different default for different port addresses, however, you can do that as well. See the following example.

The simplified httpd.conf configuration file looks like this:

```
...
<VirtualHost default:80>
DocumentRoot /www/default80
...
</VirtualHost>

<VirtualHost default:*>
DocumentRoot /www/default
...
</VirtualHost>
```

The default virtual host for port 80 (which must appear before any default virtual host with a wildcard port) catches all requests that were sent to an unspecified IP address. The primary server is never used to serve a request. If you want to provide a default virtual host only for port 80, then do not provide a wildcard port virtual host.

Migrating a Name-Based Virtual Host to an IP-Based Virtual Host

In this example, let's assume that a name-based virtual host, `www.myclient1.com`, has been assigned the IP address 192.168.0.3. In order to reflect the changes in the Apache configuration, you need to modify the virtual host setting for `www.myclient1.com` as follows:

```
...
...
NameVirtualHost 192.168.0.1

<VirtualHost 192.168.0.1 192.168.0.3>
DocumentRoot /www/client1
ServerName www.myclient1.com
...
</VirtualHost>
```

Notice that the VirtualHost directive now has both the old IP 192.168.0.1 and the new IP 192.168.0.3. This is done so that both name-based and IP-based requests for this virtual host can be serviced. It is not advisable to remove the old IP right away, because many name servers and proxies could have cached the old IP and might fail to find the site until they update their DNS data. The virtual host `www.myclient.com` can now be accessed through the new address (as an IP-based virtual host) and through the old address (as a name-based virtual host).

Debugging Virtual Host Configurations

Starting with Apache 1.3.x you can see Apache parsed settings for virtual hosts using the following command:

```
./httpd -S
```

The preceding command assumes that your current directory is where Apache executable (httpd) is located. The output of this command displays the current virtual host settings for your Apache server. You do not need to shut down a running Apache server to run the preceding command.

The Limiting Factor for Virtual Hosting

Now let's take a look at an issue that could affect servers with a large number of virtual hosts. UNIX operating systems limit the number of file descriptors (also known as file handles) a process can use. Typically, this limit is 64 and may be increased to a large hard-limit. When using a large number of virtual hosts, Apache may run out of available file descriptors.

Apache uses one file descriptor for each log file it opens, and it uses about 10 to 20 additional file descriptors for its internal use. If Apache approaches the limit set on your system, it may try to allocate more file descriptors for itself. This attempt could fail, however, if your system does not provide the setrlimit() system call, if the call does not work on your system, if the needed number of descriptors exceeds the maximum allowance on your system, or if your system has other limits that affect the number of file descriptors.

If you are faced with such a situation, you can try two options to resolve this:

- Reduce the number of log files Apache uses; you may want to look at your VirtualHost entries and remove individual log features for each virtual host.

- On most Unix systems, you could try to set the file descriptor limits manually before running Apache. Use the ulimit command as follows to set the limit to 100 descriptors:

```
ulimit -S -n 100
```

Try different numbers based on your needs. Consult the ulimit man pages for details.

Part II

Server Side Commands and Scripts

Chapter

Chapter 6

Server Side Includes

Configuring Apache for SSI

Before you can use Server Side Include (SSI) pages on your Apache server, make sure that the mod_include.c module is built into your current Apache executable (httpd). The easiest way to check this is to run the following command:

```
/path/to/your/httpd -l
```

This command enables you to see the list of all modules built into your current Apache executable. By default, you should have the SSI module compiled; if not, you need to compile and install a new httpd with mod_include.c module.

Although the mod_include.c module is compiled by default in the standard Apache distribution, the parsing of HTML pages is not enabled by default. To enable SSI support for Apache you need to perform the following steps:

1. Add a new handler for SSI pages.
2. Add a new file extension for SSI pages.
3. Enable SSI parsing for a directory.

When these steps are completed for a directory called chapter_06, under a virtual host called apache.nitec.com, the configuration appears as follows:

```
<VirtualHost 206.171.50.50>

ServerName apache.nitec.com
DocumentRoot /data/web/apache/public/htdocs
ScriptAlias /data/web/apache/public/cgi-bin

<Directory /data/web/apache/public/htdocs/chapter_06>
AddHandler server-parsed .shtml
AddType text/html .shtml
Options +Include
</Directory>

</VirtualHost>
```

WARNING

The use of Include in the Options directive enables all SSI commands. If you plan on disabling execution of external programs via SSI commands, you can use IncludesNOEXEC instead. This disables execution of external programs. However, it also disables loading of external files via the SSI command Include.

Now let's take a closer look at each step involved in enabling SSI support.

Add a New Handler for SSI Pages

By default, Apache does not parse HTML files when requested. If it did, the HTML pages that do not have SSI commands in them would still need to be parsed, and the unnecessary parsing would make the delivery of these pages slower. The solution to this problem is to identify pages that do have SSI commands with a different file extension than the typical HTML file extensions (.html or .htm). Let's say you want to use .shtml as the SSI file extension for all HTML pages that will contain one or more SSI commands. You need to tell Apache that the file extension .shtml should be treated as an SSI-enabled page. You can do that using the AddHandler directive as follows:

```
AddHandler server-parsed .shtml
```

The AddHandler directive tells Apache that an .shtml file needs to be handled by the server-parsed handler, which is found in the mod_include module.

If, for some reason, you have to use .html and .htm extension as the SSI extension, do not use:

```
AddHandler server-parsed .html
AddType text/html .html

AddHandler server-parsed .htm
AddType text/html .htm
```

This would degrade your server performance. Apache would process all the .html and .htm files, which would mean that files without any SSI commands would be parsed, therefore increasing the delay in file delivery. You should try hard to avoid using the .html or .htm extensions for SSI; if you must use them, however, then use the XbitHack directive found in the mod_include module.

The XBitHack directive controls server parsing of files associated with the MIME type text/html.

Syntax: `XBitHack on | off | full`
Default: `XBitHack off`
Context: `server config, virtual host, directory, .per-directory access control file (.htaccess)`
Override: `Options`
Module: `mod_include`

Typically, only l.html and .htm files are associated with text/html. The default value Off tells the server not to parse these files. When this is set to On, any html file that has execute permission for the file owner is considered an SSI file and is parsed. When the directive is set to Full, it makes the server check the owner and the group executable bits of the file permission settings. If the group executable bit is set, then Apache sets the last-modified date of the returned file to be the last modified time of the file. If it is not set, then no last-modified date is sent. Setting this bit enables clients and proxies to cache the result of the request. Use of the value full is not advisable for SSI pages that produce a different output when parsed and processed.

You will still have to perform the third step (Options +Includes) when using this directive.

Add a New File Extension for SSI Pages

Although Apache now knows how to handle the .shtml file, it needs to be told what to tell the Web browser about this file. Web servers send header information for each request to tell the Web browser what type of content is being sent as the response. Therefore, you need to tell Apache that when responding to an .shtml file request, it should tell the browser, by setting the content type, that the information being sent is still an HTML document. This way, the Web browser will render the content onscreen as usual. The MIME type for HTML content is text/html. The following line shows how Apache can be told to generate text/html content type header when transmitting the output of an .shtml page:

```
AddType text/html    .shtml
```

For backward compatibility, documents with the MIME type text/x-server-parsed-html or text/x-server-parsed-html3 will also be parsed (and the resulting output is given the MIME type text/html).

Enable SSI Parsing for a Directory

Both Apache and Web browsers know how to handle the new .shtml files; however, Apache is still not ready to parse the .shtml pages.

Using the Options directive, you need to tell Apache that you want to enable Includes support. First, however, you need to determine where to put this Options directive.

If you want to enable SSI support in the entire (primary) Web site, add the following directive in one of the global configuration files (such as access.conf):

```
Options +Includes
```

If you want to enable SSI support for a virtual Web site, you need to put the preceding directive inside the appropriate <VirtualHost ...> container. Or, if you want to be able to control this option from directory to directory, you can put this directive inside a <Directory ...> container or in the per-directory access control file (.htaccess).

If you use a per-directory access control file (.htaccess) to enable SSI support, make sure the AllowOverride directive for the site owning that directory allows such an operation. The AllowOverride directive for such a site must allow the Includes option to be overridden. For example, if the AllowOverride is set to None for a site, no SSI parsing will occur.

If you do not use the plus (+) sign in the Options line in the preceding example, all the options except Includes will be disabled.

Using SSI Commands

SSI commands are embedded in HTML pages in the form of comments. The base command structure looks like this:

```
<!--#command argument1=value argument2=value
argument3=value -->
```

The value is often enclosed in double quotes; many commands allow only a single attribute-value pair. Note that the comment terminator (-->) should be preceded by white space to ensure that it isn't considered part of the SSI command.

Now, let's examine the config, echo, exec, fcgi, flastmod, include, printenv, and set SSI commands.

config

The config command enables you to configure the parse error message that appears and the formatting that is used for displaying time and file size information. This is accomplished with the following lines of code:

- config errmsg="error message"
- config sizefmt=["bytes" | "abbrev"]
- config timefmt=format string

The first syntax shows how to create a custom error message:

```
config errmsg="error message"
```

This error message is displayed when a parsing error occurs. For example, Listing 6-1 shows a file called config_errmsg.shtml.

Listing 6-1 *config_errmsg.shtml*

```
<HTML>

<HEAD>
<TITLE>
Apache Server Administrator's Handbook - Chapter 6
</TITLE>
</HEAD>

<BODY BGCOLOR="white">

<FONT SIZE=+1 FACE="Arial">
```

```
Simple SSI Example #1
</FONT>

<HR SIZE=1>

<P>
Example of the SSI <STRONG>config errmsg</STRONG>
command: </P>

<P> Embedded commands: <BR><BR>

<CODE>
&lt;!—#config errmsg="This is a custom SSI error
message." —&gt;

<BR>

&lt;!—#config errmsg_typo="This is a custom SSI error
message." —&gt;

</CODE>

</P>

<P> Result: <BR>

<!--#config errmsg="This is a custom SSI error message."
-->

<BR>

<!--#config errmsg_typo="This is a custom error message."
-->

</P>
```

```
</BODY>
</HTML>
```

In this example file, there are two SSI commands. They are:

```
<!--#config errmsg="This is a custom SSI error message."
-->
```

and

```
<!--#config errmsg_typo="This is a custom error message."
-->
```

The first one is a valid config errmsg command that sets the error message to the string "This is a custom SSI error message." The second one is an invalid SSI command, which I intentionally entered into this file.

The second command caused a parse error, and the error message "This is a custom SSI error message." is displayed as a result. The message appears where the invalid command is found. It is possible to enter HTML tags or even insert client-side script in the string of the error message. For example, the following displays a popup JavaScript alert window with an error message:

```
<!— config errmsg="<SCRIPT LANGUAGE=JavaScript> alert('An
error occurred. \n Please report to
webmaster@nitec.com');</SCRIPT>" -->
```

The second syntax enables you to choose the output format for the file size:

```
config sizefmt=["bytes" | "abbrev"]
```

Acceptable format specifiers are "bytes" or "abbrev." For example:

```
<!-- config sizefmt="bytes" -->
```

This shows file sizes in bytes. To show files in kilobytes or megabytes, use:

```
<!-- config sizefmt="abbrev" -->
```

The final syntax enables you to choose the display format for time:

```
config timefmt=format string
```

The commonly used value of the format string can consist of the following identifiers:

- %a The abbreviated weekday name according to the current locale
- %A The full weekday name according to the current locale
- %b The abbreviated month name according to the current locale
- %B The full month name according to the current locale
- %c The preferred date and time representation for the current locale
- %d The day of the month as a decimal number (range 01 to 31)
- %H The hour as a decimal number using a 24-hour clock (range 00 to 23)
- %I The hour as a decimal number using a 12-hour clock (range 01 to 12)
- %j The day of the year as a decimal number (range 001 to 365)
- %m The month as a decimal number (range 01 to 12)
- %M The minute as a decimal number
- %p Either a.m. or p.m., according to the given time value or locale
- %S The second as a decimal number
- %w The day of the week as a decimal, Sunday being 0
- %x The preferred date representation for the current locale without the time
- %X The preferred time representation for the current locale without the date

%y The year as a decimal number without a century (range 00 to 99)

%Y The year as a decimal number including the century

%Z The time zone name or abbreviation

%% A literal % character

Consider this example:

```
<!--#config timefmt="%c" -->
```

This shows the time as Tue May 20 00:54:07 1998.
And the following example:

```
<!--#config timefmt="%m/%d/%Y" -->
```

This shows the time as 05/20/1998.

echo

The echo command prints one of the Include variables (defined later) or any of the CGI environment variables. The syntax is:

```
echo var="variable name"
```

If the value of the variable is not available, it prints (none) as the value. Any dates printed are subject to the currently configured timefmt. For example:

```
<!--#config timefmt="%m/%d/%Y" -->
<!--#echo var="DATE_LOCAL" -->
```

This prints a date such as 05/20/1998, due to the specified timefmt string.

exec

The exec command enables you to execute an external program. The external program can be a CGI program or any other type of executable such as shell scripts or native-binary files. The syntax for CGI programs is:

```
exec cgi="path/to/cgi/program"
```

The syntax for other programs is:

```
exec cmd="path/to/other/programs"
```

If you used the IncludesNOEXEC value for the Options directive, this command is disabled.

Let's look at how to use each of these options.

cgi

The cgi value specifies a (%-encoded) URL relative path to the CGI script. If the path does not begin with a slash (/), then it is taken to be relative to the current document. The document referenced by this path is invoked as a CGI script, even if the server would not normally recognize it as such. However, the directory containing the script must be enabled for CGI scripts (with ScriptAlias or the ExecCGI Option).

The CGI script is given the PATH_INFO and query string (QUERY_STRING) of the original request from the client; these cannot be specified in the URL path. The Include variables will be available to the script in addition to the standard CGI environment.

If the script returns a Location: header instead of output, this is translated into an HTML anchor. For example, the following code shows a simple Perl CGI script that prints out a Location: header as the output:

```
#!/usr/local/bin/perl
print "Location: http://apache.nitec.com/\n\n";
exit 0;
```

When the exec_cgi.shtml file, shown in Listing 6-2, is requested by a Web browser, the server turns the Location header into an HTML anchor instead of redirecting the browser to the `http://apache.nitec.com` site.

Listing 6-2 *exec_cgi.shtml*

```
<HTML>
<HEAD>
<TITLE>
Apache Server Administrator's Handbook - Chapter 6
</TITLE>
</HEAD>

<BODY BGCOLOR="white">

<FONT SIZE=+1 FACE="Arial">
Simple SSI Example #2
</FONT>

<HR SIZE=1>

<P>
Example of the SSI <STRONG>exec cgi</STRONG> command:
</P>

<P>
Embedded commands: <BR><BR>

<CODE>
&lt;!—#exec cgi="/cgi-bin/loc.cgi" —&gt;
<BR>
</CODE>
</P>

<P>
Result: <BR>

<!--#exec cgi="/cgi-bin/loc.cgi" --> </P>

</BODY>
</HTML>
```

As you can see in the listing, the only SSI call in the file is:

```
<!--#exec cgi="/cgi-bin/loc.cgi" -->
```

The output of this is an HTML link.

cmd

When calling a program other than a CGI program, you can use the cmd version of the exec call. The server executes the given command using the sh shell (/bin/sh) on most UNIX systems. The Include variables are available to this command. For example, Listing 6-3 shows a file called exec_cmd.shtml.

Listing 6-3 *exec_cmd.shtml*

```
<HTML>

<HEAD>
<TITLE>
Apache Server Administrator's Handbook - Chapter 6
</TITLE>
</HEAD>

<BODY BGCOLOR="white">

<FONT SIZE=+1 FACE="Arial">
Simple SSI Example #3</FONT>

<HR SIZE=1>

<P>
Example of the SSI
<STRONG>exec cmd</STRONG> command:
</P>

<P>
Embedded commands:
<BR><BR>
```

```
<CODE>

&lt;!—#exec cmd="/bin/date +%m/%d/%y" —&gt;
<BR>

&lt;!—#exec cmd="/bin/ls -l ./" —&gt;
<BR>

</CODE>

</P>

<P> Result: <BR>

<!--#exec cmd="/bin/date +%m/%d/%y" --> <BR>

<PRE>

<!--#exec cmd="/bin/ls -l ./*.html" --> <BR>

</PRE>

</P>
</BODY>
</HTML>
```

This file has two cmd calls:

```
<!--#exec cmd="/bin/date +%m/%d/%y" -->
<!--#exec cmd="/bin/ls -l ./*.html" -->
```

The first one calls the UNIX /bin/date utility with the argument +%m/%d/%y, and the second one calls the UNIX ls utility with ./*.htm.html as the argument.

The ls output is nicely formatted using the <PRE> and </PRE> pair. If you want to output something that uses new lines, you may have to use <PRE> tags to keep the output readable, as shown in the listing.

fsize

This command prints the size of the specified file. The syntax you use for this depends on whether the path to the directory is relative or virtual:

- fsize file="path"
- fsize virtual="URL"

When the first syntax is used, the path is assumed to be relative to the directory containing the current SSI document being parsed. You cannot use ../ in the path, nor can absolute paths be used. You cannot access a CGI script in this fashion. You can, however, access another parsed document. For example:

```
<!--#fsize file="download.zip"-->
```

If the second syntax is used, the virtual path is assumed to be a (%-encoded) URL path. If the path does not begin with a slash (/), then it is taken to be relative to the current document. You must access a normal file this way, but you cannot access a CGI script in this fashion. Once again, however, you can access another parsed document. For example:

```
<!--#fsize virtual="/download/free_software.zip"-->
```

The output format is subject to the sizefmt format specification. See the config command earlier in this chapter for details.

flastmod

The flastmod command prints the last modification date of the specified file. Again, there are two syntax options, depending on the path to the directory:

- flastmod file="path"
- flastmod virtual="URL"

The output is subject to the timefmt format specification. For example:

```
<!--#flastmod file="free_software.zip"-->
<!--#flastmod virtual="/download/free_software.zip"-->
```

If you are unclear about the syntax difference, see the previous section, the fsize command, as an example. To control how the modification date is printed, see the config command, earlier in this chapter.

include

The include directive inserts the text of a document into the SSI document being processed. The syntax depends on the path to the directory:

- include file="path"
- include virtual="URL"

See the fsize command, a couple of sections earlier, for the difference between file and virtual mode.

Any included file is subject to the usual access control. If the directory containing the parsed file has the Option IncludesNOEXEC set, and including the document would cause a program to be executed, then it is not included. This prevents the execution of CGI scripts. Otherwise, CGI scripts are invoked as they normally are, using the complete URL given in the command, including any query string. For example:

```
<!--#include file="copyrights.html" -->
```

This includes the copyrights.html file in the current document. This command is useful for adding repeatable HTML code in files. Many sites use a standard menu bar on each page; if this menu bar is put in an HTML file called menu.html, it can be called from all SSI pages using a similar include file call, as in the preceding example. In the future, when changes need to be made to the menu, the site administrator only needs to update the menu.html page. This will save a lot of work if there are many files in the site.

Recursive inclusions are detected and an error message is generated after the first pass. For example, if a .shtml has an SSI call such as:

```
<!--#include file="b.shtml" -->
```

And, b.SHTML has a call such as:

```
<!--#include file="a.shtml" -->
```

Then Apache logs and displays an error stating that a recursive include has been detected.

printenv

The printenv command prints out a listing of all existing variables and their values. The syntax is:

```
printenv
```

For example:

```
<!--#printenv -->
```

This prints all the Include and CGI environment variables available. Use the <PRE> tag pair to make the output more readable. Also note that displaying the output of this command in a publicly accessible page might give away somewhat sensitive information about your system. Therefore, use this command only for debugging purposes.

set

The set command sets the value of a user-defined variable. The syntax is:

```
set var="variable name" value="value of the variable"
```

For example:

```
<!--#set var="home" value="index.shtml" -->
```

Any variable set using the preceding command is not persistent. In other words, every time a page that uses the set command is loaded, all the variables will be set again.

Using SSI Variables

The SSI module makes a set of variables, in addition to the CGI environment variables, available to all SSI files. These variables are called the include variables. These can be used by SSI commands (echo, if, elif, and so on) and by any program invoked by an SSL command. The include variables are:

DATE_GMT	The current date in Greenwich Mean Time
DATE_LOCAL	The current date in the local time zone
DOCUMENT_NAME	The current SSI filename
DOCUMENT_URI	The (%-decoded) URL path of the document
LAST_MODIFIED	The last modification date of the current file. The date is subject to the config command's timefmt format.

The include variables and the CGI variables are preset and available for use. Any of the variables that are preset can be used as arguments for other commands. The syntax for using defined variables is as follows:

```
<!--#command argument1="$variable1"
argument2="$variable2" ... -->
```

As you can see, the variable name is prefixed by a $ sign. Here's another example:

```
<!--#config errmsg="An error occurred in $DOCUMENT_NAME
page." -->
```

When using variables in a var="variable" field, the $ sign is not necessary. For example:

```
<!--#echo var="DOCUMENT_NAME" -->
```

If you need to insert a literal dollar sign into the value of a variable, you can insert the dollar sign using backslash quoting. For example:

```
<!--#set var="password" value="\$cheese" -->
<!--#echo var="password" -->
```

This prints $cheese as the value of the variable "password."

Also, if you need to reference a variable name in the middle of a character sequence that might otherwise be considered a valid identifier on its own, use a pair of braces around the variable name. For example:

```
<!--#set var="uniqueid"
value="${DATE_LOCAL}_${REMOTE_HOST}" -->
```

This sets uniqueid to something like Tue May 20 06:47:48 1998_206.171.50.51, depending on the timefmt setting.

Using SSI Flow Control Commands

Like programming languages, flow control is also available in the SSI module. Using flow control commands, you can conditionally create different output. The simplest flow control (that is, conditional) statement is:

```
<!--#if expr="test_expression" -->
<!--#endif -->
```

Here, the test_expression is evaluated, and if the result of the test is true, then all the text up to the endif command is included in the output. The test_expression can be one of the following:

```
string
```

which is true if string is not empty, or

```
string1 comparison_operator string2
```

Here, the comparison_operator can be =, !=, <, >, <=, or >=.

If string2 has the form /string/, then it is compared as a regular expression. See Appendix B for details on regular expressions.

Let's look at an example of a string by itself:

```
<!--#if expr="foobar" -->
This test is successful.
<!--#endif -->
```

This syntax always prints "This test is successful" because the expression is true when the test_expression is a non-null string. If expr="foobar" is changed to expr="" or expr="""", however, then the text within the if-endif block will never be part of the output.

Now let's look at an example of a string equality test:

```
<!--#set var="quicksearch" value="yes" -->

<!--#if expr="$quicksearch = yes" -->
```

```
Quick search is  requested.
<!--#endif -->
```

Here, the variable called quicksearch is being set with the value yes, and is later being compared with yes. Since the set value and the comparison value are equal, the "Quick search is requested" line will be the output.

Using logical operators such as !, &&, and ||, you can create more complex test_expressions. For example:

```
<!--#if expr="${REMOTE_HOST} = /206\.171\.50/ &&
${DOCUMENT_NAME} = /${DATE_LOCAL}/" -->

<!--#exec cmd="/usr/local/build/timesheet/timecalc.pl">

<!--#endif -->
```

Here, the test_expression is composed of two smaller expressions. The first subexpression, ${REMOTE_HOST} = /206\.171\.50/, is evaluated to see if the server-defined variable REMOTE_HOST matches the 206.171.50 network address. Note that the address is written using the simple regular expression /206\.171\.50/, where each . (period) is escaped using a \ (backslash) character. This was necessary to undo the . character's special meaning in regular expressions. See Appendix B for more details on regular expressions.

The second subexpression, ${DOCUMENT_NAME} = ${DATE_LOCAL}, is evaluated to see if the current SSI file being processed has a name that matches today's date (this really depends on how timefmt is set up). And finally, the && (logical AND) requires that both subexpressions be true for the entire expression to be true. If the final expression is true, then the timecalc.pl script is run using the exec cmd command.

Other logical operations you can perform on the test_expression are:

```
<!--#if expr="! test_expression" -->
This is printed only when the test_expression is false.
```

```
<!--#endif -->
```

and

```
<!--#if expr="test_expression1 || test_expression2" -->
This is printed when at least one of the test_expressions
is true.
<!--#endif -->
```

The = (equal) and != (not equal) operators have higher precedence than the && (and) and the || (or) operators. The ! (not) operator has the highest priority. Note that you can use a pair of parentheses to increase priority. For example:

```
<!--#if expr="($win = yes && $loss = false) != ($profit =
yes)" -->
```

Here, the ($win = yes && $loss = false) is evaluated before the != operator.

Anything that is not recognized as a variable or an operator is treated as a string. Strings can also be quoted, like this: 'string'. Unquoted strings cannot contain white space (blanks and tabs) because they are used to separate tokens such as variables. If multiple strings are found in a row, they are concatenated using blanks.

If you require more complex flow control constructs, you can use the following:

```
<!--#if expr="test_condition1" -->

<!--#elif expr="test_condition2" -->

<!--#else -->

<!--#endif -->
```

The elif enables you to create an else-if condition. For example:

```
<!--#if expr="${HTTP_USER_AGENT} = /MSIE/" -->
```

```
        <!--#set var="browser" value="IE" -->
        <!--#include flie="vbscript.html" -->

<!--#elif expr="${HTTP_USER_AGENT} = /Lynx/" -->

        <!--#set var="browser" value="Lynx" -->
        <!--#include flie="simple-html.html" -->

<!--#else -->

        <!--#set var="browser" value="Navigator" -->
        <!--#include flie="javascript.html" -->

<!--#endif -->
```

Here, the HTTP_USER_AGENT variable is checked to see if it contains the string MSIE (a string used by Microsoft Internet Explorer browser). If it does contain this string, then the browser variable is set to IE, and a file named vbscript.html is inserted in the current document. On the other hand, if the HTTP_USER_AGENT does not contain the MSIE string, it is assumed to be the other leading browser (Netscape Navigator), and thus the browser variable is set to NAVIGATOR and the javascript.html file is inserted in the current document. By using the if-then-else construct, this example sets a different value to the same variable and loads different files.

Chapter 7

CGI Configuration

Apache's CGI support comes from the mod_cgi.c module. This module is compiled into Apache by default. Apache, a CGI-compliant Web server, uses environment variables, standard input (STDIN), and standard output (STDOUT) to transfer information to and from CGI programs. It provides a flexible set of environment variables for the CGI program developers. Using these environment variables, a CGI program not only retrieves input data, but also recognizes the type of client and server it is dealing with.

Server Specific Environment Variables

These variables are set by Apache to inform the CGI program about itself. Using server variables, a CGI program can determine various server-specific information, such as a version of the Apache software, administrator's e-mail address, and so on.

SERVER_SOFTWARE

The value of this variable is usually in the following form:

```
Apache/Version
```

Here, Apache is the name of the server software running the CGI program, and the version is the Apache version number. A sample value is as follows:

```
Apache/1.3
```

This is useful when a CGI program is to take advantage of a new feature found in a newer version of Apache and still be capable of performing in older versions.

GATEWAY_INTERFACE

This variable tells the CGI program what version of the CGI specification the server currently supports. A sample value is as follows:

```
CGI/1.1
```

A CGI program can determine the value of this variable and conditionally make use of different features available in different versions of CGI specifications. For example, if the value is CGI/1.0, the program may not use any CGI/1.1 features, or vice versa.

The first integer before the decimal point is called the *major number*, and the integer after the decimal point is called the *minor number*. Because these two integers are treated as separate numbers, CGI/2.2 is an older version than CGI/2.15.

SERVER_ADMIN

If you use the ServerAdmin directive in the httpd.conf file to set the e-mail address of the site administrator, this variable will be set up to reflect that. Also, note that if you have a ServerAdmin directive in a virtual host configuration container, the SERVER_ADMIN variable is set to that address if the CGI program being accessed is part of the virtual host.

DOCUMENT_ROOT

This variable is set to the value of the DocumentRoot directive of the Web site being accessed.

Client Request Specific Environment Variables

Apache creates a set of environment variables from the HTTP request header it receives from a client requesting a CGI program. It provides this information to the CGI program by creating the following set of environment variables.

SERVER_NAME

This variable tells a CGI program which server host is being accessed. The value is a fully qualified hostname, as follows:

```
SERVER_NAME = www.nitec.com
```

HTTP_HOST

This variable also tells a CGI program which server host is being accessed. The value is a fully qualified hostname, as follows:

```
HTTP_HOST = www.nitec.com
```

HTTP_ACCEPT

This variable is set to the list of MIME types that the client is capable of accepting, including the following:

```
HTTP_ACCEPT = image/gif, image/x-xbitmap, image/jpeg,
image/png, */*
```

Here, the client claims to be capable of handling .gif, .jpeg, .png, and other images. This enables the CGI program to determine what output will be ideal for the client. For example, a CGI program could produce either .gif or .jpeg and receive an HTTP_ACCEPT as follows:

```
HTTP_ACCEPT = image/gif, */*
```

Then, the program can send .gif output instead of .jpeg because it is not preferred by the client.

HTTP_ACCEPT_CHARSET

This variable specifies which character set is acceptable to the client, for example:

```
HTTP_ACCEPT_CHARSET = iso-8859-1,*,utf-8
```

HTTP_ACCEPT_LANGUAGE

This variable specifies which language is acceptable to the client, for example:

```
HTTP_ACCEPT_LANGUAGE = en
```

In this case, the client accepts en (English) language contents.

HTTP_USER_AGENT

This variable specifies what client software the requesting system is running and what operating system it is running on, for example:

```
HTTP_USER_AGENT = Mozilla/4.04 [en] (WinNT; I)
```

Here the information is equivalent to:

- Client Software = Netscape Navigator (as Mozilla is a keyword used by Netscape)
- Client Software Version = 4.04 (English version)

- Operating System = Windows NT (Intel)

Note that although the word Mozilla was used exclusively by Netscape browsers, many other vendors started using it as part of the HTTP header. For example, Microsoft IE 4.0 produces the following HTTP_USER_AGENT data when run from the same machine:

```
HTTP_USER_AGENT = Mozilla/4.0 (compatible; MSIE 4.0;
Windows NT)
```

This user agent information is used heavily by many Web sites. A site that is optimized for Netscape Navigator (that is, it uses a feature of HTML or JavaScript or a plug-in, that works well in Netscape Navigator) might use the HTTP_USER_AGENT information to return a different page for Microsoft IE, or any of the other less popular browsers. However, I recommend you stick to standard HTML (HTML specification for the current standard is available at www.w3.org), and not implement browser-specific features at all. Although optimizing your pages for a single browser might make them look cool on that browser — not everybody is using that particular browser. This means that your browser-specific HTML tags or plug-ins may make it harder for others who do not use your preferred browser to visit your Web site.

HTTP_REFERER

This variable is set to the URI that forwarded the request to the CGI program being called. Using this variable, you can tell if a request is coming from a link on one of your Web pages or a remote URI.

HTTP_CONNECTION

This variable is set to the type of connection being used by the client and the server, for example:

```
HTTP_CONNECTION = Keep-Alive
```

This states that the client is capable of handling persistent connections using Keep-Alive and currently using it.

SERVER_PORT

The value of this variable tells a CGI program which server port is currently being used to access the program. A sample of this is as follows:

```
SERVER_PORT = 80
```

If a CGI program creates URLs that point back to the server, it might be useful to include the port address, which is found as the value of this variable in the URL.

REMOTE_HOST

This variable tells a CGI program about the IP address or IP name of the client, as follows:

```
REMOTE_HOST = ppp-007.speedlink.net
```

If the Apache server is compiled with the MINIMAL_DNS option, this variable is not set.

REMOTE_PORT

This port number was used by the client to originate the connection to request the CGI program.

```
REMOTE_PORT = 1163
```

I have not yet seen any use for this variable.

REMOTE_ADDR

This is the IP address of the client system:

```
REMOTE_ADDR = 206.171.50.51
```

Note that if the client is behind a firewall or a proxy server, the IP address stored in this variable may not be the IP address of the client system.

REMOTE_USER

This will be set only when access to the CGI program requires HTTP basic authentication. The username used in the basic authentication is stored in this variable for the CGI program. The CGI program, however, will have no way of identifying the password used to access it. If this variable is set to a username, the CGI program can safely assume that the user supplied the appropriate password to access it.

SERVER_PROTOCOL

This is the protocol and version number the client used to send the request for the CGI program:

```
SERVER_PROTOCOL = HTTP/1.1
```

REQUEST_METHOD

This variable is set to the HTTP request method used by the client to request the CGI program. The typical values are: GET, POST, HEAD, and so on.

```
REQUEST_METHOD=GET
```

The input is stored in the QUERY_STRING variable when the request method is GET. When the method is POST, the input is stored in the STDIN of the CGI program.

REQUEST_URI

This variable is set to the URI of the request.

```
REQUEST_URI = /cgi-bin/printenv2
```

REMOTE_IDENT

This will be set only if the IdentityCheck directive is set. This variable stores the user identification information returned by the remote identd (identification daemon). Because many systems do not run this type of daemon process, it should not be considered a reliable means for identifying users.

I recommend using this in an intranet or an extranet environment in which you or your organization is running identd server.

AUTH_TYPE

If the CGI program is stored in a section of the Web site where authentication is required to gain access, this variable is set to specify the authentication method used.

CONTENT_TYPE

This variable specifies the MIME type of any data attached to the request header. For example:

```
CONTENT_TYPE = application/x-www-form-urlencoded
```

When using HTML form and the POST request method, you can specify the content type in the HTML form using the TYPE attribute of the <FORM> tag, as follows:

```
<FORM ACTION="/cgi-bin/search.cgi" METHOD="POST" TYPE=
"application/x-www-form-urlencoded">
```

CONTENT_LENGTH

When the HTTP POST request method is used, Apache stores input data (attached to the request) in the STDIN of the CGI program. The server does not, however, insert an End-of-File (EOF) marker in the STDIN. Instead, it sets the total byte-count as the value of this variable. For example, if

```
CONTENT_LENGTH = 21
```

then the CGI program should read 21 bytes of data from its STDIN.

SCRIPT_NAME

This is the URI of the requested CGI program:

```
SCRIPT_NAME = /cgi-bin/search.cgi
```

SCRIPT_FILENAME

This is the physical, fully qualified pathname of the requested CGI program:

```
SCRIPT_FILENAME = /www/kabir/public/cgi-bin/search.cgi
```

If the client uses the HTTP GET request method and provides input data after a question mark (?), the data is stored as the value of this variable. For example, a request for the following CGI program:

```
http://apache.nitec.com/cgi-bin/search.cgi?key1=
value1&key2=value2
```

will make Apache set:

```
QUERY_STRING = key1=value1&key2=value2
```

which the CGI program /cgi-bin/search.cgi can read and decode before use.

PATH_INFO

If input data for a CGI program is part of the URI, the extra path (which is really some data for the program being called) is stored as the value of the variable. For example:

```
http://apache.nitec.com/cgi-
bin/search.cgi/argument1/argument2
```

will have Apache set:

```
PATH_INFO = /argument1/argument2
```

PATH_INFO will not have anything that is part of the query string. In other words, if the URI includes a query string after a question mark (?), this part of the data will be stored in the QUERY_STRING variable. For example:

```
http://apache.nitec.com/cgi-bin/search.cgi/CA/95825?book=
apache&author=kabir
```

This will have Apache set the following variables:

```
PATH_INFO = /CA/95825
QUERY_STRING= book=apache&author=kabir
```

PATH_TRANSLATED

This is the absolute path of the requested file.

Configuring Apache for CGI

Configuring Apache to process CGI requests includes telling Apache where you store your CGI programs, setting up CGI handlers for specific file extensions, and indicating which file extensions should be considered CGI programs. It is a good idea to keep your CGI programs in one central directory; doing so permits better control of them. Scattering CGI programs all over the Web space can make the site unmanageable, and it can also create security holes that are be hard to track.

Creating a CGI Program Directory

Making a central CGI program directory is just the beginning to setting up a secured CGI environment. It is best to keep this central CGI program directory outside your DocumentRoot directory so that CGI programs cannot be accessed directly. Why? Well, when it comes to CGI programs, you want to provide as little information as possible to the outside world. This will ensure better security for your site(s). The less someone knows about where your CGI programs are physically located, the less harm that person can do.

The first step is to create a directory outside of your DocumentRoot directory. For example, if /www/mycompany/public/htdocs is the DocumentRoot directory of a Web site, then /www/mycompany/public/cgi-bin is a good candidate for the CGI program directory. To create the alias for your CGI program directory, you can use the ScriptAlias directive.

If you are setting up CGI support for the primary Web server, edit the httpd.conf file and insert a ScriptAlias line with the following syntax:

```
ScriptAlias  /alias/ /path/ \
/to/the/CGI/program/directory/ending/with/
```

For example:

```
ScriptAlias /cgi-bin/     /www/mycompany/public/cgi-bin/
```

If you are setting up CGI support for a virtual site, add a ScriptAlias line in the <VirtualHost . . . > container that defines the virtual host. For example:

```
NameVirtualHost 206.171.50.60
<VirtualHost 206.171.50.60>
ServerName blackhole.nitec.com
ScriptAlias /apps/   /www/nitec/blackhole/public/cgi-bin/
</VirtualHost>
```

Here the /apps/ alias is used to create a CGI program directory alias. If there is a CGI program called feedback.cgi in the /www/nitec/blackhole/public/cgi-bin directory, it can only be accessed via the following:

```
http://blackhole.nitec.com/apps/feedback.cgi
```

After you set up the ScriptAlias directive, make sure that the directory permission permits Apache to read and execute files found in the directory.

The directory pointed to by ScriptAlias should have very strict permission settings. No one but the CGI program developer or the server administrator should have full (read, write, and execute) permission for the directory. Note that you can define multiple CGI program directory aliases, and the ScriptAlias specified directory is not browseable (by default) for security reasons.

When requested, Apache will attempt to run any executable (file permission-wise) file found in the ScriptAliased directory. For example:

```
http://blackhole.nitec.com/apps/foo.cgi
http://blackhole.nitec.com/apps/foo.pl
http://blackhole.nitec.com/apps/foo.bak
http://blackhole.nitec.com/apps/foo.dat
```

All of the above URL requests will prompt Apache to attempt running the various FOO files.

I am not particularly fond of the idea that any file in the ScriptAlias specified directory can be run as a CGI program. I prefer a solution that enables me to restrict the CGI program names such that only files with certain extensions are treated like CGI programs. The following section discusses how you can implement this using an Apache Handler found in mod_cgi module.

Choosing Specific CGI File Extensions

In this section, I provide a sample configuration in which I enable a select set of file extensions to be treated as CGI programs. This is accomplished with the AddHandler handler.

Let's assume that the Apache server name is www.nitec.com, and its DocumentRoot directory is set to /www/nitec/public/htdocs; the CGI program directory is /www/nitec/public/cgi-bin. Notice that the CGI program directory is kept outside of the DocumentRoot specified directory intentionally. This ensures that the directory is not browseable by anyone, as Apache can see it only via the alias.

STEP 1: *Removing/disabling ScriptAlias*

The first thing to do is to disable any existing ScriptAlias directive by either removing it completely from the configuration file (httpd.conf), or by making it a comment line by inserting a pound sign (#) as the first character in that line.

STEP 2: *Creating an alias for the CGI program directory*

There is no way to access the CGI program directory without an alias (or a symbolic link), as it resides outside the document tree. You can define an alias using the Alias directive with the following syntax:

```
Alias /alias/ /path/to/cgi/dir/outside/doc/root/
```

Following this syntax, the needed alias directive looks like the following:

```
Alias /cgi-bin/ /www/nitec/public/cgi-bin/
```

Now you must instruct Apache to execute CGI programs from this directory. In order to do so, you need to define a <Directory . . . > container for this special directory.

Step 3: *Defining a directory container for the CGI program directory*

The directory container definition that is needed to make it all happen (in other words, turn the directory into a CGI program directory) follows:

```
<Directory /path/to/cgi/dir/outside/doc/root>
Options ExecCGI
AddHandler cgi-script .extension .extension ...
</Directory>
```

This directory container gives Apache instructions. First, the Options ExecCGI tells Apache to permit CGI program execution from within this directory. Second, AddHandler cgi-script .extension .extension . . . handler tells Apache to treat the list of extensions as CGI program extensions (in other words, whenever Apache encounters a URL requesting a file that has an extension listed in this directive, it must execute it as a CGI program).

The actual container definition looks like the following:

```
<Directory /www/nitec/public/cgi-bin>
Options ExecCGI
AddHandler cgi-script .cgi  .pl
</Directory>
```

Here, you have enabled .cgi and .pl as valid CGI program extensions. So, when requests, such as the following are made, Apache will attempt to execute these files as CGI programs:

```
www.nitec.com/cgi-bin/anything.cgi
www.nitec.com/cgi-bin/anything.pl
```

Of course, if these files are not really executables, Apache will display (and possibly log) error messages.

The CGI program directory permission settings mentioned earlier still apply to this configuration. The same configuration also applies to virtual host sites.

Enabling Cgi-Bin Access for Your Users

Many Internet Service Providers (ISPs) offer Web sites with user accounts. These Web sites usually have URLs, such as:

```
http://www.isp.net/~username
```

They often get requests for cgi-bin access from the users. The term cgi-bin access is a general one that is used by many to indicate CGI facility on a Web server. Traditionally, the CGI program directory has been aliased as /cgi-bin/ and, hence, this term was created.

The other common term that became very popular is homepage, which refers to the top-level index page of a Web directory of a user.

In this section, I discuss the two ways to provide cgi-bin access for users on an Apache Web server. You need to implement only one of the following methods.

Using Directory or DirectoryMatch Containers

When the UserDir directive is set to a directory name, Apache considers it as the top-level directory for a user Web site, for example:

```
ServerName www.yourcompany.com
UserDir public_html
```

Now, when a request for `www.yourcompany.com/~username` comes, Apache locates the named user's home directory (usually by checking the /etc/passwd file on UNIX systems), and then appends the UserDir specified directory to create the pathname for the top-level user Web directory. For example:

```
www.yourcompany.com/~joe
```

This makes Apache look for /home/joe/public_html (assuming /home/joe is Joe's home directory). If the directory exists, the index page for that directory will be sent to the requesting client.

One way to add CGI support for each user is to add the following configuration in one of your Apache configuration files:

```
<Directory ~ "/home/[a-z]+/public_html/cgi-bin">
Options ExecCGI
AddHandler cgi-script .cgi .pl
</Directory>
```

Or, if you are using the latest Apache server, you can use the following configuration:

```
<DirectoryMatch  "/home/[a-z]+/public_html/cgi-bin">
Options ExecCGI
AddHandler cgi-script .cgi .pl
</DirectoryMatch>
```

In both methods, Apache translates www.yourcompany.com /~username/cgi-bin/ requests to /home/username/public_html/ cgi-bin/ and permits any CGI program with the proper extension (.cgi or .pl) to execute.

Note that all usernames must be lowercase characters in order for this to work. If you have usernames that are alphanumeric, you have to use a different regular expression.

Using ScriptAliasMatch

Using the ScriptAliasMatch directive, you also can support CGI program directories for each user. For example:

```
ScriptAliasMatch ~([a-z]+)/ \
/cgi-bin/(.*)/home/$1/public_html/cgi-bin/$2
```

This directive matches username to `$1`, where `$1` is equal to ~, and matches everything followed by `/cgi-bin/` to `$2`, where `$2` is equal to `(.*)`.Then, it uses `$1` and `$2` to create the actual location of the CGI program directory. For example:

```
http://www.yourcompany.com/~joe/
cgi-bin/feedback.cgi?book=dummies&author=kabir
```

Here `~([a–z]+)` will map one or more lowercase characters following the tilde mark (~) to `$1`. In other words, the (and) pair enables us to capture everything between the tilde (~) and the trailing forward slash (/) after the username. So, `$1` is set to `kabir` and `(.*)` maps everything following the `cgi-bin/` and the parenthesis pair in this regular expression, and enables us to put everything in `$2`. So, `$2` is set to `search.cgi?book=dummies&author=kabir`.

Now Apache can create the physical path of the CGI program directory using:

```
/home/$1/public_html/cgi-bin/$2
```

This regular expression results in the following path for the previous example:

```
/home/kabir/public_html/ \
cgi-bin/search.cgi?book=dummies&author=kabir
```

Because this is where the CGI program search.CGI is kept, it executes.

If you are like me — not fond of having the CGI program directory under public_html (in other words, UserDir specified directory) — you can keep it outside by removing the public_html part of the expression as follows:

```
ScriptAliasMatch ~([a-z]+)/cgi-bin/(.*)   /home/$1/cgi- \
bin/$2
```

This will map the example call:

```
www.yourcompany.com/~joe/ \
/cgi-bin/feedback.cgi?book=dummies&author=kabir
```

to the following physical file:

```
/home/kabir/cgi-bin/search.cgi?book=dummies&author=kabir
```

Of course, if you are not too fond of keeping a user subdirectory world readable (that is, public_html), you can remedy this by creating a Web partition (or a directory) for your users, giving them individual directories to host their home pages. If you need help with regular expressions, see Appendix B.

Creating New CGI Extensions Using AddType

You learned how to create CGI program extensions using the AddHandler directive previously; however, if you want to create new CGI program extensions in a particular directory, you can also use the .htaccess (or file specified by the AccessFileName directive).

Before you can add new extensions using the per-directory access control file (.htaccess), you will have to create a <Directory> container as follows:

```
<Directory /path/to/your/directory>
Options ExecCGI
AllowOverride FileInfo
</Directory>
```

The first directive inside the preceding directory container tells Apache that you want to enable CGI program execution in this directory. The second directive tells Apache to enable the FileInfo feature in the per-directory access control file (.htaccess). This feature enables you to use an AddType directive in the per-directory access control file.

To add a new CGI program extension (.wizard), all you need to do is create an .htaccess (or whatever you specified in the Access FileName directive) file in the directory with the following:

```
AddType application/x-httpd-cgi .wizard
```

Now, rename an existing CGI program in that directory to have the .wizard extension, and request it via your browser. Make sure all of the file permission settings for the directory and the CGI programs are set to read and execute by Apache.

Running CGI Programs

Chances are that if you are an Apache administrator, you will have to set up CGI programs, or you may even have to learn to write them. In this section, I discuss only the *basics* of creating very simple CGI programs. This is a not a CGI programming book and, hence, it is not appropriate for in-depth coverage of CGI programming. My focus in this section, therefore, is to reveal things about CGI programs that will help Apache administrators better manage their CGI-capable Web sites.

A Simple CGI Script

Perl is used heavily in developing CGI programs. Because Perl is an interpreted language, it creates files that are called scripts; hence, Perl-based CGI programs are called CGI scripts. Listing 7-1 shows a very simple Perl script.

Listing 7-1 *helloworld.pl*

```
#!/usr/local/bin/perl

print "Content-type: text/html\n\n";
print <<HTML_CODE;

<HTML>
<HEAD>
<TITLE>Listing 7-1: Simple Perl-based CGI Program</TITLE>
</HEAD>
<BODY>
<CENTER>
<H1> Hello World </H1>
</CENTER>
</BODY>
</HTML>
```

If you look at the helloworld.pl script carefully, you will notice that most of the script is plain HTML text. The script can be simplified further for analysis, as follows:

```
#!/usr/local/bin/perl

print "Content-type: text/html\n\n";

print <<HTML
HTML TEXT GOES HERE
HTML
```

The first line is very important. When Apache runs this Perl script, the first line tells the system that it is a Perl script, and the Perl interpreter is /usr/local/bin/perl. This enables the system to run the interpreter and pass it the script file. Note that this method of informing the system about the interpreter is standard for all scripting languages. The following example shows the simplified helloworld.pl script as a C Shell script:

```
#!/bin/csh
echo "Content-type: text/html"
echo ""
echo "<HTML>"
echo "HTML TEXT GOES HERE"
echo  "</HTML>"
```

As you can see, the first line is similar to the Perl script. Here, the interpreter path is /bin/csh, so when you download a free script from the Web, make sure that the first line correctly points at the path of the interpreter on your system. This is the first thing to check typically.

Now, look back on the Perl script listing and you will see that the first print statement prints out Content-type: text/html\n\n, which really prints the Content-type: text/html in a line and prints a blank line (\n in Perl means new line). This is absolutely necessary. Remember from earlier discussions that parsed CGI scripts must supply header information for Apache so it can create appropriate HTTP header. The Content-type header tells Apache that the output contains text data of the HTML type. The blank line separates this declaration from the rest of the data, and it is required. The C Shell script does the same but with the help of an empty echo statement. What follows after this Content-type header is HTML text.

WARNING

Keeping an interpreter like Perl Web accessible from any directory is a bad idea. Many people suffer for this mistake. Because Perl and many other scripting language interpreters have powerful features that involve system command execution, a system abuser can attack a system if the interpreter is directly accessible from the Web. So, keep them away from your Web directories in general.

Using Widely Used CGI Modules for Perl

In the previous form generator script, I used the widely used cgi.pm package created by Lincoln D. Stein. Few other useful Perl packages can be used to do rapid Perl-based CGI script development. Let's look at a few of the popular development packages for Perl language:

- cgi.pm. This is a great Perl package to develop CGI scripts quickly and cleanly. It enables you to create CGI objects that can access the CGI query strings, create appropriate headers, read/write cookies, and write HTML forms without actually using any HTML in the script. You can find this package at:

  `www-genome.wi.mit.edu/ftp/pub/software/`
  `WWW/cgi_docs.html`

- libwww. If you are interested in developing powerful user agents, robots, or mini Web servers, do not bother writing code from scratch. Use Libwww's eight modules: HTML, LWP, MIME, WWW, HTTP, URL, File, and Font, to do it all. You can find these packages at:

  `www.perl.com/CPAN-local/modules/by-module/LWP/`

- cgi-lib.pl. If you are not yet ready for objectoriented Perl programming (both CGI.PM and libwww modules are object oriented), you can try out a simpler library called cgi-lib.pl. This library has routines to parse form inputs and create headers. You can find it at:

  `www.bio.cam.ac.uk/cgi-lib/`

Debugging CGI Programs

When you write or install someone else's CGI program, there is a chance that it might not run the right way. Debugging a CGI program is often difficult because, in most cases, you can not just run the program from the command line and feed it inputs.

TIP

If you use the CGI.PM package in your Perl-based CGI scripts, you can do a great deal of debugging from the command line. The package permits interactive mode in which you can enter key=value input pairs as if the data were coming from an HTML form.

In order to help CGI developers, Apache has logs for CGI output. For each CGI program error, the log file contains a few lines of log entries. The first two lines contain the time of the request, request URI, HTTP status, CGI program name and so on. If the CGI program cannot be run, two other additional lines contain information about the error. Alternatively, if the error is the result of the script returning incorrect header information, the information is logged in as follows: all HTTP request headers, all headers output by CGI program, STDOUT and STDIN of the CGI program. If the script failed to output anything, the STDOUT will not be included.

To log CGI output in Apache, use the following directives, which are found in the mod_cgi module (part of standard distribution).

ScriptLog

Syntax: `ScriptLog filename`

Default: none

Context: `resource config`

This directive sets the log file name for CGI program errors. If the log file name is relative (that is, it does not start with a leading /) it is taken to be relative to the server root directory set by the ServerRoot directive.

When you use this directive, make sure that the log directory is writeable by the user specified by UserDir directive. Using this directive on a daily basis might not be a good idea as far as efficiency or performance goes. I recommend using it when needed and turning it OFF when the debugging is completed.

ScriptLogLength

Syntax: `ScriptLogLength size`

Default: `10385760`

Context: `resource config`

This directive limits the size of the log file specified by the ScriptLog directive. The script log file can log a lot of information per CGI error and, therefore, can grow rapidly. Using this directive, you can limit the log so that once the file is at the maximum length, no more information will be logged.

ScriptLogBuffer

Syntax: `ScriptLogBuffer size`

Default: `1024`

Context: `resource config`

This directive limits the size of POST or PUT data that is logged.

Using these directives you can set up the logging of CGI programs that you are developing or attempting to install on your system.

Chapter 8

FastCGI

FastCGI Platforms

FastCGI currently is supported only for SunOS/Solaris, SCO, Linux, and QNX (using Static Inet sockets). It does not work with the Windows version of Apache yet. However, you should not be discouraged if your platform is not supported yet. You may want to monitor `http://www.fastcgi.com/` for availability of support for your platform.

Getting FastCGI Software Components

In order to take advantage of the FastCGI specifications, you need to get a few pieces of free, third-party software.

FastCGI Module for Apache – mod_fastcgi.c

You can get the mod_fastcgi.c module from `http://www.fastcgi.com`. This module is responsible for providing FastCGI support in Apache. The module is typically packaged in a compressed tar-ball file.

FastCGI Module for Perl – FCGI.pm

If you are planning on using Perl-based FastCGI applications, you also will need to get the FCGI.pm module for Perl. This module is available from `http://www.perl.com/CPAN-local/modules/bymodule/FCGI/`.

FastCGI Developer's Kit

If you are interested in developing your FastCGI applications in any language other than Perl (such as C), you will need to download the FastCGI developer's kit from `http://www.fastcgi.com/`. Note that the developer's kit is not often updated and instructions regarding upgrading Perl should be ignored. I recommend that you get this kit only if you are interested in developing FastCGI applications in anything other than Perl.

Compiling Apache with FastCGI Support

Adding FastCGI support in Apache is as simple as compiling it with the mod_fastcgi.c module. However, before you can compile Apache you will have to do the following:

- Extract the mod_fastcgi files contained in the compressed tar file you downloaded earlier.
- Copy or move the mod_fastcgi distribution to the src/modules/fastcgi directory of your Apache source distribution.

If you are using Apache 1.3.*x*, you have two options for building FastCGI support in Apache. However, if you are using an older version of Apache, use the old-fashioned method described in a following section.

Using APACI (Apache 1.3.*x* or Above)

This is the easiest method for compiling modules for Apache 1.3.*x*. First, change directory to your top-level Apache source distribution directory and run the configuration script as follows:

```
./configure --activate- \
module=src/modules/fastcgi/libfastcgi.a
```

If you have previously compiled Apache using APACI and want to keep the existing configuration along with the new mod_fastcgi.c module update, run the following command instead:

```
./config.status --activate- \
module=src/modules/fastcgi/libfastcgi.a
```

Now rebuild the Apache server executable (httpd) by running the make command. If you get no error messages, run the make command again with the INSTALL option to reinstall the Apache executable.

The Old-Fashioned Way (Apache 1.2.*x* or Above)

This is also known as the manual method. You have to edit the src/configuration file of your Apache source distribution as follows:

For Apache 1.3.*x*:

```
AddModule     modules/fastcgi/libfastcgi.a
```

For Apache 1.2.*x*:

```
Module fastcgi_module     modules/fastcgi/libfcgi.a
```

Now, copy or rename the modules/fastcgi/makefile.sample to modules/fastcgi/makefile and run the Configure script from the src directory.

Finally, rebuild the Apache server executable (httpd) by running the make command. If you get no error messages, run MAKE INSTALL to reinstall the Apache executable.

Verifying Your Apache Update

Once you have built the new Apache executable, you should check to verify that mod_fastcgi.c module is included in the executable. The easiest way to verify this is to run the following command:

```
/path/to/your/apache/httpd -l
```

Make sure you use the appropriate path instead of /path/to/your/apache/ as shown above. You should see mod_fastcgi.c listed in the output produced by the -l option. If you don't see it, you have missed one or more steps in compiling Apache, so go back and verify your steps.

Configuring Apache for FastCGI

Once you have built Apache with mod_fastcgi.c support, you are ready to configure Apache to run FastCGI applications. However, before you can configure Apache, you need to know the directives that are available from the mod_fastcgi.c module. They are discussed in the following section.

Using FastCGI Directives

AppClass directive

Syntax: `AppClass <path to FastCGI application> [-processes N] [-listen-queue-depth N] [-restart-delay N] [-priority N] [-port N] [-socket sock-name] [-initial-env key=value]`

Context: `server config`

This directive enables you to start FastCGI applications. For example:

```
AppClass /www/development/fcgi-devel-kit/echo.fcg -port
9000
```

This directive will enable mod_fastcgi to load the /www/development/fcgi-devel-kit/echo.fcg FastCGI application. The application will listen on port 9000. When a FastCGI application loaded by this directive dies, mod_fastcgi will restart the application and write a log entry in the error log file. The optional parameters to the AppClass directive are as follows:

- **processes**. This option specifies how many FastCGI processes to create. On a high-load scenario, loading multiple instances of the same FastCGI application can provide better performance. The default value is one (1).
- **listen-queue-depth**. This option specifies how deep the listen queue is for the FastCGI application(s) loaded with the directive. The default value is sufficient in most cases, but in a high-load scenario, you can increase the depth of the queue. This will decrease chances of a request being rejected due to application(s) being busy. However, if you expect a high load, and your server is capable of running a few extra FastCGI processes, increase the number of processes instead of the depth of the listen queue. The default value is five (5).
- **restart-delay.** This option specifies the number of seconds that will be used to delay a restart of a dead FastCGI process. This is useful only when you are using multiple instances of the same FastCGI application. In the case of a single FastCGI application, it is restarted immediately, and this option has no effect. The default value is five (5).

You might wonder why this delay is needed. Normally, a FastCGI application should not die; if it is dying, there is chance that something is wrong with it. In such a case, this delay will at least allow your server to do other useful tasks besides restarting a faulty application again and again.

- **Priority**. This option sets the process priority of a FastCGI application. The default value enables a FastCGI application to have the same priority as the Apache server itself. Other appropriate values are defined by your operating system's set-priority system call. In a RedHat Linux system, the setpriority system call permits a value in the range of -20 to 20. The lower the number, the more favorable the scheduling used for the process. However, mod_fastcgi does not allow a negative value, which means you cannot set a FastCGI process to have higher priority than the Apache server itself. So, all you can do is use a positive integer number to lower the priority of the application. The default value is zero (0).
- **Port.** This option specifies the TCP port on which the FastCGI application will listen. Because ports lower than 1024 are used for standard services, you will have to use a higher port number. Use of this option enables you to access the application from another system. No environment variable is provided by default. You need to specify port number only if you are going to run your FastCGI application on a different host machine.
- **Socket.** This option specifies the pathnamepathname of the UNIX domain socket that the application will listen on. The module creates this socket within the directory specified by the FastCgiIpcDir directive. The default value is Default Socket.

If you do not provide either the port or socket option, the module creates a Unix domain socket for the application by itself.

- **initial-env.** This option can be used to insert an environment variable (with value) in the FastCGI application's environment table. You can use this option multiple times to insert more than one key=value pair in the environment of the application. No environment variable is provided by default.

The -socket and -port options are mutually exclusive. Pathname must not equal the pathname supplied to an earlier AppClass or ExternalAppClass directive.

ExternalAppClass directive

Syntax: `ExternalAppClass <FastCGI-application-name> [-host host:port] [-socket sock-name]`
Context: `server config`

Use this directive when you have a FastCGI application running on another system. For example:

```
ExternalAppClass echo.fcg   -host fcgi.nitec.com:9090
```

Here, the echo.fcg application is running on a host called `fcgi.nitec.com` and listening to port 9090. The <FastCGI-application-name> is just an identifier that can be used to describe the application running on the remote host, so it can be any name you want. Make sure the name you choose is not already used in another AppClass or ExternalAppClasss directive. The optional parameters to the ExternalAppClass directive are listed here:

- **host.** This option enables you to specify the host and the TCP port number of the FastCGI application running on another system. Use host:port format to specify the host and port. You can use either a hostname or an IP address.
- **socket.** This option enables you to specify the pathname of the UNIX domain socket being used by a FastCGI application.

FastCgiIpcDir directive

Syntax: `FastCgiIpcDir path`

Default: `FastCgiIpcDir /tmp`

Context: `server config`

This directive specifies the default path for UNIX domain sockets created by the module. The default /tmp location is fine as long as you do not have cron jobs set up to clean up your /tmp directory from time to time. The socket name has the following format:

```
OM_WS_n.pid
```

Here, `n` is a number and `pid` is the process ID of the main Apache process. If you do set this directive to a path, make sure only Apache has read and write access to the directory.

Using the <Location> Directive for FastCGI Configuration in httpd.conf

The FastCGI module for Apache provides a handler called fastcgi-script that you can use to handle FastCGI requests. For example:

```
<Location /fcgi/>
SetHandler fastcgi-script
Options -Indexes
</Location>
```

The preceding configuration makes Apache service all requests containing /fcgi/ in the path using the fastcgi-script handler. An example of such requests is:

```
http://server.domain.tld/fcgi/script.pl
```

When the first request is made for the script.pl script, Apache will have it serviced by the fastcgi-script handler. This handler will load this script if it not already loaded by an AppClass or ExternalAppClass directive. In the preceding configuration, the script hasn't been loaded with either of these two directives, so the handler will load this script and run it. Any subsequent call for the same script will not need to load the script any more because it will remain loaded in memory as a FastCGI script.

However, this is not the case if the script is not a true FastCGI script. In fact, if I put a traditional CGI script in the FCGI directory and request it, Apache will run it via the fastcgi-script handler and keep reloading it since the CGI script will terminate after each run. This is not desirable at all since Apache will become very busy trying to start this script again and again. So, make sure you do not put any non-FastCGI scripts in a FastCGI location such as the one shown in the preceding configuration. It is also a very good idea to monitor the server's error log file when running a script for the first time. If you notice that the server is trying to restart the script again and again, stop the server and remove the script from the directory where you enabled fastcgi-script.

Also note that I have directory indexing turned off in the /fcgi/ location, because it is not a good idea to let anyone browse your script directories. That's why the ScriptAlias directive, which is typically used to create cgi-bin directory alias, automatically prohibits others from indexing CGI directories. Some administrators often put an empty index.html file (or whatever they specify as the directory index file in DirectoryIndex directive) in directories which they do not want the server to index. They do not explicitly turn off the directory indexing using the Options –Indexes directive. This trick won't work in directories that are handled by the fastcgi-script handler. Why? Well, when a request such as `http://server.domain.tld/fcg/` comes, the server will find the empty index.html file and have fastcgi-script handler load it as if it were a FastCGI script. This will cause Apache to go in a loop as the handler will repeatedly fail to load and run the script. Hence, use Options –Indexes to disable directory indexing instead of an empty index.html.

The preceding configuration does not pre-load the FastCGI scripts in the /FCG/ location, and therefore the very first request for each script in the location will take slightly more time than the subsequent ones. So, you might want to use the AppClass directive to pre-load any script you keep in such a location. For example:

```
AppClass /doc/root/fcgi/ad-engine.fcgi –intial-env
foo=bar

<Location /fcgi/>
SetHandler fastcgi-script
Options -Indexes
</Location>
```

In this configuration the ad-engine.fcgi script is pre-loaded at server start-up time. Note that there is a bug in the mod_fastcgi.c module that does not set environment variables properly unless an initial-env option is provided. Here, we use the option with a key=value pair (foo=bar) to work-around the bug.

Using AddType and AddHandler Directives for FastCGI Configuration in httpd.conf

You can also use AddType and AddHandler directives to configure Apache for FastCGI. For example:

```
AddType        application/x-httpd-fcgi     .fcgi
AddHandler     fastcgi-script       .fcgi
```

Here, the AddType directive tells Apache to consider any file ending with .fcgi as of MIME type application/x-httpd-fcgi. Then, the AddHandler directive tells Apache to handle any file ending with .fcgi via the fasctcgi-script handler. So, when a request such as `http://server.domain.tld/foo/bar.fcgi` is made, the server loads the bar.fcgi script (if it is not already loaded via an AppClass or ExternalAppClass directive) and runs it. Any subsequent call to the same script will no longer need to load it.

Running Perl-Based FastCGI Scripts

Before you can run Perl scripts as FastCGI-based Perl scripts, you will have to install a Perl module called fcgi.pm. The fcgi.pm module turns your Perl installation into a FastCGI language platform.

Installing the FCGI.pm Module for Perl

If you have installed Perl appropriately on your system, installing Perl modules can be quite easy. Just run your CPAN (Comprehensive Perl Archive Network) module as follows:

```
perl —MCPAN —eshell
```

Once you are in the CPAN shell prompt, enter the following command:

```
Install FCGI
```

If you don't have a cpan.pm module and are unable to do the preceding, you need to install the latest Perl from `http://www.perl.com`. Once you have the latest Perl installed on your system, run the preceding commands to install fcgi.pm module.

Once you have installed the fcgi.pm module, you can use the example script called echo.fpl to test your Apache/Perl FastCGI configurations. Put the echo.fpl script in your configured FastCGI directory (if you are using the <Location> method), or rename the script with the proper extension if you are using the AddType/AddHandler method to enable the FastCGI handler. In either case, you should be able to run the FastCGI script echo.fpl (or whatever you renamed it to be), and the script should show you all the environment variables that are available to it as you run it each time. This example makes it very easy to convince yourself that it is running as a FastCGI script as it shows an increasing request counter as you make subsequent requests to the same script. On most UNIX systems, you can run the ps or top utility to verify that only one copy of the echo.fpl script is running at any time.

Writing FastCGI Scripts Using FCGI.pm

The FCGI.pm module for Perl makes it very easy to write FastCGI scripts. Listing 8-1 shows a simple CGI Script that prints a "Hello World" message when requested.

Listing 8-1 *hello.pl*

```
#!/usr/bin/perl
print "Content-type: text/html\n\n";
print "Hello World";
exit 0;
```

Listing 8-2 shows hello.fcgi, which is a FastCGI version of the same script.

Listing 8-2 *hello.fcgi*

```
#!/usr/bin/perl

use FCGI;

while(FCGI::accept() >= 0) {
print "Content-type: text/html\n\n";
print "Hello World";
}
```

Simply speaking, the while loop encapsulating the two print lines keeps the script running and the FCGI::accept() method accepts a FastCGI connection from the Apache server. If FCGI::accept() is successful in accepting connection, it returns zero (0), which makes the loop continue one more time, keeping the script in service.

Writing FastCGI Scripts Using CGI.pm

cgi.pm is a very popular CGI programming module for Perl. It encapsulates many of the raw details of CGI programming from programmers and lets them focus on the actual programming task. The developer of cgi.pm has also felt the power of FastCGI and created a version of cgi.pm that allows FastCGI developers to have the same benefits. You can install the latest version of the cgi.pm as follows:

```
perl –MCPAN –eshell
```

Once you are in the CPAN shell prompt, enter the following command:

```
Install CGI
```

Once you have installed the cgi.pm module, you can develop FastCGI scripts with greater ease than using fcgi.pm itself. In fact, cgi.pm uses fcgi.pm module and hides a lot of details from the programmer, thus keeping the programmer sane in doing what the programming task was really for. Listing 8-3 shows a cgi.pm version of the hello.fcgi script:

Listing 8-3 *hello.fcgi*

```
#!/usr/bin/perl

use CGI::Fast qw(:standard);

while(new CGI::Fast) {

print header;
print "Hello World";

  }
```

Any CGI script that uses cgi.pm can be easily upgraded to run via the FastCGI handler with minimal changes. However, do not forget that FastCGI scripts are persistent, and therefore they need to be developed with much more care then typical CGI scripts. If a FastCGI script leaks memory or misuses resources, it could cause serious trouble in the long run. For example, a FastCGI script that leaks memory can eventually make the server swap more often than it should; this could slow down the server drastically. In order to avoid such circumstances, make sure that FastCGI scripts are developed carefully by skilled programmers only.

One other advantage of using cgi.pm to develop FastCGI scripts is that you can run the same script as a regular CGI script. For example, take a look at the Apache configuration shown here:

```
AppClass /doc/root/fcgi/hello.fcgi


<Location /fcgi/>
SetHandler fastcgi-script
Options -Indexes
</Location>
ScriptAlias  /cgi-bin/     /doc/root/fcgi/
```

When a request such as `http://server.domain.tld/fcgi/hello.fcgi` is made, Apache will run the hello.fcgi script as a FastCGI script. Note that the script is pre-loaded using the AppClass directive. If the request were to be `http://server.domain.tld/cgi-bin/hello.fcgi`, then the server would run this as a regular CGI script. So, the same script can be called two different ways.

Chapter 9

Embedding Perl in Apache

Preinstallation Tasks for mod_perl

Standard Apache distribution does not include mod_perl. You will have to install it. You do not need mod_perl for using the Perl interpreter (perl) in CGI scripts. This module is needed only for achieving higher performance. However, before you get started with the installation process, make sure you have completed the following preinstallation tasks.

Make sure you have the latest Perl installed on your system. Check the version number of your installed Perl using the perl –v command and verify with the latest version available at `www.perl.com site`. If you don't have the latest version, I recommend that you download and install it.

Once you have installed the latest Perl on your target system, you need to download the latest version of mod_perl source from the `perl.apache.org` Web site.

Many of the tests used for verifying mod_perl installation use the LWP Perl modules, so it may be a good idea to install LWP modules along with its prerequisite modules. If you have installed Perl properly, you can install the LWP modules quite easily using the CPAN module. Run CPAN as follows:

```
perl  -MCPAN –install LWP
```

Once you have completed these prerequisite tasks, you can install mod_perl module.

Installing mod_perl

There are many ways you can install mod_perl, but I will describe only the most flexible method here. The flexible method requires that you use both the latest version of Apache and the APACI installation procedure. Because APACI provides the easiest method for installing Apache components, I will assume that you will use it for installing mod_perl as well. If you must use the manual method, read the installation notes that comes with mod_perl.

There are two parts to installing mod_perl support into your Apache server. First, you must update your Perl distribution with mod_perl and then update Apache distribution with mod_perl. In order to make things simpler, I will also assume that you have downloaded and decompressed the mod_perl source distribution into a directory so that both Apache source and mod_perl source share the same top-level directory as their parent directory. In other words, both Apache source and mod_perl source distributions are subdirectories of a single parent directory. For the example installation discussed here, let's assume that the Apache server is in /usr/local/build/apache-1.3.2 and mod_perl source distribution is in /usr/local/build/mod_perl-1.16. Your version numbers for Apache and mod_perl may vary. Now change the directory to the mod_perl source distribution (/usr/local/build/mod_perl-1.16) and run the following command:

```
perl  Makefile.PL APACHE_SRC=../apache-1.3.2/src \
DO_HTTPD=1  \
USE_APACI=1  \
```

```
PREP_HTTPD=1   \
EVERYTHING=1
```

This will build the Perl side of mod_perl and also prepare the Apache side of mod_perl. Once you have run the preceding command, you can run the following commands as long as any error messages do not stop you:

```
make
make test
make install
```

Now you have to complete the Apache side of the mod_perl installation. If you are compiling Apache for the first time, you can run the following command from the Apache source distribution directory:

```
./configure --prefix=/path/to/where/you/want/to/install/ \
apache --activate-module=src/modules/perl/libperl.a
```

However, if you have already compiled Apache you should use the following command instead:

```
./config.status --activate-module=src/modules/perl/ \
libperl.a
```

This will preserve all the previous options that you supplied to configure command. Once you have run either version of the two preceding commands, you are ready to run the following commands:

```
make
make test
make install
```

This will install Apache with mod_perl support. You can verify that mod_perl.c is part of your Apache executable (httpd) using the httpd –l command.

Running Perl CGI Scripts via mod_perl's Apache::Registry module

mod_perl comes with a module called Apache::Registry which allows you to run Perl-based CGI scripts under mod_perl facility without any alteration. I will discuss how you can use Apache::Registry to run your existing Perl based CGI scripts. You may already know that to get CGI scripts running, you need to define a script alias directory using the ScriptAlias directive. However, when using mod_perl to run CGI scripts you cannot use ScriptAlias. Instead, you will need to create a regular alias using the Alias directive. For example, for a Web site called `apache.nitec.com` with CGI scripts in the /www/apache/public/cgi-bin directory, you can create an Alias called /perl/ as follows:

```
Alias /perl/      /www/apache/public/cgi-bin/
```

Using the <Location . . . > container, you need to set up the following:

```
<Location /alias-to-cgi-script-directory/>
SetHandler  perl-script
PerlHandler Apache::Registry
Options ExecCGI
</Location>
```

For our example, this would look like:

```
<Location /perl/>
SetHandler  perl-script
PerlHandler Apache::Registry
Options ExecCGI
</Location>
```

You should also have a ScriptAlias directive as follows:

```
ScriptAlias /cgi-bin/     /www/apache/public/cgi-bin/
```

Then you can access an application called printenv.cgi either through the traditional CGI method using the URL:

```
http://apache.nitec.com/cgi-bin/printenv/cgi
```

Or, you can use mod_perl's Apache::Registry module with the URL:

```
http://apache.nitec.com/perl/printenv.cgi
```

You might wonder how you can tell the difference between the two calls. In the mod_perl version the standard CGI variable GATEWAY_INTERFACE prints "CGI-Perl/1.1" instead of "CGI/1.1." Also, a new variable MOD_PERL is set in the mod_perl version of the call. This variable is set to the value of the version of mod_perl being used. If you need to detect how your Perl script is being run by Apache, you can use a code segment such as the following:

```
If(exists $ENV{'MOD_PERL'}){
       print "Running as a mod_perl application";
     }
else{
       print "Running as a CGI script";
     }
```

The Apache::Registry module is used to run unaltered CGI scripts under mod_perl. When the following URL is requested, this module reads the printenv.cgi script and inserts it into the body of a Perl subroutine and executes it:

```
http://apache.nitec.com/perl/printenv.cgi
```

Each Apache child server process will compile the subroutine once and store it in memory for future use. If the script gets changed in the meantime, it will be reloaded and compiled and stored in memory again.

However, you can preload your Perl scripts at server startup. With mod_perl you are provided two directives: PerlModule and PerlScript. You can use these two directives to load scripts at startup.

To load a Perl module at server startup, you can use:

```
PerlModule ModuleName . . .
```

For example:

```
PerlModule Apache::SSI  Foo::Bar Some::Other
```

This loads the SSI, Bar, and Other modules from the Apache, Foo, and Some modules. Note that using the PerlModule directive you can load a maximum of 10 modules. If you need more, you can use the PerlScript directive.

The PerlScript directive has the following syntax:

```
PerlScript /path/to/a/Perl/script
```

This will load a Perl script at server startup. If you need to load a lot of modules at startup, you can write a script such as:

```
use CGI;
use LWP::UserAgent ();
1;
```

This script loads the CGI and UserAgent modules. If you keep your modules in a location other than the default Perl module directory, you will have to specify the module location using:

```
use lib qw(/path/to/your/modules);
```

Here /path/to/your/modules should be replaced with the appropriate fully qualified pathname of the module directory.

To make use of your Perl module, you will have to use the PerlHandler directive as shown earlier. For example, say you have a PerlModule line as follows:

```
PerlModule Apache::Test
```

You want to use this module for servicing the URL:

```
http://www.myserver.com/test/
```

You can then define an Alias as follows:

```
Alias /test/     /somewhere/some/directory/
```

Then you can define a <Location . . .> container as follows:

```
<Location /test>
SetHandler perl-script
PerlHandler Apache::Test
</Location>
```

This tells mod_perl that you want to use the Apache::Test module for handling all requests that come for the specified URL.

How does mod_perl know what method to call in the Test.pm module? By default, the PerlHandler directive expects a subroutine name as the argument. If the argument is not a subroutine name, it assumes it is a module name and calls a special method called handler. So, for the PerlHandler line, when a request comes for the specified URL, mod_perl will call the method Apache::Test::handler. If this method is not defined in the module, there will be an error.

You can always use a different method name as long as you specify it in the PerlHandler line. For example, if you had a method called do it in the Test.pm module, and you wanted to invoke this method instead of handler, you can set the PerlHandler line as follows:

```
PerlHandler Apache::Test::doit
```

This will have mod_perl invoke the doit method instead of handler.

Previously, when I showed you how to use the Apache::Registry module to turn your CGI scripts into mod_perl-based scripts, for each request, mod_perl launched the Apache:Registry:handler method, which in turn runs the script requested.

Issues with Porting Perl CGI Scripts

When porting an existing Perl-based CGI script to mod_perl, make sure you pay attention to the following issues.

If you are using the latest Perl (version 5.004 or above) interpreter, it is likely that most of your CGI scripts can run under mod_perl without any major modifications. However, if you are using an older version of Perl, you might have trouble using the built-in print and read functions. I strongly suggest that you upgrade Perl.

By default, mod_perl does not send any HTTP headers; however, you can use the following directive to change this:

```
PerlSendHeader On
```

Now the response line and HTTP headers will be sent. However, your script will still have to send the following content-type header:

```
print "Content-type: text/html\n\n";
```

If you are using CGI.pm or CGI::Switch and printing the header using the header() method, you do not need to set the PerlSendHeader to On.

On the other hand, when converting non-parsed header Perl scripts (scripts with the nph- prefix) to mod_perl based scripts, you will need to force an output flush after every write or print on the output file-handle. This can be done by setting the `$|` variable to a nonzero value as follows:

```
local $| = 1;
```

Note that if you normally set the PerlSendHeader to ON, you will have to disable it for nph- files. You can use the following configuration to do that.

```
<FilesMatch */nph-*>
PerlSendHeader Off
</FilesMatch>
```

Writing a Perl Module for mod_perl

In this section, I will show you how to create a very simple Perl module for use under mod_perl that really doesn't do anything but print out the environment variables. This Perl module is called Test.pm and is shown in Listing 9-1.

Listing 9-1 *Test.pm*

```
package Apache::Test;

# Tell Perl to show warning when a variable is used
# without a declaration. This is done using 'use strict.'
# use strict;


sub handler {
#
# Purpose: this method gets called by mod_perl. So this
# is really the entry point into this module.
# In other words, this is the traditional main function.

# Assign the request object (passed as a parameter) to a
# local variable.
    my $r = shift;

# Local temporary variable
    my $key;

# Assign a local associative array variable to the hash
# returned by the request object variable's cgi_env()
# method

    my %ENV = $r->cgi_env;
```

```
# Set the content-type of the output to text/html
#
    $r->content_type("text/html");

# Print out the HTTP headers
    $r->send_http_header;

# Now loop through the %ENV array and print out the
# key=value  pair for each environment variable.
#
    foreach $key (keys %ENV){
      $r->print("$key = $ENV{$key} <BR>.");
      }

# Done
    return 1;
}
# The following line is required for a Perl module.
1;
__END__
```

In this example, there is only one subroutine called handler. When you specify a configuration line such as the following:

```
<Location /test>
SetHandler perl-script
PerlHandler Apache::Test
</Location>
```

The handler method gets called whenever Apache receives a request containing /`test`/. If you plan on messing around with Apache request processing, make sure that you have a clear understanding of the Apache API. There are several stages of a request in which the Apache API allows a module to step in and do something. The Apache documentation will tell you all about those stages and what your modules can do. By default, these hooks are disabled at compile time; see the INSTALL document for information on enabling these hooks.

There are some special programming concerns for CGI programmers developing mod_perl scripts. First, let's look at why mod_perl scripts require careful programming. Then we'll look at some special programming issues for writing mod_perl scripts.

Many CGI developers do not spend time cleaning up their code, because a CGI script runs for a short time and disappears after the request is complete. But mod_perl run scripts stay cached in memory for a long time, and therefore we need better programming practices in developing these scripts. Here are some guidelines that might help you in this regard:

- Always write script in strict mode using use strict. This will allow you to write clean scripts that do not have undefined variables lying around wasting memory or creating other confusion. Also, do not forget to use the -w switch. If you do not yet know why you should use -w, I suggest you read the man page for Perl itself. You will notice that it is suggested over and over again.
- You should also be very careful about using user input data. You can turn on Perl's taint checking using the -T switch, or you can set the PerlTaintCheck directive to ON in one of the Apache configuration files. Read the cgi_to_mod_perl man page that comes with the mod_perl distribution.
- Also note that system calls such as system(), exec(), open PIPE, |program, and so on will not work by default. If you want to use these calls, you will have to have sfio support in Perl. Also, the exit() function cannot be used. Instead, you can use the Apache::exit() method. Apache::exit() automatically overrides the built-in exit() for Apache::Registry scripts.

Apart from these general pointers, there are some programming practice-related issues that need to be considered when developing scripts for mod_perl. These issues are discussed in the following sections.

Using CGI.pm and CGI::* modules

If you use the CGI.pm module in your CGI scripts, make sure you have the very latest version. Versions earlier than 2.36 will not work with mod_perl. If you have the latest Perl version and the latest CGI.pm, you can use the use CGI command to make use of the module in your CGI script as usual. However, if you are using an older version of Perl, you will have to use the use CGI::Switch() command so that the I/O is handled via the Apache class methods.

The other CGI modules (CGI::*) can be used only with the latest version of Perl (5.004 or higher.)

If you use the CGI::Request module and the SendHeaders() method, be sure to call your $req_obj->cgi->done when you are finished with a request.

Your script will work from the command line only if you use the latest CGI::Switch or CGI.pm and the latest Perl.

Using Apache DB/DBM Authentication Modules

If you use mod_auth_dbm or mod_auth_db, you might run into problems if the order in which the dbm libraries are stored in Perl's Config.pm is not appropriate. To determine the order of the libraries, use the following command:

```
Perl -V:libs
```

By default, these libraries are linked with Perl and remembered by the Config module.When mod_perl is configured with Apache, the ExtUtils::Embed module returns these libraries to be linked with httpd for Perl extensions to work under mod_perl. However, the order in which these libraries are stored in Config.pm may confuse Apache DB/DBM modules. If -lgdbm or -ldb is before -lndbm, modify Perl's Config.pm module and move -lgdbm and -ldb to the end of the list. For example:

```
libs='-lgdbm -ldb -lndbm -ldl -lm -lc'
```

If you are not sure which Config.pm to modify, use the following short script to determine the location:

```
#!/usr/local/bin/perl
use Config;
print "Your Config.pm directory is
$Config{archlibexp}\n";
exit 0;
```

The mod_perl interface is smart enough to detect changes in a script after it is loaded. So, if you modify a script after you have already loaded it via mod_perl, you do not need to restart Apache. However, if you make changes to a Perl library or a module that has been pulled into your script via the use or require facility, mod_perl will not automatically reload it. In such a case you might want to use the Apache::StartINC module.

Another important note is that when you include the same Perl library (not a Perl module) in multiple scripts that you want mod_perl to run via the Apache::Registry facility, only one of them will work. This is true because when a required library is pulled into a script, its subroutines and variables become part of the current package. In a typical CGI environment, this is the package main. However, under the Apache::Registry facility, the script is compiled into an unique package name (based on the URL). This means that only one script will be able to use the required library; mod_perl will not compile the same library for all the other scripts that require it.

The easiest way to solve this problem is to rewrite the Perl library into an object-oriented Perl module. Because a Perl module has a package definition that gives it its own name space, the required module (which used to be a Perl library) can be used by any script.

Read the perlmodlib man page, the perlmod man page, and related perl documentation and rework your required file into a Perl module that defines a method interface. However, if rewriting the library to turn it into an object-oriented Perl module is not possible, look into exporting the functions and variables features of Perl.

Also, if you wish to use a module that is normally linked static with your Perl, it must be listed in static_ext in Perl's Config.pm to be linked with httpd during the mod_perl build.

The use of special tokens (names) is also restricted by mod_perl. As mentioned before, scripts run under Apache::Registry are not run in the default package (main). The namespace used is based on the requested URI. Therefore, these scripts cannot contain special tokens such as the __END__ token to denote the logical end of the script. The __DATA__ token is not permitted either.

Server Side Include and mod_perl Integration

So far I have talked about how you can develop CGI scripts that can take advantage of mod_perl. What about the Perl scripts that you use as Server Side Include (SSI) scripts? They can also take advantage of mod_perl features.

The mod_perl module can be well integrated with the SSI module mod_include. Either you need to make sure that when you build the Apache binary, the following line is present in the configuration file:

```
EXTRA_CFLAGS=-DUSE_PERL_SSI -I. `perl -MExtUtils::Embed -
ccopts`
```

Or, you need to make sure when you build mod_perl that you use the following command:

```
perl Makefile.PL PERL_SSI=1
Once you have built Apache, you can take advantage of
mod_perl for your Perl SSI scripts.
```

Use the following in your SSI page:

```
<!-- #perl sub="Apache::Include"
arg="/some_directory_alias/your_perlscript"-->
```

This is preferable to using an SSI command such as the following:

```
<!-- #exec cmd="/some_directory_alias/your_perlscript"-->
```

However, you will have to use the following line in the httpd.conf configuration file to preload the script:

```
PerlScript /path/to/your_perlscript
```

The value of the sub key in the preceding sample SSI call can be a subroutine name, a module name, a method name of a class, or an anonymous subroutine call (sub {}). For example:

```
<!-- #perl sub="Apache::Test" -->
```

This will call the Test::handler method by default as long as the Test.pm is preloaded with PerlModule or by some other means at server startup.

If you wanted to call a method other than the default handler, you should specify the method name as well. For example, if you want to call the doit method instead of the handler method, change the previous SSI call to the following:

```
<!-- #perl sub="Apache::Test::doit"-->
```

If arguments need to be passed to the preceding method to pass 'argument1' and 'argument2' as the arguments to the method, you can use:

```
<!-- #perl sub="Apache::Test::doit" arg="argument1"
arg="argument2" -->
```

Note that the very first argument will always be the request object reference.

Using Perl to Configure Apache

Apart from the usual advantages of having mod_perl for your CGI or SSI scripts, there is an unusual feature of mod_perl that devoted

Perl programmers and Apache administrators will enjoy—the ability to write Apache server configuration in Perl.

You can include a <Perl> container inside an Apache configuration file as follows:

```
<Perl>
# your Perl code  goes here
1;
</Perl>
```

The very last line (containing the 1;) is required. Your code can be any Perl script. The code in a <Perl> container gets compiled in a special package and mod_perl communicates the configuration information to the Apache core configuration module. Before you can use this feature, you will have to make sure you built Apache and mod_perl properly. To configure this feature for your Apache server, configure mod_perl as follows:

```
perl Makefile.PL PERL_SECTIONS=1
```

Once you have configured and recompiled mod_perl and Apache, you are ready to write Perl code in Apache configuration files. Next, I'll discuss the syntax used to describe the configuration.

The directives that take a single value are represented as scalar variables. For example:

```
User httpd
```

This User directive takes a single string value and therefore can be written as:

```
<Perl>
$User = "httpd";
1;
</Perl>
```

Here is an example configuration:

```
<Perl>
$User = "httpd";
```

```
$Group = "httpd";
$ServerAdmin = 'kabir@nitec.com';
$MinSpareServers = 5;
$MaxSpareServers = 5;
$MaxClients = 40;
1;
</Perl>
```

The directives that require multiple values can be represented as lists. For example:

```
PerlModule Apache::TestOne Apache::TestTwo can be
represented as:
@PerlModule = qw(Apache::TestOne Apache::TestTwo);
```

Containers are represented using hash, for example:

```
<VirtualHost 206.171.50.50>
ServerName www.nitec.com
ServerAdmin kabir@nitec.com
</VirtualHost>
```

This can be represented as the following:

```
$VirtualHost{"206.171.60.60"} = {
       ServerName => 'www.nitec.com',
       ServerAdmin => 'kabir@nitec.com'
      }
```

A slightly more involved example follows:

```
$Location{"/some_dir_alias/"} = {
     AuthUserFile => '/www/nitec/secret/htpasswd',
     AuthType => 'Basic',
     AuthName => 'Subscribers Only Access',
     DirectoryIndex => [qw(welcome.html welcome.htm)],
     Limit => {
         METHODS => 'POST GET',
         require => 'user reader'
```

```
    }
};
```

You can define other containers, such as <Directory>, <Files>, and so on in a similar manner. Note that in order for the <Perl> containers to work, you must define the PerlScript directive in your configuration file. If you do not need to load any Perl scripts, to take advantage of the <Perl> containers you can always set the PerlScript directive as follows:

```
PerlScript /dev/null
```

In my opinion, you should use the <Perl> containers in your configuration files only if you have one or both of the following requirements:

- You love Perl so much that you can't imagine not using <Perl> in Apache configuration files now that you know you can.
- You run multiple Apache servers and want to create a single set of configuration files that can be used in all of your Apache server systems. (This is where I would use this feature.) A scripted configuration is immensely flexible. It can read external files, use loops to automate configuration, and more. Such a configuration is limited only by the programming ability of the Apache administrator.

If you are doing it for the first reason, you should already be on your way writing fancy Perl scripts in your configuration files. However, if you want to do it for the second reason and are not yet clear how this feature can help you, let's look at an example case.

Let's say that you have three Web server systems: host_a, host_b, and host_c. Let's also say that host_a is more powerful than host_b, and host_b is more powerful than host_c. You want to define a <Perl> container that will allow you to create a single configuration for all three hosts. Here is an example of such an httpd.conf file:

```
<Perl>
# Get the host name using the UNIX hostname utility and
# store it in the $thisHost variable.
my $thisHost = '/bin/hostname';
if ($thisHost =~ /host_a/) {
       # configuration for host_a goes here
       $MinSpareServers = 10;
       $MaxSpareServers = 20;
       $StartServers = 30;
       $MaxClients   = 256;
       }
elsif ($thisHost =~ /host_b/) {
       # configuration for host_b goes here
       $MinSpareServers = 5;
       $MaxSpareServers = 10;
       $StartServers = 10;
       $MaxClients   = 50;
       }
else {
       # configuration for host_c goes here
       $MinSpareServers = 3;
       $MaxSpareServers = 5;
       $StartServers = 5;
       $MaxClients   = 30;
        }
1;
</Perl>
```

In order to make this example more interesting, let's also say that you have different virtual hosts for each of the three hosts, and you would like to configure them in an elegant manner. Take a look at this example:

```
<Perl>
# Get the host name using the UNIX hostname utility and
# store it in the $thisHost variable.
```

```
my $thisHost = '/bin/hostname';
my $thisDomain = 'mydomain.com';
my @vHosts = ();

my $anyHost;

if ($thisHost =~ /(host_a)/) {
        # configuration for host_a goes here
    @vHosts = qw(gaia, athena, romeo, juliet, shazam);
        }
elsif ($thisHost =~ /host_b/) {
        # configuration for host_b goes here
    @vHosts = qw(catbart, ratbart, dilbert);
        }
else {
  # configuration for host_c goes here
    @vHosts = qw(lonelyhost);
    }

for $anyHost (@vHosts) {
        %{$VirtualHost{"$anyHost.$domainName"}} = {
                "ServerName" => "$anyHost.$domainName",
                "ServerAdmin" =>
"webmaster\@$anyHost.$domainName"
                    }
     }
1;
</Perl>
```

Once you have created a suitable Perl-based configuration for your Apache servers, you can check your code syntax to make sure the code is syntactically correct by using the following command:

```
perl -cx httpd.conf
```

Special Concerns for Using mod_perl

So far, I have discussed how wonderful mod_perl is and how to make use of its wonders. Now let's take a look at a couple of issues that you should be aware of. These issues concern your system resources and security.

Memory Usage

Mod_perl makes your Perl scripts execute faster by taking advantage of the memory resident interpreter and cached scripts. This is great news, but where's the catch? The catch is that you use a lot of memory when you use mod_perl. Typically, when you run a CGI script in the traditional manner, it runs and disappears after the service. But in the mod_perl version, the script stays resident in memory for future use. This means that the more scripts you want to run under mod_perl, the more memory they will consume.

If your Perl scripts use a lot of common modules, you can preload these using a simple Perl script. For example, the following is a script called loader.pl that loads a module called CGI.pm:

```
#!/usr/local/bin/perl
# startup script
use lib qw(/www/perl/modules);
use CGI;
1;
```

To preload this commonly used module, load the script via the PerlScript directive as follows:

```
PerlScript /path/to/loader.pl
```

In most modern operating systems, the Apache child processes running mod_perl will be able to share CGI.pm.

In any case, the more scripts you load, the more memory you need. This can become a issue if you have limited memory and need to pay attention to your server's memory consumption. You can easily monitor memory consumption using common UNIX utilities such as ps or top. I use the following command to generate a listing of important httpd-specific information on a Linux system:

```
ps auxw | awk '{print $1, "\t", $2 , "\t", $5 , "\t",
$6}' | egrep '(httpd|SIZE)'
```

This prints out the USER, PID, SIZE / (virtual image size; size of text, data, and stack), and RSS (Resident set size; kilobytes of program in memory) of all the httpd child processes.

You can also find out what Perl packages and scripts are currently being cached by mod_perl using the Apache::Status module. However, before you can use this module, you will need to install the Devel::Symdump module. This Perl module provides a convenient way to inspect Perl's symbol table and the class hierarchies within running programs. If you have the CPAN.pm module installed, you can use the command:

```
perl -MCPAN -e 'install "Devel::Symdump"'
```

Another option is to get the source code from the URL:

```
www.perl.com/cgi-bin/cpan_mod?module=Devel::Symdump
```

Installing the module is quite easy. Just read the README file included in the module. Once you have installed the Devel: Symdump module, you can get information about the modules that have been loaded (in Apache child processes) and their symbol tables. Define the following configuration segment in one of your Apache configuration files and restart the Apache server.:

```
<Location /perl-status>
SetHandler  perl-script
PerlHandler Apache::Status
</Location>
```

You can get status information using a URL such as:

```
http://yourserver/perl-status
```

This is a really cool way of determining what is loaded by the processes.

Security Concerns

Scripts run by mod_perl have the same user and group privileges of the user and group specified by the User and Group directives in the httpd.conf file. Make sure that you keep these user/group privileges very limited.

You should also take care in developing scripts that user input data is checked before use. If you want to enable taint checking in mod_perl, make sure you set the following directive in your httpd.conf file:

```
PerlTaintCheck On
```

The -T switch usually used to enable taint checking does not work under mod_perl.

Part III

Common Administration Tasks

Chapter

Chapter 10

WWW Authentication

Using Host-Based Authentication

In this authentication scheme, access is controlled by the hostname or the host's IP address. When a request is made for a certain resource, the Web server checks to see if the requesting host is allowed access to the resource and takes action based on the findings.

The standard Apache distribution includes a module called mod_access, which enables access control based on the Internet hostname of a Web client. The hostname can be either a fully qualified domain name (FQDN), such as `blackhole.nitec.com`, or an IP address, such as 206.171.50.50. The module provides this access control support using the following Apache directives: allow, deny, order, allow from env=variable, and deny from env=variable.

allow

Syntax: `allow from host1 host2 host3`
Context: `directory, location, per-directory access control file`
Override: `Limit`

This directive enables you to define a list of hosts (containing one or more hosts or IP addresses) that are allowed access to a certain directory. When more than one host or IP address is specified, they should be separated with space characters. Table 10-1 shows the possible values for the directive.

Table 10-1 *Possible Values for the allow Directive*

Value	Example	Description
All	allow from all	This reserved word allows access for all hosts. The example shows how to use this option.
A fully qualified domain name (FQDN) of a host	allow from `wormhole.nitec.com`	Only the host that has the specified FQDN is allowed access. The allow directive in the example allows access only to `wormhole.nitec .com`. Note that this compares whole components; `toys.com` would not match `etoys.com`.
A partial domain name of a host	allow from `.mainoffice.nitec.com`	Only all the hosts that match the partial hostname are allowed access. The example permits all the hosts in `.mainoffice.nitec.com` network to access the site. For example, `developer1.main office.nitec.com` and `developer2.main office.nitec.com` have access to the site. However, `developer3.baoffice. nitec.com` is not allowed access.
A full IP address of a host	allow from 206.171.50.50	Only the specified IP address is allowed access. The example shows a full IP address (all four octets of IP are present), 206.171.50.50, that is allowed access.
A partial IP address	Example 1: allow from 206.171.50	

Value	Example	Description
	Example 2: allow from 130.86	When not all four octets of an IP address are present in the allow directive, the partial IP address is matched from left to right, and hosts that have the matching IP address pattern (that is, the address pattern is part of the same subnet) are allowed access. In the first example, all hosts with IP addresses in the range of 206.171.50.1 to 206.171.50.255 have access. In the second example, all hosts from the 130.86 network are allowed access.
A network/netmask pair	allow from 206.171.50.0/255.255.255.0	This enables you to specify a range of IP addresses using the network and the netmask address. The example allows only the hosts with IP addresses in the range of 206.171.50.1 to 206.171.50.255 to have access. This feature is available in Apache 1.3 or above.
A network/nnn CIDR specification	allow 206.171.50.0/24	Similar to the previous value, except the netmask consists of nnn high-order 1 bits. The example is equivalent to allow from 206.171.50.0/255.255.255.0. This feature is available in Apache 1.3 or above.

allow from env=variable

Syntax: `allow from env=variable`

Context: `directory, location, per-directory access control file`

Override: `Limit`

This directive, a variation of the allow directive, allows access when the named environment variable is set. This is useful only if you are using other directives, such as BrowserMatch, to set an environment variable. For example, say you want to allow Microsoft Internet Explorer 4.01, the latest version of Internet Explorer, to access a directory in which you stored some HTML files with embedded VBScript. Because the other leading Web browser, Netscape Navigator, does not support VBScript directly, you'd rather not have Navigator users go into the directory. In such a case, you can use the BrowserMatch directive to set an environment variable when Internet Explorer 4.01 is detected. The directive would be as follows:

```
BrowserMatch "MSIE 4.01" ms_browser
```

Now you can use a <Directory> container to specify the allow directive, as follows:

```
<Directory /path/to/Vbscript_directory>
order deny,allow
deny from all
allow from env=ms_browser
</Directory>
```

Here, the Apache server will set the ms_browser environment variable for all browsers that provide the "MSIE 4.01" string as part of the user-agent identifier. The allow directive will allow only browsers for which the ms_browser variable is set.

deny

Syntax: `deny from host1 host2 host3`
Context: `directory, location, per-directory access control file`
Override: `Limit`

This directive is the exact opposite of the allow directive. It enables you to define a list of hosts that are denied access to a specified directory. Like the allow directive, it can accept all the values shown in Table 12-1.

deny from env=variable

Syntax: `deny from env=variable`

Context: `directory, location, per-directory access control file`

Override: `Limit`

This directive, a variation of the deny directive, denies access capability for all hosts for which the specified environment is set. For example, if you want to deny all hosts using Microsoft Internet Explorer access, you can use the BrowserMatch directive to set a variable called ms_browser whenever a browser identified itself to the server with the string "MSIE".

```
BrowserMatch "MSIE" ms_browser
```

Now you can use a <Directory> container to specify the deny directive, as follows:

```
<Directory /path/to/Vbscript_directory>
order deny,allow
allow from all
deny from env=ms_browser
</Directory>
```

If you are interested in blocking access to a specific HTTP request method, such as GET, POST, and PUT, you can use the <Limit> container to do so. For example:

```
<Location /cgi-bin>
<Limit POST>
order deny,allow
deny from all
allow from yourdomain.com
</Location>
```

This example allows POST requests to the cgi-bin directory only if they are made by hosts in the `yourdomain.com domain`. In other words, if this site has some HTML forms that send user input data via the HTTP POST method, only the users in your domain.com will be able to use these forms effectively. Typically, CGI applications are stored in the CGI-BIN directory, and many sites feature HTML forms that use the POST method to dump data to CGI applications. Using the preceding host-based access control configuration, a site can allow anyone to run a CGI script but only allow a certain site (in this case, yourdomain.com) to actually postdata to one or more CGI scripts. This gives the CGI access in such a site a bit of read-only character. Everyone can run applications that generate output without taking any user input, but only users of a certain domain can provide input.

order

Syntax: order deny, allow | allow, deny | mutual-failure
Default: order deny, allow
Context: directory, location, per-directory access control file
Override: Limit

This directive controls how Apache evaluates both allow and deny directives. For example:

```
<Directory /mysite/myboss/rants>
order deny, allow
deny from myboss.mycompany.com
allow from all
</Directory>
```

This example denies the host myboss.mycompany.com access and allows all other hosts to access the directory. The value for the order directive is a comma-separated list, which indicates which directive takes precedence. Typically, the one that affects all hosts is given lowest priority. In the preceding example, because the allow directive affects all hosts, it is given the lower priority.

Although allow, deny and deny, allow are the most widely used values for the order directive, you can use another value, mutual-failure, to indicate that only those hosts appearing on the allow list but not on the deny list are granted access.

In all cases, every allow and deny directive is evaluated.

Using HTTP-Specified Basic Authentication

Support for HTTP-specified basic authentication in Apache has been around for quite a while. Many modules have also been written to provide basic HTTP authentication in Apache.

It is fairly simple to create a restricted area on a Web site using one or more of the authentication modules available for Apache. Along with authentication-module-specific directives, you need to use the following core directives:

- AccessFileName
- AllowOverride
- AuthType
- AuthName
- Satisfy
- Require

In the following sections, I discuss the common basic authentication modules currently available for Apache.

Using Standard mod_auth

This module is compiled by default in the standard distribution. Standard mod_auth-based basic HTTP authentication uses usernames, groups, and passwords stored in text files to confirm authentication. This works well when dealing with a small number of users. However, if you have a lot of users (thousands or more), use of mod_auth might have a performance penalty. In such a case, you can use something more advanced, such as DBM files, Berkeley DB files, or even a SQL database. (These are discussed later in the chapter.)

The standard mod_auth module offers the Apache directives AuthAuthoritative, AuthGroupFile, and AuthUserFile. Let's take a closer look at these directives and some examples that use this module.

AuthAuthoritative

Syntax: `AuthAuthoritative on | off`

Default: `on`

Context: `directory, per-directory access control file`

Override: `AuthConfig`

If you are using more than one authentication scheme for the same directory, you can set this directive to On so that when a username/password pair fails with the first scheme, it is passed on to the next (lower) level.

For example, if you are using mod_auth_db (discussed in a later section) and the standard mod_auth module to provide authentication services, and a username/password pair fails for one of them, the next module is used to authenticate the user, if possible. Which module is considered as a lower- or higher-level authentication module is determined by its appearance in the Configuration file. Say the Configuration file looks like this:

```
AddModule modules/standard/mod_auth.o
AddModule modules/standard/mod_auth_db.o
```

The mod_auth_db will have higher priority, because the modules in the Configuration file are listed in reverse priority order.

In any case, when a username/password pair fails all modules, the server reissues a 401 status header and sends the WWW-Authenticate response header for re-authentication. However, if a username/password pair is successfully authenticated by a particular module, the lower-level modules never receive the username/password pair.

AuthGroupFile

Syntax: `AuthGroupFile filename`

Context: `directory, per-directory access control file`

Override: `AuthConfig`

This directive specifies a text file to be used as the list of user groups for basic HTTP authentication. The filename is the absolute path to the group file.

You can create this file using any text editor. The format of this file is as follows:

```
groupname: username username username
```

For example:

```
startrek: kirk spock picard data
```

This creates a group called startrek, which has four users: kirk, spock, picard, and data.

It is important that the AuthUserFile-specified file resides outside the document tree of the Web site. Putting it inside a Web-accessible directory might enable someone to download it.

AuthUserFile

Syntax: `AuthUserFile filename`

Context: `directory, per-directory access control file`

Override: `AuthConfig`

This directive sets the name of the text file that contains the usernames and passwords used in the basic HTTP authentication. You must provide a fully qualified path to the file to be used. For example:

```
AuthUserFile /www/nitec/secrets/.htpasswd
```

This file is usually created using a utility called htpasswd, which is available as a support program in the standard Apache distribution. The format of this file is very simple. Each line contains a single username and an encrypted password. The password is encrypted using the standard crypt() function.

It is important that the AuthUserFile-specified file resides outside the document tree of the Web site. Putting it inside a Web-accessible directory would enable someone to download it.

Example 1: Requiring Username and Password

This example shows you how to create a restricted directory that requires a username and a password for access. To simplify the example, I will assume the following are settings for a Web site called `apache.nitec.com`:

```
DocumentRoot  /data/web/apache/public/htdocs
AccessFileName .htaccess
AllowOverride  All
```

Let's also assume that you want to restrict access to the following directory, such that only a user named "reader" with the password "bought-it" is able to access the directory:
`/data/web/apache/public/htdocs/chapter_10/`

Follow these steps to create the restricted access.

STEP 1: *Creating a user file using htpasswd*

Standard Apache distribution comes with a utility program called htpasswd, which creates the user file needed for the AuthUserFile directive. Use the program as follows:

```
htpasswd -c /data/web/apache/secrets/.htpasswd reader
```

The htpasswd utility asks for the password of "reader." Enter "bought-it," and then reenter the password again to confirm that you didn't make a typo. After you reenter the password, the utility creates a file called .htpasswd in the /data/web/apache/secrets directory. Note the following:

- Use the -c option to tell htpasswd that you want to create a new user file. If you already had the password file and wanted to add a new user, you would not want this option.

- Place the user file outside the document root directory of the `apache.nitec.com` site, because you do not want anyone to download it via the Web.
- Use a leading period (.) in the filename so that it will not appear in the output on your UNIX system. This does not provide any real benefits, but is more of a traditional UNIX habit. Many configuration files (such as .login and .profile) in UNIX systems have leading periods.

To save future headaches, execute the following command:

```
cat /data/web/apache/secrets/.htpasswd
```

This should show a line similar to the following (the password won't be exactly the same as this example):

```
reader:hulR6FFh1sxK6
```

This confirms that you have a user called "reader" in the .htpasswd file. The password "bought-it" is encrypted by the htpasswd program using the standard crypt() function.

STEP 2: *Creating an .htaccess file*

Using a text editor, add the following lines to a file named /data/web/apache/public/htdocs/chapter_10/.htaccess:

```
AuthName "Apache Server Administrator's Handbook Readers
Only"
AuthType  Basic
AuthUserFile /data/web/apache/secrets/.htpasswd
require user reader
```

The first directive, AuthName, sets the realm of the authentication. This is really just a label that is sent to the Web browser so that the user will be provided with some clue about what he or she is about to access. In this case, the "Apache Server Administrator's Handbook Readers Only" string indicates that only readers of *Apache Server Administrator's Handbook* can access this directory.

The second directive, AuthType, specifies the type of authentication to be used. Because only basic authentication is supported, AuthType is always set to "Basic." The next directive, AuthUserFile, specifies the filename for the user file. The path to the user file is provided here. The last directive, require, specifies that a user named "reader" is allowed access to this directory.

STEP 3: *Setting file permissions*

After the .htaccess and the .htpasswd files are created, it is important to make sure that only Apache can read the files. No users except the file owner and Apache should have access to these files.

STEP 4: *Testing*

Next, use a Web browser to access the following URL:

```
http://apache.nitec.com/chapter_10
```

Apache will send the 401 status header and WWW-Authenticate response header to the browser with the realm (set in AuthName) and authentication type (set in AuthType) information. The browser will display a popup dialog box that requests a username and password.

It is a good idea to see if one can get in without a username or password, so enter nothing in the entry boxes in the dialog and click OK. This should result in an authentication failure. The browser receives the same authentication challenge again, so it displays another dialog box.

Clicking Cancel results in the browser showing the standard "Authentication Required" error message from Apache.

Clicking Reload on the browser requests the same URL again, and the browser receives the same authentication challenge from the server. This time, enter "reader" as the username and "bought-it" as the password and click OK. Apache will now allow you to access the directory.

You can change the "Authentication Required" message if you want by using the ErrorDocument directive:

```
ErrorDocument 401 /nice_401message.html
```

Insert this line in your srm.conf file and create a nice message in the nice_401message.html file to make your users happy.

Example 2: Allowing a Group of Users to Access a Directory

Instead of allowing a single user called "reader" to access the restricted area, as demonstrated in the previous example, here you will allow anyone belonging to the group named "asb_readers" to access the same directory. Let's assume this group has two users: pikejb and bcaridad.

Follow these steps to give the users in group asb_readers directory access.

STEP 1: *Creating a user file using htpasswd*

Using the htpasswd utility, create the users pikejb and bcaridad.

STEP 2: *Creating a group file*

Using a text editor such as vi (available on most UNIX systems), create a file named /data/web/apache/secrets/.htgroup. This file has a single line, as follows:

```
asb_readers: pikejb bcaridad
```

STEP 3: *Creating an .htaccess file in /data/web/apache/public/htdocs/chapter_10*

Using a text editor, add the following lines to a file called /data/web/apache/public/htdocs/chapter_10/.htaccess:

```
AuthName "Apache Server Administrator's Handbook Readers
Only"
AuthType  Basic
```

```
AuthUserFile /data/web/apache/secrets/.htpasswd
AuthGroupFile /data/web/apache/secrets/.htgroup
require group  asb_readers
```

This is almost the same configuration that I discussed in the previous example but with two changes. The first change is the addition of a new directive, AuthGroupFile, which points to the .htgroup group file created earlier. The next change is in the require directive line, which now requires a group called "asb_readers." In other words, Apache will allow access to anyone that belongs to the said group. Note that you could have just as easily used the following line:

```
require user pikejb bcaridad
```

This is instead of using:

```
require group asb_readers
```

However, listing all users in the require line could become cumbersome and cause unnecessary headaches. Using group, one can easily add or remove multiple users.

STEP 4: *File permissions*

As in the previous example, it is important to make sure .htaccess, .htpasswd, and .htgroup files are readable only by Apache, and no one but the owner has write access to the files.

STEP 5: *Testing*

Testing the new setting is quite similar to the previous example, so I won't repeat the test process here.

Example 3: Mixing Host-Based Access Control with Basic HTTP Authentication

In this example, you will see how you can mix the host-based access control scheme with the basic HTTP authentication method found in Apache. For simplicity, let's assume you want to allow the "asb_readers" group to access the same directory as they do in Example 2, and you also want to allow anyone coming from a domain called `apache-training.nitec.com`, without a username/password, to have access to the same directory.

In other words, if a request for the URL `http://apache.nitec.com/chapter_10` comes from a domain named `apache-training.nitec.com`, the request is processed without HTTP authentication by using the following steps.

STEP 1: *Modifying .htaccess file*

Modify the .htaccess file (from Example 2) to look like the following:

```
AuthName "Apache Server Administrator's Handbook Readers
Only"
AuthType  Basic
AuthUserFile /data/web/apache/secrets/.htpasswd
AuthGroupFile /data/web/apache/secrets/.htgroup
require group  asb_readers
order deny, allow
deny from all
allow from apache-training.nitec.com
```

This adds three host-based access control directives discussed in earlier sections. The first one is the order directive, which tells Apache to evaluate the deny directive before it does the allow directive. The deny directive tells Apache to refuse access from all hosts. The allow directive tells Apache to allow access from the `apache-training.nitec.com` domain. This effectively tells Apache that any hosts in the `apache-training.nitec.com` domain are welcome to this directory.

STEP 2: *Testing*

Using a Web browser from a host called `user01.apache-training.nitec.com`, if you try to access the URL `apache.nitec.`

com/chapter_10, your browser will display the username/password authentication dialog box. In other words, you are required to authenticate yourself. This is not what you want to happen. So, what is going on? Well, Apache assumes that both host-based and basic HTTP authentication are required for this directory, thereby not allowing access to the directory without passing both methods. A satisfactory solution to this problem can be implemented using the satisfy directive, as follows:

```
AuthName "Apache Server Administrator's Handbook Readers
Only"
AuthType  Basic
AuthUserFile /data/web/apache/secrets/.htpasswd
AuthGroupFile /data/web/apache/secrets/.htgroup
require group  asb_readers
order deny, allow
deny from all
allow from apache-training.nitec.com
satisfy any
```

The satisfy directive takes either the all or the any value. Because you want the basic HTTP authentication to be activated only if a request comes from any host other than the apache-training. nitec.com domain, specify "any" for the satisfy directive. This effectively tells Apache to do the following:

```
If request comes from any host in the apache-
training.nitec.com domain then
  No need for basic HTTP authentication
Else
  Require  basic HTTP authentication
End
```

If you change your mind and want to allow only users of apache-training.nitec.com domain to access the directory with basic HTTP authentication, specify "all" for the satisfy directive; this tells Apache to enforce both authentication methods for all requests.

Using mod_auth_dbm

As mentioned before, .htpasswd and .htgroup text files are inefficient for high-speed processing and could negatively affect a Web server's performance when thousands of users (or more) need authenticated access to restricted areas. The mod_auth_dbm module is a better choice in such a case. This module uses DBM files instead of text files to store data. A DBM file stores data records in a key=value pair and keeps a computed index table for the keys in the file. Using the index table in a DBM file, it is possible to retrieve the record associated with the key faster than the time needed to parse a large text file with tens of thousands of records.

Many DBMs are available, the most common being GDBM, NDBM, SDBM, and Berkeley DB (BSD-DB). Table 10-2 shows a list of features for these DBMs.

Table 10-2 *DBM Features*

Features	NDBM	SDBM	GDBM	BSD-DB
Licensing restrictions	Unknown	No	Yes	No
Byte-order independent	No	No	No	Yes
Default size limits	4K	1K	None	None
Creates FTP-safe files	No	Yes	Yes	Yes
Speed	Unknown	Slow	Medium	Fast
Database size	Unknown	Small	Large	Medium
Code size	Unknown	Small	Large	Large
Source comes with Perl	No	Yes	No	No

This table is based on the information found in Perl 5 documentation. Before you can use any DBM with Apache, you will have to make sure the DBM you choose to use is already installed in your system. Do this by confirming that the DBM library files are located in your system's default library directory. You are also likely to need Perl with the same DBM support. Make sure you have the latest version of Perl compiled with the chosen DBM support.

TIP

You can get Perl from `http://www.perl.com`. Configuring Perl for DBM support is quite easy. Just run the configuration script, and it will prompt you for the DBM support. For example, if you choose NDBM or GDBM as your desired DBM and have these installed on your system, the Perl configuration script should ask you if you want to compile Perl with -lndbm, -lgdbm, and library flags.

Once you have installed the appropriate DBM libraries on your system, you then need to configure Apache for support of DBM files, because the standard Apache distribution does not enable DBM support. Before you recompile, check your Apache executable (httpd) to see if you already have this module precompiled. The following command displays all the compiled modules in a httpd executable file:

```
/usr/sbin/httpd -l
```

If you do not see mod_auth_dbm.c in the listing produced by the preceding command, you need to reconfigure and recompile Apache. First, backup your existing Apache executable so that you can restore it in case anything goes wrong in the compilation process. To add the DBM authentication module, run the configure (or config.status script if you have already compiled Apache once) with the —enable-module=auth_dbm option. Once configure or config.status script is finished, run make to compile Apache. If no error is reported, run make install to install Apache.

Once Apache is properly compiled for DBM files, you can use dbmmanage to create a DBM user file. Begin by using the dbmmanage script found in the support directory of the standard Apache distribution for creating a DBM-based user file. The dbmmanage Perl script is able to create many popular DBM files such as NDBM, GDBM, and Berkley DB files. This script can be used to create a new DBM file, add users and passwords, change passwords, delete users, or view user information. Before you use the script, you should modify the following line in the script such that the DBM you want to use is listed as the first item in the ISA array:

```
BEGIN { @AnyDBM_File::ISA = qw(DB_File, NDBM_File,
GDBM_file) }
```

For example, if you plan on using GDBM files, change the line to the following:

```
BEGIN { @AnyDBM_File::ISA = qw(GDBM_file, DB_File,
NDBM_File) }
```

To find out what options the script provides, run it as follows:

```
./dbmmanage
```

This will show you a syntax line with all the possible options. To create a new DBM file called /www/secrets/myuserdbm by adding a user named "reader." enter the following command:

```
dbmmanage /www/secrets/myuserdbm adduser reader
```

The script will ask you to enter (and re-enter) a password for the user "reader". Once you have done so, it will add the username and encrypted password to the myuserdbm DBM file.

TIP

Do not use the add option to add a user, because it does not encrypt the password.

To see a list of all users in a DBM file, use the following script:

```
dbmmanage /path/to/your/dbmfile view
```

Once you have recompiled Apache with DBM support, you can use the module mod_auth_dbm to provide DBM-based basic HTTP authentication. Note that for Berkeley DB you will have to use mod_auth_db instead of mod_auth_dbm.

The mod_auth_dbm module provides the directives AuthDBM UserFIle, AuthDBMGroupFile, and AuthDBMAuthoritative. Let's take a look at each of these directives and examples using the mod_auth_dbm module.

AuthDBMAuthoritative

Syntax: `AuthDBMAuthoritative on | off`

Default: `on`

Context: `directory, .per-directory access control file (.htaccess)`

Override: `AuthConfig`

When using multiple authentication schemes such as mod_dbm and standard mod_auth in the same directory, you can use this directive to define whether mod_auth_dbm is the authoritative authentication schema.

The default value of the directive enables mod_auth_dbm to become the authoritative authentication for the directory. This means that if the DBM-based authentication fails for a particular user, the user's credentials will not be passed on to a lower-level authentication scheme. When set to the Off value, the credentials of a failed authentication will be passed on to the next authentication level.

A common use for this is in conjunction with one of the basic auth modules, such as mod_auth.c. Whereas this DBM module supplies the bulk of the user credential checking, a few administrator-related accesses fall through to a lower level with a well-protected .htpasswd file.

AuthDBMGroupFile

Syntax: `AuthDBMGroupFile filename`

Context: `directory, per-directory access control file (.htaccess)`

Override: `AuthConfig`

This directive sets the fully qualified path name of the group file that contains the list of user groups. Each record in the file is a key=value pair, where the key is the username and the value is a comma-separated list of group names to which the user belongs.

If you prefer not to use a separate group file, you can use a single DBM file to provide both password and group information. The format of the file is as follows:

```
username: encrypted password: comma-separated group list
```

Here, username is the key, and the password and group lists are two fields of the value. Other data may be left in the DBM file after another colon, if desired; it is ignored by the authentication module. If you use a single DBM to provide both group and password information, you will have to point both AuthDBMGroup and AuthDBMUserFile directives to the same file.

AuthDBMUserFile

Syntax: `AuthDBMUserFile filename`
Context: `directory, per-directory access control file (.htaccess)`
Override: `AuthConfig`

This directive sets the fully qualified pathname of a DBM file to be used as the user file for DBM authentication. The file contains a key=value pair per record, where the username is the key and the crypt()-encrypted password is the value. Note that each field in the record is separated by a colon, and arbitrary data can be appended after the initial username and password fields.

WARNING

Never store user database files inside your Web document tree.

Example: Requiring a DBM Username and Password

Now that you have the user DBM file created, you can restrict access to any Web directory you want. In the following example, let's assume that the user DBM file is /www/secrets/myuserdbm. You can add the authentication scheme to your global or virtual server using a <Directory> container, or you can use the .htaccess file — there is no difference. The example configuration looks like this:

```
AuthName "Apache Server Administrator's Handbook Readers
Only"
AuthType  Basic
AuthUserDBMFile /www/secrets/myuserdbm
require valid-user
```

Apache will use the mod_auth_dbm module for authentication in the directory where this configuration applies.

Make sure that only Apache and the owner can read the DBM file. No one but the owner of the DBM file should be able to write to it.

Using mod_auth_db

If your system is not capable of using DBM, but Berkeley DB file support is available, you can use mod_auth_db to use DB files instead. Like the DBM module, this module is not compiled in the standard Apache distribution. You will have to recompile your Apache server with this module support to use it. However, before you recompile, you may want to check your Apache executable (httpd) to see if you already have this module precompiled. The following command displays all the compiled modules in an httpd executable file:

```
/usr/sbin/httpd -l
```

If you do not see mod_auth_db.c in the listing produced by the preceding command, you need to reconfigure and recompile Apache.

However, first make sure you know where the DB library files are stored on your system. For example, on a Linux system, the files are in the standard /usr/lib directory. If your system does not have the DB libraries, you will have to get the source code and compile DB support first. You can find DB library information at the following URL:

```
http://www.sleepycat.com/
```

Once you have made sure your system has DB libraries, you can proceed with reconfiguring and recompiling Apache. First, you will have to uncomment the following line in the Configuration file:

```
#AddModule modules/standard/mod_auth_db.o
```

Remove the # symbol, and then run the Configure script to create a new Makefile. Once you have done that, run the make utility. This should create a new HTTPD file. Using the -l command line argument, verify that you have the mod_auth_db module built into the new httpd. You can now replace the old httpd with the new one.

At this point, you should be ready to use the mod_auth_db module. This mod_auth_db module provides the directives AuthDBUserFile, AuthDBGroupFile, and AuthDBAuthoritative.

AuthDBAuthoritative

Syntax: `AuthDBAuthoritative on | off`
Default: `on`
Context: `directory, . .per-directory access control file (.htaccess)`
Override: `AuthConfig`

When using multiple authentication schemes, such as mod_db, mod_dbm, and standard mod_auth in the same directory, you can use this directive to define whether mod_auth_db is the authoritative authentication scheme. The default value of the directive allows mod_auth_db to become the authoritative authentication for the directory. Thus, if the DB-based authentication fails for a particular user, the user's credentials will not be passed on to a lower-level authentication scheme. When set to the Off value, the credentials of a failed authentication will be passed on to the next authentication level.

Although using DBM or DB files makes it easier to administer a large user base, they often are not suitable for organizations that have the user information already stored in a relational SQL database. A SQL database provides a great deal of functionality that is not available to either DBM or DB files. Apache also provides support for a popular SQL database called mSQL.

The term mSQL stands for mini-SQL. It is a lightweight Structured Query Language (SQL) database engine developed by David J. Hughes at the Bond University, Australia. Although mSQL provides only a subset of ANSI SQL, it is designed for fast access and low memory requirements. It supports various popular platforms, such as Sun OS 4.1.1, Solaris 2.*x*, Ultrix 4.3, Linux, OSF/1, most BSD-derived systems, SVR4-based systems or POSIX O/Ss, HP-UX, NeXT, SCO, Sequent, Cray, Tandem, *BSD, and so on. The database source can be downloaded from the following URL: `ftp://ftp.bond.edu.au/pub/Minerva/msql`.

AuthDBGroupFile

Syntax: `AuthDBGroupFile filename`

Context: `directory, .per-directory access control file (.htaccess)`

Override: `AuthConfig`

This directive sets the fully qualified path name of the group DB file, which contains the list of user groups for user authentication. Like the DBM counterpart, the group file uses the username as the key and the comma-separated group list is treated as the value. There must be no white space within the value, and it must never contain any colons.

If you do not prefer to use a separate group file, you can use a single DB file to provide both password and group information. The format of the file where username is the key, and the password and group lists are two fields of the value would be as follows:

```
username: encrypted password: comma-separated group list
```

Other data may be left in the DB file after another colon; it is ignored by the authentication module. If you use a single DB to provide both group and password information, you will have to point both AuthDBGroup and AuthDBUserFile directives to the same file.

AuthDBUserFile

Syntax: `AuthDBUserFile filename`

Context: `directory, .per-directory access control file (.htaccess)`

Override: `AuthConfig`

This directive sets the fully qualified path name of the user DB file that contains the list of users and encrypted passwords.

Like the DBM counterpart, the DB user file is also keyed using the username, and the value is the crypt()-encrypted password.

Always make sure your user files are kept outside the Web document tree and are readable only by Apache. No one but the owner should have write access to these files.

Using mod_auth_external

So far I have talked about various authentication methods using authentication code found in a module. What if you needed to use a third-party authentication scheme? In such a case, the solution is to use the mod_auth_external module to enable access to external authentication. This module is bundled with other contributed modules and can be downloaded from `http://www.apache.org/dist/contrib/`.

All the contributed modules are packaged in one compressed TAR file. After downloading and extracting the TAR file, you can install the mod_auth_external.c module as follows:

```
./configure —add-module=/path/to/mod_auth_external.c
```

This will add and enable the module. You can use config.status instead of configure if you have already compiled Apache before. Now run make to compile Apache again. If you get no errors, you can install the new Apache using the make install command. However, do not forget to back up your existing Apache binaries before running 'make install.'

After you have installed the new Apache, you can run the following command from the Apache executable (sbin) directory to see if the mod_auth_external.c module is included in the new executable:

```
httpd -l
```

If you see the mod_auth_external.c in the list, you have successfully installed the module.

If you prefer to write your own hard-coded C function for this module, use the following steps (skip these steps if you are not interested in writing your own function):

STEP 1: *Enable hard-coded function support in the module*

Edit the mod_auth_external.c file and uncomment appropriate lines so that you end up with the following:

```
define _HARDCODE_
ifdef HARDCODE
include "your_function_here.c"
endif
```

Replace "your_function_here.c" with your authentication function's header file. For example, if you call your authentication function source file my_auth.c and have the function's prototype in my_auth.h, you have to have the following lines in mod_auth_external.c:

```
define _HARDCODE_
ifdef HARDCODE
include "my_auth.h"
endif
```

Make sure your source code is in the same directory as the mod_auth_external.c file.

STEP 2: *Hard-code your function in the module*

Go down to the large commented section.

```
/* This is where you make your function call */
```

Start with the line above in the middle of mod_auth_external.c and follow the instructions there. Your function should start something like this:

```
int
function_name (char *user_name,char *user_passwd,char
*config_path) { }

The function call in mod_auth_external.c should look
something like:

if (strcmp(check_type,"<type>")==0) {
            code = function_name(c-
>user,sent_pw,config_file);
}
```

The <type> is what you plan to use in the AddExternalAuth directive. Do not use exit() or other such calls that will cause your function to exit abnormally or dump core. It will take the entire httpd with it and display a "no data" message to your browser. Use return() instead of exit(). You should return zero when authentication is successful and one when authentication fails.

STEP 3: *Save and compile Apache*

Run the make utility in the Apache source directory. If you do not get a clean compilation of code, debug your code. Any time you make modifications to your code file (such as my_auth.c) and do not make any changes to the mod_auth_external.c, you should use the touch utility to touch mod_auth_external.c.

If things go well, you will have successfully compiled Apache and replaced your old version.

Using External Authentication Mechanisms

Once mod_auth_external is installed, you can use three external authentication mechanisms.

system()

The first external authentication mechanism is a system() call. This is the default method. In this mode, the module calls a user-defined (that is, Apache administrator) authentication program and passes it two environment variables—USER and PASS. The client-entered username and password are passed using these two variables, respectively. The external authentication program can read its environment and perform whatever checking is necessary to determine if the client should be allowed access. The module requires that the external authentication program return an exit code of zero (0) for success and one (1) for failure.

On most UNIX systems it is possible to determine what environment variables are available to run processing using the ps utility. For example:

```
ps -auxwe
```

This shows the environment of all the running programs on a Linux system. This could allow someone on the system to see what USER and PASS variables are set to when the authcheck program is running. This could be considered a security hole.

pipe()

The second external authentication method is the pipe() call. This is similar to the system() call, but in this mode the module writes the username and the password gathered from the client on the external authentication program's standard input (STDIN). The data is stored in a key=value pair, where USER=username and PASS=password.

Hard-Coded Function Call

The third external authentication method is a hard-coded function call. In this mode, the module calls a user-defined C function and passes it the username, password, and a configuration filename. This method will allow developers to write custom gateway interfaces to existing or new authentication applications. Examples of such code are already available, including the following:

- mod_auth_external_radius.c. A Radius client using code from the publicly available Merit Radius source code.
- mod_auth_external_sybase.c. A function that queries a sybase database and compares the passwords for said user.

Now that you know what external authentication methods are available to you, let's look at the directives that this module provides and an example that uses the module.

AddExternalAuth

Syntax (system call and pipe version): `AddExternalAuth keyword path/to/authenticator`

Syntax (function version): `AddExternalAuth keyword type: path/to/configuration`

Context: `server config`

This directive associates the keyword with the specified user authenticator. For example:

```
AddExternalAuth archive_auth /usr/local/bin/authcheck
```

This associates archive_auth with an external authentication program called /usr/local/bin/authcheck. An example of the directive for a hard-coded function where RADIUS is the name of the hard-coded function, would look like:

```
AddExternalAuth archive_auth RADIUS:
```

If the function requires a configuration file, the file can be passed to it as follows:

```
AddExternalAuth archive_auth RADIUS:/usr/local/raddb
```

External user authentication programs are passed the client-entered username, the password, and, optionally, a configuration filename (only for hard-coded function-based authentication). By default the external authentication program receives the username and password as USER and PASS environment variables, respectively. If pipe mode is specified in the SetExternalAuthMethod directive, the username and password are passed as key=value pairs in the form of USER=username and PASS=password. For the hard-coded function version, the data is passed as C function parameters.

If the external user authentication program exits with an exit code of zero (0), authentication is assumed to be successful. A nonzero value indicates either a failure to authenticate or a failure to execute the authenticator.

Note that you can use multiple types of authentication in one server by providing multiple directives in the srm.conf file. Just make sure each group has a different keyword.

AddExternalGroupAuth

Syntax (system call and pipe version): `AddExternalGroupAuth keyword path/to/authenticator`

Syntax (function version): `AddExternalGroupAuth keyword type: path/to/configuration`

Context: `server config`

This directive associates the keyword with the specified group authenticator. For example, the following associates archive_auth with an external authentication program called /usr/local/bin/groupcheck:

```
AddExternalGroupAuth archive_auth \
/usr/local/bin/groupcheck
```

External group authentication programs are passed the username, the group, and, optionally, a configuration filename (only for hard-coded function-based authentication). By default the external authentication program receives the username and group as USER and GROUP environment variables, respectively. If pipe mode is specified in the SetExternalGroupMethod directive, the username and password are passed as key=value pairs in the form of USER=username and GROUP=group. For the hard-coded function version, the data is passed as C function parameters.

If the external group authentication program exits with an exit code of 0, authentication is assumed to be successful. A nonzero value indicates either a failure to authenticate or a failure to execute the authenticator.

AuthExternal

Syntax (system call and pipe version): `AddExternalAuth keyword`

Syntax (function version): AddExternalAuth function name: `path/to/configuration file`

Context: `directory, per-directory access control file (.htaccess)`

This directive is used in the directory context or per-directory access control file (.htaccess) to tell Apache which external user authenticator program to use for authentication. The server matches the keyword or the function name (in the case of hard-coded function) to determine what to do.

For example:

```
AuthExternal archive_auth
```

If this line is found in an .htaccess file, Apache will run the user authenticator associated with that keyword.

GroupExternal

Syntax (system call and pipe version): `GroupExternal keyword`

Syntax (function version): `GroupExternal function name: path/to/configuration file`

Context: `directory, per-directory access control file (.htaccess)`

This directive is used in the directory context or per-directory access control file (.htaccess) to tell Apache which external group authenticator program to use for group authentication. The server matches the keyword or the function name (in the case of hard-coded function) to determine what to do.

For example, if the following line is found in an .htaccess file, Apache will run the group authenticator associated with that keyword:

```
GroupExternal archive_auth
```

SetExternalAuthMethod

Syntax: `SetExternalAuthMethod keyword method`

Context: `server config`

This directive sets the method for passing data to the external user authentication program. Currently, there are three methods available.

environment In this method, the username and password are passed via the method environment. The USER variable contains the username, and the PASS variable contains the password. This is the default method.

Consider the following example:

```
AddExternalAuth archive_auth /usr/local/bin/authcheck
SetExternalAuthMethod archive_auth environment
```

Here, the /usr/local/bin/authcheck program will receive the client-entered username and password via environment variables USER and PASS.

function This method is used when a hard-coded function is defined to handle the authentication.

Take a look at the following:

```
AddExternalAuth archive_auth RADIUS:
SetExternalAuthMethod archive_auth function
```

Here, the hard-coded function RADIUS is used, and the function receives the data as function parameters.

pipe This method sends the data via a pipe to the external authenticator's standard input device (STDIN). The data is passed as key=value pairs, where USER=username and PASS=password.

Let's look at the following example:

```
AddExternalAuth archive_auth /usr/local/bin/authcheck
SetExternalAuthMethod archive_auth pipe
```

Here, the /usr/local/bin/authcheck program will receive the client-entered username and password via a pipe to its standard input device (STDIN), where USER=username and PASS=password.

SetExternalGroupMethod

Syntax: `SetExternalGroupMethod keyword method`
Context: `server config`

This directive sets the method, which is to be used for passing data to the external group authentication program. Currently, three methods — environment, function, and pipe — are available. See the previous section, "SetExternalAuthMethod," for examples and more details.

Example: Using a Perl Script as an External User Authenticator

In this example, you'll see how a simple Perl script can be used to provide user authentication service. To make the example a bit interesting (and perhaps controversial), let's use a Perl script that employs the /etc/passwd and /etc/group files found in most UNIX systems to perform the authentication.

Many will claim that the use of /etc/passwd and /etc/group in any Web-based authentication is not a bright idea, and I tend to agree; however, for a well-protected intranet environment (better if it is not even connected to the Internet at all), it seems very cool. Anyone who has a UNIX account on the Web server machine can authenticate using the Perl script shown in Listing 10-2.

Listing 10-2 *authcheck Script*

```
#!/usr/local/bin/perl
#
# Script Name: authcheck
# Purpose: a simple /etc/passwd and /etc/group based
# authenticator script
#

#  Variables and assignments

# Log file  to be used
my $LOG_FILE = '/tmp/authcheck.log';

# Get the username from %ENV.
my $this_user = $ENV{USER};

# Get the password from %ENV.
my $this_pwd = $ENV{PASS};

# If the user does not enter a username or
# password, exit with a nonzero value to let the
```

```
# mod_auth_external know that the authentication has
# failed.
#
exit 1 if($this_user eq "" || $this_pwd eq "");

# We want to allow only users of a certain group to
# be able to authenticate via Web When creating this
# group in your /etc/group, remember to keep power
# users out of it. For example NEVER put the 'root'
# user in this group!
#
my $WEB_USER_GROUP = 'web-users';

# Get the current time and store it in variables.
my ($sec,$min, $hr,
    $mday, $mon, $year,
    $wday, $yday, $isdst) = localtime(time);

# Increment month to take care of the 0-11 range used
# by localtime.
$mon++;

# If the user is a member of the specified Web user
# group, and his or her password is valid then we will
# consider the authentication to be a success.
if(isMember($this_user,$WEB_USER_GROUP) &&
   validPassword($this_user,$this_pwd)){

# Log the successful authentication event. However
# note that since each request from a user will
# go through this authentication code, logging
# successful authentication might create a
# performance issue. If you do not want to
# log successful logins, comment the following line:
```

```
   &log("$mon/$mday/$year $hr:$min:$sec - $this_user
login
         successful.");

# Exit with the success code value so that
# mod_auth_external will consider
# the authentication to be a complete success.
   exit 0;
   }
else{

# Well, the user didn't pass the checks, so log
# the attempt.

  &log("$mon/$mday/$year $hr:$min:$sec - $this_user login
        failed: invalid password ($this_pwd) .");

# Exit with a non-zero code to tell
# mod_auth_external that the user has failed
# authentication.
       exit 1;
       }

sub validPassword{
#
# Purpose: this subroutine checks the user's
# password against the password stored
# in the /etc/passwd file.

# Get the username and the user-entered password
# from the subroutine parameter list.
my $this_user = shift;
my $guess = shift;

# Get the user's real password record from /etc/passwd.
```

```
my (@pwdfields) = getpwnam($this_user);

# Use the crypt() to encrypt the user-entered
# password and compare it with the
# encrypted password found in the password
# record in /etc/passwd.

if(crypt($guess, $pwdfields[1]) eq $pwdfields[1]) {

# User has entered a valid password so return a
# non-zero value to caller routine.
  return 1;
  }

# Oops! User has entered an invalid password so
# return 0.
   return 0;
   }

sub isMember{
#
# Purpose: this subroutine checks the
# /etc/group file to determine if a user belongs
# to a certain group.
#

# Get the username and the group name from the
# parameter list.
my $this_user = shift;
my $web_group = shift;

# Get the member list for the group from the
# /etc/group file.
my ($groupName,
    $passwd,
```

```
    $gid,
    $memberList) = getgrnam($web_group);

# If the user is a member of this group return a
# nonzero value or else return 0.
   return 1 if ($memberList =~ /$this_user/);
   return 0;
   }

sub log{
#
# Purpose: to provide a simple log.
#

# Get the log entry from the parameter list.
my $entry = shift;

# Append the entry in the log file.
open(FP,">$LOG_FILE") || die "Can't open $LOG_FILE file";
print FP $entry, "\n";
close(FP);
}
```

This script gets a username from its USER environment variable and a password from its PASS environment variable. It then checks to see if the USER belongs to a certain group (web-users) defined in /etc/group. If the user belongs to the group, it checks to see if the password is valid. If both conditions are met, the script returns a zero (0) value or else it returns one (1). Thus the script meets the mod_auth_external module's requirements for an external user authenticator. The checking of the group is added to make sure only users in a certain group (defined in /etc/group) can be authenticated. If you use this script, make sure you never add power users (such as root) in this group.

Now let's see how this script can be used with the mod_auth_external module using the following steps:

STEP 1: *Associating the authcheck authenticator with a keyword*

In the srm.conf file, add the following lines:

```
AddExternalAuth myauth /usr/local/bin/authcheck
SetExternalAuthMethod myauth environment
```

This tells Apache that `myauth` (keyword) is associated with the Perl script authcheck, and the SetExternalAuthMethod tells Apache to use environment to pass data to the authenticator associated with `myauth`.

STEP 2: *Creating the directory access configuration*

To restrict access to a directory using the external authenticator, add the following configuration in an .htacess file:

```
AuthType Basic
AuthName Access for Everyone
AuthExternal myauth
require valid-user
```

The AuthExternal directive tells Apache that the authenticator for this directory is identified by the keyword myauth (which refers to the authcheck script). The require line tells Apache to allow valid users who pass the authentication.

STEP 3: *Testing*

Trying to access the protected directory causes the authentication dialog box to pop up. Entering a valid UNIX account username/-password pair that belongs to the group web-user allows access to the directory.

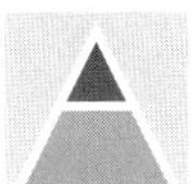

TIP

If you use this script, you can monitor user logins and attempts using the tail command, as follows:

```
tail -f /tmp/authcheck.log
```

Chapter 11

Server Status and Logging

Apache enables you to monitor two types of information via the Web. The information types are:

- Server configuration information
- Server status information

Accessing Server Configuration Status via the Web

Accessing server configuration status can be done using the mod_info module. This module provides a comprehensive overview of the server configuration, including all installed modules and directives in the configuration files. This module is contained in the mod_info.c file. It is not compiled into the server by default. You have to compile it by the usual process of adding the module to the Configuration file and then running the Configure script and the make utility.

The mod_info module provides the AddModuleInfo directive:

```
Syntax: AddModuleInfo module-name descriptive text
Context: server config, virtual host
```

This directive enables you to add descriptive text in the module listing provided by the mod_info module. The descriptive text could be anything including HTML text. For example:

```
AddModuleInfo mod_auth.c 'See <A
HREF="http://www.apache.org/docs/mod/mod_auth.html">http:
//www.apache.org/docs/mod/mod_auth.html</A>'
```

This will show an HTML link next to the listing of mod_auth.c. This link provides a quick way to get more information on the module from the Apache Web site. To view server configuration information via the Web, add the following to your access.conf file:

```
<Location /server-info>
SetHandler server-info
</Location>
```

You may wish to add a <Limit> clause inside the location directive to limit access to your server configuration information. Once configured, the server information is obtained by accessing http://your.host.dom/server-info. This returns a full configuration page for the server and all modules.

To return server configuration only, use:

```
http://your.host.dom/server-info?server
```

To return configuration for a single module, use:

```
http://your.host.dom/server-info?module_name
```

To return a quick list of included modules, use:

```
http://your.host.dom/server-info?list
```

Monitoring Server Status via the Web

Using Apache's Web-based server status monitoring capabilities, you can monitor information such as the server's uptime, total requests served, total data transfer, staus of child processes, and system resource usage. The module mod_status enables Apache administrators to monitor the server via the Web. An HTML page is created with server statistics. It also produces another page that is machine-readable. The information displayed on both pages includes:

- Server version and compilation date/time stamp.
- Current time on the server system
- Time when the server was last restarted
- Server uptime
- Total number of accesses served so far
- Total bytes transferred so far
- The number of idle servers and their status
- Averages giving the number of requests per second, the number of bytes served per second, and the average number of bytes per request
- CPU usage by each child server and total load placed on the server by Apache processes
- The list of virtual hosts and requests currently being processed.

If you do not see all the mentioned fields in the page shown by the status module, you need to add the -DSTATUS option to the AUX_CFLAGS option in the Configuration file and then reconfigure and remake Apache. Note that on some machines, there may be a small performance loss if you do this.

This module is not compiled by default in the standard Apache distribution, so you will need to compile it into your Apache executable (httpd) yourself. Also note that mod_status.c module in Apache 1.3.2 or above comes with the following directive.

```
ExtendedStatus directive
Syntax: ExtendedStatus On|Off
Default: ExtendedStatus Off
Context: server config
```

This directive turns On or Off whether the server keeps track of extended status information for each request.

Once you have the mod_status module compiled and built into your Apache server, you need to define a URL location, which Apache should use to display the information. In other words, you need to tell Apache which URL will bring up the server statistics on your Web browser.

Let's say that your domain name is `yourdomain.com`, and you want to use the following URL:

```
www.mydomain.com/apache-status
```

Using the <Location ...> container, you can tell the server that you want it to handle this URL using the server-status handler found in the mod_status module. The following will do the job:

```
<Location /apache-status>
SetHandler server-status
</Location>
```

In the code above, the SetHandler directive sets the handler (server-status) for the previously mentioned URL. This configuration segment should typically go in the access.conf file, but it really can go inside any of the three configuration files. Once you have added the configuration in one of the three files, you can restart the server and access the preceding URL from a browser. Note that the <Location ...> container in this example enables anyone to see the server status using this URL; this may not be a good thing as far as security is concerned. To make sure that only machines on your domain can access the status page, you can replace the preceding configuration with the following:

```
<Location /apache-status>
SetHandler server-status
order deny, allow
deny from all
allow from .yourdomain.com
</Location>
```

where yourdomain.com should be replaced with your own domain name. If you want only one or more selected hosts to have access to this page, you can simply list the hostnames in the allow directive line.

TIP

You can have the status page update itself automatically if you have a browser that supports the refresh command. Access http://www.yourdomain.com/server-status?refresh=N to refresh the page every N seconds.

Simplifying the Status Display

The status page displayed by the module provides extra information that makes it unsuitable for use as a data file for any data analysis program. For example, if you wanted to create a graph from your server status data using a spreadsheet program, you would need to clean up the data manually; however, the module provides a way for you to create machine-readable output from the same URL.

To simplify the status display, add ?auto at the end of the URL. This query string tells Apache to display simplified output.

Storing Server Status Information

Apache comes with a Perl script (found in the support directory of the source tree) called log_server_status, which can be used to periodically store server status information (using ?auto) in a plain text file.

You can run this script as a cron job to grab the status information on a desired time frequency. Before you can use the script, however, you may have to edit the script source to modify the value of the following configuration variables:

```
$wherelog
$port
$server
$request
```

Change the value of `$wherelog` to a path where you would like to store the file created by the script. The `$port` variable value should be the port number of the server you want to monitor. The default value of 80 is fine if your server is running on this standard HTTP port. The `$server` variable should be assigned the hostname of your server. The default value localhost is fine if the script and the server run on the same system. If the server is on another machine, however, specify the fully qualified hostname (for example, `www.mydomain.com`) as the value. The `$request` variable should be set to whatever you used in the <Location ...> directive plus the `?auto` query string.

If you do not like the record format the script uses, you can modify the following line to fit your needs:

```
print OUT "$time:$requests:$idle:$number:$cpu\n";
```

The script uses a socket connection to the Apache server to send the URL request; therefore, you need to make sure you have socket support for Perl.

Creating Server Log Files

Knowing the status and the configuration information of your server is helpful in managing the server, but knowing who or what is accessing your Web site(s) is also very important, as well as exciting. As Web server software started appearing in the market, many Web server log analysis programs started appearing as well. These programs became part of the everyday work life of many Web administrators. Along with all these came the era of log file incompatibilities, which made log analysis difficult and cumbersome; a single analysis program didn't work on all log files. Then came the Common Log Format (CLF) specification. This enabled all Web servers to write logs in a reasonably similar manner, thus making log analysis easier from one server to another.

By default, the standard Apache distribution includes a module called mod_log_config, which is responsible for the basic logging, and it writes CLF log files by default. You can alter this behavior using the LogFormat directive. However, CLF covers logging requirements in most environments.

The CLF file contains a separate line for each request. A line is composed of several tokens separated by spaces:

```
host ident authuser date request status bytes
```

If a token does not have a value, then it is represented by a hyphen (-). Tokens have the following meanings:

- **Host.** The fully qualified domain name of the client, or its IP address
- **Ident.** If the IdentityCheck directive is enabled and the client machine runs identd, then this is the identity information reported by the client
- **Authuser.** If the requested URL required a successful Basic HTTP authentication, then the username is the value of this token
- **Date.** The date and time of the request
- **Request.** The request line from the client, enclosed in double quotes (")
- **Status.** The three-digit HTTP status code returned to the client
- **bytes.** The number of bytes in the object returned to the client, excluding all HTTP headers.

See Appendix A for a list of all HTTP/1.1 status codes.

The date field can have the following format:

```
date = [day/month/year:hour:minute:second zone]
```

For example:

```
[02/Jan/1998:00:22:01 -0800]
```

Date's field sizes are:

Day	2 digits
Month	3 letters
Year	4 digits
Hour	2 digits
Minute	2 digits
Second	2 digits
Zone	(`+' | `-') 4*digit

There are four directives available in the mod_log_config module:

CookieLog

Syntax: `CookieLog filename`

Context: `server config, virtual host`

The CookieLog directive sets the filename for logging cookies. The filename is relative to the ServerRoot. This directive is included only for compatibility with mod_cookies and is deprecated. Therefore, I don't recommend that you use this directive. Use the user-tracking module's directive instead. The user-tracking module mod_usertrack is discussed later in this chapter.

CustomLog

Syntax: `CustomLog file-pipe format-or-nickname`

Context: `server config, virtual host`

Like the TransferLog directive, this directive enables you to send logging information to a log file or an external program. Unlike the TransferLog directive, however, it enables you to use a custom log format that can be specified as an argument.

The argument format specifies a format for each line of the log file. The options available for the format are exactly the same as for the argument of the LogFormat directive. If the format includes any spaces (which it will do in almost all cases), it should be enclosed in double quotes.

Instead of an actual format string, you can use a format nickname defined with the LogFormat directive.

Nicknames are available only in Apache 1.3 or later. Also, the TransferLog and CustomLog directives can be used multiple times in each server to cause each request to be logged to multiple files.

LogFormat

Syntax: `LogFormat format [nickname]`

Default: `LogFormat "%h %l %u %t \"%r\" %s %b"`

`Context: server config, virtual host`

This directive sets the format of the default log file named by the TransferLog directive. If you include a nickname for the format on the directive line, you can use it in other LogFormat and CustomLog directives rather than repeating the entire format string. A LogFormat directive that defines a nickname does nothing else — that is, it only defines the nickname, it doesn't actually apply the format.

See the "Customizing Your Log Files" section later in this chapter for details on the formatting options available.

TransferLog

Syntax: `TransferLog filename | "| \`
`/path/to/external/program"`

Default: `none`

Context: `server config, virtual host`

This directive sets the name of the log file or program where the log information is to be sent. By default, the log information is in the Common Log File (CLF) format. This format can be customized using the LogFormat directive.

When the TransferLog directive is found within a virtual host container, the log information is formatted using the LogFormat directive found within the context. If a LogFormat directive is not found in the same context, however, the server's log format is used.

The TransferLog directive takes either a log file path or a pipe to an external program as the argument. The log filename is assumed to be relative to the ServerRoot setting if no leading forward slash (/) character is found. For example, if the ServerRoot is set to /etc/httpd, then the following tells Apache to send log information to the /etc/httpd/logs/access.log file:

```
TransferLog logs/access.log
```

When the argument is a pipe to an external program, the log information is sent to the external program's standard input (STDIN).

Note that a new program is not started for a VirtualHost if it inherits the TransferLog from the main server. If a program is used, then it is run under the user who started HTTPD. This will be the root if the server was started by the root. Be sure that the program is secure.

Customizing Server Log Files

Although CLF meets most log requirements, sometimes it is useful to be able to customize logging data. For example, you may want to log the type of browsers that are accessing your site so that your Web design team can determine what type of browser-specific HTML to avoid or use. Or, perhaps you want to know which Web sites are sending (that is, referring) visitors to your sites. All this is accomplished quite easily in Apache. The default logging module, mod_log_config, supports custom logging.

Custom formats are set with the LogFormat and CustomLog directives of the module. The format argument to LogFormat and CustomLog is a string. This format string can have both literal characters and special percent sign (%) format specifiers. When literal values are used in this string, they are copied into the log file for each request. The % specifiers, however, are replaced with corresponding values. The special % specifiers are:

%b	Bytes sent, excluding HTTP headers
%f	The filename of the request
%{VARIABLE}e	The contents of the environment variable VARIABLE
%h	The remote host that made the request
%{ IncomingHeader }i	The contents of Incoming Header—that is, the header line(s) in the request sent to the server. The i character at the end denotes that this is a client (incoming) header.
%l	If the IdentityCheck directive is enabled and the client machine runs identd, then this is the identity information reported by the client.
%{MODULE_NOTE }n	The contents of the note MODULE_NOTE from another module
%{ OutgoingHeader }o	The contents of OutgoingHeader—that is, the header line(s) in the reply. The o character at the end denotes that this is a server (outgoing) header.
%p	The port to which the request was served
%P	The process ID of the child that serviced the request
%r	The first line of the request

%s	Status returned by the server in response to the request. Note that when the request gets redirected, the value of this format specifier is still the original request status. If you want to store the redirected request status, use %..>s instead.
%t	Time of the request. The format of time is the same as in CLF format.
%{format}t	The time, in the form given by format. (You can look at the man page of strftime on UNIX systems.)
%t	The time taken to serve the request, in seconds.
%u	If the requested URL required a successful Basic HTTP authentication, then the username is the value of this format specifier. The value may be bogus if the server returned a 401 status (Authentication Required) after the authentication attempt.
%u	The URL path requested
%v	The name of the server or the virtual host to which the request came

It is possible to include conditional information in each of the preceding specifiers. The conditions can be presence (or absence) of certain HTTP status code(s). For example, let's say you want to log all referring URLs that pointed a user to a nonexistent page. In such a case, the server produces a 404 status (Not Found) header. So, to log the referring URLs you can use the format specifier:

```
'%404{Referer}i'
```

Similarly, to log referring URLs that resulted in an unusual status, you can use:

```
'%!200,304,302{Referer}i'
```

Notice the use of the ! character to denote the absence of the server status list.

Similarly, to include additional information at the end of the CLF format specifier, you can extend the CLF format, which is defined by the format string:

```
"%h %l %u %t \"%r\" %s %b"
```

For example:

```
"%h %l %u %t \"%r\" %s %b \"%{Referer}i\" \"%{User- \
agent}i\""
```

This format specification logs CLF format data and adds the Referer and User-agent information found in client-provided headers in each log entry.

Creating Multiple Log Files

Sometimes it is necessary to create multiple log files. For example, if you are using a log analysis program that cannot handle non-CLF data, you may want to write the non-CLF data to a different file. You can create multiple log files very easily using the TransferLog and/or the CustomLog directive of the mod_log_config module. Simply repeat these directives to create more than one log file.

If, for example, you want to create a standard CLF access log and a custom log of all referring URLs, then you can use something like the following:

```
TransferLog logs/access_log
CustomLog   logs/referrer_log     "%{Referer}i"
```

When you have either TransferLog or CustomLog defined in the primary server configuration, and you have a virtual host defined, the virtual host-related logging also is performed in those logs. For example:

```
TransferLog logs/access_log
CustomLog   logs/agents_log     "%{User-agent}i"
<Virtual Host 206.171.50.51>
ServerName reboot.nitec.com
DocumentRoot  /www/reboot/public/htdocs
ScriptAlias /cgi-bin/ /www/reboot/public/cgi-bin/
</VirtualHost>
```

Here, the virtual host `reboot.nitec.com` does not have a TransferLog or CustomLog directive defined within the virtual host container tags. All logging information will be stored in the LOG/ACCESS_LOG and the LOGS/AGENTS_LOG. If the following line is added inside the virtual host container:

```
TransferLog vhost_logs/reboot_access_log
```

then all logging for the virtual host `reboot.nitec.com` is done in vhost_logs/reboot_access_log file. None of the log/access_log and logs/agents_log files will be used for `reboot.nitec.com`.

Storing Specific Information

This section introduces you to a few more logging-specific modules that provide features that are already available from the default logging module (mod_log_config). The information is provided for completeness and backward compatibility purposes.

Storing User-Agent Information

Apache provides another module called mod_log_agent to enable you to store user agent (Web browsers, robots) information in a separate log file. This module is not compiled into standard Apache distribution, so you need to add it to your Apache executable as usual. The module provides a single directive, the AgentLog directive:

```
Syntax: AgentLog filename | "| /path/to/external/program"
Default: AgentLog logs/agent_log
Context: server config, virtual host
```

This directive tells Apache the file or program name to be used to send the UserAgent header for incoming requests. As with the TransferLog directive, you can provide either a log filename or a fully qualified pathname to a program.

When using the CustomLog directive, you can add the %{User agent}i format specifier to log the UserAgent header without the use of this module. In other words, this module does not provide any functionality that is not present in the standard mod_log_config module. If this module had a way of ignoring local accesses made by you and people on your network, then the data would be more interesting.

Storing Referer Information

Knowing who referred a visitor to your Web site is helpful, because it gives you an idea of who your friends are on the Web. It also may help you decide where you should spend your advertising dollars.

Being able to tell who forwarded a request to your Web site is a great advantage in establishing Web relationships with others. If you are receiving many referrals from a particular Web site, you may want to be courteous and provide a link from your Web site to theirs. Remember to ask their permission first, however. On the other hand, if you are getting referrals from Web sites that you either do not care for or do not want to be associated with, you can determine these Web sites from your log and politely request that they remove references that point to your site.

The mod_log_referer provides you with the facility to log the incoming Referer headers from requests. Of course, the standard mod_log_config with the CustomLog directive enables you to do the same using the %{Referer}I format specifier. So, what's the advantage of using this module? Well, this module, unlike mod_log_config, enables you to ignore certain hosts. This way, you can log only your real users and not references from your own host(s).

You need to compile this module into your Apache executable by yourself. It provides the following directives.

RefererLog

Syntax: `RefererLog filename | "| \`
`/path/to/external/program"`
Default: `RefererLog logs/referer_log`
Context: `server config, virtual host`

This directive sets the name of the log file or program that receives the Referer headers of incoming requests.

See the TransferLog details later in this chapter for more information about the path restrictions and how to use the external program.

RefererIgnore

Syntax: `RefererIgnore string string ...`
Context: `server config, virtual host`

The RefererIgnore directive adds to the list of strings to be ignored in Referer headers. If any of the strings in the list are contained in the Referer header, then no referrer information will be logged for the request. For example:

```
RefererIgnore yourcompany.com
```

This avoids logging references from `yourcompany.com`. If `yourcompany.com` is the domain name for your internal network, you will be able to ignore all references that have been generated from within your network.

The log file format is quite simple. It contains a separate line for each referral. Each line has the following format:

```
uri -> document
```

where uri is the (%-escaped) URI for the document that references the one requested by the client, and document is the (%-decoded) local URL to the document being referred to.

Storing Cookies

So far, I have talked about quite a few logging options. None of these enable you to uniquely identify visitors. This is important, because if you know which requests are made by which visitor, it gives you a better idea of how your content is being used. For example, say that you have a really cool page on your Web site, and you have a way to identify the visitors in your logs. If you look at your log and see that many visitors have to go from one page to another to find the cool page at the end, you might reconsider your site design and make that cool page available sooner in the click stream. Apache has a module called mod_usertrack that enables you to track your Web site visitor by logging HTTP cookies.

An HTTP cookie is not made with cookie dough. It is simply a piece of information that the server gives to the Web browser. This information is usually stored in a key=value pair and can be associated with an entire Web site or a particular URL on a Web site. Once a cookie is issued by the server and accepted by the Web browser, the cookie resides in the Web browser system. Every time the Web browser requests the same URL, or any URL that falls under the domain or path of the cookie URL, the cookie information is returned to the server. When setting the cookie, the server can tell the Web browser to expire the cookie after a certain time. The time can be specified so that the cookie is never used in a later session, or it can be used for a long period of time.

There has been much controversy over the use of cookies. Many consider cookies as a intrusion of privacy. Using cookies to track user behavior has become widely popular. In fact, several advertisement companies on the Internet make heavy use of cookies to track users. It should be stressed that cookies themselves cannot cause any harm. The cookie data is usually written in a text file in a directory of your browser software.

There used to be a module called mod_cookies, which is now known as mod_usertrack. However, the previous version of the module performed its own logging using the CookieLog directive, which is no longer supported in this module. Instead, a much better way of logging cookies is available in the standard mod_log_config module.

For example, using the CustomLog directive in the standard logging module, you can store the cookies in a separate file:

```
CustomLog logs/clickstream "%{cookie}n %r %t"
```

For backward compatibility, the configurable log module implements the old CookieLog directive, but this should be upgraded to the preceding CustomLog directive.

Remember that mod_usertrack does not save a log of cookies; it just generates unique cookies for each visitor. You can use CustomLog (as shown earlier) to store these cookies in a log file for analysis.

The mod_usertrack directive is not compiled into the standard distribution version of Apache, so you need to compile it before you can use it. The module provides the following directives.

CookieExpires

Syntax: `CookieExpires expiry-period`
Context: `server config, virtual host`

This directive is used to set the expiration period of the cookies that are generated by the module. The expiration period can be defined in terms of number of seconds, or in a format such as "1 month 2 days 3 hours." For example:

```
CookieExpires 3600
CookieExpires "2 days 3 hours"
```

In the code above, the first directive defines the expiration period in seconds, and the second one defines the expiration period using the special format. Note that when the expiration period is not defined in a numeric form, the special form is assumed. However, the special format requires that you put double quotes around the format string. If this directive is not used, cookies last only for the current browser session.

CookieTracking

Syntax: `CookieTracking on | off`
Context: `server config, virtual host, directory, per-directory configuration file ( .htaccess)`
Override: `FileInfo`

This directive enables or disables the generation of automatic cookies. When it is set to on, Apache starts sending a user-tracking cookie for all new requests.

The CookieTracking directive can be used to turn this behavior on or off on a per-server or per-directory basis. By default, compiling mod_usertrack does not activate cookies.

Using Error Logs

In this chapter I have talked about many ways of logging various interesting data. However, one important logging feature you must enable on your Web site is error logs. Without logging errors, you will be unable to determine what's wrong and where the error occurs.

Interestingly, error logging is supported in the core Apache. The ErrorLog directive enables you to log all types of errors that Apache encounters.

In this section, we look at how you can incorporate your Apache error logs into the widely used syslog facility found on almost all UNIX platforms.

Syslog is the traditional way of logging messages sent out by daemon (server) processes. You may ask, "Apache is a daemon, so why can't it write to syslog?" It can, actually. All you need to do is replace your existing ErrorLog directive in the configuration file with the message below and then restart Apache.:

```
ErrorLog syslog
```

Using a Web browser, access a nonexistent page on your Web server and watch the syslog log file to see if it shows an httpd entry. You should take a look at your /etc/syslog.conf file for clues about where the httpd messages will appear.

For example, Listing 11-1 shows /etc/syslog.conf for a Linux system.

Listing 11-1 */etc/syslog.conf*

```
# Log all kernel messages to the console.
# Logging much else clutters up the screen.
 kern.*                                         /dev/console

# Log anything (except mail) of level info or higher.
# Don't log private authentication messages!
*.info;mail.none;authpriv.none             /var/log/messages

# The authpriv file has restricted access.
authpriv.*                                   /var/log/secure

# Log all the mail messages in one place.
mail.*                                     /var/log/maillog

# Write emergency messages on each file.
# machine.
*.emerg                                      *

# Save mail and news errors of level err and higher in a
# special file.
uucp,news.crit                             /var/log/spooler
```

There are two important lines (as far as Apache is concerned) in this listing. They are:

```
*.info;mail.none;authpriv.none          /var/log/messages
*.emerg                                 *
```

The first line tells syslog to write all messages of the info type (except for mail and private authentication) to the /var/log/messages file, and the second line states that all emergency messages should be written to all log files. Using the LogLevel directive, you can specify what type of messages Apache should send to syslog. For example:

```
ErrorLog syslog
LogLevel debug
```

Above, Apache is instructed to send debug messages to syslog. If you want to store debug messages in a different file via syslog, then you need to modify /etc/syslog.conf. For example:

```
*.debug                          /var/log/debug
```

Add this line in /etc/syslog.conf, restart syslogd (kill -HUP syslogd PID), and Apache will enable you to store all Apache debug messages to the /var/log/debug file. There are several log level settings:

- **Emerg.** Emergency messages
- **Alert.** Alert messages
- **Crit.** Critical messages
- **Error.** Error messages
- **Warn.** Warnings
- **Notice.** Notification messages
- **Info.** Information messages
- **Debug.** Messages logged at debug level will also include the source file and line number where the message is generated to help debugging and code development.

TIP

If you wanted to see updates to your syslog or any other log files as they happen, you can use the tail utility found on most UNIX systems. For example, if you wanted to see updates for a log called /VAR/LOG/HTTPD_ERRORS as they occur, use:

```
tail -f /var/log/httpd_errors
```

Analyzing Server Log Files

Your log analysis needs may vary. Sometimes you may need to produce extensive reports, or maybe you just want to do a simple checking on the logs. For simple tasks, it is best to use whatever is available at hand. Most UNIX systems have enough utilities and scripting tools available to do the job.

Let's take a look at using a UNIX utility to get a list of all the hosts. If you use the default logging facility or a custom log with CLF support, you can find a list of all the hosts quite easily. For example:

```
cat /path/to/httpd/access_log | awk '{print $1}'
```

prints out all the host IP addresses (if you have DNS lookup enabled, then host aliases are shown). The cat utility lists the access_log file, and the resulting output is piped to the awk interpreter, which prints out only the first field in each line using the print statement. This prints all the hosts — but what if you wanted to exclude the hosts on your network? In that case, you would use:

```
cat /path/to/httpd/access_log | awk '{print $1}'  | egrep\
-v '(^206.171.50)'
```

where 206.171.50 should be replaced with your network address. Note that here, I assume you have a class C network. If you have a class B network, you need to use only the first two octets of your IP addresses. This version enables you to exclude your own hosts using the egrep utility, which is told to display (via -v) only the hosts that do not start with the 206.171.50 network address. This still may not be satisfactory, however, because there are likely to be repeats. Therefore, thc final version is as follows:

```
cat /path/to/httpd/access_log | awk '{print $1}'  | uniq\
| egrep -v '(^206.171.50)'
```

Here, the uniq utility filters out repeats and shows you only one listing per host. Of course, if you wanted to see the total number of unique hosts that have accessed your Web site, you can pipe the final result to the wc utility with a -l option as follows:

```
cat /path/to/httpd/access_log | awk '{print $1}'  | uniq\
| egrep -v '(^206.171.50)' | wc -l
```

This gives you the total line count (that is, the number of unique host accesses).

Using UNIX utilities, you can quickly grab needed information; however, this method requires some UNIX know-how, and is not always convenient because your boss may want a pretty report instead of some dry textual listing. In such a case, you can either develop your own analysis programs or use third-party analysis tools.

Many third-party Web server log analysis tools are available. Most of these tools expect the log files to be in CLF format, so make sure you have CLF formatting in your logs. Here are some of those tools and where you can find them:

WebTrends	`www.webtrends.com/`
Wusage	`www.boutell.com/wusage/`
wwwstat	`www.ics.uci.edu/pub/websoft/wwwstat/`
http-analyze	`www.netstore.de/Supply/http-analyze/`
pwebstats	`www.unimelb.edu.au/pwebstats.html`
WebStat Explorer	`www.webstat.com/`
AccessWatch	`http://netpressence.com/accesswatch/`

The best way to find out which one will work for you is to try them out, or at least visit their Web sites for feature comparisons. Two utilities that I find very useful are Wusage and wwwstat.

Wusage is my favorite commercial log analysis application. It is highly configurable and produces great graphical reports using the company's well-known GD graphics library. Wusage is distributed in a binary format. Evaluation copies of Wusage are provided free for many UNIX and Windows platform.

One of the freely available analysis programs that I prefer is wwwstat. It is written in Perl, so you need to have Perl installed on the system on which you want to run this application. The wwwstat output summaries can be read by gwstat to produce fancy graphs of the summarized statistics.

Maintaining Server Log Files

Creating logs in Apache is easy and useful, and they help you learn more about what's going on with your Apache server. Logs can help you detect problems, identify your site's problems, find out about your site's best features, and much more. Can something so beneficial come without a catch? If you said no, you guessed right. Log files take up a lot of valuable disk space, so they must be maintained regularly.

On Apache sites with high hit rates or many virtual domains, the log files can become huge in a very short time, which could easily cause a disk crisis. When log files become very large, you should rotate them.

You have two options for rotating your logs: you can use a utility that comes with Apache called rotatelog, or you can use logrotate, a facility that is available on most Linux systems.

Using rotatelog

Apache comes with a support tool called rotatelog. You can use this program as follows:

```
TransferLog "| /path/to/rotatelogs <logfile> <rotation
time in seconds>"
```

For example, if you want to rotate the access log every 86,400 seconds (that is, 24 hours), use the following line:

```
TransferLog "| /path/to/rotatelogs /var/logs/httpd 86400"
```

You will have each day's access log information stored in a file called /var/logs/httpd.nnnn, where nnnn represents a long number.

Using logrotate

The logrotate utility rotates, compresses, and mails log files. It is designed to ease the system administration of log files. It enables the automatic rotation, compression, removal, and mailing of log files on a daily, weekly, or monthly basis or on a size basis. Normally, logrotate is run as a daily cron job. Read the man pages for logrotate to learn more about it.

If your system supports the logrotate facility, you should have a configuration similar to what is shown in your /etc/logrotate.conf file:

```
/path/to/httpd/access_log {
compress
rotate 5
main webmaster@yourdomain.com
   errors root@yourdomain.com
size=1024K
postrotate
               kill -HUP 'cat /path/to/httpd.pid'
endscript
}
```

This configuration specifies that the /path/to/httpd/access_log file be rotated whenever it grows over one megabyte (1024K) in size, and that the old log files be compressed and mailed to `webmaster@yourdomain.com` after going through five rotations, rather than being removed. Any errors that occur during processing of the log file are mailed to `root@yourdomain.com`.

Chapter 12

Web Security

Reducing CGI Risks

The biggest security risk on the Web comes in the form of CGI applications. CGI (Common Gateway Interface) is not inherently insecure, but poorly written CGI applications are a major source of Web security holes. Actually, the simplicity of the CGI specification makes it easy for many inexperienced programmers to write CGI applications. These inexperienced programmers, being unaware of the security aspects of Internetworking, create applications that work but also create hidden back doors and holes on the system on which the applications run.

Following are the three most common security risks that CGI applications may create:

- **Information leaks.** Such leaks help hackers break into a system. The more information a hacker knows about a system, the better he or she gets at breaking into the system.
- **Execution of system commands via CGI applications.** In many cases, remote users have successfully tricked an HTML form-based mailer script to run a system command or give out confidential system information.
- **Consumption of system resources.** A poorly written CGI application can be made to consume so many system resources that the server becomes virtually unresponsive.

Of course, you should take careful steps in developing or installing CGI applications when your Apache server will run these applications as an unprivileged user, but even carefully written applications can be a security risk.

Most of the security holes created by CGI applications are caused by user input.

Protecting CGI Applications from Bad User Input

One type of user input problem occurs when coding practices permit buffers to overflow when reading input. This can create a major security hole, because a program that overflows a buffer will crash, allowing many expert hackers to take advantage of the crashed program to gain access to a system. Character buffer overflow is actually more common in languages such as C and C++.

Listing 12-1 shows a C function that makes an assumption that user-posted (via the HTTP POST method) input can be only up to 1,024 characters (bytes) and, therefore, is sufficient to declare an array of size 1,024. This wrong assumption forces this program to crash or behave wildly when a user enters a great deal of data in the input.

Listing 12-1 *A risky C function to get POST data*

```
#include <stdio.h>
#include <stdlib.h>
static char query_string[1024];

char* POST() {
/*
Function to read input that has been POSTED
from an HTML form.
*/
```

```
/*Local integer variable */
int size;

/*
Use getenv() function to get the value of
the environment variable CONTENT_LENGTH
which holds the byte count for the form input
data stored in the STDIN. Convert the
resulting string value of genet() to an integer
using the atoi() function and return the value
to the size variable.
*/

size=atoi(getenv("CONTENT_LENGTH"));

/*
Read the input data from the standard input.
*/
fread(query_string, size,1,stdin);

/* Return the string buffer
holding the data.
*/

return query_string;
}
```

When a user enters data exceeding 1,024 bytes, this routine will break the program and increase the possibility of a major security hole. In some circumstances, the crash can be exploited by the hacker to execute commands remotely.

This problem can be removed by making sure the memory allocation for the data storage (query_string) happens dynamically using a call to the malloc() or calloc() function.

Stopping Systems Calls Embedded in Bad User Input

Another user-input problem results when a user makes a request in which a system call opens subshells to process a command. For example, in Perl (a widely used CGI programming language) such a call could be made using system(), exec(), piped open() function, and eval() functions. Similarly, in C, the popen(), and system() functions are potential security hazards. All of these functions/commands typically invoke a subshell (such as /bin/sh) to process the user command.

Even shell scripts using system(), exec() calls are likely to open entry portals for hackers. Note that backtick quotes, available in shell interpreters and Perl for capturing the output of programs as text strings, also are dangerous.

To illustrate the importance of careful use of system calls, take a look at this innocent-looking Perl code segment shown in Listing 12-2.

Listing 12-2 *Example of bad system calls in a Perl script*

```
#!/usr/local/bin/perl
#
# Purpose: to demonstrate security risks in
# poorly written CGI scripts.
#

# Get the domain name from query string
# environment variable.
#
my $domain = $ENV{'QUERY_STRING'};

# Print the appropriate content type. Since
# whois output is in plain text
# we choose to use text/plain as the
# content-type here.
```

```
#
print "Content-type: text/plain\n\n";

# Here is the bad system call:
system("/usr/bin/whois $domain");

# Here is another bad system call using
# back-ticks:
#
# my $output = `/usr/bin/whois $domain`;
#
# print $output;
exit 0;
```

This little Perl script is supposed to be a Web-based WHOIS gateway. If this script is called script.pl and is kept in the cgi-bin directory of a Web site called `www.notsecured.com`, a user can call this script as follows:

```
http://domain/cgi-bin/script.pl?anydomain.com
```

The script will take the `anydomain.com` as the $domain variable via the QUERY_STRING variable and launch the /usr/bin/whois program with the $domain value as the argument. This will return the data from the WHOIS database that InterNIC maintains. This is all very innocent and good, but the script is a disaster waiting to happen.

Consider the following line:

```
http://domain/cgi-bin/script.pl?nitec.com;ps
```

This does a WHOIS lookup on a domain called `nitec.com` and also provides the output of the UNIX ps utility that shows process status. This reveals information about the system that should not be available to the requesting party. Using this technique, anyone can find out a great deal about your system. For example, replacing the ps command with df (a common UNIX utility that prints a summary of disk space) will enable anyone to determine what partitions you have and how full they are. I will leave to your imagination the real dangers this security hole could pose.

What is the lesson here? The lesson is not to trust any input and not to make system calls an easy target for abuse. Next, I show you how you can achieve these goals.

Scan for Illegal Characters

There are two approaches in making sure user input is safe. One of these approaches is to scan the input for illegal characters and replace or remove them. For example, for the previous whois.pl script, you can add the following line:

```
$domain =~ s/[\/ ;\[\]\<\>&\t]//g;
```

This will remove illegal metacharacters. This is a common but inadvisable approach, as it requires that the programmer be aware of all possible combinations of characters that could cause trouble. If the user uses input not predicted by the programmer, there is the possibility that the program may be used in a manner not intended by the programmer.

Define Acceptable Characters

A better approach is to define a list of acceptable characters and replace or remove any character that is not acceptable. The list of valid input values is typically a predictable, well-defined set of manageable size.

This approach does not require the programmer to trap all characters that are unacceptable, leaving no margin for error. In the recommended approach, a programmer must only ensure that acceptable characters are identified, and can be less concerned about the characters an attacker may try in an attempt to bypass security checks.

Building on this philosophy, the Perl program presented earlier could be sanitized to contain only those characters allowed, for example:

```
#!/usr/local/bin/perl
#
# This is a better version of the previous
# whois.pl script.
#
# Assign a variable the acceptable character
# set for domain names.
#
my $DOMAIN_CHAR_SET='-a-zA-Z0-9_.';

# Get the domain name from query string
# environment variable.
#
my $domain = $ENV{'QUERY_STRING'};

# Now remove any character that does not belong to the
# acceptable character set.
$domain =~ s/[^$DOMAIN_CHAR_SET]//g;

# Print the appropriate content type.
# Since whois output is in plain text, we
# choose to use text/plain as the content-type
# here.
#
print "Content-type: text/plain\n\n";

# Here is the system call:
system("/usr/bin/whois $domain");

# Here is another system call using back-ticks:
#
# my $output = `/usr/bin/whois $domain`;
#
# print $output;
exit 0;
```

The $DOMAIN_CHAR_SET variable holds the acceptable character set, and the user-input variable $domain is searched for anything that does not fall in the set. The unacceptable character is removed.

The best way to go about user input is to establish rules for each input (that is, what you expect and how you can determine what you have received is acceptable). If you are expecting an e-mail address as input, rather than just scanning it blindly for shell metacharacters, for example, use a regular expression such as the following to detect the validity of the input as a possible e-mail address:

```
$email = $input{'email-addr'};
if ($email=~ /^[\w-\.]+\@[\w-\.]+$/) {
       print "Possibly valid address."
       }
else {
       print "Invalid email address.";
       }
```

Invoke External Programs Carefully

Just sanitizing user input is not enough. You need to be careful about how you invoke external programs. There are many ways you can invoke external programs in Perl.

Using backticks, you can capture the output of an external program, such as:

```
$list = "/bin/ls -l /etc";
```

This captures the /etc directory listing. Or, you can open a pipe to a program, such as:

```
open (FP, " | /usr/bin/sort");
```

You also can invoke an external program and wait for it to return with system():

```
system "/usr/bin/lpr data.dat";
```

or you can invoke an external program and never return with exec():

```
exec "/usr/bin/sort < data.dat";
```

All of these constructions can be risky if they involve user input that may contain shell metacharacters. For system() and exec(), there's a somewhat obscure syntactical feature that enables you to call external programs directly rather than going through a shell. If you pass the arguments to the external program (not in one long string, but as separate elements in a list), Perl will not go through the shell, and shell metacharacters will have no unwanted side effects, as follows:

```
system "/usr/bin/sort", "data.dat";
```

You can take advantage of this feature to open up a pipe without going through a shell. By calling open the character sequence -|, you fork a copy of Perl and open a pipe to the copy. Then, the child copy immediately forks another program using the first argument of the exec function call.

To read from a pipe without opening up a shell, you can do something similar with the sequence -|:

```
open(GREP,"-|") || exec
"/usr/bin/grep",$userpattern,$filename;
while (<GREP>) {
  print "match: $_";
  }
close GREP;
```

These forms of open()s are more secure than the piped open()s and, therefore, you should use these whenever applicable.

There are many other obscure features in Perl that enable you to call an external program and lie to it about its name. This is useful for calling programs that behave differently depending on the name by which they were invoked. The syntax is as follows:

```
system $real_name "fake_name","argument1","argument2"
```

One trick used by hackers is to alter the PATH environment variable so it points to the program they want your script to execute, rather than the program you're expecting. You should invoke programs using full pathnames rather than relying on the PATH environment variable. That is, instead of this fragment of Perl code:

```
system("cat /tmp/shopping.cart.txt");
```

use this:

```
system "/bin/cat" , "/tmp/shopping.cart.txt";
```

If you must rely on the PATH, set it yourself at the beginning of your CGI application, as follows:

```
$ENV{'PATH'}="bin:/usr/bin:/usr/local/bin";
```

Even if you don't rely on the path when you invoke an external program, there's a chance that the invoked program will; therefore, you need to include the previous line toward the top of your script whenever you use taint checks. Note that you will have to adjust the line as necessary for the list of directories you want searched. Also note that in general, it's not a good idea to put the current directory (.) into the path.

Use Perl's Taint Checking

One of the most frequent security problems in CGI applications is inadvertently passing unchecked user variables to the shell. Perl provides a *taint-checking* mechanism that prevents you from doing this. Any variable assigned data from outside the program (including data from the environment, from standard input, and from the command line) is considered tainted and cannot be used to affect anything else outside your program. The taint can spread. If you use a tainted variable to set the value of another variable, the second variable also becomes tainted. Tainted variables cannot be used in eval(), system(), exec(), or piped open() calls. If you try to do so, Perl exits with a warning message. Perl also will exit if you attempt to call an external program without explicitly setting the PATH environment variable.

You turn on taint checks in Perl 5 by using a -T flag in the interpreter call line:

```
#!/usr/local/bin/perl -T
```

As mentioned before, once a variable is tainted, Perl won't permit you to use it in a system(), exec(), piped open, eval(), or backtick command (or any other function that affects something outside of the program, such as unlink). You can't use it even if you scan it for shell metacharacters or use the tr/// or s/// commands to remove metacharacters. The only way to untaint a tainted variable is to perform a pattern-matching operation on it and extract the matched substrings. For example, if you expect a variable to contain an e-mail address, you can extract an untainted copy of the address in this way:

```
$e-mail=~/([\w-\.]+\@[\w-\.]+)/;
$untainted_address = $1;
```

Therefore, turning on taint checking in Perl is a good idea.

The rule of thumb is to avoid passing direct user input to external programs, because they might contain hidden commands that do harm. Try to avoid using system calls that open subshells to do the work. Always scan the input for shell metacharacters and remove them from the input.

User Sees HIDDEN Data

Another form of input-related danger has to do with the misconception about the HIDDEN HTML input fields. CGI applications that require a lot of user input often ask the user for a few inputs, do some processing based on the input, and later ask for another set of inputs. Because CGI applications are run per request, they are unable to maintain what the user has entered in the last invocation. To solve this problem, many CGI programmers store the previous input data in the output HTML using HIDDEN input fields. An HTML hidden-input record looks like the following:

```
<INPUT TYPE=HIDDEN NAME="variable" VALUE="value">
```

There is nothing wrong with using this method, but beware that, although supposedly hidden, they are not. Any user can see these using the View Source option found in many browsers. Make sure that the data you store to maintain the state between CGI application invocations is not sensitive. In other words, do not store any PATH, filename, username, or password in these fields.

Stopping Denial of Service Attacks

The most common type of security attack is the denial of service (DOS) attack. This type of attack makes a system unavailable or nonresponsive to honest users or paying customers. Such an attack can be mounted on CGI applications, as well.

Most CGI applications take user-input data, perform some processing, and later return some output. Because these programs can be run by anyone via the Web, they are game for DOS attacks. An ill-minded user need only call a CGI application on your Web server with whatever input it needs to process and get it started. Then he or she can make repetitive calls to the same, or other, CGI applications to make your Web server launch many CGI processes along with child server processes.

This can potentially consume a lot of resources on your server system and make it less responsive to the good-natured users. This type of attack is easy to launch from any university computer laboratory where there are a lot of computers and a great deal of bandwidth available. A small Perl script can launch an HTTP request to your server and keep repeating the same request over and over. If this is done from multiple machines, it can bring the Web server system to a crawl. How can you correct this situation?

Unfortunately, there is not much you can do to prevent this; however, once such an incident takes place, you can ban the hosts that were responsible. You can use Apache's <Limit ..> container to deny access to these hosts.

You also can use the RLimitCPU and RLimitMEM directives to fine-tune Apache's CPU and memory usage.

Disabling HTML Posting on Your Site

Another common form of CGI vandalism rampant on the Web is seen on Web sites that enable any user to write texts that later get posted on the Web site. For example, Web sites that use Web-based CGI discussion groups or CGI guest books are likely to fall victim to vandalism. If any of your CGI applications enable users to write anything that gets posted on your Web site, make sure you have disabled HTML tag entries in any input a user can enter. The simplest way to disable HTML in Perl is to replace the less-than symbol (<) with <. This way, when rendered on a Web browser, the actual HTML tag appears instead of its being interpreted by the browser. The following Perl code segment does exactly that:

```
$user_input=~ s/</&lt;/g;
```

Many vandals finds sites that permit writing to guest books, usually entering HTML tags that link to obscene sites or a large image to make each real user suffer the time it takes to load the page. It also is possible to embed a JavaScript in a guest book entry, which could cause serious annoyance to a good user. Replacing the < character with < will take care of all these nuisances.

Limiting CGI Risks with Wrappers

The best way to reduce CGI-related risks is not to run any CGI applications at all; however, in the days of dynamic Web content, this could be suicide! Perhaps you can centralize all CGI applications in one location and closely monitor their development to ensure they are well written.

In many cases, especially on Internet Service Provider systems, all of the users with Web sites want CGI access. In this case, it might be a good idea to run CGI applications under the user ID of the user who owns the CGI application. By default, CGI applications that Apache runs use the Apache user ID. If you run these applications using the owner's user ID, all possible damage is limited to what the user ID is permitted to access. In other words, a bad CGI application run with a user ID other than the Apache server user ID, can only damage the user's files. The user responsible for the CGI application will now be more careful because the possible damage will affect his or her content solely. In one shot, you get increased user responsibility and awareness and, at the same time, a limited area for potential damage. To run a CGI application using a different user ID than the Apache server, you need a special type of program called a wrapper. A wrapper program will enable you to run a CGI application as the user who owns the file rather than the Apache server user. Some CGI wrappers do other security checks before they run the requested CGI applications. In the following sections, I cover two popular CGI wrappers.

suEXEC

Apache comes with a support application called suEXEC that provides Apache users the ability to run CGI and SSI programs under user IDs that are different from the user ID of Apache. Note, however, that suEXEC may work only on UNIX or UNIX-like platforms.

This setuid wrapper program is called when an HTTP request is made for a CGI or SSI program that the administrator designates to run as a user ID other than that of the Apache server. When such a request is made, Apache provides the suEXEC wrapper with the program's name and the user and group IDs. suEXEC runs the program using the given user and group ID.

Before running the CGI or SSI command, the suEXEC wrapper performs a set of tests to ensure that the request is valid. Among other things, this testing procedure ensures that the following things are considered:

- The request was called with an appropriate number of arguments.
- The request is being executed by a valid user who is permitted to run the wrapper. Typically, only the Apache user will be permitted to run the wrapper.

- The request passed a CGI application or SSI command (target of the exec command) that resides within Apache Web space. The requested application must reside within the current site's DocumentRoot-specified directory. This directory, or the application itself, cannot be writable by anyone but the owner. The application cannot be a setuid or setgid program, because these types of applications will change the user ID or group ID when run.
- The request is asked to run the CGI application or SSI command (target of the exec command) using a user ID and group ID that are valid. Note that suEXEC does not permit root user or root group to execute any program. Both the user ID and group ID must be below the user ID and group ID numbers specified during configuration. This allows blocking of system accounts and groups.

Once the preceding checks are successful, the suEXEC wrapper changes user ID and group ID to the target user and group ID via setuid and setgid calls. The group-access list is also initialized with all groups of which the user is a member. suEXEC cleans the process's environment by establishing a safe execution PATH (defined during configuration), as well as passing through only those variables whose names are listed in the safe environment list (also created during configuration). The suEXEC process then becomes the target CGI application or SSI command and executes.

This may seem like a lot of work—and it is; but this provides a greater security coefficient as well.

Configuring and Installing suEXEC If you are interested in installing suEXEC support in Apache, you will need to run the configure (or config.status) script as follows:

You need to run the configure (or config.status) script from your Apache source distribution as follows:

```
./configure --prefix=/path/to/apache \
            --enable-suexec \
```

```
            --suexec-caller=httpd \
            --suexec-userdir=public_html\
            --suexec-uidmin=100 \
            --suexec-gidmin=100 \
            --suexec-safepath="/usr/local/bin: \
/usr/bin:/bin"
```

Here is the detailed explanation of this configuration:

```
--enable-suexec
This option enables the suEXEC support.
```

```
--suexec-caller=httpd
```

Change "httpd" to the user ID you use for the User directive in the Apache configuration file. This is the only user that will be permitted to run the suEXEC program:

```
--suexec-userdir=public_html
```

This option defines the subdirectory under users' home directories where suEXEC executables are to be kept. Change the public_html to whatever you use as the value for the UserDir directive which specifies the document root directory for a user's Web site:

```
--suexec-uidmin=100
```

This option defines the lowest user ID (uid) permitted to run suEXEC-based CGI scripts. In other words, user IDs below this number will not be able to run CGI or SSI commands via suEXEC. You should take a look at your /etc/passwd file to make sure the range you chose does not include the system accounts that are usually lower than 100.

```
--suexec-gidmin=100
```

This option defines the lowest group ID permitted to be a target group. In other words, group IDs below this number will not be able to run CGI or SSI commands via suEXEC. You should take a look at your /etc/group file to make sure that the range you chose does not include the system account groups that are usually lower than 100.

```
--suexec-safepath="/usr/local/bin:/usr/bin:/bin"
```

This option defines the PATH environment variable that gets executed by suEXEC for CGI applications and SSI commands:

Enabling and Testing suEXEC Once you have installed both the suexec wrapper and the new Apache executable in the proper location, restart Apache. When the Apache server starts up, it will write a message similar to this:

```
[notice] suEXEC mechanism enabled (wrapper:
/usr/local/sbin/suexec)
```

This notifies that the suEXEC is active. Now let's test suEXEC functionality. In the srm.conf file, add the following lines

```
UserDir public_html
AddHandler cgi-script  .pl
```

The first directive (UserDir) sets the document root of a user's Web site to be ~username/public_html, where username can be any user on the system. The second directive associates the cgi-script handler with the .pl files. This is done to run Perl scripts with .pl extensions as CGI scripts. For this test, you will need a user account. In this example, I will use the host `wormhole.nitec.com` and a user called kabir. Copy the script shown in Listing 12-3 in a file called test.pl and put it in a user's public_html directory. In my case, I put the file in the~kabir/public_html directory.

Listing 12-3 *A CGI script to test suEXEC support*

```
#!/usr/bin/perl
#
# Make sure the preceding line is pointing to the
# right location. Some people keep perl in
# /usr/local/bin.
```

```
my ($key,$value);
print "Content-type: text/html\n\n";
print "<h1>Test of  suEXEC<h1>";

foreach $key (sort keys %ENV){
    $value = $ENV{$key};
    print "$key = $value <br>";
    }
exit 0;
```

To access the script via a Web browser, I request the following URL:

```
http://wormhole.nitec.com/~kabir/test.pl
```

Only after a CGI script passes all the security checks performed by suEXEC is it executed. suEXEC will also log the script request in its log file. The log entry for my request looks like this:

```
[1998-10-23 16:00:22]: uid: (kabir/kabir) gid:
(kabir/kabir) cmd: test.pl
```

If you are really interested in knowing that the script is running under the user's uid, you can insert a sleep command (such as sleep(10);) inside the foreach loop, which will slow down the execution and allow you to run commands like 'top' or 'ps' on your Web server console to find out the uid of the process running test.pl. You also can change the ownership of the script using chown command and try to access the script via your Web browser and see the error message that suEXEC logs. For example, when I change the ownership of the test.pl script in the ~kabir/public_html directory as follows:

```
chown root test.pl
```

I get a server error, and the log file shows the following line:

```
[1998-10-23 16:00:22]: uid/gid (500/500) mismatch with
directory (500/500) or program (0/500)
```

Here, the program is owned by user ID 0, and the group is still kabir (500), so the suEXEC refuses to run it. As you can see, suEXEC is doing what it is supposed to do.

To ensure that suEXEC is going to run the test.pl program in other directories, I created a cgi-bin directory in ~kabir/public_html and put test.pl in that directory. After determining that the user and group ownership of the new directory and file are set to user ID kabir and group ID kabir, I accessed the script using:

```
http://wormhole.nitec.com/~kabir/cgi-bin/test.pl
```

If you have virtual hosts and want to run the CGI programs and/or SSI commands using suEXEC, you must use User and Group directives inside the <VirtualHost ...> container. Set these directives to user and group IDs other than those the Apache server is currently using. If only one, or neither, of these directives is specified for a <VirtualHost> container, the server user ID or group ID is assumed.

For security and efficiency reasons, all suexec requests must remain within either a top-level document root for virtual host requests or one top-level personal document root for userdir requests. For example, if you have four virtual hosts configured, you would need to structure all of your virtual host document roots off of one main Apache document hierarchy to take advantage of suEXEC for virtual hosts.

CGIWrap

CGIWrap is like the suEXEC program in that it permits users to use CGI applications without compromising the security of the Web server. CGI programs are run with the file owner's permission. In addition, CGIWrap performs several security checks on the CGI application and will not be executed if any checks fail.

CGIWrap is written by Nathan Neulinger, and the latest version of CGIWrap is available from the primary ftp site on `ftp://ftp.cc.umr.edu/pub/cgi/cgiwrap/`. CGIWrap is used via a URL in an HTML document. As distributed, CGIWrap is configured to run user scripts that are located in the ~/public_html/cgi-bin/ directory.

Configuring and Installing CGIWrap CGIwrap is distributed as a gzip compressed tar file. You can decompress it using gzip, and extract it using the tar utility.

Run the Configure script, and it will prompt you to answer many questions. Most of these questions are self-explanatory; however, there is a feature in this wrapper that differs from suEXEC. It enables you to create allow and deny files that can be used to restrict access to your CGI applications. Both of these files have the same format, as shown in the following:

```
User ID
mailto:Username@subnet1/mask1,subnet2/mask2...
```

You can either have a single username (nonnumeric user ID) or a user mailto:ID@subnet/mask line where one or more subnet/mask pairs can be defined, for example:

```
mailto:Myuser@1.2.3.4/255.255.255.255
```

If this line is found in the allow file (file name is specified by you), the user kabir's CGI applications are permitted to be run by hosts that belong in the 206.171.50.0 network with netmask 255.255.255.0.

Once you run the Configure script, you must run the make utility to create the CGIWrap executable.

Enabling CGIWrap To use the wrapper application, copy the CGIWrap executable to the user's cgi-bin directory. Note that this directory must match what you have specified in the configuration process. The simplest way to get things going is to keep the ~username/public_html/cgi-bin type of directory structure for the CGI application directory.

Once you have copied the CGIWrap executable, change the ownership and permission bits as follows:

```
chown root CGIWrap
chmod 4755 CGIWrap
```

Create hard link or symbolic link nph-cgiwrap, nph-cgiwrapd, cgiwrapd to CGIWrap in the cgi-bin directory as follows:

```
ln [-s] CGIWrap cgiwrapd
ln [-s] CGIWrap nph-cgiwrap
ln [-s] CGIWrap nph-cgiwrapd
```

On my Apache server, I specify only the cgi extension as a CGI application and, therefore, I renamed my CGIWrap executable to cgiwrap.cgi to get it working. If you have similar restrictions, you might try this approach or make a link instead.

Now you can execute a CGI application as follows:

```
http://www.yourdomain.com/cgi-bin/cgiwrap/username/ \
scriptname
```

To access user kabir's CGI application test.cgi on the `wormhole.nitec.com` site, for example, I would have to use the following:

```
http://wormhole.nitec.com/cgi-bin/cgiwrap/kabir/test.cgi
```

If you wish to see debugging output for your CGI, specify cgiwrapd instead of CGIWrap, as in the following URL:

```
http://www.yourdomain.com/cgi-bin/cgiwrapd/username/ \
scriptname
```

If the script is an nph- style script, you must run it using the following URL:

```
www.yourdomain.com/cgi-bin/nph-cgiwrap/username/ \
scriptname
```

Reducing Server Side Includes Risks

Many administrators consider Server Side Includes (SSI) as much a security risk as CGI applications. This is true in some ways, and in some ways it is not.

If you run external applications using SSI commands such as exec, the security risk is virtually the same as with the CGI applications. However, you can disable this command very easily under Apache, using the Options directive as follows:

```
<Directory />
Options IncludesNOEXEC

</Directory>
```

This disables exec and includes SSI commands everywhere on your Web space; however, you can enable these commands whenever necessary by defining a narrower-scoping directory container. Following is an example:

```
<Directory />
Options IncludesNOEXEC

</Directory>


<Directory /ssi>
Options +Include

</Directory>
```

This configuration segment disables the exec command everywhere but the /SSI directory.

Chapter 13

Secured Socket Layer for Apache

Finding the Right SSL Solution for Apache

Currently, there are multiple choices for SSL software for Apache. Table 13-1 should help you pick the right one for your needs.

Table 13-1 *SSL Solutions for Apache*

Software	Distribution	Restriction	Comments
Apache-SSL	Free	Commercial use in the USA might be restricted by copyright and patent laws.	Not recommended, because this is not the cleanest solution. Apache-SSL is basically a set of patches for Apache and is not well documented.
mod_ssl	Free	Commercial use in the USA might be restricted by copyright and patent laws	Clean solution. Although partly based on Apache-SSL, much cleaner and better documented. Recommended by the author.

Continued

Table 13-1 *(continued)*

Software	Distribution	Restriction	Comments
Raven SSL module	Commercial	None	Cheapest commercial solution.
Stronghold Web Server	Commercial	None	Great solution for serious e-commerce sites.

Patching Apache with Apache-SSL

Apache-SSL is a secure, noncommercial Apache Web server based on Apache and the free implementation of the SSL library called SSLeay. This library supports SSL versions 2 and 3. Before you explore Apache-SSL any further, make sure you understand the following legal issues.

If you plan to use Apache-SSL outside the United States, you should have no legal restrictions according to the SSLeay documentation. If you use the RSA algorithms provided by RSAREF, however, you can use Apache-SSL for noncommercial purposes. For commercial purposes, you need to make agreements with RSA, because they hold patents in the United States. Also, there may be restrictions on the use of IDEA algorithms in Europe and RC4 in the United States.

If you are still able (legally, that is) and willing to give Apache-SSL a try, the first step is to set up SSLeay in your system. You can get SSLeay at:

```
ftp://ftp.psy.uq.oz.au/pub/Crypto/SSL
```

Setting Up SSLeay

First, get the SSLeay compressed tar file from the preceding site. The easiest way to build SSLeay is to run the Perl script called Configure, which is provided in the distribution. You need to specify your operating system name when you run the script. If you run the system without any parameters, you will see a list of supported operating system names.

For example, to create appropriate Makefile configurations for an ELF-based Linux system such as RedHat 5.0, run the script as follows:

```
perl Configure linux-elf
```

Once you have run the configuration script successfully, run the following:

```
make clean
make
make rehash
make test
```

The first make command cleans up any leftover object files from previous compilations. The second make command compiles the library; the third one fixes demo certificates; and the fourth make command tests everything.

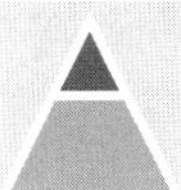

Tip

If you are on a Windows platform or are having problems with the installation, you can get more information on how to build SSLeay from the following Web site:

```
http://www.cryptsoft.com/ssleay/doc/Building.html
```

Once you have tested SSLeay successfully, run the following command to install the software:

```
make install
```

The single executable is called ssleay and can be found in the APPS subdirectory. Run the following to see the version information:

```
./ssleay version
```

Now that you have SSLeay support built for your system, you can continue with setting up Apache-SSL.

Setting Up Apache-SSL

Getting Apache-SSL files is as easy as going to the `www.apache-ssl.org/` site and finding a nearby FTP site. One such site is:

```
ftp://ftp.ox.ac.uk/pub/crypto/SSL/
```

Once you have obtained the latest Apache-SSL compressed tar file, copy this file to your current Apache distribution directory (that is, the top directory in your Apache distribution) and extract it. Now you can patch the original Apache files as follows:

```
./FixPatch
```

This will fix the original SSLpatch and ask you if you want to apply the fixed patch. Enter y, and once the patch is applied, run Apache's configure script as usual. For example:

```
./configure --prefix=/usr/local/apache
```

Once you have configured Apache as usual, run the make and make install commands to compile and install Apache in your desired destination directory. This compilation process will create an Apache-SSL executable called httpsd. To verify that the executable is the right version, try:

```
httpsd -v
```

Along with the Apache version, you also should see the Ben-SSL version number. Now you're ready to create a temporary certificate for your secured Apache server.

Creating a Temporary Certificate

The certificate creation process requires random numbers. To supply some random data for this process, create a file with arbitrary text data. You can simply copy an existing text file from anywhere or type one yourself. Then, set an environment variable called RANDFILE to point to the file you want to use. For example:

```
setenv RANDFILE /tmp/random.txt
```

This command points the RANDFILE environment variable to the /tmp/random.txt file. You should consult your shell documentation regarding how to set environment variables. The preceding command works for the tcsh shell. Once you've set this variable, run the following command from the SRC directory of your Apache distribution:

```
make certificate
```

This prompts you to enter some general information, such as your company's name, your name, and your e-mail address. The certificate is stored in the SSLconf/conf/httpsd.pem file.

Directives for Configuring Apache-SSL

You're almost ready to configure Apache for SSL. First, however, you need to know about the following directives provided by Apache-SSL. You'll use these for the configuration.

SSLBanCipher

Syntax: `SSLBanCipher cipher`

Context: `per-directory config (.htaccess)`

This directive bans a cipher from being used in a per-directory configuration. With this directive, you can disallow clients that want to use the banned cipher.

SSLCACertificateFile

Syntax: `SSLCACertificateFile CA_certificate_filename`

Default: `none`

Context: `server config, virtual host`

This directive specifies the file that contains the Certificate Authority certificate.

SSLCACertificatePath

Syntax: `SSLCertificatePath path/to/CA/certificates`

Default: none

Context: `server config, virtual host`

This directive specifies the directory in which you keep the Certificate Authority certificate files.

SSLCacheServerPath

Syntax: `SSLCacheServerPath filename`

Context: `server config, virtual host`

This directive sets the path for the global cache server executable. If you have installed Apache using APACI configure script, then the cache executable file is in the sbin subdirectory of your top-level Apache installation directory. For example, if you provided the configure script with --prefix=/usr/local/apache option, then the path for the cache executable should be set as follows:

```
SSLCacheServerPath /usr/local/apache/sbin/gcache
```

SSLCacheServerPort

Syntax: `SSLCacheServerPort port | filename`

Context: `server config, virtual host`

This directive configures the TCP/IP port (numeric) or UNIX domain socket (filename) for the global SSL Session Cache server process. For example, the following sets the TCP port 1234 as the global cache server port.:

```
SSLCacheServerPort 1234
```

Another example is as follows:

```
SSLCacheServerPort logs/gcache_port
```

Here, the UNIX domain socket named logs/gcache_prt is used.

SSLCertificateFile

Syntax: `SSLCertificateFile certificate_filename`

Context: `server config, virtual host`

This directive specifies the certificate filename for a Web site host. Note that you need a separate certificate for each Web site; so, if you plan to provide SSL connectivity for a virtual host, you need a separate certificate for the virtual host.

SSLCertificateKeyFile

Syntax: `SSLCertificateKeyFile certificate_key_filename`

Default: `none`

Context: `server config, virtual host`

This directive specifies the certificate private key file. If you do not use this directive, the key is assumed to be in SSLCertificateFile specified file.

SSLDisable

Syntax: `SSLDisable`

Context: `server config, virtual host`

This directive disables SSL. It does not require any arguments.

SSLEnable

Syntax: `SSLEnable`

Context: `server config, virtual host`

This directive enables SSL. It does not require any arguments.

SSLFakeBasicAuth

Syntax: `SSLFakeBasicAuth`

Context: `server config, virtual host`

This directive translates client's X509 certificate to a user name that can be used in authentication. I do not recommend that you use this directive.

SSLLogFile

Syntax: `SSLLogFile log_filename`

Context: `server config, virtual host`

This directive specifies where to write information about SSL connections. Most of the information written to the specified file will also be written in the server's error log file. You might not want to use this directive at all.

SSLRequireCipher

Syntax: `SSLRequiredCipher cipher`

Context: `per-directory config (.htaccess)`

This directive adds a cipher to the per-directory list of required ciphers.

SSLRequireSSL

Syntax: `SSLRequireSSL`

Context: `directory, per-directory config file`

This directive disables access unless an SSL conection is in use. It does not require any arguments.

SSLRequiredCiphers

Syntax: `SSLRequiredCiphers cipher1:cipher2:cipher3:...`

Context: `server config, virtual host, per-directory config (.htaccess)`

This directive specifies a colon-separated list of ciphers (cryptographic algorithms such as RC4-MD5 and RC4-SHA).

SSLSessionCacheTimeout

Syntax: `SSLSessionCacheTimeout seconds`

Context: `server config, virtual host`

This directive sets the cache time-out session for an SSL session. For example:

```
SSLSessionCacheTimeout 300
```

SSLVerifyClient

Syntax: `SSLVerifyClient numeric_option`
Default: `SSLVerifyClient 0`
Context: `server config, virtual host`

This directive sets the client certificate policy for the server. If you require client certificates, set this to two (2). If client certificates are optional, set this to one (1). If client certificates are not required, use zero (0).

SSLVerifyDepth

Syntax: `SSLVerifyDepth  number`
Default: `SSLVerifyDepth 0`
Context: `server config, virtual host`

Because a CA certificate can be certified by another CA, a chain of CA certificates can be formed. This directive specifies how many CA certificates the server should consult when verifying client certificates. If you are not using client certificates, do not change the default.

Configuring Apache for Apache-SSL

The author of Apache-SSL, Ben Laurie, provides an example of an httpd.conf file, shown in Listing 13-1. This file can be found in the SSLconf/conf directory of your Apache source distribution where you applied the Apache-SSL patch. The access.conf and srm.conf files are empty because all the SSL-specific configuration used in the author's example is in httpd.conf.

In this sample configuration, Ben gives an example of how Apache-SSL can be used for both secured and nonsecured document-serving purposes. Instead of the default SSL port 443, he uses port 8887 for secured (https) connection and port 8888 for regular (http) connections. The example configuration is not ready to be tested, since you need to replace directory paths and uncomment a few directives.

Listing 13-1 *httpd.conf*

```
# This is an example configuration file
# for Apache-SSL.
# Copyright (C) 1995,6,7 Ben Laurie

# By popular demand, this file now illustrates the
# way to create two websites, one secured
# (on port 8887), the other not (on port 8888).

# You may need to change
# the following user and group names.
User ben
Group group

LogLevel debug

# SSL Servers MUST be standalone, currently.
ServerType standalone

# The default port for SSL is 443...
Port 8887
Listen 8887
Listen 8888

# My test document root
#DocumentRoot /u/ben/www/1/docs.
DocumentRoot /u/ben/apache/apache_1.3.0-ssl/htdocs

<Directory /u/ben/apache/apache_1.3.0-ssl/htdocs/manual>
# This directive forbids access except when
# SSL is in use. Very handy for defending
```

```
# against configuration errors that expose stuff
# that should be protected.
SSLRequireSSL
</Directory>

# Watch what's going on.
TransferLog logs/transfer_log

# Note that all SSL options can apply to
# virtual hosts.

# Disable SSL. Useful in combination with
# virtual hosts. Note that SSLEnable is
# now also supported.
SSLDisable

# Set the path for the global cache server executable.
# If this facility gives you trouble, you can
# disable it by setting
# CACHE_SESSIONS to FALSE in apache_ssl.c.
SSLCacheServerPath ../src/modules/ssl/gcache

# Set the global cache server port number, or
# path. If it is a path, a UNIX domain socket is
# used. If a number, a TCP socket.
SSLCacheServerPort logs/gcache_port
#SSLCacheServerPort 1234

# Directory for the cache server to run in
# (in case of crashes). Optional.
SSLCacheServerRunDir /tmp

# Set the session cache timeout, in seconds
# (set to 15 for testing, use a
```

Continued

Listing 13-1 *(continued)*

```
# higher value in real life).
SSLSessionCacheTimeout 15

# Set the CA certificate verification
# path (must be PEM encoded).
# (in addition to getenv("SSL_CERT_DIR")).
# SSLCACertificatePath /u/ben/apache/apache_1.2.5-
ssl/SSLconf/conf

# Set the CA certificate verification file
# (must be PEM encoded).(in addition to
# getenv("SSL_CERT_FILE"), I think).
# SSLCACertificateFile /some/where/somefile
# SSLCACertificateFile /u/ben/apache/apache_1.2.5-
ssl/SSLconf/conf/httpsd.pem

# Point SSLCertificateFile at a PEM encoded
# certificate. If the certificate is encrypted,
# then you will be prompted for a pass phrase.
# Note that a kill -1 will prompt again.
# A test certificate can be generated with
# "make certificate."
SSLCertificateFile /u/ben/apache/apache_1.3.0-\
ssl/SSLconf/conf/httpsd.pem
# SSLCertificateFile /u/ben/apache/apache_1.2.6-\
ssl/SSLconf/conf/t1.pem


# If the key is not combined with the certificate,
# use this directive to point at the key file.
# If this starts with a '/' it specifies an absolute
# path, otherwise it is relative to the default
# certificate area. That is, it
# means "<default>/private/<keyfile>".
```

```
# SSLCertificateKeyFile /some/place/with/your.key

# Set SSLVerifyClient to:
# 0 if no certicate is required
# 1 if the client may present a valid certificate
# 2 if the client must present a valid certificate
# 3 if the client may present a valid certificate
# but it is not required to have a valid CA
SSLVerifyClient 3
# How deeply to verify before deciding they don't
# have a valid certificate
SSLVerifyDepth 10

# If you have enables client cert exports (in buff.h)
# you need to use
# SSLExportClientCertificates to enable them.
# Note that the server still has to mess about with
# certs even if this is disabled (and exports are
# enabled)
# because the cert chain is received before we can
# know whether it is needed or not.
<Location /scripts>
SSLExportClientCertificates
</Location>

# Translate the client X509 into a Basic
# authorisation. This means that the standard
# Auth/DBMAuth methods can be used for access control.
# The user name is the "one line" version of the
# client's X509 certificate. Note that no
# password is obtained from the user. Every entry in
# the user file needs this
# password: xxj31ZMTZzkVA. See the code for
# further explanation.
```

Continued

Listing 13-1 *(continued)*

```
SSLFakeBasicAuth

# List the ciphers that the client is permitted to
# negotiate. See the source
# for a definitive list. For example:
# SSLRequiredCiphers RC4-MD5:RC4-SHA:IDEA-CBC-MD5:DES-
#CBC3-SHA

# These two can be used per-directory to require
# or ban ciphers. Note that (at
# least in the current version) Apache-SSL will
# not attempt to renegotiate if a
# cipher is banned (or not required).
# SSLRequireCipher
# SSLBanCipher

# A home for miscellaneous rubbish generated by SSL.
# Much of it is duplicated
# in the error log file. Put this somewhere where
# it cannot be used for symlink
# attacks on a real server (i.e., somewhere where
# only root can write).
# Don't use this anymore! Now everything is
# logged in the error log.
# SSLLogFile /tmp/ssl.log

# Custom logging
CustomLog logs/ssl_log "%t %{version}c %{cipher}c \
%{clientcert}c"

<VirtualHost scuzzy:8888>
#SSLDisable
SSLEnable
</VirtualHost>
```

```
# If you want, you can disable SSL globally and
# enable it in a virtual host...
# <VirtualHost scuzzy:8887>
# SSLEnable
# and the rest of the SSL stuf...
# </VirtualHost>

# Experiment with authorization...
# <Directory /u/ben/www/1/docs>
#AuthType Basic
#AuthName Experimental
#AuthGroupFile /dev/null
#AuthUserFile /u/ben/www/1/users
#<Limit PUT GET>
#allow from all
#require valid-user
#</Limit>
#</Directory>

ScriptAlias   /scripts      /u/ben/www/scripts
```

To provide you with a simpler configuration example, I created the httpd.conf file shown in Listing 13-2. In this configuration, there are two virtual hosts. One listens to the standard 80 port, and another listens to the standard SSL port 443. The virtual host on port 80 uses the SSLDisable directive.

Listing 13-2 *httpd.conf*

```
ServerType standalone
ServerName picaso.nitec.com
Port 443
Listen 80
HostnameLookups off
User httpd
Group httpd
```

Continued

Listing 13-2 *(continued)*

```
ServerAdmin kabir@picaso.nitec.com
ServerRoot /usr/local/apache132
ErrorLog /usr/local/apache132/var/log/error_log
LogLevel warn
LogFormat "%h %l %u %t \"%r\" %>s %b \"%{Referer}i\"\
"%{User-Agent}i\"" combined
LogFormat "%h %l %u %t \"%r\" %>s %b" common
LogFormat "%{Referer}i -> %U" referer
LogFormat "%{User-agent}i" agent
CustomLog /usr/local/apache132/var/log/access_log common
PidFile /usr/local/apache132/var/run/httpd.pid
ScoreBoardFile
/usr/local/apache132/var/run/httpd.scoreboard
ServerSignature on
UseCanonicalName on
Timeout 300
KeepAlive On
MaxKeepAliveRequests 100
KeepAliveTimeout 15
MinSpareServers 5
MaxSpareServers 10
StartServers 5
MaxClients 150
MaxRequestsPerChild 30

SSLCacheServerPath sbin/gcache
SSLCacheServerPort logs/gcache_port
SSLCacheServerRunDir /tmp
SSLSessionCacheTimeout 15
SSLCertificateFile /usr/local/build/apache_1.3.2/ \
SSLconf/conf/httpsd.pem
SSLVerifyClient 3
SSLVerifyDepth 10
```

```
NameVirtualHost 206.171.50.50

<VirtualHost 206.171.50.50:80>
  SSLDisable
  ServerName picaso.nitec.com
  DocumentRoot /www/nitec/public/htdocs
</VirtualHost>

<VirtualHost 206.171.50.50:443>
  SSLEnable
  ServerName picaso.nitec.com
  DocumentRoot /www/nitec/secure/htdocs
</VirtualHost>
```

If you are only interested in creating virtual hosts that are secured, and you want to leave the main server on port 80 as it is, you can use the following in your main server configuration section (outside a virtual host container):

```
Port 80
SSLDisable
```

To create secured virtual hosts, you use a configuration similar to the following:

```
<VirtualHost host.domain.com:443>
DocumentRoot /path/to/secure/pages
ServerAdmin webmaster@host.domain.com
ServerName host.domain.com
SSLCACertificatePath /usr/local/ssl/certs
SSLCACertificateFile\
/usr/local/ssl/certs/virtual.host.com.pem
SSLCertificateFile\
/usr/local/ssl/certs/virtual.host.com.pem
SSLLogFile /path/to/ssl.log
</VirtualHost>
```

The SSLDisable directive in the main server configuration section disables SSL for everything but the virtual hosts that list SSL directives. Now you are ready to test your secured site.

Testing the Secured Server

Start or restart your Apache server. Also make sure you have the latest Netscape Navigator or Microsoft Internet Explorer browser. Some of the older browsers do not support SSL.

To test a secured Web site, point your browser to:

```
https://your.secure.domain.tld/
```

Remember that you must use https:// instead of http:// for all secured server URLs. For the preceding configuration, I can use the following for secured server access:

```
https://picaso.nitec.com/
```

For regular Web access, I can use:

```
http:// picaso.nitec.com/
```

If you created a self-generated certificate by running make certificate earlier, and you try to access your secured site, you will get a warning message from your browser.

Unless you obtain a certificate from a commercial Certificate Authority that the browsers know, this type of warning message will pop up for each user trying to access the secured site.

Once you get past the warning dialog windows and accept the certificate manually by clicking one or more buttons (OK or Finish), the browser establishes a secured communication channel with the server.

If you are interested in seeing what happens when a client such as a browser connects to a secured server, you can run the s_client application that comes with the SSLeay package. For an Apache-SSL site called `blackhole.nitec.com`, the s_client can be run as follows:

```
ssleay s_client -host blackhole.nitec.com -port 443
```

This produces the output shown in Listing 13-3.

Listing 13-3 *Output of s_client connecting toblackhole.nitec.com on port 443*

```
CONNECTED(00000003)
depth=0
/C=US/ST=California/L=Sacramento/O=Nitec/CN=blackhole.nit
ec.com/Email=kabir@nitec.com
verify error:num=18:self signed certificate
verify return:1
depth=0 /C=US/ST=California/L=Sacramento/O=Nitec/
CN=blackhole.nitec.com/Email=kabir@nitec.com
verify return:1
--
Certificate chain
 0 s:/C=US/ST=California/L=Sacramento/O=Nitec/
CN=blackhole.nitec.com/Email=kabir@nitec.com
   i:/C=US/ST=California/L=Sacramento/O=Nitec/
CN=blackhole.nitec.com/Email=kabir@nitec.com
--
Server certificate
---BEGIN CERTIFICATE---
MIICezCCAeQCAQAwDQYJKoZIhvcNAQEEBQAwgYUxCzAJBgNVBAYTAlVTM
RMwEQYD
VQQIEwpDYWxpZm9ybmlhMRMwEQYDVQQHEwpTYWNyYW1lbnRvMQ4wDAYDV
QQKEwVO
aXRlYzEcMBoGA1UEAxMTYmxhY2tob2xlLm5pdGVjLmNvbTEeMBwGCSqGS
Ib3DQEJ
ARYPa2FiaXJAbml0ZWMuY29tMB4XDTk3MDQyMjA4NDAwNFoXDTk3MDUyM
jA4NDAw
NFowgYUxCzAJBgNVBAYTAlVTMRMwEQYDVQQIEwpDYWxpZm9ybmlhMRMwE
QYDVQQH
EwpTYWNyYW1lbnRvMQ4wDAYDVQQKEwVOaXRlYzEcMBoGA1UEAxMTYmxhY
2tob2xl
```

Continued

Listing 13-3 *(continued)*

```
Lm5pdGVjLmNvbTEeMBwGCSqGSIb3DQEJARYPa2FiaXJAbml0ZWMuY29tM
IGfMA0G
CSqGSIb3DQEBAQUAA4GNADCBiQKBgQDVuXIKqg7p9eS1xVIRyglaLTSZ+
Ge+CESR
HUBUQiGuiU+eo97CaKze4B19AM4ZV3xnloJrS8LKTnLmkJ95A++6ymrhH
VIVgmXZ
DgkczjQ2LKInWCJ9QZntoEu/1mPUY2KnXbbQo5v/gtf/J6tbhuRJKtLgz
2dK4CWM
/OPQzzrYjQIDAQABMA0GCSqGSIb3DQEBBAUAA4GBAIT2FA3Je7Q+tnu3K
jBj7NLT
VDG5YsEyGXZKBEWJEzpAzOywnqndiTwwdUgocYl/EADidHsrgiYDsYPD3
oVFkWOw
evHLwxBE++6FIcLkRty3C/bfgrdJWWFsrd14nZq3Vy8y/xFQkZJ9Ob0cp
o6ac0qm
5HrrSatn6DBaWuDXdEI5
---END CERTIFICATE---
subject=/C=US/ST=California/L=Sacramento/O=Nitec/CN=black
hole.nitec.com/Email=kabir@nitec.com
issuer=/C=US/ST=California/L=Sacramento/O=Nitec/CN=blackh
ole.nitec.com/Email=kabir@nitec.com
SSL handshake has read 813 bytes and written 317 bytes
--
New, SSLv3, Cipher is RC4-SHA
SSL-Session:
    Cipher    : RC4-SHA
    Session-ID:
C26196B7FC9C2DBE664FC5C55AD4C89887BC9703B98F9441362853E42
8C4D67F
    Master-Key:
303EBE61E04175F81C605E02A2CC264022F6E55F7714FA32DB3A37852
A4AD6C85B2748ED3FAD06FDD733CDD098B443D6
    Key-Arg   : None
    Start Time: 861699068
    Timeout   : 7200 (sec)
```

The preceding output contains a lot of information. The server provides a distinguished name associated with the output, in abbreviated form. Distinguished names are defined by the X.509 standard, which defines the fields, field names, and abbreviations used to refer to the fields. Table 13-2 lists some of the fields shown in the preceding output.

Table 13-2 *Distinguished Name Fields*

Field	Abbreviation	Description	Example
Common Name	CN	Name being certified. This is the fully qualified domain name of the system.	CN=blackhole.nitec.com
Organization or Company	O	Name is associated with this organization.	O=Nitec
Organizational Unit	OU	Name is associated with this organizational unit, such as a department.	OU= I didn't specify one.
City/Locality	L	Name is located in this city.	L=Sacramento
State/Province	ST	Name is located in this state/province	ST=California
Country	C	Name is located in this country (ISO code).	C=US

The Certificate Authorities define which fields are required and which are optional. There may even be restrictions on the content of a field. For example, Netscape browsers require that the Common Name field for a certificate be the server name or a regular expression for the domain.

The binary format of a certificate is defined using the Abstract Syntax Notation 1 (ASN.1). This notation defines how to specify the contents, and the encoding rules define how this information is translated into binary form. ASN.1 can be encoded in many ways, but the emerging standard is a very simple encoding scheme called Direct Encoding Rules (DER), which results in a compact binary certificate. For e-mail exchange purposes, the binary certificate is often Base64 encoded, resulting in ASCII text lines such as the one appearing between the -BEGIN CERTIFICATE- and -END CERTIFICATE- lines.

Information about certificate chains also appears. When a certificate is issued by a CA whose certificate is issued by another CA, a chain is created and the server reveals information regarding the chain so the client can decide to investigate the certificates mentioned in the chain. In this particular example, the chain is not present.

After displaying the output shown in Listing 13-3, the s_client program remains connected to the server. If you enter the following HTTP request followed by a blank line, you get the output shown in Listing 13-4.:

```
GET / HTTP/1.0
```

Listing 13-4 *Output of a GET request on a secured server*

```
HTTP/1.1 200 OK
Date: Tue, 22 Apr 1997 08:51:56 GMT
Server: Apache/1.3.3 Ben-SSL/1.13
Connection: close
Content-Type: text/html

<HTML><HEAD>
<TITLE>Index of /</TITLE>
</HEAD><BODY>
<H1>Index of /</H1>
<UL><LI> <A HREF="/"> Parent Directory</A>
<LI> <A HREF="development"> development</A>
<LI> <A HREF="future"> future</A>
<LI> <A HREF="public"> public</A>
</UL></BODY></HTML>
```

There was no directory index file in the top-level directory of the secured server `blackhole.nitec.com`, so a dynamically generated directory listing was produced by the server as usual.

If you've been able to perform similar tests on your Apache-SSL server, you have successfully created a secured Web server.

Using mod_ssl

The mod_ssl module is a much cleaner approach than Apache-SSL. Although it is partly based on Apache-SSL, it is yet another well-documented module by Ralf S. Engelschall. I recommend using this if you are using the latest version of Apache.

Getting mod_ssl

The mod_ssl module is not distributed with the standard Apache source distribution. You will have to download it from the following Web site:

```
http://www.engelschall.com/sw/mod_ssl/
```

Since this module depends on the SSLeay package (like Apache-SSL), you will also have to get the SSLeay package from the following FTP site:

```
ftp://ftp.psy.uq.oz.au/pub/Crypto/SSL/
```

If you are a U.S. citizen and plan on using the SSL support in the United States, you will need to obtain the RSA Reference Implementation package from the following FTP site:

```
ftp://ftp.rsa.com/rsaref/
```

Read the README file at the FTP site to locate the US citizen only directory where rsaref20.tar.Z package is kept.

You also will need a working Perl 5 interpreter and to make sure that you have the latest Apache source from the Apache Web site or one of its mirror sites.

Compiling and Installing mod_ssl

Extract all the packages into an appropriate directory. I typically use /usr/local/src for such purposes. Once you have extracted each of the previously mentioned packages, you are ready to compile and install them per the following steps.

I will assume that you have extracted the necessary packages into the following directories:

/usr/local/src/apache_1.3.3	— for the Apache source distribution
/usr/local/src/mod_ssl-2.0.13-1.3.3	— for the mod_ssl source distribution
/usr/local/src/SSLeay-0.9.0B	— for the mod_ssl source distribution
/usr/local/src/rsaref-2.0/	— for the RSAref package for U.S. citizens only

TIP

Your version numbers might vary since this software is always being updated, so make sure you replace appropriate version numbers as you follow the instructions in this book.

Building the RSAref Library

You do not need the RSAref package for mod_ssl if you are not in the United States. If you are in the United States and do not already have the librsaref.a library module, follow these steps:

Change directories to /usr/local/src/rsaref-2.0, and run the following commands:

```
cp -rp install/unix local
cd local
make
mv rsaref.a librsaref.a
```

Once you have created the librsaref.a library file, you can compile SSLeay.

Building SSLeay

Change directories to /usr/local/src/SSLeay-0.9.0B, and run the following command:

```
make -f Makefile.ssl links
```

If you are in the United States, you will need to tell SSLeay about the rsaref library package. So, run the following commands:

```
perl ./Configure gcc -DNO_IDEA -DRSAref -lRSAglue \
-L`pwd`/../rsaref-2.0/local/ -lrsaref
cp rsaref/rsaref.h include/
```

Everyone else should run the following command, which does not specify the RSAref library package:

```
perl ./Configure gcc  -DNO_IDEA
```

Now you should compile and test the package by running the following commands:

```
make
make test
```

Building mod_ssl and Apache

Change directories to /usr/local/src/mod_ssl-2.0.13-1.3.3, and run the configure script as follows:

```
./configure  \
--with-apache=../apache_1.3.3   \
--with-ssleay=../ SSLeay-0.9.0b \
--with-rsaref=../rsaref-2.0/local  \
--prefix=/usr/local/apache
```

You do not need the --with-rsaref option if you are not in the United States. Also make sure you use the appropriate --prefix value for your desired Apache destination.

If you already have a working server certificate and a private key, you can supply the following options to the configure script:

```
--with-key=/path/to/your/server.key
--with-crt=/path/to/your/server.crt
```

Now you can compile Apache as follows:

Change your dcurrent directory to /usr/local/src/apache_1.3.3, and run the make comand.

If you do not have a real server certificate and private key, you can make a test certificate using the make certificate command.

Now run the make install command to install the Apache server.

You now have an SSL-enabled Apache server. All that remains is the Apache configuration.

Configuring Apache for mod_ssl

The mod_ssl package installs a copy of httpd.conf.default file in the ETC subdirectory of your Apache installation directory. You can use this file to test and configure your Apache server. An example of this file is listed in Listing 13-5.

Listing 13-5 *Default httpd.conf installed with mod_ssl*

```
##
## httpd.conf — Apache HTTP server configuration file
##

# This is the main server configuration file. See URL
# http://www.apache.org/ for instructions.

# Do NOT simply read the instructions in here
# without understanding what they do. If you are
# unsure, consult the online docs. You have been
```

```
# warned.

# Originally by Rob McCool

# Dynamic Shared Object (DSO) Support
#
# To be able to use the functionality of a
# module that was built as a DSO. you
# have to place corresponding LoadModule lines
# at this location so the
# directives contained in it are actually available
# before they are used.
#
# Please read the file README.DSO in the Apache
# 1.3 distribution for more details about the DSO
# mechanism and run httpd -l for the list of already
# built-in (statically linked and thus always available)
# modules in your httpd binary.
#
# Example:
# LoadModule foo_module libexec/mod_foo.so

# ServerType is either inetd, or standalone.

ServerType standalone

# If you are running from inetd, go to "ServerAdmin".

# Port: The port the standalone listens to.
# For ports < 1023, you will
# need httpd to be run as root initially.

Port 80
```

Continued

Listing 13-5 *(continued)*

```
##
##  SSL Support
##
##  When we also provide SSL, we have to listen to the
##  standard HTTP port (see previous) and to the HTTPS
port
##
<IfDefine SSL>
Listen 80
Listen 443
</IfDefine>

# HostnameLookups: Log the names of clients or
# just their IP numbers—e.g., www.apache.org (on) or
# 204.62.129.132 (off). The default is off because
# it'd be overall better for the Net if people
# had to knowingly turn this feature on.

HostnameLookups off

# If you wish httpd to run as a different user or
# group, you must run httpd as root initially, and
# it will switch.

# User/Group: The name (or #number) of the
# user/group to run httpd as.
# On SCO (ODT 3), use User nouser and Group nogroup.
# On HPUX, you may not be able to use shared memory
# as nobody, and the
# suggested workaround is to create a user www and
# use that user. Note that some kernels refuse to
# setgid(Group) or semctl(IPC_SET)
# when the value of (unsigned)Group is above 60000;
# don't use Group nobody on these systems!
```

```
User nobody
Group nobody

# ServerAdmin: Your address, where problems with
# the server should be e-mailed.

ServerAdmin kabir@picaso.nitec.com

# ServerRoot: The directory the server's config,
# error, and log files are kept in.
# Note! If you intend to place this on an NFS
# (or otherwise network) mounted file system, then
# please read the LockFile documentation,
# you will save yourself a lot of trouble.

ServerRoot "/usr/local/apache"

# BindAddress: You can support virtual hosts with
# this option. This option is used to tell the
# server which IP address to listen to. It can
# contain "*", an IP address, or a fully qualified
# Internet domain name.
# See also the VirtualHost directive.

# BindAddress *

# ErrorLog: The location of the error log file.
# If this does not start
# with /, ServerRoot is prepended to it.

ErrorLog /usr/local/apache/var/log/error_log

# LogLevel: Control the number of messages logged to
# the error_log. Possible values include: debug, info,
```

Continued

Listing 13-5 *(continued)*

```
# notice, warn, error, crit, alert, emerg.

LogLevel warn

# The following directives define some format
# nicknames for use with a CustomLog directive (see
later).

LogFormat "%h %l %u %t \"%r\" %>s %b \"%{Referer}i\" \
"%{User-Agent}i\"" combined
LogFormat "%h %l %u %t \"%r\" %>s %b" common
LogFormat "%{Referer}i -> %U" referer
LogFormat "%{User-agent}i" agent

# The location of the access logfile
# (Common Logfile Format). If this does not start
# with /, ServerRoot is prepended to it.

CustomLog /usr/local/apache/var/log/access_log common

# If you would like to have an agent and
# referer logfile, uncomment the
# following directives.

#CustomLog /usr/local/apache/var/log/referer_log referer
#CustomLog /usr/local/apache/var/log/agent_log agent

# If you prefer a single logfile with access,
# agent and referer information
# (Combined Logfile Format), you can use the following
# directive.

#CustomLog /usr/local/apache/var/log/access_log combined
```

```
# PidFile: The file the server should log its pid to
PidFile /usr/local/apache/var/run/httpd.pid

# ScoreBoardFile: File used to store internal
# server process information. Not all architectures
# require this.  But if yours does (you'll know because
# this file is created when you run Apache), then
# you *must* ensure that no two invocations of Apache
# share the same scoreboard file.
ScoreBoardFile /usr/local/apache/var/run/httpd.scoreboard

# The LockFile directive sets the path to the
# lockfile used when Apache
# is compiled with either USE_FCNTL_SERIALIZED_ACCEPT or
# USE_FLOCK_SERIALIZED_ACCEPT. This directive
# should normally be left at its default value.
# The main reason for changing it is if the logs
# directory is NFS mounted, since the lockfile
# MUST BE STORED ON A LOCAL DISK. The PID of the
# main server process is automatically appended to
# the filename.
#
# LockFile /usr/local/apache/var/run/httpd.lock

# ExtendedStatus controls whether Apache will
# generate "full" status
# information (ExtendedStatus On) or just basic
# information (ExtendedStatus
# Off) when the server-status Handler is called.
# The default is Off.
#
# ExtendedStatus On
```

Continued

Listing 13-5 *(continued)*

```
# ServerName allows you to set a host name which
# is sent back to clients for
# your server if it's different from the one the
# program would get (i.e., use "www" instead of the
# host's real name).
#
# Note: You cannot just invent host names and hope
# they work. The name you define here must be a valid
# DNS name for your host. If you don't understand
# this, ask your network administrator.
#
# If your host doesn't have a registered DNS
# name, enter its IP address here.
# You will have to access it by its address
# (e.g., http://123.45.67.89) anyway, and this
# will make redirections work in a sensible way.

# ServerName picaso.nitec.com

# Optionally, add a line containing the server
# version and virtual host name to server-generated
# pages (error documents, ftp directory listings,
# mod_status and mod_info output etc., but not SSI
# generated documents).
# Set to "EMail" to also include a mailto: link to
# the ServerAdmin. Set to one of:  On | Off | Email
#
ServerSignature on

# UseCanonicalName (new for 1.3): With this
# setting turned on, whenever
# Apache needs to construct a self-referencing
# URL (a url that refers back
# to the server the response is coming from), it
```

```
# will use ServerName and Port to form a "canonical"
# name.
# With this setting off, Apache will
# use the hostname:port that the client supplied,
# when possible.  This
# also affects SERVER_NAME and SERVER_PORT
# in CGIs.
UseCanonicalName on

# CacheNegotiatedDocs: By default, Apache sends
# Pragma: no-cache with each document that was
# negotiated on the basis of content. This asks proxy
# servers not to cache the document. Uncommenting
# the following line disables
# this behavior, and proxies will be allowed to cache the
# documents.

#CacheNegotiatedDocs

# Timeout: The number of seconds before receives
# and sends time out.

Timeout 300

# KeepAlive: Whether or not to allow persistent
# connections (more than
# one request per connection). Set to "off" to
# deactivate.

KeepAlive on

# MaxKeepAliveRequests: The maximum number of requests to
# allow
# during a persistent connection. Set to 0 to allow
```

Continued

Listing 13-5 *(continued)*

```
# an unlimited amount. We reccomend you leave this number
# high, for maximum performance.

MaxKeepAliveRequests 100

# KeepAliveTimeout: Number of seconds to wait for
# the next request.

KeepAliveTimeout 15

# Server-pool size regulation.  Rather than making
# you guess how many
# server processes you need, Apache dynamically adapts
# to the load it
# sees -- that is, it tries to maintain enough server
# processes to handle the current load, plus a few
# spare servers to handle transient
# load spikes (e.g., multiple simultaneous requests
# from a single Netscape browser).

# It does this by periodically checking how many
# servers are waiting for a request.  If there are
# fewer than MinSpareServers, it creates
# a new spare.  If there are more than MaxSpareServers,
# some of the spares die off.  These values are probably
# OK for most sites:

MinSpareServers 5
MaxSpareServers 10

# Number of servers to start—should be a
# reasonable ballpark figure.

StartServers 5
```

```
# Limit on total number of servers running, i.e.,
# limit on the number of clients who can simultaneously
# connect; if this limit is ever
# reached, clients will be LOCKED OUT, so it should
# NOT BE SET TOO LOW.
# It is intended mainly as a brake to keep a runaway
# server from taking
# UNIX with it as it spirals down.

MaxClients 150

# MaxRequestsPerChild: The number of requests each
# child process is allowed to process before the
# child dies. The child will exit so as to avoid
# problems after prolonged use when Apache (and maybe
# the libraries it uses) leak.  On most systems, this
# isn't really needed, but a few (such as Solaris)
# do have notable leaks
# in the libraries.

MaxRequestsPerChild 30

# Proxy Server directives. Uncomment the following
# line to enable the proxy server:

#ProxyRequests on

# Enable/disable the handling of HTTP/1.1
# "Via:" headers.
# ("Full" adds the server version; "Block" removes
# all outgoing Via: headers.) Set to one of:
# off | on | full | block
# ProxyVia on
```

Continued

Listing 13-5 *(continued)*

```
# To enable the cache as well, edit and
# uncomment the following lines:
# (no cacheing without CacheRoot).

#CacheRoot /usr/local/apache/var/proxy

#CacheSize 5
#CacheGcInterval 4
#CacheMaxExpire 24
#CacheLastModifiedFactor 0.1
#CacheDefaultExpire 1
#NoCache a_domain.com another_domain.edu
#joes.garage_sale.com

# Listen: Allows you to bind Apache to specific
# IP addresses and/or ports, in addition to the
# default. See also the VirtualHost command

# Listen 3000
#Listen 12.34.56.78:80

# VirtualHost: Allows the daemon to respond
# to requests for more than one server address,
# if your server machine is configured to accept
# IP packets for multiple addresses. This can be
# accomplished with the ifconfig
# alias flag, or through kernel patches like VIF.

# Any httpd.conf or srm.conf directive may go
# into a VirtualHost command.
# See also the BindAddress entry.

#<VirtualHost host.some_domain.com>
#ServerAdmin webmaster@host.some_domain.com
```

```
#DocumentRoot /www/docs/host.some_domain.com
#ServerName host.some_domain.com
#ErrorLog logs/host.some_domain.com-error_log
#TransferLog logs/host.some_domain.com-access_log
#</VirtualHost>


##
##  SSL Support
##
##  Note that all SSL options can apply to
##  virtual hosts, which
##  is where we are going to put them now. We disable
##  SSL globally
##  and enable only inside a virtual host.
##

<IfModule mod_ssl.c>
# We disable SSL globally.
SSLDisable
# Configure the path/port for the SSL session
# cache server [RECOMMENDED].
# Additionally sets the session cache timeout,
# in seconds (set to 15 for
# testing, use a higher value in real life)
[RECOMMENDED].
SSLCacheServerPath     /usr/local/apache/sbin/ssl_gcache
SSLCacheServerPort     /usr/local/apache/var/run/ \
ssl_gcache_port
SSLSessionCacheTimeout 300

<IfDefine SSL>
<VirtualHost _default_:443>
```

Continued

Listing 13-5 *(continued)*

```
# Set up the general virtual server configuration.
DocumentRoot /usr/local/apache/share/htdocs
ServerName picaso.nitec.com
ServerAdmin kabir@picaso.nitec.com
ErrorLog /usr/local/apache/var/log/error_log
TransferLog /usr/local/apache/var/log/access_log

# Enable SSL for this virtual host.
SSLEnable

# This forbids access except when SSL is in use.
# Very handy for defending
# against configuration errors that expose stuff
# that should be protected.
SSLRequireSSL

# Point SSLCertificateFile at a PEM-encoded certificate.
# If the certificate is encrypted, then you will be
# prompted for a pass phrase. Note that a kill -HUP
# will prompt again. A test certificate can be
# generated with `make certificate' underbuilt time
# [RECOMMENDED].
SSLCertificateFile     /usr/local/apache/etc/ssl.crt/ \
server.crt

#   If the key is not combined with the certificate, use
#   this directive to point at the key file [OPTIONAL].
SSLCertificateKeyFile  /usr/local/apache/etc/ssl.key/ \
server.key

#  set the CA certificate verification path where
#  to find CA certificates for client authentication or
#  alternatively one huge file containing all of them
#  (file must be PEM encoded) [OPTIONAL].
```

```
#  Note: Inside SSLCACertificatePath you need hash
#  symlinks to point to the certificate files.
#  Use the provided Makefile to update the hash symlinks
#  after changes.
# SSLCACertificatePath  /usr/local/apache/etc/ssl.crt
#SSLCACertificateFile  /usr/local/apache/etc/ssl.crt/
#ca-bundle.crt

#Set client verification level [RECOMMENDED]:
# 0|none:           no certificate is required
# 1|optional:
#   the client may  present a valid certificate
# 2|required:
#   the client must present a valid certificate
# 3|optional_no_ca:
#   the client may  present a valid certificate
#   but it is not required to have a valid CA
SSLVerifyClient none

# Set how deeply to verify the certificate issuer chain
# before deciding the certificate is not valid
# [OPTIONAL].
# SSLVerifyDepth 10

# List the ciphers that the client is permitted to
# negotiate.
# See the mod_ssl documentation for a complete list
# [OPTIONAL].
# SSLRequiredCiphers RC4-MD5:RC4-SHA:IDEA-CBC-MD5:
# DES-CBC3-SHA

#  These two can be used on a per-directory basis to
# require or
#  ban specific ciphers. Note that (at least in the
```

Continued

Listing 13-5 *(continued)*

```
#  current version)
#  SSL will not attempt to renegotiate if a cipher is
# banned
#  (or not required) [OPTIONAL].
# SSLRequiredCipher RC4-MD5
# SSLBanCipher RC4-MD5

#  Translate the client X.509 into a Basic Authorisation.
#  This means that the standard Auth/DBMAuth methods
#  can be used for
#  access control. The user name is the `one line'
# version of
#  the client's X.509 certificate. Note that no password
# is obtained from the user. Every entry in the
#  user file needs
#  this password: `xxj31ZMTZzkVA' [OPTIONAL].
# SSLFakeBasicAuth

#  A home for miscellaneous rubbish generated by SSL.
#  Much of it is duplicated in the error log file.
#  Put this somewhere where it cannot be used for
#  symlink attacks on a real server (i.e.
#  somewhere where only root can write) [RECOMMENDED].
SSLLogFile /usr/local/apache/var/log/ssl_misc_log

#  Define custom SSL logging [RECOMMENDED].
CustomLog /usr/local/apache/var/log/ssl_log "%t %h \
%{version}c %{cipher}c %{subjectdn}c %{issuerdn}c \"%r\"\
%b"

</VirtualHost>
</IfDefine>

</IfModule>
```

The first configuration segment in the file is as follows

```
<IfDefine SSL>
Listen 80
Listen 443
</IfDefine>
```

In the code above, Apache is made to listen to port 80 and 443 only if a label called SSL is defined in the command line of the Apache executable (httpd.) You can define the label when running Apache executable directly as follows:

```
httpd -DSSL
```

Or, you can use the apachectrl script from the sbin subdirectory of your Apache installation as follows:

```
apachectl -sslstart
```

If this lable is not defined, Apache listens only to port 80, which is set by the Port directive earlier in the configuration.

The next set of mod_ssl related directives that are found in the default httpd.conf file is as shown here without comments:

```
<IfModule mod_ssl.c>
SSLDisable
SSLCacheServerPath     /usr/local/apache/sbin/ssl_gcache
SSLCacheServerPort     /usr/local/apache/var/run/\
                       ssl_gcache_port
SSLSessionCacheTimeout 300

<IfDefine SSL>
<VirtualHost _default_:443>
  DocumentRoot /usr/local/apache/share/htdocs
  ServerName picaso.nitec.com
  ServerAdmin kabir@picaso.nitec.com
  ErrorLog /usr/local/apache/var/log/error_log
  TransferLog /usr/local/apache/var/log/access_log
```

```
  SSLEnable
  SSLRequireSSL
  SSLCertificateFile/usr/local/apache/etc/ssl.crt/\
  server.crt
  SSLCertificateKeyFile  /usr/local/apache/etc/\
  ssl.key/server.key
  SSLVerifyClient none
  SSLLogFile /usr/local/apache/var/log/ssl_misc_log
  CustomLog /usr/local/apache/var/log/ssl_log "%t %h \
%{version}c \ %{cipher}c %{subjectdn}c %{issuerdn}c \
\"%r\" %b"
</VirtualHost>
</IfDefine>

</IfModule>
```

Now the <IfModule modulename> container is used to make sure the enclosed directives are taken into consideration only if the mod_ssl.c module is compliled into the running Apache executable.

```
SSLDisable
```

This directive is used to disable SSL support everywhere. This is done to be able to enable SSL support where needed. In this example, SSL support is enabled for the mail server listening on port 443 and not on port 80.

```
SSLCacheServerPath      /usr/local/apache/sbin/ssl_gcache
SSLCacheServerPort      /usr/local/apache/var/run/\
ssl_gcache_port
SSLSessionCacheTimeout 300
```

These three directives are used to set up path, port, and timeout values for the SSL session cache server. Than again the <IfDefine Label> container is used to make sure that the server was intended to run in SSL mode using –DSSL or sslstart option provided at command-line. Next comes the virtual host configuration for the default server running on port 443. This is the SSL enabled server.

After the usual DocumentRoot, ServerName, ServerAdmin, ErrorLog, TransferLog directives, the SSLEnable directive is used to turn on SSL support for this virtual host. Next the SSLRequireSSL directive is used to ensure that only SSL-based access is permited for this virtual host.

```
SSLCertificateFile     /usr/local/apache/etc/ \
ssl.crt/server.crt
SSLCertificateKeyFile  /usr/local/apache/etc/ \
ssl.key/server.key
```

These two directives set the server's certificate and private key file path. If you already have a real certificate and private key for your server, you should use them here.

The next directive, SSLVerifyClient, is set to 'none' to allow any SSL-capable client to access the site. If you want to allow only clients with client certificates, you can set this to 'require.'

The SSLLogFile and the CustomLog directives are used to write SSL-related logging data in a custom file. This is really not needed since most of the SSL data is automatically written to the error log file of the virtual host.

If you are interested in running your main server as an SSL-enabled server, you can just put the following directives outside any virtual host configuration:

```
Listen 443
SSLEnable
SSLRequireSSL
SSLCertificateFile     /usr/local/apache/etc/ \
ssl.crt/server.crt
SSLCertificateKeyFile  /usr/local/apache/etc/ \
ssl.key/server.key
SSLVerifyClient none
```

The directives used in mod_ssl are the same as the Apache-SSL directives.

Testing Apache Built with mod_ssl

Testing your mod_ssl-enabled server is quite simple. You just restart the server using the apachectl script with 'sslstart' or 'startssl' option and access it as `https://yourserver.domain.tld`. If you are using a certificate created using the make certificate command, the Web browser will display warning dialog windows stating that the server is using SSL but the certificate is not issued by any known Certificate Authority. In such a case, you should apply for a real certificate from a known CA such as Verisign, Thawte, and so on.

Getting a CA-Signed Certificate

All you need to do is get a browser-recognizable certificate from one of the well-known Certificate Authorities. Here are a few CAs that are likely to provide you with a certificate for Apache-SSL:

- VeriSign at `www.verisign.com/`
- Thawte Consulting, at `www.thawte.com/certs/server/request.html`
- CertiSign Certificadora Digital Ltda., at `www.certisign.com.br`
- IKS GmbH, at `www.iks-jena.de/produkte/ca/`
- Uptime Commerce Ltd., at `www.uptimecommerce.com`
- ID-Pro GmbH, CA-Projekt, at www.id-pro.de/security/CA

The certification process requires that you produce paper documents proving the authenticity of your business. Such documents also will have to be accompanied by letters from high authorities in your organization. It is possible to get a certificate for your personal Web server; you do not have to have a legally founded company. For personal server certificates, only proof of an existing bank account is required by most CAs.

Chapter 14

Rewriting Your URLs

Installing mod_rewrite with Apache

By default, mod_rewrite module is not turned on in the standard Apache distribution. To enable the mod_rewrite module, use the --enable-module=rewrite option with configure (or config.status) script and recompile and install Apache again by running the make and the make install commands.

The Standard Variables for mod_rewrite

You should familiarize yourself with the server variables that can be used in many rewrite rules and conditions:

API_VERSION	Version of API used
AUTH_TYPE	Type of authentication used
DOCUMENT_ROOT	Top-level document directory of the Web site
HTTP_ACCEPT	MIME types that are acceptable by the Web client

HTTP_COOKIE	Cookie received from the Web client
HTTP_FORWARDED	Forwarding URL
HTTP_HOST	Web server's hostname
HTTP_PROXY_CONNECTION	The HTTP proxy connection information
HTTP_REFERER	The URL that referred to the current URL
HTTP_USER_AGENT	Information about the Web client
IS_SUBREQ	Set if request is a subrequest
PATH_INFO	Path of the requested URL
QUERY_STRING	Query data sent along with the requested URL
REMOTE_ADDR	IP address of the Web client
REMOTE_HOST	Host name of the Web client
REMOTE_USER	Username of the authenticated user
REMOTE_IDENT	Information about the remote user's identification
REQUEST_URI	Requested URI
REQUEST_FILENAME	Same as SCRIPT_FILENAME
REQUEST_METHOD	HTTP request method used to request the current URL
SCRIPT_FILENAME	Physical path of the requested script file
SERVER_ADMIN	Web server administrator's e-mail address
SERVER_NAME	Hostname of the Web server
SERVER_PORT	Port address of the Web server

SERVER_PROTOCOL	Version of HTTP protocol being used by the Web server
SERVER_SOFTWARE	Name of the Web server vendor
SERVER_VERSION	Version of the Web server software
THE_REQUEST	Requested URL
TIME	Current time
TIME_DAY	Current day
TIME_HOUR	Current hour
TIME_MIN	Current minute
TIME_MON	Current month
TIME_SEC	Current second
TIME_WDAY	Current weekday
TIME_YEAR	Current year

The mod_rewrite Directives

The following directives are available from mod_rewrite module:

RewriteBase

```
Syntax: RewriteBase <base URL>
Default: current directory path of per-directory config
(.htaccess)
Context: per-directory config (.htaccess)
```

This directive is useful only if you are using rewrite rules in per-directory configuration files. It is also required only for URL paths that do not map to the physical directory of the target file. Set this directive to whatever alias you used for the directory. This will ensure that mod_rewrite will use the alias instead of the physical path in the final (substituted) URL. For example, when an alias is set as follows:

```
Alias /icons/   /www/nitec/htdocs/icons/
```

and rewrite rules are enabled in the /www/nitec/htdocs/icons/ .htaccess file, the RewriteBase directive should be set as follows:

```
RewriteBase/icons/
```

RewriteCond

Syntax: `RewriteCond test-string condition-pattern [flag list]`
Context: `server config, virtual host, perl-directory config (.htaccess)`

This directive is useful when you want to add an extra condition for a rewrite rule specified by the RewriteRule directive. You can have several RewriteCond directives per RewriteRule. All rewrite conditions must be defined before the rule itself.

The test string may be constructed with plain text, server variables, or back-references from both the current rewrite rule and the last rewrite condition. To access the first back-reference from the current RewriteRule directive, use $1, and to access the first back-reference from the last RewriteCond directive, use %1.

To access a server variable, use the %{variable name} format. For example, to access the REMOTE_USER variable, specify %{REMOTE_USER} in the test string.

There are a few special data access formats:

- **%{ENV:variable}.** Use this to access any environment variable that is available to the Apache process.
- **%{HTTP:header}.** Use this to access the HTTP header used in the request.
- **%{LA-U:variable}.** Use this to access the value of a variable that is not available in the current stage of processing. For

example, if you need to make use of the REMOTE_USER server variable in a rewrite condition stored in the server's configuration file (httpd.conf), you cannot use %{REMOTE_USER} because this variable is defined only after the server has performed the authentication phase, which comes after mod_rewrite's URL-processing phase. To look ahead at what the username of the successfully authenticated user is, you can use %{LA-U:REMOTE_USER} instead. However, if you are accessing the REMOTE_USER data from a RewriteCond in a per-directory configuration file, you can use %{REMOTE_USER}, because the authorization phase has already finished and the server variable has become available as usual. The lookup is performed by generating a URL-based internal subrequest.

- **%{LA-F:variable}.** Same as the %{LA-U:variable} in most cases, but lookup is performed using a filename-based internal subrequest.

The condition pattern also can use some special notations, in addition to being a regular expression. For example, you can perform lexical comparisons between the test string and the condition pattern by prefixing the condition pattern with a <, >, or = character. In such a case, the condition pattern is compared with the test-string as plain text string.

Also, there may be times when you want to check whether the test-string is a file, directory, or symbolic link. In such a case, you can replace the condition pattern with the following special strings:

- **-d.** Tests whether the test-string specified directory exists
- **-f.** Tests whether the test-string specified file exists
- **-s.** Tests whether the test-string specified non-zero size file exists
- **-l.** Tests whether the test-string specified symbolic link exists
- **-F.** Tests the existence and accessibility of the test string-specified file

- **-U.** Tests the validity and accessibility of the test string-specified URL

The optional flag list can consist of one or more comma-separated strings as follows:

- **NC | nocase.** Performs a case-insensitive condition test.
- **OR | ornext.** Normally, when you have more than one RewriteCond for a RewriteRule directive, these conditions are ANDed together for the final substitution to occur. However, if you need to create an OR relationship between two conditions, use this flag.

RewriteEngine

Syntax: `RewriteEngine on | off`

Default: `RewriteEngine off`

Context: `server config, virtual host, per-directory config(.htaccess)`

This directive provides you with the On/Off switch for the URL rewrite engine in the mod_rewrite module. By default, all rewriting is turned Off. To use the rewrite engine, you must turn the engine on by setting this directive to On.

When enabling URL rewriting per-directory configuration (.htaccess) files, you must enable (set to On) this directive inside the per-directory configuration file and make sure that you have enabled the following directive in the appropriate context for the directory:

```
Options FollowSymLinks
```

In other words, if the directory belongs to a virtual host site, make sure this option is enabled inside the appropriate virtual host container. Similarly, if the directory in question is part of the main server's Web document space, make sure this option is enabled in the main server configuration.

Enabling rewrite rules in per-directory configurations could degrade the performance of your Apache server. This is because mod_rewrite employs a trick to support per-directory rewrite rules, and this trick involves increasing the server's processing load. Therefore, you should avoid using rewrite rules in per-directory configuration files whenever possible.

RewriteLock

Syntax: `RewriteLock filename`

Context: `server config, virtual host`

If you use an external mapping program for creating rewrite maps, you will need to specify a filename with this directive. This file is used as a lock file for synchronizing communication with external mapping programs.

RewriteLog

Syntax: `RewriteLog path/to/logfile`

Context: `server config, virtual host`

If you want to log the applications of your rewrite rules, use this directive to set a log filename. Like all other log directives, it assumes that a path without a leading slash (/) means that you want to write the log file in the server's root directory, for example:

```
RewriteLog logs/rewrite.log
```

This will write a log file in the logss subdirectory under your server's root directory. As mentioned before, a log written by the server should be writeable only by the server user.

RewriteLogLevel

Syntax: `RewriteLogLevel level`

Default: `RewriteLogLevel 0`

Context: `server config, virtual host`

This directive allows you to specify what gets logged in the log file. A default value of zero (0) means that nothing will be logged. In fact, a log level of zero (0) means no log-related processing is done inside the module. Therefore, if you wanted to disable logging, keep it set to zero (0).

If you set the RewriteLog directive to /dev/null and the RewriteLogLevel to a nonzero value, the internal log-related processing will still be done, but no log will be produced. This is a waste of your system's computing resources, so if you don't want logging, keep this directive set to its default value. You have a choice between zero (0) and nine (9) for log levels. The higher the level, the more logging data is written.

RewriteMap

Syntax: `RewriteMap name-of-map type-of-map: source-of-map`

Context: `server config, virtual host`

This directive facilitates a key-to-value lookup through the use of a map. Think of a map as a table of data where each row has a key and a value. Typically, a map will be stored in a file. However, the map can be either a text file, a DBM file, internal Apache functions, or an external program. The type of the map corresponds to the source of the map. The applicable types are:

- **txt.** Plain text file that has key value lines such that each key and value pair are on a single line and are separated by at least one whitespace character. The file can contain comment lines starting with # characters or can have blank lines. Both comments and blank lines are ignored.

```
Key1    value1
Key2    value2
```

The example above defines two key value pairs. Note that text file-based maps are read during Apache startup and reread only if the file has been updated after the server is already up and running. The files are also reread during server restarts.

- **rnd**. A special plain text file that has all the restrictions of txt type but allows flexibility in defining the value. The value for each key can be defined as a set of ORed values using the | (vertical bar) character.

```
Key1    first_value_for_key1 | second_value_for_key1
Key2    first_value_for_key2 | second_value_for_key2
```

The example above defines two key value pairs where each key has multiple values. The value selected is decided randomly.

- **int**. The internal Apache functions toupper(key) or tolower(key) can be used as a map source. The first function converts the key into all uppercase characters and the second one converts the key to lowercase characters.
- **dbm**. A DBM file can be used as a map source. This can be very useful and fast (compared to text files) when you have a large number of key value pairs. Note that DBM-file-based maps are read during Apache startup and reread only if the file has been updated after the server is already up and running. The files are also reread during server restarts.
- **prg**. An external program can generate the value. When a program is used, it is started at Apache startup, and data (key, value) is transferred between Apache and the program via standard input (stdin) and standard output (stdout). Make sure you use the RewriteLock directive to define a lock file when using an external program. When constructing such a program, make sure you read the input from the stdin and write it on stdout in a nonbuffered I/O mode.

RewriteOptions

Syntax: `RewriteOptions option1 option2 ...`

Default: none

Context: `server config, virtual host, per-directory config (.htaccess)`

This directive enables you to specify options to change the rewrite engine's behavior. Currently, the only available option is inherit. By setting this directive to the inherit option, you can force a higher-level configuration to be inherited by a lower-level one. For example, if you set this directive in your main server configuration area, a virtual host defined in the configuration file will inherit all the rewrite configurations, such as the rewrite rules, conditions, maps, and so on.

Similarly, when this directive is set as mentioned in a per-directory configuration file (.htaccess), it will inherit the parent directory's rewrite rules, conditions, and maps. By default, the rewrite engine does not permit inheritance of rewrite configuration, but this directive permits you to alter the default.

RewriteRule

Syntax: `RewriteRule search-pattern substitution-string [flag list]`

Context: `server config, virtual host, per-directory config (.htaccess)`

This directive enables you to define a rewrite rule. The rule must have two arguments. The first argument is the search pattern that must be met to apply the substitution string. The search pattern is written using regular expression (see Appendix B for basics of regular expression). The substitution string can be constructed with plain text, back-references to substrings in the search pattern, values from server variables, or even map functions. The flag list can contain one or more flag strings, separated by commas, to inform the rewrite engine about what to do next with the substitution. Let's take a look back at the previous example:

```
RewriteRule /~([^/]+)/?(.*)   /users/$1/$2 [R]
```

Here, the search pattern is /~([^/]+)/?(.*) and the substitution string is /users/$1/$2. Notice the use of back-references in the substitution string. The first back-reference string $1 corresponds to the string found in the first set of parentheses (from the left). So, $1 is set to whatever is matched in ([^/]+) and $2 is set to the next string found in (.*). When a URL request is as follows:

```
http://blackhole.nitec.com/~kabir/welcome.html
```

The value of $1 is kabir, and $2 is welcome.html; so the substitution string looks like:

```
/users/kabir/welcome.html
```

When you have more than one RewriteRule specified, the first RewriteRule operates on the original URL, and if a match occurs, the second rule will no longer operate on the original URL. Instead, it gets the URL substituted by first rule as the URL on which to apply rules. In a scenario in which a match occurs at every step, a set of three rewrite rules will function as follows:

```
RewriteRule  search-pattern-for-original-URL\
substitution-string-1  [flags]
RewriteRule  search-pattern-for-substitution-string-1\
substitution-string-2  [flags]
RewriteRule  search-pattern-for-substitution-string-2\
substitution-string-3  [flags]
```

Is it possible to apply more than one rule to the original URL? Yes, you can use the C flag to instruct the rewrite engine to chain multiple rules. In such a case, you may not want to substitute until all rules arc matched so you can use a special substitution string to disable a substitution in a rule.

The details of the possible flags are as follows:

- **C | chain.** This flag specifies that the current rule be chained with the next rule. When chained by a C flag, a rule is looked at if and only if the previous rule in the chain results in a match. Each rule in the chain must contain the flag, and if the first rule does not match, the entire chain of rules is ignored.
- **E=var:value | env=var:value.** You can set an environment variable using this directive. The variable is accessible from rewrite conditions, Server Side Includes, CGI scripts, and so on.
- **F | forbidden.** When a rule using this flag is matched, an HTTP response header called FORBIDDEN (status code 403) is sent back to the browser. This effectively disallows the requested URL.
- **G | gone.** When a rule using this flag is matched, an HTTP response header called GONE (status code 410) is sent back to the browser. This informs the browser that the requested URL is no longer available on this server.
- **L | last.** This tells the rewrite engine to end rule processing immediately so that no other rules are applied to the last substituted URL.
- **N | next.** This tells the rewrite engine to restart from the first rule. However, the first rule no longer tries to match the original URL, because it now operates on the last substituted URL. This effectively creates a loop. You must have terminating conditions in the loop to avoid an infinite loop.
- **NS | nosubreq.** Use this flag to avoid applying a rule on an internally generated URL request.
- **P | proxy.** Using this flag will convert a URL request to a proxy request internally. This will work only if you have compiled Apache with the mod_proxy module and configured it to use the proxy module.

- **PT | passthrough.** This is a hack and likely to disappear in a later version of Apache. This flag forces the rewrite engine to modify the internal request record structure such that the URL member variable of the structure is set to the value of the filename member variable. Use this directive only when you are using directives from mod_rewrite with other modules that contain URL-to-filename translators. An example of such module is the mod_alias module.
- **QSA | qsappend.** This flag allows you to append data (such as key=value pairs) to the query string part of the substituted URL.
- **R [=HTTP status code] | redirect |.** Using this flag, you can send an external HTTP redirect request to the Web browser. When this flag is used in a rule that matches, the substitute URL is prefixed with http://server[:port]/ and a default HTTP status code of 302 (MOVED TEMPORARILY) is sent to the Web browser. If you would like to use other valid HTTP status code, use the optional 'code=' option.
- **S=n | skip=n.** Skips n rules.
- **T=mime-type | type=mime-type.** Forces the specified MIME-type to be the MIME-type of the target file of the request.

You can add conditions to your rules by preceding them with one or more RewriteCond directives, which are discussed in the RewriteCond section above.

Examples of Rewrite Rules

In the following sections, I demonstrate various practical uses of the mod_rewrite module.

URL Layout

In this section, you will find examples of URL rewrites that deal with the layout of URLs. Often you will need to redirect or expand a URL request to another URL. In the following examples, you will see how mod_rewrite can help in such cases.

Expanding requested URL to canonical URL

Web sites that offer user home pages usually support a URL scheme such as:

```
http://hostname/~username
```

This is a shortcut URL and needs to be mapped to a canonical URL. You also may have other shortcuts or internal URLs that need to be expended to their canonical URLs. In this example, you will see how the ~username gets translated to /u/username.

When a request for `http://hostname/~username` is received, the rewrite rule will translate that into /u/username and redirect the new URL to the browser. The browser then rerequests the `http://hostname/u/username` URL, and the usual Apache request processing completes the request.

The external HTTP redirect is necessary because any subsequent requests also must use the translated canonical URL instead of ~username. The rule needed to do this is:

```
RewriteRule    ^/~([^/]+)/?(.*)     /u/$1/$2  [R]
```

Many ISP sites with thousand of users use a structured home directory layout; that is, each home directory is in a subdirectory that begins, for instance, with the first character of the username. So, /~foo/anypath is /home/f/foo/www/anypath while /~bar/anypath is /home/b/bar/www/anypath. To implement a translation scheme from shortcut URLs to canonical URLs in this case, the following rule can be used:

```
RewriteRule    ^/~(([a-z])[a-z0-9]+)(.*) /home/$2/$1/www$3
```

Redirecting a user home directory to a new Web server

If you had a lot of user home pages on a Web server and needed to move them to a new machine for some reason, you would need to have a redirect rule like this:

```
RewriteRule   ^/~(.+)  http://newserver/~$1  [R,L]
```

This rule redirects all /~user/anypath URLs from the old server to `http://newserver/~user/anypath`. The L flag is used to indicate that no other rewrite rule can be applied to the substituted URL.

Searching for a page in multiple directories

Sometimes it is necessary to let the Web server search for pages in more than one directory. Here MultiViews or other techniques cannot help. For example, say you want to handle a request for `http://hostname/filename.html` such that if filename.html is not present in the dir1 directory of your Web server, you want the server to try a subdirectory called dir2. The rules needed to implement this are as follows:

```
RewriteCond   /your/docroot/dir1/%{REQUEST_FILENAME}  -f
RewriteRule   ^(.+)  /your/docroot/dir1/$1  [L]

RewriteCond   /your/docroot/dir2/%{REQUEST_FILENAME}  -f
RewriteRule   ^(.+)  /your/docroot/dir2/$1  [L]

RewriteRule   ^(.+)  -      [PT]
```

The first rule substitutes the requested URL with `/your/docroot/dir1/$1` (where $1 is the target file in the request) only if the requested file exists in your/docroot/dir1/subdirectory. If the condition is met, this is the last rule applied to this URL. However, if no match is found, then the next rule applies. This rule does the same thing as the first one, but this time a subdirectory DIR2 is used for the path. This rule is also final if a match is found. In the event that none of the rules match, the request is not substituted and is passed on to Apache as usual.

Setting an environment variable based on a URL

You might want to keep status information between requests and use the URL to encode it. But you don't want to use a CGI wrapper script for all pages just to strip out this information. You can use a rewrite rule to strip out the status information and store it via an environment variable that can be later dereferenced from within XSSI or CGI. This way, a URL `/foo/S=java/bar/` gets translated to `/foo/bar/`, and the environment variable named STATUS is set to the value java. The following rewrite rule does just that:

```
RewriteRule   ^(.*)/S=([^/]+)/(.*)    $1/$3 [E=STATUS:$2]
```

Here, the value of $3 gets stored in the environment variable called STATUS using the E flag.

Creating www.username.host.com sites

Assume that you want to provide `www.username.host.com` for the home page of username via just DNS address (A) records to the same machine and without any virtual hosts on this machine. For HTTP/1.0 requests, there is no solution, but for HTTP/1.1 requests that contain a Host: HTTP header, you can use the following rule set to rewrite `http://www.username.host.com/anypath` internally to `/home/username/anypath`:

```
RewriteCond   %{HTTP_HOST}  ^www\.[^.]+\.host\.com$
RewriteRule   ^(.+)  %{HTTP_HOST}$1  [C]
RewriteRule   ^www\.([^.]+)\.host\.com(.*)   /home/$1$2
```

This is an example of a chained rule set. The first rule has a condition that checks to see if the environment variable HTTP_HOST matches a pattern such as `www.username.host.com`. If it does, the rule is applied. In other words, a request such as `www.username.host.com/anypath` gets substituted with `www.username.host.com`

/anypath. This could be a bit confusing because whether or not the substitution is needed is not quite obvious. It is needed so that the username can be extracted using the second rule. The second rule extracts the username part from the substituted request and creates a new URL /home/username/anypath for an internal subrequest.

Redirecting a failing URL to another Web server

If you have a multiserver Web network, and you often move contents from one server to another, you might face a problem in which you need to redirect failing URL requests to from Web server A to Web server B. There are many ways of doing this: you can use the ErrorDocument directive, write a CGI script to handle this, or use mod_rewrite to rewrite the failing URLs to the other server. Using this mod_rewrite-based solution is less preferable than using an ErrorDocument CGI script. The first solution performs the best but is less flexible and not as error-safe:

```
RewriteCond   /your/docroot/%{REQUEST_FILENAME}  !-f
RewriteRule   ^(.+)  http://Web serverB.dom/$1
```

The problem here is that this will work only for pages inside the DocumentRoot. While you can add more conditions (to also handle home directories, for example), there is a better variant:

```
RewriteCond   %{REQUEST_URI}  !-U
RewriteRule   ^(.+)  http://Web serverB.dom/$1
```

This uses the URL look-ahead feature of mod_rewrite, and will work for all types of URLs. This does have a performance impact on the Web server, however, because for every request there is one more internal subrequest. If your Web server runs on a powerful CPU, use this one. If it is a slow machine, use the first approach or, better, an ErrorDocument CGI script.

Creating an access multiplexer

This example will show you how to create a rule set to redirect requests based on a domain type, such as .com, .net, .edu, .org, .uk,

.de, and so on. The idea is to redirect the visitor to the geographically nearest Web site. This technique is employed by many large corporations to redirect international customers to an appropriate Web site or FTP server.

The first step in creating such a solution is to create a map file. For example, the following shows a text-based map file called site-redirect.map:

```
com     http://www.mydomain.com/download/
net     http://www.mydomain.com/download/
edu     http://www.mydomain.com/download/
org     http://www.mydomain.com/download/
uk      http://www.mydomain.uk/download/
de      http://www.mydomain.de/download/
ch      http://www.mydomain.ch/download/
```

When a request is received for `http://www.mycompany.com/download/anypath` from a host called `dialup001.demon.uk`, the request needs to be redirected to the Web site `www.mydomain.uk/download/`, and similarly, any request from hosts that belong to the top-level domains (TLD) `.com`, `.net`, `.edu`, and `.org` is routed to the `www.mycompany.com/download/` site.

Here are the rules that are needed for the preceding setup:

```
RewriteMap      sitemap    txt:/path/to/site-redirect.map
RewriteRule     ^/download/(.*)     %{REMOTE_HOST}::$1  [C]
RewriteRule     ^.+\.([a-zA-Z]+)::(.*)$\
%{sitemap:$1|www.mydomain.com/download/}$2  [R,L]
```

When a host such as `dialup001.demon.uk` requests the `www.mydomain.com/download/index.html` page, the first rule rewrites the request using the hostname of the requesting host as follows:

```
dialup001.demon.uk::index.html
```

Then the next rule in the chain is applied. This rule gets applied when the search pattern matches, and the substitution URL is created by looking up the map file for the TLD. If no matches are found, the default www.mydomain.com is used. This is done by the | (or) operator in the substitution URL string. Perhaps it is easier to understand the second rule using the algorithm shown in Listing 14-1.

Listing 14-1 *Algorithm for the second rewrite rule*

```
if(current URL matches a fully-qualified-
hostname::anything) then

       Substitute the current URL using the domain-type
       information stored in $1; perform a lookup in
       the map file.

If  (map file has a key that
     matches the domain type) then

      Use the key's value as follows:
      Substituted URL = value-of-the-key$2  where $2 is
      anything after
      the fully qualified hostname:: pattern.



Else
      Use default value www.mydomain.com/download/$2
      Substituted URL = www.mydomain.com/download/$2
endif

Endif
```

The R flag makes this an external URL redirect, and the L flag makes this the last rule for the substituted URL.

Creating time-sensitive URLs

Ever wonder if it would be possible to have a URL that would point to different files based on time? Well, mod_rewrite makes it easy to create such a URL. There are a lot of variables named TIME_xxx for rewrite conditions. Using the special lexicographic comparison patterns <STRING, >STRING, and =STRING you can do time-dependent redirects, for example:

```
RewriteCond   %{TIME_HOUR}%{TIME_MIN} >0700
RewriteCond   %{TIME_HOUR}%{TIME_MIN} <1900
RewriteRule   ^foo\.html$             foo.day.html
RewriteRule   ^foo\.html$             foo.night.html
```

This provides the content of foo.day.html under the URL foo.html from 07:00 to19:00 and the remaining time provides the contents of foo.night.html.

Content Handling

The examples in this section deal with content-specific rewriting rules.

Adding Backward Compatibility in URLs

Assume that you have recently renamed the page bar.html to foo.html, and now you want to provide the old URL for backward compatibility. Additionally, you do not want the users of the old URL to even recognize that the page was renamed. How can this be done? Here is how:

```
RewriteRule    ^foo\.html$  bar.html
```

If you want to let the browser know about the change, you can do an external rewrite so the browser will display the new URL. All you need to do is add the R flag as follows:

```
RewriteRule    ^foo\.html$  bar.html [R]
```

Creating Browser-Matched Content URLs

You can use rewrite rules to dish out different contents (using internal subrequests) to different browsers. You cannot use content negotiation for this because browsers do not provide their types in that form. Instead you have to act on the HTTP header User-Agent. For example, if a browser's User-Agent header matched Mozilla/4 then you can send out a Netscape Navigator 4 (or above) features-friendly page, or you can send out a different page if the browser is an older version of Navigator or another type of browser. For example:

```
RewriteCond %{HTTP_USER_AGENT}  ^Mozilla/4.*
RewriteRule ^foo\.html$         foo.4x.html       [L]
RewriteCond %{HTTP_USER_AGENT}  ^Lynx/.*          [OR]
RewriteCond %{HTTP_USER_AGENT}  ^Mozilla/[123]. *
RewriteRule ^foo\.html$         foo.old.html      [L]
```

Here, when a request for a URL such as `http://hostname/foo.html` is received, the first condition tests to see if the environment variable HTTP_USER_AGENT has a value that contains the string Mozilla/4. If it does, the first rule is applied. This rule substitutes `foo.4x.html` for the original URL, and all rewriting is complete. When the first rule is not applied, the second rule is invoked. There are two conditions that are ORed. In other words, one of these conditions must match before this rule can be applied.

The first condition tests the same environment variable for the substring Lynx/, and the second condition tests the same environment variable for the substring Mozilla/1 or Mozilla/2 or Mozilla/3. If any of these conditions is met, the rule is applied. The rule substitutes `foo.old.html` for the original URL. The substituted URL is turned into a subrequest and processed by Apache as usual.

Creating an HTML-to-CGI Gateway

You may want to transform a static page foo.html into a dynamic variant foo.cgi in a seamless way—that is, without informing the browser or user. Here is how:

```
RewriteRule    ^foo\.html$  foo.cgi\
[T=application/x-httpd-cgi]
```

The rule rewrites a request for foo.html to a request for foo.cgi. It also forces the correct MIME-type so it gets run as a CGI script. A request, such as `http://hostname/foo.html`, is internally translated into a request for the CGI script. The browser does not know that its request has been redirected.

Access Restriction

These examples deal with access control issues.

Blocking Robots

It's easy to block an annoying robot from retrieving pages of a specific Web site. You might try a robots.txt file containing entries of the Robot Exclusion Protocol, but that is typically not enough to get rid of such a robot. A sample solution follows:

```
RewriteCond   %{HTTP_USER_AGENT}   ^NameOfBadRobot.*
RewriteCond   %{REMOTE_ADDR}       ^123\.45\.67\.[8-9]$
RewriteRule   ^/not/to/be/indexed/by/robots/.+   -   [F]
```

This rule has two conditions, as follows:

```
If  (HTTP_USER_AGENT of the robot
     matches a pattern "NameOfBadRobot") and
    (REMOTE_ADDR of the requesting host
     is 123.45.67.8 to 123.45.67.9)
Then
    No substitution
    but send an HTTP "Forbidden" header
    (status code 403)

endif
```

As you can see, the robot's User-Agent header is matched, along with the IP address of the host it uses. These conditions allow for multiple IP addresses (123.45.67.8 and 123.45.67.9) to be checked.

Creating an HTTP Referer-Based URL Deflector

You can program a flexible URL deflector that acts on the Referer HTTP header and configure it with as many referring pages as you like. Here is how:

```
RewriteMap    deflector        txt:/path/to/deflector.map
RewriteRule   ^/(.*) ${deflector:%{HTTP_REFERER}|/$1}
RewriteRule   ^/DEFLECTED          %{HTTP_REFERER}  [R,L]
RewriteRule   .* - [PT]
This is used in conjunction with a corresponding rewrite
map such as:
http://www.badguys.com/bad/index.html \ DEFLECTED
http://www.badguys.com/bad/index2.html  DEFLECTED
http://www.badguys.com/bad/index3.html \
http://somewhere.com/
```

This automatically redirects the request back to the referring page if the URL matches the DEFLECTED value in the map file. In all other cases, the requests are redirected to specified URLs.

Chapter 15

Proxy in Apache

Compiling the Proxy Module

Proxy support in Apache comes from the mod_proxy module, which is not compiled by default.

If you are using the APACI interface for compiling and installing Apache, then building a new Apache executable with proxy module is as easy as performing the following steps in your Apache source distribution directory.

If you are running the configure script for the first time, then enter the following command:

```
./configure --prefix=/dir/where/you/want/to/install/ \
apache --enable-mode=proxy
```

On the other hand, if you have already run the configure script before to compile Apache, run:

```
./config.status  --enable-module=proxy
```

This way your previous configuration options will be applied in creating a new configuration file.

Now run the make command. If it returns no error messages, run the make command with the install option to install the newly compiled Apache executable in the appropriate directory.

However, if you are using the old-fashioned method for compiling Apache, you will have to edit the src/Configuration file such that the `AddModule modules/proxy/libproxy.a` line is uncommented. You will then run the src/Configure script to create the new Makefile. Once src/Configure is finished, you will need to run the make command. If the make command returns without any error messages, then change directories to the top-level of your Apache distribution and run make again with the install option to install the new Apache executable in the appropriate directory.

Once you have compiled and installed the new Apache executable (httpd) in the appropriate directory, you can verify that the mod_proxy.c module is built into your current server. Run the following and make sure that the mod_proxy.c is listed in the output:

```
httpd -l
```

Proxy Module Directives

The proxy module for Apache comes with the following set of directives, which are needed to make use of the module.

ProxyBlock

Syntax: `ProxyBlock <partial or full host name> ...`
Default: `None`
Context: `server config, virtual host`

This directive enables you block access to a named host or domain, for example:

```
ProxyBlock gates
```

This will block access to any host that has the word *gates* in its name. This way, access to `http://gates.ms.com` or `http://gates.friendsofbill.com` will be blocked. You also can specify multiple hosts as follows:

```
ProxyBlock apple orange.com banana.com
```

This blocks all access to any host that matches any of the preceding words or domain names. The mod_proxy module attempts to determine the IP addresses for these hosts during server start-up, and caches them for matching later.

To block access to all hosts, use:

```
ProxyBlock *
```

This effectively disables your proxy server.

ProxyDomain

Syntax: `ProxyDomain <Domain>`

Default: `None`

Context: `server config, virtual host`

This directive specifies the default domain name for the proxy server. When this directive is set to the local domain name on an intranet, any request that does not include a domain name will get this domain name appended in the request, for example:

```
ProxyDomain     .nitec.com
```

When a user of `nitec.com` domain sends a request for an URL such as `http://marketing/us.html`, the request will be regenerated as the following URL:

```
http://marketing.nitec.com/us.html
```

Note that the domain name you specify must have a leading period.

ProxyPass

Syntax: `ProxyPass <relative-URL> <destination-URL>`

Default: `None`

Context: `server config, virtual host`

This directive enables you to map a Web server's document tree onto your proxy server's document space. For example:

```
ProxyPass /internet/microsoft      www.microsoft.com/
```

This directive found in the HTTPD.CONF file of a proxy server called `proxy.nitec.com` will permit users of the proxy server to access the Microsoft Web site using the URL:

```
http://proxy.nitec.com/internet/microsoft
```

This acts like a mirror of the remote Web site. Any request that uses the <relative-URL> will be converted internally into a proxy request for the <destination-URL>.

Mirroring another Web site without permission is illegal; therefore, make sure you have written permission from a Web site owner before creating a mirror site.

ProxyPassReverse

Syntax: `ProxyPassReverse <relative-URL> <destination-URL>`

Default: `None`

Context: `server config, virtual host`

This directive is useful when you want to create a reverse proxy server using Apache. In such a reverse proxy setup, this directive fixes the Location headers that might be returned by the actual Web server.

```
<Virtualhost 206.171.50.50>
ServerName www.nitec.com
ProxyRequests  on
ProxyPass / realserver.nitec.com/
ProxyPassReverse / realserver.nitec.com/
</VirtualHost>
```

In the preceding example, the `www.nitec.com` is the proxy server that gets all the pages from another server called `realserver.nitec.com`. The ProxyPass directive enables this feature. However, if a page on the `realserver.nitec.com` sends a Location header in response, the ProxyPassReverse directive fixes it so that the proxy server `www.nitec.com` is not bypassed by the client.

ProxyReceiveBufferSize

Syntax: `ProxyReceiveBufferSize <bytes>`

Default: `None`

Context: `server config, virtual host`

This directive sets the network buffer size for outgoing requests from the proxy server. It has to be greater than 512. However, to use the system's default buffer size, set this directive to zero (0).

ProxyRequests

Syntax: `ProxyRequests on/off`

Default: `ProxyRequests off`

Context: `server config, virtual host`

This directive allows you to enable or disable the caching proxy service. However, it does not affect the functionality of the ProxyPass directive.

ProxyRemote

Syntax: `ProxyRemote <match> <remote-proxy-server-URL>`

Default: `None`

Context: `server config, virtual host`

This directive enables you to interface your proxy server with another proxy server. The value of match can be one of the following:

- The name of an URL scheme that the remote server supports
- A partial URL for which the remote server should be used
- To indicate the server should be contacted for all requests

The <remove-proxy-server-URL> can be `http://remove-proxy-hostname:port`. Note that, currently, only the HTTP protocol is supported. In other words, you can only specify a proxy server that deals with the HTTP protocol; however, you can forward FTP requests from your proxy server to one that supports both HTTP and FTP protocols as follows:

```
ProxyRemote ftp http://ftp.proxy.nitec.com:8000
```

This will send all FTP requests that come to the local proxy server to `ftp://ftp.proxy.nitec.com`. The requests will be send via HTTP, so the actual FTP transaction will occur at the remote proxy server.

If you just want to forward all proxy requests for a certain Web site to its proxy server directly, you can do that with this directive. For example:

```
ProxyRemote http://www.bigisp.com/  http://web-\
proxy.bigisp.com:8000
```

This will send all requests that match `www.bigisp.com` to `web-proxy.bigisp.com`. If you want to forward all of your proxy requests to another proxy, however, you can use the asterisk as the match phrase, for example:

```
ProxyRemote * http://proxy.domain.com
```

This will send all local proxy requests to the proxy server at `proxy.domain.com`.

NoProxy

Syntax: `NoProxy <Domain name|  Subnet | IP Address | Hostname>`
Default: `None`
Context: `server config, virtual host`

This directive gives you some control over the ProxyRemote directive in an intranet environment. You can specify a domain name, subnet, IP address, or hostname not to be served by the proxy server specified in the ProxyRemote directive. For example:

```
ProxyRemote  *  http://firewall.yourcompany.com:8080
NoProxy         .yourcompany.com
```

In the code above, all requests for <anything>.yourcompany.com (such as www.yourcompany.com) will be served by the local proxy server, and everything else will go to the firewall.yourcompany.com proxy server.

CacheDefaultExpire

Syntax: `CacheDefaultExpire <n hours>`

Default: `CacheDefaultExpire 1`

Context: `server config, virtual host`

This directive provides a default time (in hours) that is used to expire a cached file when the last modification time of the file is unknown. CacheMaxExpire does not override this setting.

CacheDirLength

Syntax: `CacheDirLength <length>`

Default: `CacheDirLength 1`

Context: `server config, virtual host`

When disk caching is On, Apache creates subdirectories in the directory specified by the CacheRoot directive. This directive specifies the number of characters used in creating the subdirectory names. You really do not need to change the default for this directive. For curious users who want to know how or why these subdirectories are created, a simplified answer follows.

Apache uses a hashing scheme when creating the path and filename for a URL's data to be cached. For example, when you have caching turned On and access a URL (such as www.microsoft.com) via your proxy Apache server, the server hashes this URL so it can retrieve the data quickly later on. This hash could look like `1YSRxSmB20Q_HkqkTuXeqvw`. If the defaults are used for both the CacheDirLength and CacheDirLevels directives, Apache will store the data found on www.microsoft.com in a file called:

```
%CacheRoot%/1/Y/S/RRxSmB20Q_HkqkTuXeqvw
```

Here, %CACHEROOT% is the directory specified by the CacheRoot directive. The 1/Y/S directories get created because of the default value of the CacheDirLevels directive. When this document is requested again using the same URL, Apache needs to only recalculate the hash and retrieve the page from the specified path.

By spreading files over multiple directories, Apache reduces the total number of files per directory, which makes file lookups faster.

CacheDirLevels

Syntax: `CacheDirLevels <levels>`

Default: `CacheDirLevels 3`

Context: `server config, virtual host`

This specifies the number of subdirectories that Apache will create to store cache data files. See the "CacheDirLength" section for related information.

CacheForceCompletion

Syntax: `CacheForceCompletion <percentage>`

Default: `CacheForceCompletion 90`

Context: `server config, virtual host`

This directive tells the proxy server to continue transferring a document from the remote HTTP/FTP server, even if the request is cancelled. The percentage specified in the directive makes the proxy server determine if it should continue or not with the transfer. The default value is 90 percent, which tells the proxy server to continue transferring when 90 percent of the document is already cached. You can change the value from 1 to 100.

CacheGcInterval

Syntax: `CacheGcInterval <n hours>`

Default: `None`

Context: `server config, virtual host`

This directive specifies the time (in hours) when Apache should check the cache directories for deleting expired files. This is also when Apache will enforce the disk space usage limit specified by the CacheSize directive.

CacheLastModifiedFactor

Syntax: `CacheLastModifiedFactor <floating point number>`

Default: `CacheLastModifiedFactor 0.1`

Context: `server config, virtual host`

This directive specifies a factor used to calculate expiration time when the original Web server does not supply an expiration date for a document. The calculation is done using the following formula:

```
expiry-period = (last modification time for the
document) * (floating point number)
```

So, if a document was last modified 24 hours ago, then the default factor of 0.1 will make Apache calculate the expiration time for this document to be 2.4 hours. If the calculated expiration period is longer than that set by CacheMaxExpire, then the latter takes precedence.

CacheMaxExpire

Syntax: `CacheMaxExpire <n hours>`

Default: `CacheMaxExpire 24`

Context: `server config, virtual host`

This directive specifies the time (in hours) when all cached documents expire. In other words, if you specify this directive as written below then all the cached documents will expire in 48 hours, or two days:

```
CacheMaxExpire 48
```

This directive overrides any expiration date specified in the document itself; so if a document has a expiration date later than the maximum specified by this directive, the document is still removed.

CacheRoot

Syntax: `CacheRoot <directory>`

Default: `None`

Context: `server config, virtual host`

This directive allows you to enable disk caching. You can specify a directory name where the proxy server can write cached files. The Apache server running the proxy module must have write permission for the directory, for example:

```
CacheRoot /www/proxy/cache
```

This will tell Apache to write proxy cache data to the /www/proxy/cache directory. Note that you will need to specify the size of the cache using the CacheSize directory before the proxy server can start using this directory for caching. You also may need to use other cache directives such as CacheSize, CacheMaxExpire, CacheDefault Expire, CacheGcInterval, CacheDirLength, and so on to create a usable disk caching proxy solution.

CacheSize

Syntax: `CacheSize <n kilobytes>`

Default: `CacheSize 5`

Context: `server config, virtual host`

This directive specifies the amount of disk space (in K) that should be used for disk caching. The cached files are written in the directory specified by the CacheRoot directive. Note that it is possible for the proxy server to write more data than the specified limit, but the proxy server's garbage collection scheme will delete files until the usage is at or below this setting. The default setting (5K) is unrealistic; I recommend anywhere from 10MB to 1GB depending on your user load.

NoCache

Syntax: `NoCache <Domain name| Subnet | IP Address | \`
`Hostname> ...`
Default: `None`
Context: `server config, virtual host`

The NoCache directive specifies a list of hosts, domain names, and IP addresses, separated by spaces, for which no caching is performed. This directive should be used to disable caching of local Web servers on an intranet. Note that the proxy server also matches partial names of a host. If you want to disable caching altogether, use the following:

```
NoCache *
```

Configuring the Proxy Server

To enable the proxy server, you need to set the ProxyRequests to On. After that, the additional configuration depends on what you want to do with your proxy server. Whatever you decide to do with it, any proxy configuration that you choose should go inside a special <Directory . . .> container that looks like the following:

```
<Directory proxy:*>
. . .
</Directory>
```

Any directives that you want to use to control the proxy server's behavior should go inside this container. The asterisk is a wild card for the requested URL. In other words, when a request for `www.nitec.com` is processed by the Apache server, it looks like:

```
<Directory proxy:http://www.nitec.com/>
. . .
</Directory>
```

You also can use the <Directory ~ /RE/> container, which uses regular expressions, for example:

```
<Directory ~ proxy:http://[^:/]+/.*>
. . .
</Directory>
```

Now let's look at a few commonly used proxy configurations.

Connecting a Private IP Network to the Internet

If you have a network of computers using private nonroutable IP addresses, and you want to provide Internet connectivity such as HTTP/FTP services for these systems, all you need is a single computer with a valid IP address running Apache with a proxy module. This computer needs to run the Apache proxy server with the ProxyRequest set to ON, and no additional proxy configuration is needed. All HTTP/FTP requests can be serviced by this proxy server.

In such a configuration, the proxy server needs to be multihomed. In other words, it needs to have access to both the nonroutable private network and the routable IP network. In a way, this proxy acts like a firewall for the private network although the chosen nonroutable IP pool does that already.

Caching Remote Web Sites

Because a great deal of Web content on both the Internet and intranets is likely to be static, caching them on a local proxy server could save valuable network bandwidth. A cache-enabled proxy server will fetch requested documents only when the cache contains an expired document or when the requested document is not present in the cache. To enable caching on your proxy server, you need to specify caching directives inside a special directory container, for example:

```
<Directory proxy:*>
CacheRoot /www/cache
CacheSize 1024
CacheMaxExpire 24
</Directory>
```

This configuration defines a caching proxy server that writes cache files to the /www/cache directory. It is permitted to write 1,024K of data (1MB), and the cache must expire after each day (24 hours).

If you do not want to permit outside people to abuse your proxy, you can restrict proxy access either by host or by username/password authentication.

To control which hosts have access to the proxy server, you can create a configuration such as the following:

```
<Directory proxy:*>
AuthType Basic
AuthName Proxy
order deny,allow
deny from all
allow from myhost.nitec.com
</Directory>
```

This configuration denies access to all but `myhost.nitec.com`. If you want to use username/password authentication, you can use something similar to the following:

```
<Directory proxy:*>
       AuthType Basic
```

```
AuthName Proxy
AuthUserFile /path/to/proxy/.htpasswd
AuthName Proxy
require valid-user
</Directory>
```

Create the .htpasswd file using the htpasswd utility that comes with Apache. It also is possible to restrict access for a protocol, for example:

```
<Directory proxy:http:*>
. . .
</Directory>
```

This will enable you to control how HTTP requests are processed by your proxy server. Similarly, you can use the following to control how each of these protocols is handled by the proxy server:

```
<Directory proxy:ftp:*>
. . .
</Directory>
```

or

```
<Directory proxy:https:*>
. . .
</Directory>
```

You can also create a virtual host exclusively for proxy server. In that case, the directives should go inside the proxy host's <VirtualHost> container:

```
<VirtualHost proxy.host.com:*>
. . .
</VirtualHost>
```

Mirroring a Web Site

A mirror Web site is a local copy of a remote Web site. For example, if you wanted to mirror the www.apache.org Web site so your users can connect to your mirror site for quick access to Apache information, you can use the proxy server to create such a mirror, as follows:

```
ProxyPass      /        www.apache.org/
ProxyPassReverse        /        www.apache.org/
CacheRoot      /        www/cache
CacheDefaultExpire    24
```

This makes a proxy server a mirror of the www.apache.org Web site. For example, this configuration turns my proxy server blackhole.nitec.com into a www.apache.org mirror. Users who enter as the URL receive the Apache mirror's index page as if they had gone to.

WARNING

Before you mirror someone else's Web site, it is important that you get permission, because there may be copyright issues involved.

Creating a Reverse Proxy Server

Reverse proxy servers are needed when the real HTTP/FTP server is behind a firewall or some load-balancing scheme needs to be in place to speed up or distribute delivery of the content. Creating a reverse proxy server is quite easy with the latest proxy module found in Apache 1.3.*x*. Say that you have a Web server with hostname realserver.yourcompany.com and you want to have everyone visit it via a reverse proxy server called www.yourcompany.com (11.22.33.44.) You can create the following virtual host on .yourcompany.com server:

```
<VirtualHost 11.22.33.44>
ServerName www.yourcompany.com
```

```
ProxyPass     /      realserver.yourcompany.com/
ProxyPassReverse     /      realserver.yourcompany.com/
CacheRoot / www/cache
CacheDefaultExpire   24
</VirtualHost>
```

This makes the proxy server a reverse proxy for `realserver.yourcompany.com`. To your visitors, they are accessing `www.yourcompany.com`.

Setting Up Web Browsers to Use Proxy Servers

The popular Web browsers make it quite easy to use proxy servers. In this section, I will show you how to configure the latest versions of Netscape Navigator and Microsoft Internet Explorer (IE) for proxy. There are two ways you can set up a proxy server for these browsers: manual or automatic proxy configuration.

You want to do manual proxy configuration in situations in which you have only a few clients and your proxy configurations do not change often. If your needs are different, you should skip to the section on "Automatic Proxy Configuration."

Manual Proxy Configuration

The following steps will guide you through the manual proxy configuration for Netscape Navigator 4:

1. Select the Preference option under the Edit menu from the Navigator menu bar.
2. Click the Advanced category.
3. Click the Proxies category.
4. Select the Manual proxy configuration radio button and click View.

5. Enter the proxy server URLs for the HTTP, FTP, and Security (HTTPS) data entry fields along with the port information. Because I am using a single proxy server for all of these protocols, the URL (`http://proxy.nitec.com/`) and the port (8080) are the same. If you have different proxy servers for each of these services, you should specify them accordingly.
6. Once you have entered the information, make a request for a remote document and see if your proxy is working as it should. A good way to determine what's going on is to monitor the proxy server's access and error logs. On most UNIX systems, you can use a command such as the following to view log entries as they get written to the file:

   ```
   tail -f /path/to/access/log
   ```

To configure Microsoft Internet Explorer 4 for manual proxy, follow these steps:

1. Click the View menu and select Internet options. This brings up the dialog window.
2. Select the Connection tab.
3. Select the Access the Internet Using a Proxy Server radio button.
4. Enter the proxy server URL and port number in the fields provided.
5. Click OK to complete configuration.

If you want to specify different proxy server information for different protocols, then you can use the Advanced button to bring up the window.

Here, as in Netscape Navigator, you can specify different proxy server settings. Once you click OK and use the Apply button to apply the new settings, your browser is configured to use the proxy server.

As you can see, manually configuring Web browsers for proxy is not that complicated. However, if you have a lot of user computers that need to be configured, this could become a big hassle every time you needed to change your proxy configuration. This is where automatic proxy configuration for browsers comes in handy.

Automatic Proxy Configuration

The good folks at Netscape thought about the problems involved with manually configuring a proxy for several client computers and came up with a way to get around this type of hassle. Microsoft has also caught up with auto-configuring options for Internet Explorer. Unfortunately, they have made auto-configuring a bit harder to incorporate in the browser. You must obtain the Internet Explorer Administrator Kit (IEAK) to create auto-configuration files. Because getting IEAK requires a licensing agreement that asks each IEAK licensee to report quarterly to Microsoft regarding IEAK-related use, this author didn't feel like getting one. However, I have confirmation from a good source that the IEAK documentation discusses a Netscape-like automatic proxy configuration scenario and can even use the same scripts.

This section applies to both IE and Navigator. The only difference is that if you want this to work with IE, you must figure out how to create the appropriate files using IEAK.

The proxy auto-configuration is done using a special JavaScript. This is true for both Netscape Navigator and IE. Requirements for the special JavaScript follow below.

The proxy auto-config JavaScript must implement a function called FindProxyForURL. This function has the following skeleton:

```
function FindProxyForURL(url, host)
        {
           // java script code goes here
```

```
            return "proxy to use for servicing the URL";

        }
```

The arguments that this function receives are url and host. The url is the full URL being requested and the host is the hostname extracted from the URL. For example, when a request for `http://www.nitec.com` is detected by the Web browser, it will call the function as follows:

```
ret = FindProxyForURL("http://www.nitec.com",
"www.nitec.com")
```

The host argument in the function call is really the substring between the colon and two slashes (://) and the first colon (:) or slash (/). The port number is not included in this (host) parameter.

The function must return a string containing the necessary proxy configuration for a particular URL request. The acceptable string values that represent a proxy configuration arc:

NULL	When a NULL value (not the string NULL) is returned, it tells the browser not to use any proxy for this request.
DIRECT	Connections should be made directly, without any proxies.
PROXY host:port;	The specified proxy should be used.
SOCKS host:port;	The specified SOCKS server should be used.

Obviously, the really interesting return values are DIRECT and PROXY. When you have multiple PROXY or SOCKS servers, you can return a list instead of a single host:port pair. For example:

```
PROXY best-proxy.nitec.com:8080; PROXY good-
proxy.nitec.com:8081; PROXY soso-proxy.nitec.com:8082
```

This proxy configuration will tell the browser to first try `best-proxy.nitec.com`, and if it fails, to then try the next one (`good-proxy.nitec.com`), and so on. Note that each host:port pair is separated by a semicolon (;) and the keyword PROXY is repeated for each pair. If all the proxy servers fail, the user will be asked before attempting a direct connection.

When all proxies fail and there is no DIRECT option specified, the browser will ask the user if proxies should be temporarily ignored and direct connections attempted. To avoid such user interaction, the configuration can be replaced with the following:

```
PROXY best-proxy.nitec.com:8080; PROXY goodproxy.nitec. \
com:8081; PROXY soso-proxy.nitec.com:8082; DIRECT
```

Because direct connection is already specified as the last resort, the user will not be asked before making such a connection in case of total proxy failure. You also can mix PROXY and SOCKS. For example:

```
PROXY best-proxy.nitec.com:8080; SOCKS socks4.nitec.com: \
1080; DIRECT
```

Here, the SOCKS-based proxy will be used when the primary proxy server `best-proxy.nitec.com` fails to respond.

When a proxy fails to respond, Netscape Navigator retries the proxy after 30 minutes. Each subsequent time it fails, the interval is lengthened by another 30 minutes.

In order to help Web administrators (who also must know JavaScript programming), a set of pre-defined functions are available. These functions and their descriptions are listed in Table 15-1.

Table 15-1 *Predefined functions for programming automatic proxy configuration script*

Function Name	Explanation	Examples
isPlainHostName(host)	Returns TRUE if there is no dot in host. In other words, if the domain name is not included.	isPlainHostName("`blackhole`") returns TRUE. IsPlainHostName("`blackhole. nitec.com`") returns FALSE.
dnsDomainIs(host, domain)	Returns TRUE if host belongs to the domain. Note that the domain name must contain a leading period.	dnsDomainIs("`www.nitec.com`", "`.nitec.com`") returns TRUE. dnsDomainIs("`www.apache. org`","`.nitec.com`") returns FALSE.
localHostOrDomainIs(host, fqdnhost)	Returns TRUE if host part of fqdnhost (fully qualified hostname) matches with host.	localHostOrDomainIs("`a.b.com`", "`a.b.com`") returns TRUE; localHostOrDomainIs("`a.b`", "`a.b.com`") returns TRUE; localHostOrDomainIs("`a.b.org`", "`a.c.com`") returns FALSE.
isResolvable(host)	If DNS server can resolve the hostname to an IP, returns TRUE or else FALSE. Note that use of this function can slow down browsers, because a DNS query will be required to perform the test.	isResolvable("`www.nitec.com`"); returns TRUE, because `www.nitec.com` has DNS records.

Continued

Table 15-1 *(continued)*

Function Name	Explanation	Examples
isInNet(host, IP address pattern, netmask)	Returns TRUE if the IP address of the host matches the pattern specified in the second argument. The match is done using the netmask as follows: if one of the octets of the mask is a 255, the same octet of the IP address of the host must match. If an octet of the mask is zero (0), the same octet of the IP address of the host is ignored. Note that use of this function can slow down browsers, because a DNS query will be required to perform the test.	If the host has an IP address of 206.171.50.51: isInNet(host, "206.171.50.50", "255.255.255.0"); returns TRUE because according to the netmask only the first three octets must match and the last one should be ignored.
dnsResolve(host)	Returns the IP address of the host if successful. Note that use of this function can slow down browsers, because a DNS query will be required to perform the test.	dnsResolve("`proxy.nitec.com`") returns "`206.171.50.50`"
myIpAddress()	Returns the IP address of the host the Web browser is running. Note that use of this function can slow down browsers because a DNS query will be required to perform the test.	var hostIP = myIpAddress() returns the IP of the Web browser host and stores it in a variable called hostIP.
dnsDomainLevels(host)	Returns number of domain levels in the hostname.	dnsDomainLevels("`www.nitec. com`") returns 2.

Function Name	Explanation	Examples
shExpMatch(string, shellExpression)	Returns true if string matches the shell expression.	shExpMatch("`path/to/dir`", "`*/to/*`") returns TRUE. shExpMatch("`abcdef`", "`123`") returns FALSE.
weekdayRange(weekday1, weekday2, gmt)	Only the first argument, weekday1, is required. Returns TRUE if the day this function is executed is equal to weekday1 or in the range of weekday1 to weekday2. If the third parameter gmt is GMT, then GMT time is used instead of local time. Acceptable weekday values for weekday1 or weekday2 are: SUN, MON, TUE, WED, THU, FRI, or SAT.	weekdayRange("FRI") returns TRUE if day is Friday in local time. weekdayRange("MON", "FRI", "GMT") returns true if day is in the Monday-Friday range in GMT time.
dateRange(day) dateRange(day1, day2) dateRange(month) dateRange(month1, month2) dateRange(year) dateRange(year1, year2) dateRange(day1, month1, day2, month2) dateRange(month1, year1, month2, year2) dateRange(day1, month1, year1, day2, month2, year2) dateRange(day1, month1, year1, day2, month2, year2, gmt)	Returns true if current day, month, year, or all three, are in the range. The value of day can be 1–31; month can be JAN, FEB, MAR, APR, MAY, JUN, JUL, AUG, SEP, OCT, NOV, or DEC; year is a four-digit number; gmt is GMT or nothing (local time).	dateRange(31) returns TRUE if current day is the 31st dateRange("JAN", "APR") returns TRUE if current month is in the January to April range. dateRange(1995) returns TRUE if current year is 1995.

Continued

Table 15-1 *(continued)*

Function Name	Explanation	Examples
imeRange(hour) timeRange(hour1, hour2) timeRange(hour1, min1, hour2, min2) timeRange(hour1, min1, sec1, hour2, min2, sec2) timeRange(hour1, min1, sec1, hour2, min2, sec2, gmt)	Returns TRUE if hour, min, or sec specified is current. If a range is specified, then returns TRUE when the current corresponding unit of time is in be 0-23; min can be 0-59, second can be 0-59, and gmt is GMT or nothing (local time).	timeRange(9, 17) returns TRUE if current hour is in the 9 AM-5 PM range. the range specified. The value of hour can

With the help of the predefined functions and your custom functions, you can write FindProxyForURL so that it returns an appropriate proxy configuration string for each request.

When the Web browser starts, it loads the function from the JavaScript file (how the file is made available to the Web browser will be discussed later) and calls FindProxyForURL for each URL request. The browser supplies the host and URL arguments to the function so that it can return the most appropriate proxy configuration.

Let's take a look at some example scenarios where the FindProxyForURL function can be written in different ways.

Using Proxy Only for Remote URL Requests

If you want to use proxy service only for remote URLs, then you need to use a FindProxyForURL function like Listing 15-1 in your automatic proxy configuration JavaScript file.

Listing 15-1 *Using proxy only for remote URL requests*

```
function FindProxyForURL(url, host) {

// Check to see if the host is a local host. If it is a
// local
// host, specify DIRECT connection (i.e., no proxy)
// or else use the proxy.
if (isPlainHostName(host) ||
    dnsDomainIs(host, ".nitec.com"))
       return "DIRECT";
else
      return "PROXY proxy.nitec.com:8081; DIRECT";
}
```

When a request for a URL such as `http://www.ad-engine.com` is made by the Web browser user, the browser calls FindProxyForURL with the url argument set to `http://www.ad-engine.com` and the host set to `www.ad-engine.com`. The function first calls the isPlainHostName function to see if `www.ad-engine.com` is a plain host (just www) or not. Because it is not, isPlainHostName returns FALSE. Now the dnsDomainIs function is called to test if `www.ad-engine.com` is in the `.nitec.com` domain. This also returns FALSE. Because both of these tests return FALSE, the else part of the conditional statement is executed. In other words, the URL request for `www.ad-engine.com` returns the following proxy configuration to the Web browser:

```
PROXY proxy.nitec.com:8081; DIRECT
```

This tells the Web browser to use the proxy server named `proxy.nitec.com` on port 8081 if it is not down. In case it is down, the request should be serviced by a direct HTTP request to `www.ad-engine.com`. For most proxy server installations, this configuration is sufficient. Let's take a look at more complex scenario.

Using Multiple Proxy Servers

In this scenario, there are three proxy servers: `http-proxy.nitec.com` is used for all remote HTTP URL requests, `ftp-proxy.nitec.com` is used for all remote FTP URL requests, and `ssl-proxy.nitec.com` is used for all remote HTTPS URL requests. All other remote URL requests using other protocols such as GOPHER, NEWS, and so on are directly connected. All types of local requests are serviced directly as well.

To implement this configuration, FindProxyForURL becomes a bit complex and looks like Listing 15-2.

Listing 15-2 *FindProxyForURL for multiproxy server configuration*

```
function FindProxyForURL(url, host) {

  // Is the URL local? If it is then use a DIRECT
  // connection
   if (isPlainHostName(host) ||
       dnsDomainIs(host, ".nitec.com")) {
```

```
    return "DIRECT";
    }

// Okay, the URL is remote so check which proxy to use.
else{

   if(url.substring(0, 5) == "http:") {
      return "PROXY http-proxy.nitec.com:8080";
      }
   else if(url.substring(0, 4) == "ftp:") {
        return "PROXY ftp-proxy.nitec.com:8080";
        }
   else if(url.substring(0, 6) == "https:") {
        return "PROXY ssl-proxy.nitec.com:8080";
        }
   else{
       return "DIRECT";
       }
   }
}
```

This function first checks to see if the URL request is a local one. If it is local, then it is serviced directly. If the request is for a remote server, the URL protocol is matched to locate the appropriate proxy server. However, only HTTP, FTP, and HTTPS protocols are recognized, and URLs requesting remote resources using such protocols are directed to proxy servers. When a remote URL request does not match any of the stated protocols, it is connected directly.

It is also possible to customize your proxy server configuration based on the host that is accessing the proxy server. This can be done using a CGI script that outputs the FindProxyForURL differently depending on the REMOTE_HOST (the browser host). Listing 15-3 shows one such script called proxy.pl written in Perl.

Listing 15-3 *proxy.pl script*

```
#!/usr/bin/perl
#
# A Perl script that outputs proxy server configuration.
# $Author$
# $Revision$
# $Id$

# Get the remote host IP from the CGI environment
# variable
# REMOTE_HOST.
my $client = $ENV{REMOTE_HOST};

# Print out the necessary content-type to let the browser
# know that this is a proxy configuration.
print "Content-type: application/x-ns-proxy-\
autoconfig\n\n";

# If the request came from a host with IP address
# 206.171.50.51, then output proxy configuration
# from subroutine &specialClient
#
if ($client =~ /206\.171\.50\.51/){ &specialClient; }

# If the request came from any other clients, then
# output proxy configuration from the subroutine
# &otherClients.
else { &otherClients;      }

exit 0;

sub specialClient{
#
# This subroutine outputs a proxy server configuration
#
```

```
print <<FUNC;

    function FindProxyForURL(url, host)
    {
        if (isPlainHostName(host) ||
            dnsDomainIs(host, ".nitec.com"))
            return "DIRECT";
        else if (shExpMatch(host, "*.com"))
            return "PROXY com-proxy.nitec.com:8080; "

        else if (shExpMatch(host, "*.edu"))
            return "PROXY edu-proxy.nitec.com:8080; "

        else
            return "DIRECT";
     }
FUNC
}

sub otherClients{
#
# This subroutine outputs a proxy server configuration
#

print <<FUNC;

    function FindProxyForURL(url, host)    {
      return "DIRECT";
      }

FUNC

}
```

This script outputs a special proxy server configuration for a host with the IP address `206.171.50.51`, and all other hosts get a different configuration. To access this proxy configuration, I can set up the browser (Navigator) to point to this script at `http://servername/cgi-bin/proxy.pl`. This is done exactly the same way you would specify the .pac file. In this case, you are asking the browser to request a CGI script instead of a .pac file. But because the script sends out the content-type of a .pac file, the browser has no quarrel about why it got the proxy configuration from a CGI script and not a .pac file. Although the example script does not do much, you can use similar scripts for complex proxy configurations.

Appendix A

HTTP/1.1 Status Codes

For each request from a Web client, the Web server must return to the client an HTTP status code, which consists of a three-digit number. A Web client can attempt to understand the server's response by looking at this status code which is sent in the HTTP Status-Line header. The code is accompanied by a short phrase, called a reason phrase, which is intended to provide a brief explanation for the user. For example, an HTTP Status-Line header may look like this:

```
HTTP/1.1 404 Not Found
```

Here, "404" is the status code, and "Not Found" is the reason phrase. On a typical Web client, a Web browser will display the "Not Found" phrase in the browser window. Five different classes of status codes are available from the latest HTTP/1.1 specifications, and these are discussed in the following sections.

Informational Status Codes (100–199)

The purpose of this type of status code is to let the client know the server is in the process of fulfilling a request. These status codes are only informational; the client does not have to act on any of them. Note that HTTP/1.0 does not define 1*xx* status codes, so 1*xx* status codes must not be sent to HTTP/1.0 clients. The currently defined 1*xx* status codes are as follows:

100 Continue	The server sends this code to let the client know it is ready to receive the rest of the request.
101 Switching Protocols	The server sends this code when it is willing to switch the application protocol to one specified in an Upgrade request header provided by the client. Switching should take place only if the new protocol provides an advantage over the existing one. For example, the client may request that the server use a newer HTTP protocol than what it is currently using. In such a case, the server should switch if possible.

Client Request Successful (200–299)

If the server returns a status code in the 200–299 range, the client's request was successfully received and accepted. The currently defined 2*xx* status codes are as follows:

200 OK	The server has succeeded in processing the request, and the requested document is attached.
201 Created	The server has successfully created a new URI, specified in a Location header.
202 Accepted	The request has been accepted for processing, but the server has not yet completed processing it.

203 Non-Authoritative Information	The metainformation in the response header did not originate with the server; it was copied from another server.
204 No Content	The request is complete, but no new information needs to be sent back. The client should continue to display the current document.
205 Reset Content	The client should reset the current document. This is useful when an HTML form needs to be reset to clear all existing values of input fields.
206 Partial Content	The server has fulfilled the partial GET request for the resource. This code is used to respond to Range requests. The server sends a Content-Range header to indicate which data segment is attached.

Request Redirected (300–399)

Status codes in the 300–399 range are sent to a client to let it know it needs to perform further action to complete the request. The currently defined 3*xx* status codes are as follows:

300 Multiple Choices	The requested resource corresponds to a set of documents. The server can send information about each document with its own specific location and content negotiation information to enable the client to choose one.
301 Moved Permanently	The requested resource does not exist on the server. A Location header is sent to redirect the client to the new

	URL. The client directs all future requests to the new URI.
302 Moved Temporarily	The requested resource has temporarily moved. A Location header is sent to redirect the client to the new URL. The client continues to use the old URI in future requests.
303 See Other	The requested resource can be found in a different location indicated by the Location header, and the client should use the GET method to retrieve it.
304 Not Modified	The server uses this code to respond to the If-Modified-Since request header. This indicates the requested document has not been modified since the specified date, and the client should use its cached copy.
305 Use Proxy	The client should use a proxy, specified by the Location header, to retrieve the requested resource.
307 Temporary Redirect	The requested resource has been temporarily redirected to a different location. A Location header is sent to redirect the client to the new URL. The client continues to use the old URL in future requests.

Client Request Incomplete (400–499)

The status codes in the 400–499 range are sent to indicate the client request is not complete and more information is needed to complete the resource request. The currently defined 4*xx* status codes are as follows:

400 Bad Request	The server detected a syntax error in the client request.
401 Unauthorized	The request requires user authentication. The server sends the WWW-Authenticate header to indicate the authentication type and realm for the requested resource.
402 Payment Required	This code is reserved for future use.
403 Forbidden	Access to requested resource is forbidden. The request should not be repeated by the client.
404 Not Found	The requested document does not exist on the server.
405 Method Not Allowed	The request method used by the client is unacceptable. The server sends the Allow header stating what methods are acceptable to access the requested resource.
406 Not Acceptable	The requested resource is not available in a format that the client can accept, based on the accept headers received by the server. If the request was not a HEAD request, the server can send Content-Language, Content-Encoding, and Content-Type headers to indicate which formats are available.
407 Proxy Authentication Required	Unauthorized access request to a proxy server. The client must first authenticate itself with the proxy. The server sends the Proxy-Authenticate

	header indicating the authentication scheme and realm for the requested resource.
408 Request Time-Out	The client has failed to complete its request within the request timeout period used by the server. However, the client can repeat the request.
409 Conflict	The client request conflicts with another request. The server can add information about the type of conflict along with the status code.
410 Gone	The requested resource is permanently gone from the server.
411 Length Required	The client must supply a Content-Length header in its request.
412 Precondition Failed	When a client sends a request with one or more If. . . headers, the server uses this code to indicate that one or more of the conditions specified in these headers is FALSE.
413 Request Entity Too Large	The server refuses to process the request because its message body is too large. The server can close connection to stop the client from continuing the request.
414 Request-URI Too Long	The server refuses to process the request, because the specified URI is too long.
415 Unsupported Media Type	The server refuses to process the request, because it does not support the message body's format.
417 Expectation Failed	The server failed to meet the requirements of the Expect request-header.

Server Errors (500-599)

The status codes in the 500–599 range are returned when the server encounters an error and cannot fulfill the request. The currently defined 5*xx* status codes are as follows:

500 Internal Server Error	A server configuration setting or an external program has caused an error.
501 Not Implemented	The server does not support the functionality required to fulfill the request.
502 Bad Gateway	The server encountered an invalid response from an upstream server or proxy.
503 Service Unavailable	The service is temporarily unavailable. The server can send a Retry-After header to indicate when the service may become available again.
504 Gateway Time-Out	The gateway or proxy has timed out.
505 HTTP Version Not Supported	The version of HTTP used by client is not supported.

Appendix B

Basics of Regular Expression

A regular expression is typically composed of both normal and special characters to create a pattern. This pattern is used to match one or more substrings or an entire string, for example:

```
([a-z]+)\.([a-z]+)\.([a-z]+)
```

This regular expression matches `www.idgbooks.com`, `www.apache.org`, and so on. The special characters used in a regular expression are often called metacharacters. Following are commonly used metacharacters:

.	Matches any character (except Newline)
^	Matches the start of the string
$	Matches the end of the string
\b	Matches a word boundary
x?	Matches 0 or 1 x's, where x is any regular expression
x*	Matches 0 or more x's
x+	Matches 1 or more x's
foo|bar	Matches one of foo or bar
[abc]	Matches any character in the set abc
[A–Z]	Matches any character in the range A to Z.
[^xyz]	Matches any single character not in the set xyz

\w	Matches an alphanumeric character (for instance, [a–zA–Z0–9_])
\s	Matches a white-space character
\t	Tab character
\n	Newline character
\r	Return character
\f	Form feed character
\v	Vertical tab (whatever that is!)
\a	Bell character
\e	Escape character
\077	Octal char
\x9f	Hex char
\c[	Control char
\l	Lowercase next char
\L	Lowercase till \E
\U	Uppercase till \E
\E	End case modification
\u	Uppercase next char
\Q	Quote metacharacters till \E

If you need to use a metacharacter as a normal character in the regular expression, you can use \metachar format to take away the special meaning. An example of this is \$, which is a regular dollar sign character. The standard quantifiers used in regular expressions are as follows:

*	Match 0 or more times.
+	Match 1 or more times
?	Match 1 or 0 times
{n}	Match exactly n times
{n,}	Match at least n times
{n, m}	Match at least n but not more than m times

A pipe (|) character is treated as an OR operator. A pair of parentheses () enables you to define the area used for the search match strings in a regular expression. A pair of square brackets [] creates a character class or range.

Let's revisit the first example again:

```
([a-z]+)\.([a-z]+)\.([a-z]+)
```

As mentioned before, this expression can be used to match strings such as `www.idgbooks.com`. The first [a–z]+ specifies that one or more characters in the a to z range is needed to match the group specified by the first pair of parenthesss. If a match is found, whatever is matched can be accessed using $1. There are three pairs of parentheses in this expression. The first one (starting from the left) is $1, the second one is $2, and the third one is $3. Notice that a backslash (\) is used to escape the dot (.) metacharacter between the groups.

Here are two more examples:

- ^foo\.htm$. This will match a string foo.htm. It would not match afoo.htm, because the ^ metacharacter is used to specify that the matching string must start with the f character. It also would not match foo.html, because the $ metacharacter is used to specify that the matching string must end with the m character.
- ^www\.([^.]+)\.host\.com(.*). This will match a string, such as `www.username.host.com STATUS=java` and the $1 will be assigned to host and $2 will hold everything followed by the `www.username.host.com` part of the string. The $2 will hold `STATUS=java`.

Appendix C

Internet Resources for Apache

Free Resources

Following are some of the free Internet resources for Apache.

Web Sites

Official Apache Web site: `http://www.apache.org`

Apache Module Registry: `http://modules.apache.org/`

Apache-SSL: `http://www.apache-ssl.org/`

Apache/Perl Integration Project: `http://perl.apache.org/`

Java-Apache Project: `http://java.apache.org/`

Apache for OS/2: `http://www.slink.com/ApacheOS2/`

Apache for Amiga: `http://www.xs4all.nl/~albertv/apache/`

Usenet Newsgroups

You also can find information about World Wide Web topics in 15 distinct newsgroups. They are subdivided for good reason—please use the newsgroup that is most relevant to your topic. Before you post anything, make sure you are posting to the right newsgroup(s), and always read the FAQ of the newsgroup, if available.

Web Server-Related Newsgroups

These newsgroups discuss Web servers and related issues. Possible subjects include: configuration questions/solutions, security issues, directory structure, and bug reports.

Unix platforms: `comp.infosystems.www.servers.unix`

Windows platforms: `comp.infosystems.www.servers.ms-windows`

Macintosh: `comp.infosystems.www.servers.mac`

Other platforms: `comp.infosystems.www.servers.misc`

Authoring-Related Newsgroups

These newsgroups cover issues related to Web authoring. Possible subjects include how to handle forms and their results, creating and manipulating images and image maps, interactive Web applications, formatting HTML, standards, audio and video, and other similar subjects.

CGI: `comp.infosystems.www.authoring.cgi`

HTML: `comp.infosystems.www.authoring.html`

Images: `comp.infosystems.www.authoring.images`

Other subjects: `comp.infosystems.www.authoring.misc`

Web-Browser-Related Newsgroups

These newsgroups discuss Web browsers. Possible subjects include: configuration questions/solutions, external viewers (helper applications), and bug reports.

Windows platforms: `comp.infosystems.www.browsers.ms-windows`

Macintosh platforms: `comp.infosystems.www.browsers.mac`

X-Windows platforms: comp.infosystems.www.browsers.x

Other platforms: comp.infosystems.www.browsers.misc

Announcements Newsgroups

This is a newsgroup in which new, Web-related resources can be announced.

Announcements: comp.infosystems.www.announce

Tip

Read this group first to find the posting guidelines.

Other WWW Newsgroups

These groups discuss issues surrounding Web browsers, servers, and software.

Opinions and comparisons: comp.infosystems.www.advocacy

General discussions: comp.infosystems.www.misc

Perl Newsgroups

These newsgroups are devoted to discussions about Perl; they include everything from bug reports to new features to history, humor, and trivia. This is the best source of information about anything Perl related, especially what's new with Perl5.

Information: comp.lang.perl.misc

Announcements: comp.lang.perl.announce

WWW Resources for Usenet Newsgroups

DejaNews: http://www.dejanews.com/

The Reference Archive: http://www.reference.com/

Critical Mass Communications: http://www.critical-mass.com/concord/index.htm

Mailing Lists

If you would like to receive Apache-related announcements on a timely basis, you can subscribe to this mailing list. To subscribe, send a message to `apache-announce-request@apache.org` with the word "subscribe" in the body of the message. Note that this is not a forum for asking questions.

To subscribe for general discussions, send the command "subscribe apache" to `majordomo@geek.net`. There is also a digested version of the list, to which you can subscribe with the command "subscribe apache-digest."

Commercial Resources

A growing number of Apache users (especially corporate users) are always looking for commercial resources that offer Apache software or services. Following are some well-known commercial resources for Apache:

The Apache Week online free magazine: `http://www.apacheweek.com`

US/Canada Stronghold: `http://www.c2.net`

Outside US/Canada Stronghold: `http://www.uk.web.com`

Covalent Raven: `http://raven.covalent.net`

Rovis: `http://www.rovis.com/warpaint/`

Other Related Resources

WWW Consortium: `http://www.w3.org/`

Netcraft Survey Report Web site: `http://www.netcraft.co.uk/Survey/`

All RFC documents: `http://ds.internic.net/ds/dspg1intdoc.html`

Server Watch: `http://www.ServerWatch.com`

Search Engine Watch: `http://www.SearchEngineWatch.com`

Browser Watch: `http://www.BrowserWatch.com`

Web Compare: `http://www.WebCompare.com`

Web Developer: `http://www.WebDeveloper.com`

Web Reference: `http://www.WebReference.com`

Electronic Commerce on Internet: `http://e-comm.internet.com`

ISP Buyer's Guide: `http://www.thelist.com`

Internet News: `http://www.InternetNews.com`

CGI Specification: `http://hoohoo.ncsa.uiuc.edu/cgi/interface.html`

FastCGI Web site: `http://www.fastcgi.com`

Perl Language Site: `http://www.perl.com`

Appendix D

Apache Quick Reference

Mark this page! This appendix is your one-stop, quick reference for using Apache Server. It summarizes information from the Apache documentation, version 1.3.3, which can be found at `http://www.apache.org/docs/`. No more wading through documentation—all the important information you need is here.

Each directive is listed with its arguments. Defaults are given in parentheses where appropriate at the end of the line, followed by an indication of the directive status as follows:

C = core

B = base

E = extension

The contexts in which the directive is valid are indicated by:

c =in a configuration file

v = within a virtual host section

d = within a directory section

a = in an access control file

NOTE

Options and directives that are new for Apache 1.3 are marked 1.3N. Options that have changed for Apache 1.3 are marked 1.3C.

Command Line Options

`Httpd`	`[-d directory] [-f file] [-C directive]` [-c *directive]* [-h] [-l] [-S] [-v] [-V] [-X]
-d	directory initial value for ServerRoot
-D	*parameter* define parameter for <*IfDefine*>
-f	*file* configuration file (*conf/httpd.conf*)
-C	*directive* process *directive* before reading config files 1.3N
-c	*directive* process *directive* after reading config files 1.3N
-h	list available configuration directives and exit
-l	list compiled-in modules and exit
-S	show *vhost* settings
-t	test syntax of configuration files and exit
-v	print version and exit
-V	show compilation settings and exit 1.3N
-X	debug mode

General Configuration Directives

DocumentRoot *directory*	(/usr/local/apache/htdocs)Ccv	
ServerRoot *directory*	(/usr/local/apache)Ccv	
AccessConfig *filename*	(conf/access.conf)Ccv	
ResourceConfig *filename*	(conf/srm.conf)Ccv	
Include *filename*	Ccv	1.3N
TypesConfig *filename*	(conf/mime.types)Bcv	
PidFile *filename*	(logs/httpd.pid)Ccv	
LockFile *filename*	(logs/accept.lock)Ccv	
ScoreBoardFile *file*	(logs/apache_status)Ccv	
ServerAdmin *email-addr*	Ccv	
ServerType{inetdstandalone}	(standalone)Ccv	
ServerName *name*	(*determined automatically*)Ccv	
ServerAlias *fqdn*	Ccv	

ServerSignature	(Off)Ccvda {OnOffEmail}	1.3N
ServerPath *pathname*	Ccv	
ServerTokens	(Full)Ccv {Min[imal]OSFull}	1.3N
BindAddress {**IP-addr*}	(*)Ccv	
Listen [*IP-addr*:]*port-number*	Ccv	
Port *portno*	(80)Ccv	
User {*username#userid*}	(#-1)Ccv	
Group {*group-name#group-id*}	(#-1)Ccv	
NameVirtualHost addr[:port]	Ccv	1.3N
UseCanonicalName {OnOff}	(On)Ccvda	1.3N
CoreDumpDirectory *directory*	(*as ServerRoot*)Ccv	1.3N
IdentityCheck {OnOff}	(Off)Ccvd	
ClearModuleList	Ccv	
AddModule *module...*	Ccv	
AddModuleInfo *module* text	Ecv	1.3N
ExtendedStatus {OnOff}	(Off)Ecv	1.3N

Sectional Directives

<Directory *pattern*> ... </Directory>	Ecv	1.3C
<DirectoryMatch *pattern*> ... </DirectoryMatch>	Ecv	1.3N
<Files *pattern*> ... </Files>	Ecv	1.3C
<FilesMatch *pattern*> ... </FilesMatch>	Ecv	1.3N
<Location *pattern*> ... </Location>	Ecv	1.3C
<LocationMatch *pattern*> ... </LocationMatch>	Ecv	1.3N
<VirtualHost *pattern*> ... </VirtualHost>	Ecv	
<IfDefine *parameter*> ... </IfDefine>	Ecv	1.3N
<IfModule *module*> ... </IfModule>	Ecv	
<Limit *method*> ... </Limit>	Ecv	

Logging Directives

ErrorLog {*filename*|syslog}	(logs/error_log)Ccv		
CustomLog *file-or-pipe*	{*format*-string|*format*-name}	Bcv	1.3C
TransferLog *file-or-pipe*	(logs/access_log)	Bcv	
HostnameLookups {On|Off|Double}	(Off)Ccvd		1.3C
RefererIgnore *hostname* ...	Ecv		
LogFormat *format-string* [*format-name*]	("%h %l %u %t \"%r\" %s %b")	Bcv	1.3C
LogLevel {emergalertcriterrorwarnnotice = infodebug}	(error)Ccv		1.3N

format-string can contain literal text and format specifiers:

%a	Remote IP address
%b	Number of bytes sent (excluding headers)
%{*var*}e	Environment variable value
%f	Filename
%h	Remote host
%{*hdr*}i	Incoming header value
%l	Remote logname (from identd)
%{*hdr*}o	Outgoing header value
%p	Canonical port number of server
%P	Process ID of child server process
%r	First line of request
%s	Status
%t	Time in Common Log Format (CLF) format
%{*format*}t	Time (*format* is strftime format)
%T	Time taken to serve the request (in seconds)
%u	Remote username
%U	URL requested
%v	Canonical ServerName of server

Performance Tuning Directives

Timeout *secs*	(300)Ccv	
KeepAlive {OnOff}	(On)Ccv Note:	
KeepAliveTimeout *seconds*	(15)Ccv	
MaxKeepAliveRequests *number*	(100)Ccv	
MaxClients *number*	(256)Ccv	
MaxRequestsPerChild *number*	Ccv	
ExcessRequestsPerChild *number*	Ecv	1.3N
MaxSpareServers *number*	(10)Ccv	
MinSpareServers *number*	(5)Ccv	
StartServers *number*	(5)Ccv	
ListenBacklog *number*	(511)Ccv	1.3N
RLimitCPU {*secs*max} [{*secs*max}]	Ccvda	
RLimitMEM {*bytes*max} [{*bytes*max}]	Ccvda	
RLimitNPROC {*nprocs*max} [{*nprocs*max}]	Ccvda	
SendBufferSize *bytes*	Ccv	
ThreadsPerChild *number*	(50)Ccv	1.3N

File Typing Directives

DefaultType *MIME-type*	(text/html) Ccvda	
ForceType *MIME-type*	Bcvda	
AddHandler *handler-name extension ...*	Bcvda	
AddType *MIME-type extension ...*	Bcvda	
AddEncoding *MIME-enc extension ...*	Bcvda	
AddLanguage *MIME-language extension ...*	Bcvda	
LanguagePriority *lang ...*	Bcvda	
XbitHack {OnOffFull}	(Off)Bcvda	
MetaFiles {OnOff}	(Off)Ecvda	1.3N
MetaDir *dir-name*	(.web)Ecvda	1.3C
MetaSuffix *suffix*	(.meta)Ecvda	1.3C

MimeMagicFile *filename*	Ecv	1.3N
ExpiresActive {OnOff}	Ecvda	
ExpiresBytype *MIME-type expiry-code*	Ecvda	
ExpiresDefault *expiry-code*	Ecvda	
Header {setappendaddunset} *header value*	Ecvda	

Mapping Directives

Action *MIME-type script*	Bcvda	
Alias *url-path real-path*	Bcv	
AliasMatch *url-regex path-*replacement	Bcv	1.3N
Redirect [*status*] *url-path url*	Bcvda	
RedirectMatch [*status*] *url-regex dest-url*	Bcvda	1.3N
RedirectPermanent *url-path url-dest*	Bcvda	
RedirectTemp *url-path url-dest*	Bcvda	
Script *method script*	Bcvd	
ScriptAlias *url-path script-dir*	Bcv	
ScriptAliasMatch *url-regex script-dir*	Bcv	1.3N
SetHandler *handler-name*	Bcvda	
UserDir {DISABLEDDISABLED *user* ... ENABLED *user* ...}	(public_html)Bcv	1.3C
ErrorDocument *error-code* {*stringurl*}	Ccvda	
ImapBase {mapreferer*url*} (http://*server*)	Bcvda	
ImapDefault {errornocontentreferer menu*url*}	(nocontent)Bcvda	
ImapMenu {noneformattedsemi-formattedunformatted}	Bcvda	
RewriteBase *url*	Ecvda	
RewriteCond *test-string cond-pattern* [*flags*]	Ecvda	

RewriteEngine {OnOff}	(Off)Ecvda	
RewriteLock filename	Ecv	1.3N
RewriteLog *filename*	Ecv	
RewriteLogLevel *digit*	Ecv	
RewriteMap *map-name map-type:map*-source	Ecv	1.3C
RewriteOptions *option*	Ecvda	
RewriteRule *pattern substitution* [*flags*]	Ecvda	1.3C

Scripting Directives

BrowserMatch *regexp var*[*=value*] ...	Bcv	
BrowserMatchNoCase *regexp var*[*=value*] ...	Bcv	
PassEnv *varname* ...	Bcv	
SetEnv *varname value*	Bcv	
SetEnvIf *headername regex var*[*=value*] ...	Bcv	1.3N
SetEnvIfNoCase *headername regex var*[*=value*]...	Bcv	1.3N
UnsetEnv *varname* ...	Bcv	
ScriptLog *filename*	Bcv	
ScriptLogBuffer *size-bytes*	Bcv	
ScriptLogLength *length-bytes*	Bcv	

Directory Indexing Directives

DirectoryIndex *file*	(index.html)Bcvda	
ReadmeName filename	Bcvda	
HeaderName filename	Bcvda	
IndexIgnore pattern ...	Bcvda	
DefaultIcon url	Bcvda	
AddAlt "string" file ...	Bcvda	
AddAltByEncoding "string" MIME-encoding ...	Bcvda	

AddAltByType "string" MIME-type ...	Bcvda	
AddIcon icon file ...	Bcvda	
AddIconByType icon MIME-type ...	Bcvda	
AddIconByEncoding icon MIME-encoding ...	Bcvda	
AddDescription "description" file-pattern	Bcvda	
IndexOptions option ...	(no options) Bcvda	1.3C

Valid index options are: FancyIndexing, IconsHeight=*pixels*, IconsWidth=*pixels*, IconsAreLinks, ScanHTMLTitles, SupressColumnSorting, SupressDescription, SupressHTMLPreamble, SupressLastModified, SupressSize

Access Control Directives

AccessFileName *filename* ...	(.htaccess)Ccv	1.3C
AllowOverride *directive-group* ...	(All)Cd	

Valid directive groups are: None, All, AuthConfig, FileInfo, Indexes, Limit, Options

Options {+*feature*-*feature*}...	(All)Ccvda	

Valid options are: None, All, ExecCGI, FollowSymLinks, Includes, IncludesNOEXEC, Indexes, MultiViews, SymLinksIfOwnerMatch

AuthName realm-name	Cda	
AuthType type	Cda	
AuthUserFile filename	Eda	
AuthGroupFile filename	Eda	
AuthAuthoritative {OnOff}	(On)Bda	
allow from {allhost ...env=var}	Bda	
deny from {allhost ...env=var}	Bda	
order {allow,denydeny,allow mutual-failure}	(deny,allow)Bda	
Require {user user ...group group ...valid-user}	Cda	
Satisfy {AllAny}	(All)Cda	

Apache-SSL/mod ssl Directives

SSLBanCipher cipher	Ecvda
SSLCACertificateFile file	Ecv
SSLCACertificatePath path	E
SSLCertificateFile filename	Ecv
SSLCertificateKeyFile filename	Ecv
SSLDisable	Ecv
SSLEnable	Ecv
SSLFakeBasicAuth	Ecv
SSLLogFile file	Ecv
SSLRequireCipher cipher	Ecvda
SSLRequiredCiphers list	Ecv
SSLVerifyClient number	Ecv
SSLVerifyDepth *number*	Ecv

Common Gateway Interface (CGI) Variables

AUTH_TYPE	Authentication method used
CONTENT_LENGTH	Length of input stream data
CONTENT_TYPE	Internet media type of input stream
GATEWAY_INTERFACE	CGI version
PATH_INFO	URL part after script identifier
PATH_TRANSLATED	PATH_INFO translated into filesystem
QUERY_STRING	Query string from URL (if present)
REMOTE_ADDR	IP address of client
REMOTE_HOST	DNS name of client
REMOTE_IDENT	Remote user id (unreliable)
REMOTE_USER	Name of the authenticated user
REQUEST_METHOD	HTTP request method
SCRIPT_NAME	Virtual path of the script
SERVER_NAME	Host-name of the server

SERVER_PORT	Port number of server
SERVER_PROTOCOL	Name and version of the protocol
SERVER_SOFTWARE	Server software name and version
HTTP_ACCEPT	MIME types the browser will accept
HTTP_REFERER	URL of referring document
HTTP_USER_AGENT	Client software identification
MOD_PERL	Defined if running under mod_perl

Apache-SSL/mod ssl Extensions

HTTPS	Set if HTTPS is being used
HTTPS_CIPHER	SSL/TLS cipherspec
SSL_CIPHER	The same as HTTPS_CIPHER
SSL_PROTOCOL_VERSION	SSL protocol version
SSL_SSLEAY_VERSION	Version of SSLEAY library
HTTPS_KEYSIZE	Number of bits in the session key
HTTPS_SECRETKEYSIZE	Number of bits in the secret key
SSL_CLIENT_DN	DN in client's certificate
SSL_CLIENT_<x509>	Component of client's DN
SSL_CLIENT_I_DN	DN of issuer of client's certificate
SSL_CLIENT_I_<x509>	Component of client's issuer's DN
SSL_SERVER_DN	DN in server's certificate
SSL_SERVER_<x509>	Component of server's DN
SSL_SERVER_I_DN	DN of issuer of server's certificate
SSL_SERVER_I_<x509>	Component of server's issuer's DN

Server Side Includes (SSI)

Format is:	<!–#*element attr=value* ... –>
Elements are:	
Config	controls parsing; attributes: errmsg, sizefmt (one of bytes or abbrev)
echo	print the value of a variable; attribute var (can be a CGI variable or one of: DATE_GMT, DATE_LOCAL, DOCUMENT_NAME, DOCUMENT_URI or LAST_MODIFIED)

set	set the value of a variable; attributes: var, value
printenv	print a list of all variables and their values
exec	execute a shell command or CGI script; attribute: cmd or cgi (IncludesNOEXEC option disables exec)
fsize	print size of file; attribute: file or virtual
flastmod	print file modification time; attribute file or virtual
include	include another document; attribute file or virtual
if	conditional; attribute: expr
elif	conditional; attribute: expr
else	conditional
endif	conditional

HTTP 1.1 Status Codes

100 Continue

101 Switching protocols

200 OK

201 Created

202 Accepted

203 Non-authoritative information

204 No content

205 Reset content

206 Partial content

300 Multiple choices

301 Moved permanently

302 Moved temporarily

303 See other

304 Not modified

305 Use proxy

400 Bad request

401 Unauthorized

402 Payment required

403 Forbidden

404 Not found

405 Method not allowed

406 Not acceptable

407 Proxy authentication required

408 Request timeout

409 Conflict

410 Gone

411 Length required

412 Precondition failed

413 Request entity too large

414 Request-URI too long

415 Unsupported media type

500 Internal server error

501 Not implemented

502 Bad gateway

503 Service unavailable

504 Gateway timeout

505 HTTP version not supported

Apache Web Resources

`http://www.apache.org/`	Apache home page
`http://www.apache.org/docs/`	Apache documentation
`http://modules.apache.org/`	Apache Module Registry
`http://www.apache-ssl.org/`	Apache-SSL home page
`http://www.engelschall.com/sw/mod_ssl`	mod_ssl page
`http://java.apache.org/`	The Java-Apache Project
`http://perl.apache.org/`	The Apache/Perl Integration Project
`http://www.php.net/`	PHP: Hypertext Processor
`http://www.apacheweek.com/`	Apache Week
`http://www.netcraft.com/Survey/`	Netcraft Server Survey

Index

Continued

L

M

Continued